SHAKESPEARE, MUSIC AND PERFORMANCE

Music has been an essential constituent of Shakespeare's plays from the sixteenth century to the present day, yet its significance has often been overlooked or underplayed in the history of Shakespearean performance. Providing a long chronological sweep, this collection of essays traces the different uses of music in the theatre and in film from the days of the first Globe and Blackfriars to contemporary, global productions. With a unique concentration on the performance aspects of the subject, the volume offers a wide range of voices, from scholars to contemporary practitioners (including an interview with the critically-acclaimed composer Stephen Warbeck), and thus provides a rich exploration of this fascinating history from diverse perspectives.

BILL BARCLAY is the Director of Music at Shakespeare's Globe. His original scores for the Globe include *Romeo and Juliet, The Taming of the Shrew* and *Hamlet* Globe-to-Globe, which toured 197 countries from 2014–2016. He has directed or adapted concerts for the Boston Symphony Orchestra, the Los Angeles Philharmonic, the BBC Symphony Orchestra, the British Film Institute, and the Tanglewood Music Center, and has lectured on Shakespeare and the Music of the Spheres on three continents. He is editor of *The Plays of Jon Lipsky* (with Jonah Lipsky, 2015).

DAVID LINDLEY is a Professor Emeritus at the University of Leeds, where he taught in the School of English. He has published books and articles on court masques, on the scandalous history of Frances Howard, and on Thomas Campion. He edited eleven Jonson masques for the *Cambridge Edition of the Works of Ben Jonson* (2012). His study *Shakespeare and Music* appeared in 2006, and his substantially revised second edition of *The Tempest* for The New Cambridge Shakespeare was published in 2013.

SHAKESPEARE, MUSIC AND PERFORMANCE

EDITED BY

BILL BARCLAY

Shakespeare's Globe, London

DAVID LINDLEY

University of Leeds

CAMBRIDGE
UNIVERSITY PRESS

CAMBRIDGE
UNIVERSITY PRESS

University Printing House, Cambridge CB2 8BS, United Kingdom

One Liberty Plaza, 20th Floor, New York, NY 10006, USA

477 Williamstown Road, Port Melbourne, VIC 3207, Australia

4843/24, 2nd Floor, Ansari Road, Daryaganj, Delhi – 110002, India

79 Anson Road, #06–04/06, Singapore 079906

Cambridge University Press is part of the University of Cambridge.

It furthers the University's mission by disseminating knowledge in the pursuit of education, learning, and research at the highest international levels of excellence.

www.cambridge.org
Information on this title: www.cambridge.org/9781107139336
DOI: 10.1017/9781316488768

First published 2017

Printed in the United Kingdom by TJ International Ltd. Padstow Cornwall

A catalogue record for this publication is available from the British Library.

ISBN 978-1-107-13933-6 Hardback

Contents

Illustrations, Tables and Music Examples

Illustrations

Tables

Music Examples

Contributors

LINDA PHYLLIS AUSTERN is Associate Professor of Musicology at Northwestern University in Evanston, Illinois. She is the author of *Music in English Children's Drama of the Later Renaissance*, and has published over thirty articles, the most recent of which are '"Lo Here I Burn": Musical Figurations and Fantasies of Male Desire in Early Modern England', in *Eroticism in Early Modern Music*, ed. by Bonnie Blackburn and Laurie Stras (2015) and '"The Mystic Pow'r of Music's Unison": The Conjuncture of Word, Music, and Performance Practice in the Era of Katherine Philips', in *The Noble Flame of Katherine Philips: A Poetics of Culture, Politics and Friendship*, ed. by David L. Orvis and Ryan Singh Paul (2015). She has also edited, or co-edited, four collections of essays, most recently *Beyond Boundaries: Rethinking Music Circulation in Early Modern England* (with Candace Bailey and Amanda Eubanks Winkler, 2017).

BILL BARCLAY is the Director of Music at Shakespeare's Globe. His original scores for the Globe include *Romeo and Juliet*, *The Taming of the Shrew* and *Hamlet* Globe-to-Globe, which toured 197 countries from 2014–16. He has directed or adapted concerts for the Boston Symphony Orchestra, the Los Angeles Philharmonic, the BBC Symphony Orchestra, the British Film Institute, and the Tanglewood Music Center, and has lectured on Shakespeare and the Music of the Spheres on three continents. He is editor of *The Plays of Jon Lipsky* (with Jonah Lipsky, 2015).

VAL BRODIE is a freelance musician and musical director. She gained her PhD at the Shakespeare Institute, University of Birmingham and was awarded the Louis Marder Scholarship by the Shakespeare Birthplace Trust for her research into theatre music manuscripts in their collection. In 1997, she received an MBE for services to music education.

MICHAEL BURDEN Michael Burden is Professor in Opera Studies at Oxford University, and Fellow and Dean at New College. His published research is on the stage music of Henry Purcell, and on aspects of dance and theatre in the London theatres of the seventeenth, eighteenth, and nineteenth centuries. He is currently completing a volume on the staging of opera in London between 1660 and 1860; his five-volume collection of opera documents, *London Opera Observed*, and study of the London years of the soprano Regina Mingotti were both published in 2013. *The works of Monsieur Noverre translated from the French: Noverre, his circle, and the English Lettres sur la danse*, edited with Jennifer Thorp, was published in 2014. He is the Past President of the British Society for Eighteenth-century Studies, a Visitor to the Ashmolean Museum in Oxford, and Director of Productions of New Chamber Opera, www.newchamberopera.co.uk

JOHN CUNNINGHAM is a Senior Lecturer in Music at Bangor University. His main research area is secular music in the British Isles, c.1600–1800. He has published on various aspects of seventeenth-century instrumental music and its sources in England, and is the author of *The Consort Music of William Lawes, 1602–45* (2010). He was also contributing music editor to *The Cambridge Edition of the Works of Ben Jonson* (2014), and took the same role in *The New Oxford Shakespeare Edition* (2016, 2017).

PAUL L. FABER is an instructor in the Department of English at Pearson College UWC, Victoria, Canada. He is also Music Editor for the University of Victoria's online resource, *Internet Shakespeare Editions*. He has published essays on early modern dramatic music in *Early Theatre* and *The Ben Jonson Journal*. He has also enjoyed a successful career as professional musician supporting some of Canada's top recording artists for over a decade.

ADAM HANSEN is Senior Lecturer in English at Northumbria University. In addition to publishing numerous articles on early modern culture in its own time and ours, he is author of *Shakespeare and Popular Music* (2010), and co-editor of *Litpop: Writing and Popular Music* (2014) and *Shakespearean Echoes* (2015).

PETER HOLLAND is McMeel Family Professor in Shakespeare Studies in the Department of Film, Television and Theatre and Associate Dean for the Arts at the University of Notre Dame. He was Director of the Shakespeare Institute in Stratford-upon-Avon from 1997 to 2002. He is Editor of *Shakespeare Survey*, co-General Editor of *Oxford Shakespeare Topics* and of *Great Shakespeareans*.

KATHERINE HUNT is a Career Development Fellow in Early Modern English Literature at The Queen's College, University of Oxford. She works on the intersection of early modern literary, material, and aural culture and is completing a monograph about the resonances of bells in seventeenth-century English writing. She is one of the editors of Sir Thomas Browne's notebooks for the new edition of his complete works, from Oxford University Press.

CLAIRE VAN KAMPEN, Senior Research Fellow and Associate for Early Modern Theatre music at Shakespeare's Globe, is a composer, director and playwright. She was the first female music director of the RSC in 1986, and of the National Theatre in 1987. At the opening of Shakespeare's Globe in 1997 she was Mark Rylance's Associate artistic director. In addition she was the Founding Director of Theatre Music, creating scores for more than thirty-five Globe productions. Since 2007 she has continued to be the Globe Associate for early Modern Music, creating music for ten productions, including *The Duchess of Malfi* which opened the Wanamaker Playhouse in 2014. She is also a lecturer on the Education faculty of the Globe's MA courses. Work in the U.S. includes scores for Matthew Warchus's Broadway productions of *True West* (2000), *Boeing-Boeing* (2008) and *La Bete* (2010). Her new play, *Farinelli and the King*, received multiple Olivier nominations in 2016. Film scores include *Anonymous, Days and Nights, Wolf Hall* (historical music arranger) for the mini-series on BBC/PBS.

ELIZABETH KENNY is Professor of Musical Performance at the University of Southampton, and Professor of Lute at the Royal Academy of Music. She has played with many of the world's best period instrument groups, including Les Arts Florissants and the Orchestra of the Age of Enlightenment. Her research interests have led to critically acclaimed recordings of Lawes, Purcell and Dowland, and to the formation of her ensemble *Theatre of the Ayre*. As well as regular collaborations with singers such as Robin Blaze, Ian Bostridge and Nicholas Mulroy in recital, she has a fondness for the viol consort repertory and has recorded William Lawes' *Royal Consort* with Phantasm, as well as Dowland's *Lachrimae*. She guest-edited a Dowland-themed issue of *Early Music*, bringing performers and scholars together in celebration of the 450th anniversary of the composer's birth in 2013. She was an artistic advisor to the York Early Music Festival from 2011 to 2014.

DAVID LINDLEY is a Professor Emeritus at the University of Leeds, where he taught in the School of English. He has published books and articles on court masques, on the scandalous history of Frances Howard, and on Thomas Campion. He edited eleven Jonson masques for the Cambridge Edition of the Works of Ben Jonson (2012). His study *Shakespeare and Music* appeared in 2006, and his substantially revised second edition of *The Tempest* for The New Cambridge Shakespeare was published in 2013.

WILLIAM LYONS is a specialist performer and teacher of Historically Informed Performance. He has a long association with Shakespeare's Globe, having worked there as a musical director, composer and historical advisor since 1998. He is a Leverhulme Research Fellow and is editor of the *wait* and *türmusik* entries in the Grove Dictionary of Music and Musicians. He directs the acclaimed early music ensemble The Dufay Collective with whom he has toured the world and produced a series of critically acclaimed recordings. He is also founder and director of The City Musick, an ensemble formed to explore the repertoire and performance practices of urban and court musicians in Early Modern Europe.

LUCY MUNRO is a Reader in Shakespeare and Early Modern Literature at King's College London. Her books include *Children of the Queen's Revels: A Jacobean Theatre Repertory* (2005) and *Archaic Style in English Literature, 1590–1674* (2013), and editions of plays by Sharpham, Shakespeare and Wilkins, Brome and Fletcher. Her edition of *The Witch of Edmonton* recently appeared with Arden Early Modern Drama and she is currently working on a study of the King's Men.

CAROL CHILLINGTON RUTTER is Professor of Shakespeare and Performance Studies, University of Warwick, and a National Teaching Fellow. Her monographs include *Shakespeare and Child's Play: Performing Lost Boys on Stage and Screen* and *Enter the Body: Women and Representation on Shakespeare's Stage*. She has contributed essays to *Great Shakespeareans* ('Peggy Ashcroft'), *The Oxford Middleton Handbook, Shakespeare Beyond Doubt*, and *The Shakespeare Circle*, and reviewed Shakespeare performed in England for *Shakespeare Survey* (2007–2014). Her practice as research film, 'Unpinning Desdemona: The Movie' is online.

SIMON SMITH is Leverhulme Early Career Fellow at the Shakespeare Institute, Stratford-upon-Avon and the Department of English

Literature, University of Birmingham. His research is concerned with early modern playhouse music, and with early modern audiences. Recent publications include *The Senses in Early Modern England, 1558–1660*, co-edited with Jackie Watson and Amy Kenny (2015), as well as articles on music in *The Winter's Tale*, in *Antony and Cleopatra*, and in *Richard III*. His monograph, *Musical Response in the Early Modern Playhouse, 1603–1625*, is forthcoming with Cambridge University Press.

JON TRENCHARD is an actor, musician, singer, musical director and composer. He was a choral scholar, an organist, and a Cathedral lay clerk, before training at the London Academy of Performing Arts. Since then, he has appeared on stages across the world, as well as extensive touring around the UK. Whilst an actor in Edward Hall's all-male Shakespeare company Propeller he also arranged, composed and provided musical direction for their productions of *Richard III, The Comedy of Errors, The Merchant of Venice, Twelfth Night* and *The Taming of the Shrew* (nominated for the NYC Drama Desk Award for Best Music For A Play in 2007). He has been musical director for productions at the Bristol Old Vic, for Bruiser, and for Hotspur Theatre Company. As an actor-musician, he plays piano, flute, piccolo, accordion and saxophone.

STEPHEN WARBECK scores music across theatre, film and television. Work for Shakespeare's Globe includes *The Tempest, Richard II, Much Ado About Nothing, As You Like It, Othello* and *Pericles*. Scores for the RSC include *Wolf Hall* and *Bring up the Bodies* (also Broadway), *The Tempest, Romeo and Juliet, The Taming of the Shrew*, and *Cymbeline*. Stephen has also scored many theatrical productions for other theatres including the Royal Court, the National Theatre, the Almeida, in the West End, and on Broadway. He completed his first ballet score, *Peter Pan*, in 2005 for Northern Ballet. Film scores include *Le Secret Des Banquises, Mon Roi* (César nomination), *Polisse, There Be Dragons, Billy Elliott, Charlotte Gray, Captain Corelli's Mandolin* and *Shakespeare in Love* (winner of the Academy award for best original musical or comedy score). His television work includes *Indian Summers, The Dresser, Fungus the Bogeyman, A Young Doctor's Notebook, Skellig, Fallout* and *Prime Suspect* (BAFTA nomination). Stephen also writes music for his band, the hKippers.

RAMONA WRAY is Reader in Renaissance Literature at Queen's University, Belfast. She is the editor of the Arden Early Modern Drama edition of Elizabeth Cary's *The Tragedy of Mariam* (2012), the author of *Women Writers in the Seventeenth Century* (2004) and the co-author of *Great Shakespeareans: Welles, Kurosawa, Kozintsev, Zeffirelli* (2013). She has published articles on Shakespeare appropriation and early modern women's writing and is also the co-editor of *The Edinburgh Companion to Shakespeare and the Arts* (2011), *Screening Shakespeare in the Twenty-First Century* (2006), *Reconceiving the Renaissance: A Critical Reader* (2005), *Shakespeare, Film, Fin de Siècle* (2000) and *Shakespeare and Ireland: History, Politics, Culture* (1997).

Acknowledgements

The origins of this book lie in a conference organised by the editors at Shakespeare's Globe in 2013. We wish to thank Dr. Farah Karim-Cooper, Head of Higher Education and Research, and Adam Sibbald, then Education Events Manager, for all their work in making the conference possible. The Modern Humanities Research Association and the journal Music and Letters generously sponsored the event, for which we are very grateful.

Our gratitude goes to Michelle Morton of the RSC for help in locating and permission to use the image of *The Winter's Tale*, and especially to Carol McKay and Propeller Theatre Company, Mark Sullivan at Shakespeare's Globe, and Melanie Leung at the Folger Shakespeare Library for their generosity in supplying photographs without charge.

Unless otherwise specified, all Shakespeare quotations are taken from the volumes in the *New Cambridge Shakespeare* series.

Introduction

David Lindley and Bill Barclay

Music has played a vital part in theatrical entertainment since the very beginnings of drama. The theatre of Shakespeare's own time was no exception, and music has continued to make a highly significant contribution to the performance of his plays up to the present day. Exactly what sort of contribution, however, has been dictated by a variety of factors: by the number and range of musicians available; by the changing architecture of theatres themselves; by the historical evolution of musical styles; by the changing expectations of audiences; and latterly through the influences of film and television, and of sophisticated technology. It is the aim of this collection of essays to explore the nature and implication of these developments from the time of the plays' composition through to contemporary performance both on film and in the theatre.

In the late sixteenth and early seventeenth centuries competition and rivalry between the outdoor, amphitheatre playhouses and their mostly adult actors, and the more select and expensive indoor theatres, where companies of boy actors performed, was an important stimulus to musical activity. Adult actors were, as William Lyons's essay demonstrates, often versatile musicians, and probably played a range of instruments not dissimilar to those of the civic bands, the waits, who themselves might be employed in the theatres on an occasional basis. The boys' companies, initially at least made up of choristers, and performing less frequently than their adult competitors, offered more extensive musical fare. The practical necessities of the indoor theatres dictated that there needed to be breaks at the ends of each act to attend to the candles, and these breaks were covered by music; but the boys also seem to have offered a pre-show concert of some elaboration, as well as offering rather more songs as part of the plays' entertainment. It may be that the flurry of songs in Shakespeare's turn-of-the-century comedies reflects an attempt to compete with the more music-heavy offerings of the 'little eyases' (as Hamlet calls them), but in any event,

I

after the King's Men took over the Blackfriars hall theatre in 1608 the musical practices at both kinds of theatre, as Simon Smith and Lucy Munro argue, gradually converged.

There are a number of ways in which the issues raised in the sixteenth and seventeenth centuries reverberate right up to the present day. In the first place, theatrical competition has always been a spur to innovatory performance practice, and the increasing musical elaboration of the post-Restoration theatre reflects the competition between the two principal theatrical companies as Katherine Lowerre's detailed study of the years 1695–1705 indicates.[1] In the later eighteenth century, as theatres were enlarged, similar rivalries were an important stimulus to the staging of ever-more extensive musical processions, as Michael Burden demonstrates. In the nineteenth century there was continued reliance on the crowded stages and extended musical interludes that Val Brodie's essay describes.

Secondly, the questions of who, exactly, played the music and of where they were situated in the theatre, is an open one in the seventeenth century, and remains significant in considering the way music functions in Shakespearean performance throughout the centuries. In the Jacobean and Caroline theatre the musicians would not have been numerous. Any notion of an 'orchestra' lay in the future, and only in the Royal Music was it possible to collect together a sizeable amalgamation of the different groups of instrumentalists. The forty-two voices and instruments that played for Campion's *Lord Hay's Masque* of 1607, or the sixty or so musicians that Bulstrode Whitlocke managed to put together for Shirley's *Triumph of Peace*, presented by the Inns of Court to Charles and Henrietta Maria in 1634, could not be imitated in the public theatre. Yet, though the range of instruments in the children's theatres was initially more extensive than that to be found in the adult amphitheatres, after 1608 there was a more varied instrumental palette across the theatrical world, as William Lyons makes clear.

After the Restoration the makeup of the theatre band changed, with increased reliance on strings, and the number of players grew. Curtis Price suggests that between twelve and eighteen players made up the usual theatre band in the Restoration – though it might on occasion have grown to as many as thirty musicians.[2] This remained the standard

---

[1] K Lowerre, *Music and Musicians on the London Stage, 1695–1705* (Farnham: Ashgate, 2009).
[2] C. A. Price, *Music in the Restoration Theatre* (Ann Arbor: UMI Research Press, 1979), 81–2.

ensemble for smaller theatres, but in the latter part of the eighteenth century and into the nineteenth, the predominance of operatic entertainment at the principal theatres, and the expansion of processions, tableaux and interludes in the performances, called for larger instrumental resources, so that one might end up with substantial forces both in an orchestra pit and simultaneously on stage.[3] Henry Irving's orchestra in the late nineteenth century consisted of thirty to thirty-five players.[4] An important question then concerns the location of these the musicians. Simon Smith shows that the old assumption that musicians in the seventeenth century were confined to a music-room above the stage is a simplification of theatrical reality, but nonetheless, the fact that musicians could be curtained off, separated physically from the action they accompanied, marked an important moment of change.

During the Restoration, Curtis Price suggests, musicians might still have occupied boxes at the side of the proscenium arch, but increasingly were placed in the pit, immediately in front of the thrust stage that was still part of standard theatre architecture.[5] There, sitting facing the stage, they would have been visible to the audience. As the century progressed, and into the nineteenth century, so the orchestra pit, sometimes extending below the stage and largely out of sight of the audience, became conventional. The physical and visual separation of instrumentalists from the stage action is significant for the understanding of the ways in which music might work in the theatre. From the sixteenth century onwards the expectation of music before the play and between the acts embodied a distinction between music which is part of the action of the play itself – what film criticism calls 'diegetic' music – and music which is simply part of the experience of going to the theatre. For much of this time it was not required that such music – properly called 'incidental' – should connect directly to the action of the play that it introduced and interleaved. In the eighteenth century and beyond entr'actes might be occupied by substantial musical compositions, or by songs or dances with no relevance to the play. John Marston, however, writing for the boys' companies in the early seventeenth century, seems already to have wanted the 'act music' to provide some kind of affective continuity with the action that it followed or preceded, and over time composers increasingly attempted in their overtures and entr'actes to comment on, or prepare for the drama itself.

---

[3] See M. Burden's essay below.
[4] M. Pisani, *Music of the Melodramatic Theatre in Nineteenth-Century London and New York* (University of Iowa Press, 2014), 253.
[5] Price, 81–7.

Even more significant to the experience of the plays in the theatre, however, is the extension of the term 'incidental music' to the provision of musical underscore not explicitly called for in the action of the drama, nor heard by the onstage actors, but intended solely to work its emotional affect upon the audience. It is a matter of some dispute as to when, exactly, underscoring of this sort began. In Shakespeare's plays, though he calls on occasion for music to play under dialogue – Sneak's Noise accompanying the melancholy dialogue of Falstaff and Mistress Quickly in *2 Henry IV*, or the solitary instrumentalist playing outside Richard II's prison cell, for example – it seems always to be assumed that the actors as well as the audience can hear the music. The same, by and large, is true of the Restoration and early eighteenth-century theatre, where, though there was ever more pressure on playwrights to make opportunity for song and for instrumental sound, almost always some pretext is given in the action of the play itself for its introduction.

Towards the end of the eighteenth century and into the nineteenth, as Michael Pisani's study amply demonstrates, the practice begins of giving emotional shape to action with underscore that deployed often short fragments of music to support or intensify the emotional affect of the action. Found in its most full-blown form in melodrama and various popular forms of theatre, it rapidly reached the 'high-art' end of the market, and was pervasive in Shakespearean theatre at the end of the nineteenth and into the early twentieth centuries. Pisani quotes a critic as late as 1910 asserting that '[A] running accompaniment of music, half-heard, half-guessed, that moves to the mood of the play … may do much toward keeping the audience in tune with the emotional significance of the action.'[6] Not everyone agreed – an anonymous reviewer of Beerbohm Tree's *Tempest* complained that '[A]t the rare moments when Shakespeare's lines emerge from the prevailing racket, they drag, they limp, … as [the actors] always speak to a musical accompaniment, generally slow, it is surprising if they make a single speech intelligible.'[7] This comment testifies to the way that actors increasingly played off the underscore in the delivery of their speeches. Paradoxically, then, the music that existed entirely outside the world of the drama increasingly dictated both the presentation of that world and the audience's response to it.

[6] Pisani, 310.
[7] D. Lindley, '"Sounds and Sweet Airs": Music in Shakespearian Performance History', *Shakespeare Survey*, 64 (2011), 62–3.

In the twentieth century, the nature of theatrical music changed under two different pressures. In the first place, the growth of the early music movement complemented the interest in Shakespearean stage practice evidenced, for example, in the experiments of William Poel. He turned to the musical pioneer Arnold Dolmetsch to provide the scores for his productions, using a small band playing music of the period on recorder, viol and harpsichord, or else musical pastiche of its style.[8] As the essays by Elizabeth Kenny and Claire van Kampen show, exploration of the possibilities of using period music in contemporary productions continues, even if underpinned by a more self-conscious awareness of the theoretical problems in re-creating what would once have been called 'authentic' performance practices.

Music, indeed, occupies an especially problematic space in terms of the representation of historical periods. In the Victorian era, though enormous efforts might be made to achieve 'authenticity' in the detail of costumes and setting, music only rarely gestured towards a period style. The same is often true in more recent times, where the precise historical location of the visual elements of a production is not often matched by similar musical fidelity.

The main pressures towards the reduction in size of the instrumental band in the twentieth century, however, came from simple economics on the one hand, and the growth of electronic and then digital means of presenting music in the theatre on the other. When the Shakespeare Memorial Theatre (as it then was) experimented with recorded music in the 1940s they simply recorded new scores by Lennox Berkeley and others, and played them through what turned out to be an inadequate speaker system. The music was itself being deployed in an entirely traditional manner. Technology has improved, and we will return to the implications of digital media later, but the ease of deploying music from across the entire historical and stylistic spectrum means that it is now easily possible to yoke together music of many kinds in a 'compilation score'. Such scores are not, in fact, new. Throughout stage history music of different periods and styles could be pressed into service, as Val Brodie's essay demonstrates, but a purposeful mash-up of different types of music characterises many modern productions and is discussed in relation to the practice of the theatre company Propeller, in Carol Rutter and Jonny Trenchard's essay, and extended in Adam Hansen's exploration of the place of popular music

[8] See Marion O'Connor, *William Poel and the Elizabethan Stage Society* (Cambridge: Chadwick-Healey, 1987).

in contemporary productions. Film, of course, has always used both through-composed scores by a single composer and compilations which exploit the cultural resonances of different musical genres and styles, and Shakespearean film has been no exception – as the essays by Peter Holland and Ramona Wray demonstrate.

The overlap between theatrical and cinematic practice has been of fundamental importance in the twentieth and twenty-first centuries. So, for example, in 1957 Peter Brook declared that:

> It is no longer the ideal to go to an eminent composer … and ask him to write a score to accompany a play … A good incidental score nowadays is more a matter of timbre and tone colour than of harmony or even of rhythm; it has to appeal to a mind which has at least one and three-quarter ears fully occupied with following the dramatic narrative; it is, in fact, quarter-ear music.[9]

This view overlaps with the notion one frequently finds in film music criticism, that the best music is that which is not memorable in itself and is scarcely consciously recognised by the audience. Hence the disappearance of musicians from view in theatrical performance, either in a retreat to recorded sound, or else by the physical concealment of musicians which reached its symbolic apogee in arrangements like that of the 'Bandbox' at the Royal Shakespeare Theatre, where musicians sat in a studio connected only electronically with the stage. Such separation suited the assumptions about music's place as emotional encouragement; heard but not seen.

In recent years, this tendency for theatre music to aspire to the condition of the cinema has been reversed. A production of *The Winter's Tale* at Stratford in 2009 illustrated this tendency, but also some of the conceptual problems which attend it. Here musicians were not only brought onstage in the sheep-shearing scenes, but named as 'characters' and given a line or two of invented dialogue. While this was straightforwardly acceptable in the scenes of merrymaking, later these same still-visible musicians played what was clearly 'non-diegetic' music to accompany the action. As a result their status became somewhat confusing – were they, as actors, responding to the action they witnessed before them, or were they reverting to their cinematic function of conditioning our response, telling us musically how to react to the scene? Their onstage presence highlighted their ambiguous nature in a way that only live theatre can.

---

[9] *Sunday Times*, 22 September 1957.

Illustration 1 Musicians in *The Winter's Tale*, Act 4 (RSC, 2009) Photograph by
Alessandra Evangelista, ©Royal Shakespeare Company

We will return to current practice shortly, but if thus far we have been
considering in the main instrumental music, some of the same ambivalence
which attended the *Winter's Tale* musicians in 2009 may be said to
surround the singer of songs in Shakespearean drama throughout its history.
W. H. Auden's distinction between performed and impromptu song remains
a useful one, distinguishing the character who sings because it is his (or more
rarely her) profession or place to do so, from the character who bursts into
song as an expression of their personal feelings at a particular moment.[10]
In the former case the singer must be reasonably adept (even if gentlemen
such as Amiens in *As You Like It* and Balthazar in *Much Ado About Nothing*
make fashionably modest disclaimers of their abilities – in contrast to Feste
who asserts that he 'take[s] pleasure in singing' (2.4.67)). In the latter case,
they need not. Two interesting borderline examples are the subjects of the
essays by Linda Phyllis Austern and Paul Faber. Merrythought, a central
figure in Beaumont's *Knight of the Burning Pestle*, is an impromptu singer *par
excellence*, but a performance in which he did not at least sing moderately well
would be a very long haul for the audience. Shakespeare's Ophelia begins the

---

[10] W. H. Auden, 'Music in Shakespeare', in *The Dyer's Hand* (London: Faber, 1962), 511, 522.

tradition of female madness being demonstrated through distracted singing, but during the theatrical history of the play she has at times sung her songs with some skill – the First Quarto, after all, has her play upon a lute – while, especially in more recent performances informed by naturalistic acting styles, she has barely sung her words at all. These two 'borderline' cases expose the tension between singer-as-character and singer-as-performer.

That tension, of course, informs an audience's relationship with any acted part. As spectators and listeners, we are both immersing ourselves in the world actors are creating, and simultaneously observing, and taking self-conscious pleasure in, their skill in taking us into that world; but the tension is more particularly marked by the action of singing. Song occupies a peculiarly liminal space in theatrical entertainment. As Mark Booth observes, '[A] song, set in a play, but set out of the play too by its music, facilitates our indulgence in feelings that may be undercut before and after the music plays.'[11] As song settings became more elaborate, so the question of the relationship between actor-as-character and actor/singer-as-performer becomes ever more problematic.[12] How, exactly, music generates emotional response is a matter of much debate, but undoubtedly part of its effect in Early Modern theatre was generated by the way in which songs were frequently borrowed from, or alluded to, the tunes and words made popular by their circulation in ballads. The complexity of response this might generate is the subject of Linda Austern's essay. But though it would seem likely that most of the songs in Shakespeare's plays were written to fit existing tunes, in his late plays, and in the revivals which followed in the years before the Civil War, composers might provide new and fashionable settings for the songs. Robert Johnson's settings of songs in *Cymbeline*, *Winter's Tale*, and *The Tempest* may or may not have been used in their first stagings, but they mark out the direction in which song settings were to go in the centuries that followed. There is an important distinction to be made between the responses of an audience who know the tune they hear, but perhaps not the words, and the situation of a modern audience in particular, for whom the words of a Shakespeare song are probably well-known, but who might delight in the novelty of the fresh setting that contemporary performance demands. It is, of course, also true that the pleasure of recognition and familiarity were generally available to audiences in the eighteenth and nineteenth centuries, when settings of the songs by Arne and others had a remarkable tenacity on the stage.

---

[11] M. W. Booth, *The Experience of Songs* (New Haven and London: Yale University Press, 1981), 15.
[12] See Elizabeth Kenny's essay, 124–5 below.

Songs were, from their beginning, in important respects eminently detachable from the particular context in which they are first found. Tiffany Stern has argued that the lyrics of songs were separated from the playbook, and not necessarily available to the printers of the first editions of the plays – hence the number of 'blank songs' in published plays, where there is an instruction for a song to be provided, but no lyrics are given.[13] Equally, however, dramatists may not have worried too much about precisely what song was inserted, accepting any generally appropriate selection from the singing actor's repertoire. But be that as it may, there is no doubt that soon after first performances new songs were being created and dovetailed into existing scripts. So, for example, 'Take, O take those lips away' in *Measure for Measure* (4.1.1ff.) is an importation into a version of the play revised after Shakespeare's death, as is almost certainly the case with the Hecate scenes and songs in *Macbeth*.[14]

After the Restoration the addition of new songs, or borrowings of songs from one play into another became the norm, satisfying the tastes of a theatre audience for whom an evening's entertainment was made up of a varied programme of dramatic, musical and other genres. So, for example, the 'Cuckoo Song', a setting of the first stanza of *Love's Labour's Lost*'s Epilogue, found its way into *As You Like It*, where it was allocated, according to the singing abilities of the actresses, to either Celia or Rosalind. It was Thomas Arne's setting of the song that achieved this fame, and it continued to be used for at least a hundred years after its composition. As John Cunningham's essay demonstrates, Arne was particularly successful in his settings of Shakespeare, not least because he carefully controlled the publication of his songs, reaching out beyond the theatre to a domestic market. Though Arne's songs are, as it were, framed off from the action that might surround them, they are, in general, not particularly demanding of their singers. (Part of the reason, no doubt, for their popularity in the theatre for nearly two hundred years.) By contrast the young Thomas Linley, composing the music for a Sheridan revival of *The Tempest* at Drury Lane in 1777, though he took over some of Arne's airs, provided for his father's new protégé, Miss Field, acting the part of Ariel, extended arias that require great singerly expertise, with a wide vocal

---

[13] T. Stern, *Documents of Performance in Early Modern England* (Cambridge University Press, 2009), Ch. 5.
[14] D. Lindley, 'Music in the English Theatre of 1616', in T. Y. Tan, P. Edmondson and S-P Wang, eds., *1616: Shakespeare and Tang Xianzu's China* (London: Bloomsbury Arden Shakespeare, 2016), 226–8.

range and many dazzling melismata.[15] New songs, with words probably by Sheridan, were inserted, so that Charles Burney described the production as 'more a musical masque than opera or play'.[16] If Linley's settings mark a high point in the vocal elaboration of Shakespeare's songs, the possibility of treating any song as an occasion for a big 'production number' is one which contemporary performances, for all that they are much less ready to insert new material than their eighteenth- and nineteenth-century predecessors, cannot always resist. *As You Like It*, for example, has seen frequent amplifications of 'It was a lover and his lass', and the reintroduction of a musical epilogue at Shakespeare's Globe, drawing on the Elizabethan practice of the concluding jig, has been imitated elsewhere.[17]

A particularly important strand in the essays which follow is the series we have headed 'In Practice'. Throughout the history of Shakespearean performance music has often been in the hands of orchestra leaders, who might assemble scores from stock material, adding pieces of their own composition as required. Some theatre composers, such as Thomas Arne or Stephen Storace in the eighteenth century, were among the most important musicians of their day. Increasingly in the latter part of the nineteenth-century theatres recruited eminent composers to provide music for individual productions – Arthur Sullivan or Edward German, for example. In the twentieth century composers well known in other fields might provide music for the theatre – Lennox Berkeley and Harrison Birtwistle are two such. Evidencing this trend as alive and well, recent years have seen three notable new scores for different productions of *As You Like It* by a trio of well-known figures from popular culture: the actor/comedian and bluegrass connoisseur, Steve Martin (Shakespeare in the Park, New York City, 2012), and pop icons Laura Marling (RSC, 2013), and Johnny Flynn (Shakespeare's Globe, 2015). There have also been composers doubling as musical directors for leading Shakespearean companies, such as Guy Woolfenden and Stephen Warbeck in Stratford, Todd Barton at the Oregon Shakespeare Festival, and both Claire van Kampen and Bill Barclay at Shakespeare's Globe. Four essays printed here explore the diverse relationships that exist between composers and the theatrical productions or films for which they write. If in many ways these relationships are not profoundly different from that between Thomas Linley the

---

[15] Can be heard in the recording by The Parley of Instruments, dir. Paul Nicholson on Helios CDH55256.
[16] Quoted in Neighbarger.   [17] See Claire van Kampen's essay, 53, below.

elder and his theatre manager, Sheridan, modern technology has generated a very significant shift in the responsibilities of a director of music.

Since the birth of modern theatrical sound design in the 1970s and the progressively increasing ease and accessibility of digital audio editing, productions of Shakespeare in all but the largest theatres have mostly followed the trend in theatre generally to engage a sound designer for all the requisite sound and music. This development has fully embraced the ability of digital-savvy composers to provide synthetic instrumental accompaniment that, particularly since the rise of Apple computing, has steadily proved both more affordable and user friendly. The power of one clever sound designer armed with a battery of digital instrument libraries and sound manipulation software has increased music's amplitude and flexibility on the one hand, while on the other it has de-emphasised music's role as an active constituent in the world of the play that its characters can hear, and in many cases, discuss. As a consequence, the cinematic role of music as unseen emotional narrator has been assimilated fully in the theatre, where, as signaller of transitions and moods, it becomes Brook's quarter-ear music, out of sight and mind. The consequences of disembodied music in Shakespeare mark a substantial departure from the rich and live musical accompaniment that this volume documents, particularly since the early twentieth century when the last of the great theatre orchestras became the provenance solely of musical theatre, opera, and ballet, where they are still shrinking in size today.[18]

In performing arts economies such as that of the United States where state subsidy is virtually nil, the sound designer's cost-effective contribution has taken an almost universal hold. Yet in this stripped-down paradigm problems persist. In spite of the rash of graduate programmes that have been initiated in the US and the UK for theatre sound design, the tasks a composing sound designer may be called to perform can be daunting. Sound designers may not read music and therefore struggle to compose songs, which frequently enough are excised from the action. Some cannot effectively provide musical direction for actors or collaborate dynamically with choreographers while at the same time providing the competent audio engineering expected in a full production. When in the last decades, sound designers have demonstrated an ability to merge more of these abilities together, the industry at large has enthusiastically

---

[18] The end of this performance lineage is often marked with Kurt Weill's *Die Silbersee* in 1933, the last such play that featured a nineteenth-century-style orchestra and big name composer to so richly flesh out the entertainment.

responded, causing others to upskill quickly and race to keep up.
The clear result, for both small films and straight plays in all but the
largest of companies, is to look to fewer sound experts with slimmer
budgets to shoulder what used to be the weight of a larger group of
people. That such a condensing of sound's role renders it both less visible
and poorly understood is surely evidenced by the American Theatre
Wing's elimination of both the Tony Awards for Sound Design in
a Play and Sound Design in a Musical in 2014, a surprise announcement
met with dismay and consternation in the Broadway community and in
American theatre at large.

Critically, not all theatres are universally wooed by the belief in less as
more. As we have seen, the Royal Shakespeare Company has hired live
musicians in nearly all of its own productions in recent decades, even if
their long-standing practice of employing salaried players has yielded to
a less expensive freelance model. Shakespeare's Globe makes visible, costumed, memorised, and embodied musical accompaniment a hallmark of
its creative style, and has seen a nearly 300 percent increase in the number
of musicians per season from 2011–2015.[19] There and elsewhere, a robust
practice of actor-musicianship, vital to the distinct energies of myriad
smaller companies, has become central to the identities of a few large and
successful outfits; Propeller's widely acclaimed company aesthetic of musical actors is richly detailed in this volume. Their aggressive touring model,
alongside that of the RSC and Globe, has surely been one reason that more
companies appear to follow suit. Director John Doyle's high-profile
Broadway and London revivals of *Sweeney Todd, Company,* and *Merrily
We Roll Along*, which feature actors simultaneously playing the musical
score, have greatly contributed to a recent fad for actor-musicianship in
straight theatre on both sides of the Atlantic, though at the expense of
traditional employment for musicians. In a compelling counterexample,
van Kampen's historical music for the Globe's 2012–13 Broadway and
West End hits *Twelfth Night* and *Richard III* discussed below, played by
a band of seven period music specialists, demonstrated that a full dynamic
partnership between live music and straight theatre is possible even in the
face of its attendant costs. In sum, a detectable evolution towards making
music visible again has newly and convincingly established itself against the
technologically driven trends of audio playback. Such visibility resuscitates
music's natural role in the lives and psyches of Shakespeare's characters,

---

[19] The 2011 season featured forty-six musicians on the books, while the 2015 season of over twenty
productions included 148.

counteracting the powerful influence of non-diegetic emotional guidance inherited from a century of film, and restoring what is truly theatrical about theatre music.

The final chapter of this volume examines music in the 2012 Globe-to-Globe Festival, surveying the thirty-eight productions of Shakespeare from around the world that formed the heart of the World Shakespeare Festival in the Cultural Olympiad. The great diversity of musical approaches among these multilingual productions makes a compelling case that vibrant live music in full partnership with storytelling (outside the genre of musical theatre) is perhaps healthier around the world than in the English-speaking theatre. The festival dynamically showcased the undeniable charms and benefits of imaginatively reintegrating music with the performers, and provided evidence that Shakespeare's musical DNA – embodied, integrated, and central to both the characters' and audience's experience of his stories – still lives on in the fabric of Shakespearean production whether in English or Māori.

The pendulums of fashion and economy in the last 400 years have certainly swung Shakespeare's music to far-flung polarities of approach, style, and personnel. While there is certainly no single wrong or right approach, this volume implicitly asserts the pleasure and creative advantage in understanding music's immense possibility in Shakespeare, so that it can fully play on in his stories everywhere.

CHAPTER I

Theatre Bands and Their Music in Shakespeare's London

William Lyons

Introduction

With the rise in popularity of public and private theatres in Early Modern London, the opportunity arose for professional musicians to find employment in many of the bespoke playhouses that sprung up on both sides of the Thames. This essay considers the various styles and sound worlds incorporated into plays, and in particular the question of who actually played the music. When musicians could be afforded, it was important to engage the very best available and in early seventeenth-century London the principal professional band outside of the royal court was the civic 'waits', a type of band whose skill and versatility were well attested. Whilst it is clear that waits were far from being the only musicians to be employed in theatres, I will suggest that it was the waits who contributed more significantly to the high standards of playing remarked upon by visitors to London's theatres than hitherto recognised.

Waits were employed principally to provide music for civic ceremony and procession, particularly attending the Lord Mayor on such occasions. In a sense, the waits provided a 'civic soundtrack that distinguished town from country'.[1] This aural emblem of the city came with considerable perks; the official status achieved by being accepted into the waits (usually after a lengthy apprenticeship, period of probation and then interview) meant that the musician could wear the civic livery, which signified an official and elevated social status.[2] They were also allowed to accept non-civic employment. As highly skilled and usually multi-instrumental professionals, the waits were able to provide a variety of sonorities and volume depending on what was required of them.

---

[1] C. Marsh, *Music and Society in Early Modern England* (Cambridge University Press, 2010), 117.

[2] W. L. Woodfill, *Musicians in English Society from Elizabeth to Charles I* (New York: Da Capo Press, 1953), 33–53.

Theatre Bands and Their Music

In his dedication to *The First Booke of Consort Lessons* Thomas Morley refers to the '*ancient custome*' of maintaining a waits band '*to adorne your honors favors, Feasts and Solemne meetings*' and '*your Lordships Wayts*', these '*excellent and expert Musitians*' with their '*carefull and skilfull handling*' are recommended the publication as much as is their employer, the Lord Mayor of London. Morley goes on to suggest that the waits can improve upon the arrangements '*by their melodious additions*' and hints of a second volume of pieces '*to give them more testimonie of my love towards them*'.[3] Here is a publication that is unique, firstly for its precise specification of instruments – the 'Treble Lute, the Pandora, the Citterne, the Base-Violl, the flute, and the Treble-Violl', and in its recommendation to a specific group of musicians. What Morley fails to reveal, however, is the purpose of this compilation of twenty-three arrangements or why he recommends them to the waits in particular. The assumption has to be that these pieces reflect a repertoire of an already-established ensemble and one that was, at least in the case of Morley's collection, particularly associated with the waits.

The earliest dramatic reference to the Consort comes in George Gascoigne's *Jocasta*, performed at Gray's Inn in 1566. For the 'dumbe shewe' before the first Act 'did sounde a dolefull and straunge noyse of violles, cytheren, bandurion, and such like. . . '[4] The ensemble is also noted in the musical accounts of the wealthy houses of Hengrave Hall, Ingatestone Hall and most notably at Elvetham Hall, seat of Edward Seymour, Earl of Hertford.[5] In 1591, he organised a lavish four-day entertainment for Elizabeth I as she was on 'progress' in order to regain favour after a period spent in disgrace in the Tower of London. On two occasions a 'consort' played before the Queen, much to her delight:

> After supper was ended hir Majestie graciously admitted into her presence a notable consort of six Musitions, which the Earl of Harford had provided to entertain her Majestie. Their Musicke highly pleased her, that in grace and favour thereof, she gave a new name unto one of their Pavans, made long since by Maister Morley, then organiste at Paule's Church.

And:

---

[3] T. Morley, *The First Booke* (London, 1599), sig. A2.
[4] G. Gascoigne, *The Pleasauntest Works* (London, 1587), 71.
[5] D.C. Price, *Patrons and Musicians of the English Renaissance* (Cambridge University Press, 1981), 77–88, 126–7.

> The Fairy Queene and her maides daunced about the Garden, singing a Song of sixe parts, with the music of an exquisite consort, wherein was the Lute, Bandora, Base-violl, Citterne, Treble-violl and Flute, . . . This spectacle and Musicke, so delighted her Majesty, that shee desired to see and hear it twise over.[6]

The Queen's enjoyment seems to have expanded in the telling, as the second edition claims: 'that shee commanded to here it sung and to be daunced three times over and called for divers Lords and Ladies to behold it'.

Whatever the extent of her pleasure, it is clear that the Queen had an affection for this ensemble which must have done wonders for its social standing. Morley's publication was reprinted in a posthumous 1611 edition, while two years earlier, in 1609, Philip Rosseter had produced his own *Lessons for Consort*. Consort books also survive from the hand of Matthew Holmes, who was Precentor and Singing Man of Christ Church in Oxford from 1588 and then in Westminster Abbey in London from 1597 until his death in 1621. The surviving consort books (the treble viol and bandora part books are missing) contain a similar mixture of dances, masque pieces, instrumental versions of songs, and ballad tunes as are found in the Morley and Rosseter books, and are thought to have been used to teach the choristers in Oxford and Westminster. In general, Holmes' consort part books and the solo lute music he copied out tend towards music by composers associated with the Court or London theatres of the early seventeenth century.[7]

Philip Rosseter (1567/68–1623) was a court lutenist, and is significant for this essay in that of those who produced the surviving consort books he has the clearest line of contact with the theatrical world of the time. In 1609, the same year that he published the *Lessons for Consort*, Rosseter, along with a goldsmith, Robert Keysar, became associated with the management of a company of boy actors, previously known as the Children of the Queen's Revels but – following an injunction due to their performing certain plays considered offensive to the royal family – now called the Children of Whitefriars, the theatre at which they performed. Rosseter and Keysar secured the patent to have the old name restored and the company performed five times at court during 1612–13.[8]

---

[6] R. Laneham, *Laneham's Letter Describing the Magnificent Pageants Presented Before Queen Elizabeth in 1575, At Kenilworth Castle* (London: J.H. Burn, 1822).

[7] John H. Robinson, Lute Society http://cudl.lib.cam.ac.uk/view/MS-DD-00009–00033/1.

[8] A. Ashbee, and D. Lasocki *A Biographical Dictionary of English Court Musicians 1485–1714* (Aldershot: Ashgate Press, 1998), vol. 2.

Rosseter's publication of his *Lessons for Consort* in the same year that he took over management of a boys' company, if not designed, certainly seems fortuitously coincidental. Companies of boy actors had their heyday in the 1590s until around 1615, and performed a considerable number of the plays staged in the private indoor playhouses. The convention of boys performing interludes and plays at court had long been established and the three main boys companies, The Children of Paul's, The Children of the Chapel and the Children of the King's Revels, all used their courtly association to their advantage, justifying the higher prices of admission by promoting their royal credentials.[9] The Paul's and Chapel boys were selected from choristers and grammar school students, and it seems likely that they would therefore offer a high standard of musicianship. If the suggestion that Matthew Holmes did indeed use his consort books to train his students is right, then the likely connection between the consort and boys' companies is strengthened. More concrete evidence exists in the account of a visit to the Blackfriars in 1602 by the German Frederic Gerschow:

> From there we went to a children's play. Now this is the situation with these children's plays: The Queen has a number of young boys, who are required to devote themselves earnestly to the art of singing and learn to play all sorts of instruments, while they continue their [other] studies. These boys have excellent instructors in all subjects, especially outstanding music teachers . . . For an entire hour before [a play] one hears an exquisite concert of organs, lutes, pandoras, mandoras, bowed strings, and woodwinds, such as this time when a boy sang so beautifully in a warbling voice to a bass viol, that unless the nuns in Milan may have outdone him, we did not hear the like on our travels.[10]

All of these instruments, with the exception of the organ, are those of the Consort, and that the performers probably were the boy players themselves contributed to the charm that Gerschow obviously felt with regard to the performance. If Matthew Holmes had copied his consort part books from other sources used by the boys' companies then these could perhaps represent the repertoire Gerschow heard at the Blackfriars Playhouse. If not the boys, then the musicians playing for this concert would have been professional musicians, most likely drawn at least in part from the waits of the City of London, so lauded by Thomas Morley. If that were the

[9] See L. P. Austern, *Music in English Children's Drama of the Late Renaissance* (Philadelphia: Gordon & Breach, 1992), 15.

[10] E. Chambers, *The Elizabethan Stage Volumes I-IV* (Oxford University Press, 1923), vol. 2, 46–7.

case, then Morley's consort book forms not only a probable source of theatre music but reveals also something of the repertoire of the waits themselves, something so frustratingly scant in other areas.

From within the plays themselves is to be found more indication that the Consort was well established as a theatre band by the 1580s, associated at first with royal entertainment (as were the boys' companies), noble households, and then in the private and public playhouses, in jigs and masques. In Thomas Dekker's *Old Fortunatus* of 1599, performed by the Admiral's Men at the Rose Theatre, Shadow enters:

> Musicke still: Enter Sadow [*sic*] very gallant, reading a Bill, with emptie bags in his hand, singing.
>
> . . .
>
> [SHADOW] Musicke? O delicate warble: O these Courtiers are most sweete triumphant creatures! Seignior, Sir, Monsieur, Sweete Seignior: this is the language of the accomplishment. O delicious strings; these heavenly wyredrawers have stretcht my master even out at length: yet at length he must wake.[11]

The 'delicate warble', 'delicious strings' and 'heavenly wire drawers' must surely be the Consort again: flute, viols and lute, and the metal strung cittern and bandora.[12] The term 'consort' crops up several times in plays denoting the mixed consort. In Antony Munday's translation of an Italian play we find:

The first Act being ended, the Consorte of Musique soundeth a pleasant Galliard.
The Consorte soundeth again.
The third Act being done, the Consort sounds a sollemne Dump.
The fourth Act being ended, the Consort soundeth a pleasant Allemaigne.[13]

In Middleton's *A Mad World My Masters* '*A strain played by the consort*' leads to Sir Bouteous's boast that he has 'no ordinary Musitians'.[14] Marston in *The Fawne* (1606, sig. B2) refers to a '*Consort of Musicke*'; as do Dekker and Massinger in *The Virgin Martyr* (1622, sig. K3 v). In Webster and Rowley's *The Thracian Wonder*, performed before 1625, after a '*Mad dance*' follows '*Consort a Lesson*' (1661, sig. D1 v).

The term 'lesson' was used to describe pieces for solo and ensemble instruments, not exclusively for the Consort, but it could be that the

[11] *The Pleasant Comedie of Old Fortunatus* (London, 1600), sig. G3r-v.
[12] J. Stevens, 'Shakespeare and the Music of the Elizabethan Stage', in P. Hartnoll, ed., *Shakespeare in Music* (London: Macmillan 1966), 22–29.
[13] A. Munday, *Two Italian Gentlemen* (London, 1586), sigs. C2, D3v, E3v, G1.
[14] T. Middleton, *A Mad World, My Masters* (London, 1608), sig C1.

Morley or Rosseter books were being referenced here. The collective term 'consort' would explain why, amongst all the instruments that are referred to in public and private theatres, cittern and bandora are nowhere mentioned by name, in spite of their being fundamental to the sound of the consort. Recorder, flute, viol and lute are all referred to because of their separate identities but, despite having solo repertoire of their own, both cittern and bandora appear to be regarded in theatrical terms as consort instruments without the need for further definition in stage directions.

The English Consort was not just a success at home. The reports of visitors from the continent to London theatres led to something of a vogue for English acting companies and musicians finding patronage abroad. On their semi-official excursions to London, including a trip to the theatre, the sight of high class professional musicians and actors performing in a purpose-built theatre would have made a significant impression on continental visitors. Especially remarked upon were the music and dance heard before, during and after plays which would culminate in the *jigs*: skits, often comedic that would follow the end of the play.[15] From the 1580s, companies of actors and musicians, including the famous comic actor Will Kemp, had been travelling to perform on the continent. Interestingly, Kemp is referred to in the accounts of the Danish court in 1585 as '*Wilhelm Kempe instrumentist*' and in 1586 five other English '*instrumentiste och springere*', named as Thomas Stiwens (Stevens), Jurgenn Brienn (George Bryan[t]), Thomas Koning (King), Thomas Pape (Pope) and Robert Percj (Percy) were at the Danish court. Their contract for performance states that they are '*Auß Engelandt, Geigen und Instrumentisten*' and were to entertain on their instruments and with *springere*[16] at banquets. Pope and Bryan, however, are best known in England as actors for Strange's Men and The Chamberlain's Men and therefore associated with Shakespeare. Pope was also known as a clown, like Kemp. In 1601, when an English company arrived on tour in Münster 'They had with them many different instruments, on which they played, such as lutes, citterns, fiddles, pipes and such like. . .'[17]

---

[15] See R. Clegg and L. Skeaping *Singing Simpkin and Other Bawdy Jigs: Musical Comedy on the Shakespearean Stage* (Exeter University Press, 2014). Moritz, Landgraf von Hessen-Kassel (1572–1632) was so enthused that in 1605 he had erected the first purpose-built theatre in Germany, the *Ottoneum* in the courtyard of his palace at Kassel.

[16] The term *springere* has been interpreted as referring to dancing and acrobatics. It might, however, mean 'jig' in the sense of the short entertainment.

[17] 'sie hetten bi sich vielle vershieden instrumente, dar sie uf speleten, als luten, zitteren, fiolen, pipen und dergleichen' (Chambers, 1923) II, 273.

It would appear, therefore, that on tour at least, actors-as-musicians (or vice versa) were chosen to be able to perform music to a high standard. When Robert Browne arrived with his company in Kassel in 1594/95 they were to perform 'all sorts of merry comedies, tragedies, and other plays' and to 'perform vocal, as well as instrumental music'. Thomas Sackville ran a troupe of English actors at the court of the Duke of Brunswick for twenty years and in 1597 'Thomas Sackfeit und Consorten' performed at Augsburg. In 1605, also at Kassel, the company led by Richard Machin was feted because 'they have such musicians as can hardly be found anywhere'. A recently discovered Kassel manuscript (*D-Kl*, 4° MS mus. 125, 1–5) of fifty-three pavans and six contrapuntal pieces contains eight pavans that have concordances with the consort repertoire found in the Morley and Rosseter books and the Holmes and Walsingham manuscripts.[18] These pieces strongly suggest that the English consort repertoire had travelled abroad with the players and was then arranged, perhaps by Machin himself (a lutenist of sorts) – which again gives a clear signal that these consort books did indeed provide repertoire for musicians to use in play performances. Plays in England would often end with a jig, and from the several surviving foreign language versions, the jig appears to have been very popular, with its straightforward plot, catchy tunes, and clowning.

The Consort was of course not the only ensemble heard in public and private theatres. Wind instruments such as the shawm (and its other names 'hoboy' or 'hautboy') and cornett are called for, the latter frequently in playhouse texts. On much rarer occasions sackbuts and bagpipes are named. The sackbut is only cited twice: in Fletcher's *The Mad Lover,* 1617 we find '*A Dead March within of Drum and Sackbuts*' and in Fletcher and Massinger's *The Little French Lawyer,* 1619 '*A strange Music, Sackbut and Troupe Music*' is called for.[19] However, given that collective terminology (as with 'consort') was often used when 'shawms' and 'cornetts' (both referring to a wind band that could include sackbut) were called for, the sackbut could have been, like the cittern and bandora, more common than might appear from the evidence to hand. Recorders frequently, and flutes occasionally, are called for, the former often associated with funereal

---

[18] P. Holman, *Four and Twenty Fiddlers* (Oxford: Clarendon Press, 1993), 158–9.

[19] A. C. Dessen and L. Thomson, *A Dictionary of Stage Direction in English Drama 1580–1642* (Cambridge University Press, 1999), 186.

or 'infernal' music. With those plays performed in the private play-houses, both child and adult companies employed music liberally in the plays produced between roughly 1590 and 1640. Of interest is the number and variety of instruments called for in many of the plays, when recorders, viols, organs, a Consort, lute, bass lute, treble viol, and hoboys can be demanded at various points, with those changes sometimes occurring within a matter of lines. For example, in Rowley's *When You See Me You Know Me* (1604) we have:

> *Tye.* Tis ready for your Grace, giue breath to your loud-tun'd instruments.
> *Loude Musicke*
> *Pr[ince].* 'Tis well, me thinkes in this sound I prooue a compleat age;
> As Musicke, So is man gouern'd by stops.
> Aw'd by diuiding notes, sometimes aloft,
> Sometimes below, and when he hath attained
> His high and loftie pitch, breathed his sharpest and most
> Shrillest ayre, yet at length tis gone,
> And fals downe flat to his conclusion. (*Soft Musicke.*)
> Another sweetnesse, and harmonious sound,
> A milder straine, another kinde agreement,
> Yet mong'st these many stringes, be one vntun'd,
> Or jarreth low, or hyer than his course,
> Not keeping steddie meane among'st the rest,
> Corrupts them all, so doth bad men the best.
> *Tye.* Enough! Let voices now delight his princely ear!
> *A Song.*[20]

First, 'loud music' is called for, presumably on cornetts and hoboys. Six lines later 'soft' music on recorders or Consort is required, followed by a song, either solo, with lute or most practically with the same ensemble that plays the soft music. In order for this to be executed smoothly either different ensembles of instrumentalists are required, or a few players need to be able to play loud and soft wind as well as bowed and plucked strings. The actors themselves could have provided some of the music (this play was performed by the Prince's Men at the Fortune theatre) in conjunction with professionals. If the waits had been hired, then this multi-instrumental ability would have been something they specialised and were trained in to a high standard. Their very versatility would have been an attractive asset for theatre companies that could afford to hire musicians but were mindful of space and finances. Other evidence

---

[20] S. Rowley, *When You See Me* (London, 1605), sig G4v.

exists within play texts to support the likely employment of the waits: for example, in *The Booke of Sir Thomas Moore* (c.1595), '*The waits plays, Enters Lord Mayor*',[21] while in Heminges's *The Fatal Contract*, we read '*Enter the* Eunuch, *whilst the waits play softly*'.[22] One might imagine the entrance for the Lord Mayor to be loud and ceremonial, if not on trumpets (rarely used in indoor theatres) then on cornetts or hoboys. The 'soft' music would be played on recorders, viols or the consort.

Further references can be found in Heywood's *If you know not me Part II*: '*Enter ... the Weights in Sergeants gowns*',[23] and in Robert Armin's *The Historie of the two Maides of More-clacke*:

HUM. What are the waits of London come?
MAN. Yes sir.
HUM. Play in their highest key then. *hoboyes play.*
MAN. sound Hoboyes.'[24]

An intriguing direction appears in *The Late Lancashire Witches*: 'Enter an invisible spirit. J. Adson with a brace of greyhounds'.[25] John Adson, City Wait, composer and later member of the Royal Musick, appears, not in a musical role but rather as a walk-on ghost and dog handler. The fact that he is named, whilst not unique, is of interest. The inference is that here we have an example of a musician being incorporated into the action of the play, suggesting that musicians were expected to participate in non-musical roles, just as actors would be prepared to perform music. The 'actor-musician' function that was essential for those in the touring companies may well have applied even when professional musicians were employed in theatres in London. One clear piece of evidence for the waits' connection with theatres comes not from a play text but in the form of an official complaint in 1613 which states that they failed to play for the wedding of a magistrate's daughter because they had instead taken on (more lucrative?) employment in a public playhouse.[26]

The identity of those professional musicians is largely lost. Companies rarely made record of musicians they employed, but there are some

---

[21] W.W. Greg, ed., *The Booke of Sir Thomas More* (Oxford: The Malone Society, 1911) lines 944–54.
[22] W. Heminges, *The Fatal Contract* (London, 1653), sig. H3r:, 1654.
[23] T. Heywood, *The Second Part of If You Know Not Me* (London, 1609), sig. F4v.
[24] R. Armin, *The History of the Two Maids of More-clacke* (London, 1609), sig. A1v.
[25] T. Heywood, *The Late Lancashire Witches* (London, 1634), sig. D4.
[26] Woodfill, Musicians, p.41.

documents that give at least a partial picture of who performed and where. These come largely from the list of Sir Henry Herbert, *de facto* Master of the Revels, compiled on 27 December 1624, of the twenty-one 'hired' men associated with the King's Men. These 'musitions and other necessary attendantes' were listed so as to avoid arrest or being 'pressed for soldiers' without the permission of the Master of the Revels or the Lord Chamberlain:

JOHN ADSON: City Wait, one of the Blackfriars Musick. Recorder, flute and cornett player.

FRANCIS BALLS: c1631, hired man; possibly a musician and walk-on actor. He had a non-speaking role in *Believe as You List* in 1631.

RICHARD BALLS: Blackfriars Musick and City Wait, 1608–22.

AMBROSE BEELAND: 'winde instrumentes and consorts' as City Wait, violin for the King's Musick, 1640.

JEFFREY COLLINS: member of the Cockpit Theatre music in the *Triumph of Peace*, 1634.

EDWARD HORTON: Boy player and singer, 1629–30.

JOHN RHODES: Possibly a musician, 1624.

WILLIAM SAUNDERS: City Wait, 1634/41.

WILLIAM TAWYER/TOYER: d.1625, in *A Midsummer Night's Dream* F1 stage direction: '*Tawyer with a Trumpet before them.*

THOMAS TUCKFIELD: Probably the same 'T. Tucke' mentioned in the revival of *The Two Noble Kinsmen*, 1624.

NICHOLAS UNDERHILL: Boy player. Violin. Apprentice to Ambrose Beeland 1620, Played as part of the Cockpit Theatre music in the *Triumph of Peace*, 1634.

HENRY WILSON: Named as lutenist in *Believe as You List* in 1631.

JOHN WILSON: also 'Iacke Wilson' in F1 of *Much Ado About Nothing* 'Enter *Balthaser with musicke*'. He was a City Wait 1622–41+.

To this list can be added the 'actor-musicians':

THOMAS DOWNTON: Strange's Men, 1593; Admiral's-Henry's-Palgrave's, 1594-c.1618.

SAMUEL GILBURNE: Apprentice. Left a bass viol in the will of Augustine Philips, 1605.

JAMES SANDS: Apprentice. Left a cittern, bandora and a lute in the will of Augustine Philips, 1605.

RICHARD SCARLETT: d.1609, came from a family of Royal Trumpeters.

THOMAS UNDERELL: Worcester's Men, 1602. One of the same name was a royal trumpeter, 1609–24.

James Shirley's Inns of Court masque *The Triumph of Peace*, managed by Bulstrode Whitelocke in 1634, included, initially at least, named players from the bands of the Blackfriars and Cockpit theatres:

The Blackfriars Theatre Band

JOHN ADSON: see above

AMBROSE BEELAND: see above

HENRY FIELD: City Wait from 1625. Woodwind and treble 'viollen'.

THOMAS HUTTON/SUTTON: lutenist. City Wait from 1625.

FRANCIS PARKER: City Wait from 1616.

RALPH STRACHEY (STREACHY, STREET): City Wait from 1611?

The Cockpit Theatre Band

JEFFREY COLLINS: see above

THOMAS HUNTER: no information

JOHN LEVASHER: no information

JOHN STRONG: winds and violins. Became King's musician for the winds
    in November 1634. He was never a City Wait, but frequently substituted for
    Robert Parker, the City Wait.

NICHOLAS UNDERHILL: see above

EDWARD WRIGHT: no information

Of these musicians, the Blackfriars Musick are all registered as waits. Those
whose backgrounds are traceable from the Cockpit list are associated with
the theatre, and in the cases of Strong and Underhill, with the waits.
The inclusion of these two theatre bands in the procession for
The Triumph of Peace is probably due to the involvement of Bulstrode
Whitelocke, a noted devotee of the music at Blackfriars, and James Shirley,
resident dramatist at the Cockpit from 1625–35.

The Repertoire and Role of Theatre Bands

We have seen already that the music for the consort contained in
the Morley and Rosseter publications and in the Holmes part books
can be regarded as a reliable source of theatre music. After around 1615,
the mixed consort began to be replaced by violins (fiddles) and possibly theorbos and lutes.[27] Simon Ives (1600–61) collaborated with
William Lawes on the music for Shirley's *The Triumph of Peace* in
1634 and was a wait by 1637. He had an association with the Blackfriars
Playhouse before then, for in his memoir of 1634 Bulstrode Whitelocke
wrote:

> I was so conuersant with the musitians, & so willing to gaine their favour,
> especially att this time, that I composed an aier my selfe, with the assistance
> of M^r [Simon] Iues, and called it, Whitelockes Coranto, which being cryed

---

[27] Holman, Fiddlers, 131–40.

up, was first played publiquely by the Blackefryars Musicke, who were then esteemed the best of Common Musicke in all London.

    Whensoeuer I came to that house (as I did sometimes in those dayes) though not often to see a play, the Musitians would presently play Whitelocke's Coranto, & it was so often called for, that they would haue it played, twice or thrice in an afternoon.[28]

From this account, it is clear that to go to the theatre did not necessarily involve seeing a play, the attraction of the best band in town being sufficient draw in itself, regardless of the drama to which it was attached.

    Identifying specific music, other than the surviving play songs and snatches of ballads with their popular tunes, is harder to achieve. Usually actors would have sung their songs and, if accompanied, a lutenist or fiddler might have come on to stage with them. Apart from Whitelocke's account of hearing his own music, eye-witness accounts refer to the performance itself but not the actual music heard. Much of the musical content in terms of songs from the boys' company plays has been identified[29] and in the plays themselves there are indicators of pieces well known as perhaps stock repertoire. In Beaumont's 1607 play for the Blackfriars, *The Knight of the Burning Pestle*, for example, the Citizen and his wife refer to 'Lachrymae' and 'Baloo', two pieces contained in Morley's Consort books.[30] Who would have made the choices on music selection and how much there was a set repertoire for act music and pre-performance is not clear. The waits would rehearse twice a week and give public concerts for half the year, so a substantial amount of music would have been available to hand. Songs for the plays, if accompanied by the musicians, could be prepared separately from the acting rehearsals. The instrumental colours available from a band of six players would have been considerable. In *The Tragedie of Tancred and Gismund*, a play presented by Gentlemen of the Inns of Court, there are more details than usual of the music heard between acts:

> *Before the second Act there was heard a sweete noice of stil pipes*
> *Before this Acte* [Act 3] *the Hobaies sounded a lofty Almain*
> *Before this Act* [Act 4] *there was heard a consort of sweet musick*
> *Before this Act* [Act 5] *was a dead march plaid*[31]

---

[28] Ibid., 142   [29] Austern, 1992, passim.   [30] See L. Austern's essay, 91–2 below.
[31] *The Tragedie of Tancred and Gismund* (London, 1591). In both this and the 1592 edition these details about the music between acts are placed at the end, after the epilogue.

Recorders, shawms (and probably sackbut) and mixed consort are all used, with a variety of different styles and textures.

Musical Realism

Generally, music served the functions of realism, effect and affect. Realism includes songs that are part of the drama, for instance when a song is called for by a character. Dancing as part of a scene again involves music as a realistic element. In martial scenes trumpets sound various calls: *parley*, *tucket*, *sennet*, *alarum*, *flourish*. They are often sounded 'afar' to denote distance, action occurring elsewhere, or the imminent arrival of royalty or opposing armies. It is possible that professional trumpeters were hired to play not only the realistic martial calls but also to sound the advent of the play by playing the same short fanfare three times before the players entered. In *The Merrie Conceited Jests of George Peele* is the account of how George Peele waited until a single 'trumpet had sounded thrise' before going on to the stage to recite the Prologue. Trumpets and drums would go about the streets to proclaim the opening of a new play, the trumpeter most likely having a banner attached to his instrument to denote the particular theatre he was promoting, as can be seen in the copy of the well-known De Witt sketch of the Swan Theatre, where the trumpeter's banner is emblazoned with the same Swan emblem as the flag that flies from the top of the building.[32] In *A Midsummer Night's Dream* the mechanicals enter to perform their play preceded by a trumpeter (William Tawyer, see above). In the indoor play-houses cornetts take on the role of the trumpet, possibly because they were felt to be too loud for the enclosed space but equally possibly because the cornett was regarded as a 'proper' professional instrument, as opposed to the trumpet, an expensive piece of military hardware. The cornett was much more versatile, capable of everything from fanfares to accompanying voices, and perhaps rendered the employment of a trumpeter unnecessary.[33]

Musical Effect

Effect in the theatre could be achieved in various ways. In 1620, an eyewitness account of *Faustus* as performed at the Fortune states that

---

[32] See T. Stern, 'Before the beginning; after the end. When did plays start and stop?', in M.J. Kidnie and S. Massai, eds., *Shakespeare and Textual Studies* (Cambridge University Press, 2015), 359–61.

[33] See D. Lindley, 'Music in the English theatre of 1616', in Tian Yuan Tan, Paul Edmondson and Shih-Pe Wang, eds., *1616: Shakespeare and Tang Xianzu's China* (London: Bloomsbury, 2016), 222–3.

'Drummers make Thunder in the Tyring-house'.[34] *The Pilgrim*, performed by the King's Men in 1621 has *'Musick afar off. [Singing of] Pot
birds.'*[35] These 'pot birds' are devices whereby birdsong is imitated by
blowing a pipe through water in an earthenware pot. Then there are the
other-worldly effects to evoke the heavens, spirits and sombre funerals.
Dead Marches play for funeral processions and recorders often play
a role in the same solemn moments. For example, Marston's *Sophonisba*,
1606 instructs: *'Orgaine and Recorders play to a single voice: Enter in the
mean time the mournful solemnity of Massinissas presenting Sophon.
Body:'*.[36]
   This leads to another question, that of whether or not musicians ever felt
the need or desire to respond to the historical or geographical elements of
the narrative. Most probably they did not, as an awareness of, and exposure
to, other musical styles and traditions would not have been expected of
professional players. Just as the actors wore contemporary clothing, with
very little added to indicate historical period, the same was true of the
music. In the music for masques, 'antic' music or that for satyrs' dances and
other fantastical characters would have had much the same musical style as
for other more mundane figures. So it would have been in the theatre; even
when cues call for a *'phantastique measure'*, this would still be within the
tonal and cultural reference of player and listener.

Musical Affect

Music has an immense theatrical power; it can enhance the emotional level
of a scene, stir the blood with harsh bold fanfares and alarums, lull the
listener into a reverie and produce tears through the melody of a song.
Modern usage of music in film and television means that a soundtrack, or
'underscore' is often more or less constant. In early modern theatre this
would not have been the case and yet it was still appreciated that music
could lend force and support to particular moments in the play if needed.
In the indoor playhouses music on occasion was played underneath
dialogue or action. In *Sophonisba* there are several instances where
Marston appears to be indicating music as underscore to the text and in
his *The Malcontent* (1603), the very first entry is prefaced with the cue

[34] John Melton, *Astrologaster* (London, 1620), E4r.
[35] F. Bowers, ed., *The Dramatic Works in the Beaumont and Fletcher Canon* (Cambridge, 2008, 10 vols),
vol. 6, 196 (5.4.16. SD).
[36] J. Marston, *The Wonder of Women* (London, 1605), sig. G3.

'*The vilest out of tune Musicke being heard*'. Considering that this would probably have followed a consort playing exquisitely, the effect, describing aurally the inner working of the mind of Malevole, would have been powerful. We can only speculate as to the way such a cue might be interpreted by the musicians: what would constitute 'vile' and 'out of tune'? A chaotic mess or something more organised but deliberately badly played?

The musicians would normally play behind a curtain in the music room but could move easily enough to other points in the theatre for dramatic purposes.[37] Musical effects could be specific in their location, as in *Sophonisba*:

> *Infernall Musique softly*
> [Syphax] Harke, harke, now rise infernall tones
> The depe fetch'd grones of labouring spirits . . .[38]

In Shakespeare's *Antony and Cleopatra* we find the instruction: '*Music of the hautboys is under the stage*' (4.3.12. SD). The latter example proves that it was not just in the private indoor playhouses that use was made of spatial effect, placing the musicians for maximum impact in the infernal regions of the underworld, literally under the stage. In Fletcher's *The Double Marriage* the '*Strange Music within, Hoboys*' is then referred to as '*a hideous Dirge*', then: '*Within strange Cries, horrid Noise, Trumpets*'.[39]

Whoever played and whatever, exactly, they performed, it is a fact that music has been an essential and integral element of dramatic performance for millennia. Its power to give an aural manifestation of inner feelings was a vital aspect of renaissance humanist thought and of the Platonic doctrine that the order of a man's spirit could be reflected in the harmony of music. As Lucy Munro's essay in this volume demonstrates, theatres both indoor and outdoor were increasingly able to draw on the musical versatility of actors and professionals to ensure the variety and potency of musical effect in the drama of the period.

---

[37] See Simon Smith's essay, below.   [38] The Wonder of Women, sig E.
[39] Bowers, ed. Vol. 9, 137 (2.4.79SD-81).

CHAPTER 2

The Many Performance Spaces for Music at Jacobean Indoor Playhouses

Simon Smith

'Where breath's that musique?' So asks Duke Pietro upon hearing the *'vilest out of tune Musicke'* that so memorably opens John Marston's *The Malcontent* (CQR, c.1603, Blackfriars).[1] The most likely location for music at a Jacobean indoor playhouse would be the music room above the stage, as seen in Illustration 2, and indeed these out-of-tune sounds emanate from 'the Malecontent *Maleuoles* chamber', an unseen space on the upper level from which the title character will later emerge. Scholars of early modern drama are often quick to focus on the music room as the locus of music, and of instrumental performance in particular, at indoor venues, be that in adult company plays by Shakespeare and others after 1609, or in youth company drama before 1613. Andrew Gurr, for instance, sees Blackfriars' 'consort of professional musicians' as synonymous with the music room above the stage, two components of a 'ready-made musical accessory' for Shakespearean performance after 1609.[2] The music room was certainly an important location, but as Linda Phyllis Austern reminds us, 'music also sounded from within, below, and afar off' at Jacobean indoor playhouses.[3] This chapter investigates the many musical performance spaces of these venues, arguing that instrumentalists were far more itinerant, flexible and indeed visible at Blackfriars, Paul's, Whitefriars and the Cockpit than a close focus on the music room would suggest. It will also ask whether performances in the music

---

[1] J. Marston, *The Malcontent* (London, 1604), B1r. Since precise dates and places are important to the argument, details of the first performance including company, date and venue are given in parentheses, following *DEEP: Database of Early English Playbooks*, ed. by A. B. Farmer and Z. Lesser (2007), http://deep.sas.upenn.edu (accessed 18 September 2015). Company abbreviations are: CKR – Children of the King's Revels; CQR – Children of the Queen's Revels; LCM – Lord Chamberlain's Men; LEM – Lady Elizabeth's Men; KM – King's Men; PB – Paul's Boys; QAM – Queen Anna's Men.

[2] A. Gurr, *The Shakespeare Company, 1594–1642* (Cambridge University Press, 2004), 80–81, 84.

[3] L. P. Austern, *Music in English Children's Drama of the Later Renaissance* (Philadelphia: Gordon and Breach, 1992), 28.

Illustration 2 Musicians occupying the gallery above the actors in rehearsal for the
Globe production of *Knight of the Burning Pestle* (Sam Wanamaker Playhouse, 2013)
Photograph by Alastair Muir, © Shakespeare's Globe

room were hidden from sight as often as is currently assumed. The chapter's
'musicians' include actors playing a range of instruments, and hired or
retained professionals. Our knowledge of musical expertise amongst early
modern actors, and of the extent to which professional musicians were used
in commercial theatres, is partial, but this chapter is not an intervention in
recent debates about playhouse musical personnel.[4] This is, rather, an attempt
to chart some of the relationships between music and space at Jacobean
indoor playhouses, investigating the conventions of indoor music use that
informed Shakespeare's dramaturgy when writing for Blackfriars, as well as
shaping indoor performances of earlier Shakespeare plays that remained in
the King's Men's repertory after 1609.[5]

---

[4] D. Lindley offers the best recent account of the surviving evidence in *Shakespeare and Music*
(London: Thomson, 2006), 90–103. D. Mann has recently challenged prevailing opinion, particu-
larly concerning music outdoors pre-1609, in 'Reinstating Shakespeare's Instrumental Music', *Early
Theatre*, 15 (2012), 67–91. See W. Lyons's essay in this volume.

[5] The significance of Shakespeare to the company's later repertory is clear from a payment of £5 for the
Master of the Revels to 'forbid the playinge of any of Shakespeare's playes to the Red Bull company'
on 11 April 1627. N.W. Bawcutt, ed., *The Control and Censorship of Caroline Drama: The Records of
Sir Henry Herbert, Master of the Revels 1623–73* (Oxford University Press, 1996), 165.

Musical performers were not exclusively confined to the playhouse music room. Singers on the lower stage are well documented both indoors and out, youth company repertories being particularly renowned for such inclusions.[6] Less remarked upon, however, is the common appearance of instruments on indoor stages. In John Day's *Humour out of Breath* (CKR, 1608, Whitefriars), the gullish Hortensio removes his blindfold (having believed he was playing blind man's buff), and spies a musical instrument conveniently placed '*on the Lower stage*':

> **HORTENSIO**
> what haue we here? a base violl! though I cannot tickle the
> mynnikyn within, ile (though it be somewhat base) giue them a
> song without, and the name of the Ditty shall be;
> > *The Gentleman Vshers Voluntarie.*
> > He sings.[7]

Day places a musical performer and his large viol ostentatiously upon the relatively small Whitefriars stage, drawing visual attention to the instrument even as Hortensio's punning on 'base' and 'bass' evokes the intimate encounter occurring 'within'.[8] This viol is momentarily a stage property, to be seen as well as heard. After the song, Hortensio shouts towards the tiring house until a servant enters '*aboue*'.[9] This entrance inverts the expected placement of instrument (and musician) in the music room and dramatic character below, an inversion elsewhere used to great effect in *The Insatiate Countess* (CQR, c.1607–1608, Blackfriars; revised 1609–1613, Whitefriars).[10] To see an actor on the upper stage was not unusual, and neither was it unexpected to see instruments below. But by inverting the most *common* respective locations of musician and actor, such scenes draw attention to the movement of musical instruments and performers, emphasising music's contribution not just as sound but as sight.

Scenes of self-accompaniment require relatively modest musical resources, but Shakespeare's *Cymbeline* (KM, c.1608–1611, Blackfriars & Globe) is more demanding of its playhouse musicians. The play is usually thought to post-date the company's move to Blackfriars, although if

---

[6] See, for instance: Austern, *Children's Drama*, 50–59; M. Shapiro, *Children of the Revels: The Boy Companies of Shakespeare's Time and Their Plays* (New York: Columbia University Press, 1977), 236.

[7] John Day, *Humour Out of Breath* (London, 1608), G1r–G2r.

[8] See J. McIntyre, 'Production Resources at the Whitefriars Playhouse', *Early Modern Literary Studies*, 2.3 (1996), 21–35.

[9] Day, *Humour*, G2r.

[10] L. Machin, W. Barkstead and J. Marston, *The Insatiate Countess* (London, 1613), D4v.

earlier, it would nonetheless have been performed at both of the King's Men's venues after 1609 and before its 1623 publication.[11] In the second act, Cloten seeks to seduce Innogen, and so prepares a serenade beneath her window:

> **CLOTEN**
> I would this music would come. I am advised to giue her music o' mornings; they say it will penetrate.
>   *Enter* MUSICIANS
>   Come on, tune. If you can penetrate her with your fingering, so; we'll try with tongue too. If none will do, let her remain; but I'll neuer give o'er. First, a very excellent good-conceited thing; after, a wonderful sweet air, with admirable rich words to it, and then let her consider.
>
> **[SONG]**
> So, get you gone. If this penetrate, I will consider your music the better: if it do not, it is a vice in her ears which horsehairs and calves' guts, nor the voice of unpaved eunuch to boot, can never amend. (2.3.10–27)

A 'very excellent good conceited' piece of instrumental music precedes a 'wonderful sweet' song, 'Hark, Hark, the Lark', selected by Cloten to 'penetrate' Innogen, in his own unpleasant, punning phrase. Precisely which instruments are used is unclear, although 'horsehairs' and 'calves' guts' indicate bowed strings. Cloten's advice to try 'with tongue' perhaps suggests wind instruments too, or may simply mean singing. Where Hortensio's verbal delight upon spying the bass viol foregrounds the materiality of a single instrument, here the rigmarole of many musicians coming on stage and 'tun[ing]' their instruments before playing, coupled with Cloten's extended musical innuendos, emphasise the musicians-as-bodies and instruments-as-objects moving in and out of the tiring house in the immediate proximity of Blackfriars' onstage playgoers.

   Where Hortensio's bass viol and Cloten's musicians are displayed ostentatiously, other plays hide music in the lower tiring house. Cues for music 'within' are generally taken to indicate performance below, although this assumption has been destabilised by Mariko Ichikawa's observation that 'within' can also mean out of sight above.[12] The safest examples of lower tiring house music therefore involve a musician either entering or visible through the stage doors, or explicitly cued as 'below'. For instance, *The Spanish Gypsy* (LEM, 1623, Cockpit) instantly follows a '*Florish*' with

[11] See M. Butler, ed., *Cymbeline* (Cambridge University Press, 2005), 3–6.
[12] M. Ichikawa, *The Shakespearean Stage Space* (Cambridge University Press, 2013), 52–67.

the entrance of the performer: '*Enter Soto, with a Cornet in his hand.*'[13] Cornetts (or sometimes hautboys) were generally preferred to trumpets for fanfares and signals at indoor playhouses, although as Linda Phyllis Austern has demonstrated, trumpets were not entirely absent.[14] Soto's cornett confirms this preference at the Cockpit in 1623, whilst his entrance from the lower tiring house clarifies the performance location. Soto is probably the performer who again sounds a '*Florish within*' to announce the start of the gypsies' play-within-a-play in act four, presumably upon the cornett and at the lower level; he enters from the tiring house a few lines later to act the part of Lollio.[15] It is notable that *The Spanish Gypsy* uses a cornett here, for whilst, as David Lindley observes, playing 'basic fanfares and signals' on the natural trumpet is 'not a particularly difficult task', cornetts require more practice.[16] Like the youth playing Hortensio, this adult actor – possibly a clown, for Soto is 'A merry fellow' – fulfils a significant dramatic role, as well as demonstrating instrumental competence.[17] That said, these cornett flourishes were probably less demanding than the bass viol accompaniment required of Hortensio. Robert Daborne's *The Poor Man's Comfort* (QAM, 1615–1617, Cockpit), performed 'divers times' at the same venue as *The Spanish Gypsy*, similarly calls for a '*Horn within*' immediately followed by the stage-door appearance of the messenger who sounded it: '*Enter Post.*'[18] It is a stretch to classify a blast on a post-horn as 'music', however.

Two Blackfriars plays place sophisticated and varied musical performances in the lower tiring house. Marston's *The Wonder of Women, or Sophonisba* (CQR, 1605–1606, Blackfriars), a particularly musical play, requires at least two groups of musicians, or some extremely hasty movement between levels. In a scene of dubious witchcraft, Erichtho casts a 'spell' that will supposedly summon the play's eponymous heroine to a bed just offstage, allowing the villain Syphax to have sex with her. Erichtho's conjuring requires significant assistance from the Blackfriars' musicians, beginning with some '*Infernall Musique softly*' from an unspecified location. The next cue is precisely placed: '*A treble Violl and a base Lute play softlyd [sic] within the Canopy.*' That the canopy is the discovery

---

[13] T. Dekker, J. Ford, T. Middleton and W. Rowley, *The Spanish Gipsie* (London, 1653), E2r.

[14] Austern, *Children's Drama*, 67–8. See also Mann, 'Instrumental Music', 69–70, and Lyons' essay, 26, above.

[15] Dekker, Ford, Middleton and Rowley, *Spanish Gipsie*, G4r.

[16] Lindley, *Shakespeare and Music*, 102.

[17] Dekker, Ford, Middleton and Rowley, *Spanish Gipsie*, A2r.

[18] R. Daborne, *The Poor-Mans Comfort* (London, 1655), A1r, E4r.

space curtain on the lower level is clear from entrance and exit cues: Syphax exits into '*the Canopy*' from the main stage, having entered '*Through the vautes mouth*' (described also as '*a caues mouth*') represented either by one of the flanking stage doors or, more probably, the trapdoor. The canopy is put to practical use at the opening of the fifth act when Syphax '*drawes the curtaines and discouers Erictho lying with him*' in a particularly memorable bed-trick. With viol and lute '*within the Canopy*', it might seem logical to place further cues 'below', yet ten lines later the text calls for '*A short song to soft Musique aboue*'. Not only singers (Syphax can hear the harmonious voices of several 'inforced Spirits') but also players of '*soft Musique*' are required on the upper level, raising questions of practicality. Unless the viol and lute players could move between levels with remarkable swiftness they presumably remain '*within the Canopy*', leaving singers and instrumentalists above, two instrumentalists below, and possibly yet more musicians elsewhere, if the '*Infernall Musique*' sounded from a third location. Syphax's observation that 'Hell and Heauen ringes | With Musique' hints at a rationale for this precise placement of music at upper and lower levels, given the association of music under 'th'earth' and 'i'th air' (*The Tempest*, 1.2.387) with the respective abodes of the Devil and God.[19] It is also possible that the infernal music heard earlier in the scene sounded from underneath the stage, making this the music that 'rings' through 'hell', although it is not clear that Shakespeare's contemporaneous and unique cue in *Antony and Cleopatra* (KM, 1606–1608, Globe) for '*Music of the Hoboyes ... under the stage*' (4.3.12.) reflects wider playhouse practice rather than the playwright and company's idiosyncratic choice.

A similarly swift juxtaposition occurs in Nathan Field and Philip Massinger's *The Fatal Dowry* (KM, 1617–1619, Blackfriars & Globe), when a '*Song Aboue*' is shortly followed by a '*Song Below*'. Both are sung on the stage by Aymer, but accompanied by offstage and out of sight 'instruments'; Charalois has come to hear this famed singer, but is disappointed he 'Shall ... not see' the musicians too.[20] Quite how the songs were performed at Blackfriars, then, is far from clear. Aymer is onstage and

---

[19] J. Marston, *The Wonder of Women or The tragedie of Sophonisba* (London, 1606), E2v–F2r. On the early modern associations of music above and below, see: S. Smith, '"I see no instruments, nor hands that play": *Antony and Cleopatra* and visual musical experience', in S. Smith, J. Watson and A. Kenny, eds., *The Senses in Early Modern England, 1558–1660* (Manchester University Press, 2015), 167–84 (177–8).

[20] N. Field and P. Massinger, *The Fatall Dowry* (London, 1632), I1r.

not directed to be above; moreover, with less than ten lines between singing the first song and introducing the second, there does not seem to be time for him to move unremarked from the upper stage down through the tiring house and out onto the lower stage in a fit state to sing again. It seems more likely that '*Aboue*' and '*Below*' refer to the accompanying musicians, presumably two separate groups located out of sight and awaiting Aymer's cues, for if the singer cannot quite move between levels in time, multiple instrumentalists would certainly struggle. The dramatic purpose of this apparent dual location of invisible musicians is opaque, but once more it places instrumentalists in the lower tiring house.

One particularly tantalising location for drums, trumpets and cornetts is '*afar off,*' *Sophonisba*, for instance, calling for '*A march far off,*' '*Cornets a march far off*' and '*The Cornets a far off sounding a charge*'.[21] The phrase could pertain to the diegetic world rather than to playhouse space, as a Caroline Blackfriars retreat '*sounded as from far*' suggests, but John Fletcher's calls for '*Drums within at one place afar off*', followed by '*Drums and Trumpets in severall places afar off, as at a main Battell*' in *Bonduca* (KM, 1611–1614, Blackfriars & Globe) imply that the effect was achieved at least in part through physical location at a particular '*place*' or '*places*' in Jacobean performance.[22] Alan C. Dessen and Leslie Thomson note a cue in Folio *Hamlet* (LCM, 1600–1601, Globe) for a '*March afar off, and shout within*' (5.2.328.1; TLN 3836), suggesting that the former is 'a sound in the distance', presumably at the back of the tiring house, the latter 'just offstage' at the lower level.[23] This seems persuasive, assuming that *Hamlet*'s insidious hendiadys has not spread to the stage directions here, although as the Folio text is thought to predate the move to Blackfriars by six years, it cannot be said to preserve conventions of musical staging specifically indoors.[24] Dessen and Thomson also note two Blackfriars cues to stand afar off on the stage itself, which would suggest 'afar' need not be any great distance: Fletcher and Massinger's *The Double Marriage* (KM, 1619–1623, Blackfriars & Globe) requires two citizens to enter '*at both dores, saluting afar off*'; Thomas Middleton directs the '*Nobles afarr of*' from the '*Tirant*' who enters '*wondrous discontentedly*' in *The Second*

[21] Marston, *Sophonisba*, F3r-v, G1r.

[22] W. Davenant, *Love and Honovr* (London, 1649), A2r (my emphasis); J. Fletcher, 'The Tragedie of Bonduca', in *Comedies and Tragedies* (London, 1647), 4H1v–4H2r. Cornetts could possibly have replaced trumpets for Blackfriars performances of *Bonduca*, but this is uncertain (see note 14).

[23] Alan C. Dessen and Leslie Thomson, *A Dictionary of Stage Directions in English Drama, 1580–1642* (Cambridge University Press, 1999), 2.

[24] See Ann Thompson and Neil Taylor, eds., *Hamlet*, The Arden Shakespeare Third Series (London: Thomson, 2006), 74–86.

Maiden's Tragedy (KM, 1611, Blackfriars & Globe).[25] On the balance of probability, then, it seems likely that musicians afar off at Jacobean indoor playhouses stood at the very back of the tiring house, perhaps also moderating the volume of their instruments. In the case of the highly directional trumpet, this could even have involved facing away from the *frons scenae*.

So far, this investigation has considered musicians on the stage, in the lower tiring house and (briefly) at the upper level. Having explored a range of locations other than the music room, the remainder of the chapter will ask how far the most familiar of musical performance spaces might have contributed to the itinerancy, flexibility and visibility of music at Jacobean indoor playhouses. Music rooms were located in the 'gallery or galleries that fronted the tiring house at the second storey', and scholars generally imagine a single, central music room.[26] Nonetheless, the only direct reference in a pre-Caroline indoor play-text actually describes two music rooms flanking a central 'upper stage' performance space at the tiny Paul's playhouse: '*Andrugios ghost is placed betwixt the musick houses*' in Marston's *Antonio's Revenge* (PB, 1600–1601, Paul's).[27] Scholars often argue that music room curtains were normally only opened when musicians played 'for the Act' whilst the wicks of the candles were trimmed, act breaks being observed at indoor venues throughout the Jacobean period.[28] Richard Hosley has been influential in suggesting that 'the chief function of the curtains over the stage . . . was to conceal musicians, a possible secondary function . . . being to reveal the musicians between the acts and before and after the play', drawing upon pictorial sources of 1640 and 1662.[29] Andrew Gurr argues that '[s]ome of Fletcher's stage directions assume a curtain across the central section of the balcony behind which the invisible musicians played', and notes a 1631 reference to 'the encurtain'd musique'.[30] Linda Phyllis Austern takes 'verbal directions for music to begin' in plays staged at Paul's and Blackfriars similarly to indicate that during dramatic

[25] Dessen and Thomson, *Stage Directions*, 3. J. Fletcher and P. Massinger, 'The Double Marriage', in *Comedies and Tragedies*, 5D4v; T. Middleton, *The Second Maiden's Tragedy*, The Malone Society Reprints (Oxford: Malone Society, 1909), TLN 1655–6.

[26] Austern, *Children's Drama*, 26.

[27] J. Marston, *Antonios Reuenge* (London, 1602), K1v; R. Bowers, 'The Playhouse of the Choristers of Paul's, c.1575-1608', *Theatre Notebook*, 54 (2000), 70–85.

[28] Marston, *Sophonisba*, B4v. For a recent account of the practicalities of candle use at indoor playhouses, see: M. White, '"When Torchlight Made an Artificial Noon": Light and Darkness in the Indoor Jacobean Theatre', in A. Gurr and F. Karim-Cooper, eds., *Moving Shakespeare Indoors: Performance and Repertoire in the Jacobean Playhouse* (Cambridge, 2014), 115–36.

[29] R. Hosley, 'Was There a Music Room at Shakespeare's Globe?', *Shakespeare Survey*, 13 (1966), 115.

[30] Gurr, *Shakespeare Company*, 80.

performance, '[t]he music room was undoubtedly located behind a curtain that could be pulled aside when the musicians were to be made visible'.[31] As Gurr and Hosley demonstrate, the evidence for habitual curtaining of musicians by the Caroline period is reasonably strong, but similar evidence from earlier years is lacking. Austern's 1600s play-text evidence indicates that musicians could have played many of their mid-scene cues from behind a curtain, but it does not necessarily follow that they must, therefore, have done so. In fact, a closer look at certain dramatic and non-dramatic texts suggests rather different music room practices in the first decade or so of the seventeenth century.

Francis Beaumont's *The Knight of the Burning Pestle* (CQR, 1607, Blackfriars) places a 'Grocer' and his 'Wife' amongst genuine playgoers on stage stools; they interrupt the play with scripted, comic and often meta-theatrical interjections. The Wife in particular struggles not just with the conventions of decorous playgoing, but even, in places, with distinguishing dramatic performance from reality. At one point, she seeks to amass witnesses with a view to detaining one of the dramatic characters, Jasper, who has just stolen his mother's casket of jewels; she 'do[es] not like that this vnthrifty youth should embecill away the money'.[32] She believes she could easily substantiate her accusation that Jasper is a thief, noting, 'heere are a number of sufficient Gentlemen can witnesse, and my selfe, and your selfe [her husband], and the Musitians, if we be cal'd in question' (D3ʳ). Critically, she can see the musicians from where she sits, and she is also adamant that they have a clear view of the stage from their place in the music room above, sufficient for them to act as 'witnesse[s]' to the preceding events. *The Knight of the Burning Pestle* is preoccupied with playhouse conventions; the Grocer's Wife's unfamiliarity with these conventions leads to much meta-theatrical comedy, but she also provides helpfully clear observations of details that more seasoned playgoers may not bother to mention. In so doing, she offers strong evidence for visible musicians not just during act breaks but also in the middle of a scene at Blackfriars.

The Grocer's Wife's remarks are supported by two broadly contemporaneous and generally overlooked references to music rooms by dramatist Thomas Dekker, in texts not written for the commercial stage. Dekker's *The Bellman of London* (1608), a rogue pamphlet, opens with Envy and Avarice running amok through contemporary society in the form of furies

---

[31] Austern, *Children's Drama*, 26, 29.
[32] F. Beaumont, *The Knight of the Burning Pestle* (London, 1613), D3r.

'begotten by a player' and 'a Dutch Burger'. The narrator seeks respite in 'the Country', where he stumbles upon a remarkable feature of the natural landscape:

> It was a Groue set thicke with Trees, which grew in such order, that they made a perfect circle, insomuch that I stood in feare, it was kept by Fayries, and that I was brought into it by enchantment. The branches of the Trees (like so many handes) reached ouer one to another and in their embrace-ments held so fast together, that their boughes made a goodly greene roofe, which being touched by the winde, it was pleasure to behold so large a seeling to mooue: vpon euerie branch sat a consort of singers, so that euerie Tree shewed like a Musick room.

He resolves to dwell in 'this goodly Theater', dividing each 'day into acts, as if the ground had beene a stage, and that the life which there I ment to leade, should haue bene but as a play', but is swiftly distracted by a plume of putrid smoke that leads him to a hellish scene of food preparation in a nearby cottage. Dekker's rich, fantastical description draws upon design features of both indoor and outdoor playhouses. The perfectly circular shape of this living wooden 'O' imitates the polygonal construction of the Globe and the Swan, yet the 'seeling' or 'roofe' of interwoven green branches echoes the enclosed form of an indoor theatre. Continuing his theatrical comparison, Dekker suggests that the trees look like music rooms because one can see musical performers therein: the 'consort of singers' (in fact, 'birds') visible on each branch means that every tree 'shewed' – that is, looked – 'like a Musick room'.[33] Dekker's simile suggests that playgoers could see as well as hear musical performers in real music rooms, as could the Grocer's Wife mid-scene at Blackfriars.

Dekker makes further comparisons with music rooms in his 1604 account of the entertainment offered to the new monarch, James I, in the City of London on 15 March. With expansive transcriptions and descriptions of his own contributions, and minimal references to those of Ben Jonson, Dekker's printed text is a rich, if partisan, account of this day of celebration. In recounting the fifth pageant, he offers an extremely detailed description, corroborated by Stephen Harrison's printed image, of the arch erected at Little Conduit (known widely as the Pissing Conduit) alongside Paul's churchyard at the western end of Cheapside.[34] Dekker explains that the upper-middle part of the arch is best understood through reference to playhouse design:

---

[33] T. Dekker, *The Belman of London* (London, 1608), B1r–B2r, B3v–B4r.
[34] S. Harrison, *The Arch's of Trivmph* (London, 1604), G2r.

> Wee might (that day) haue called it, *The Musicke roome*, by reason of the chaunge of tunes, that danced round about it; for in one place were heard a noyse of cornets, in a second, a consort, the third, (which sate in sight) a set of Viols, to which the Muses sang.[35]

This 'music room' contains a variety of instruments including wind, bowed strings, and a 'consort' perhaps of mixed instruments, contrasting with another consort, or 'set', of viols. This tallies with Austern's view of the Blackfriars music room as 'large enough to accommodate an organ, a consort of viols, and a chorus of singers at one time'.[36] Once again, Dekker implies that music rooms have at least some musicians 'sate in sight', in this case, the viol players. Such spaces are apparently characterised by the variety of musical possibilities they house, by their location on an upper level, and by the visual display of musical performers.

Dekker wrote a number of plays for indoor, youth company performance at Paul's in the 1600s, so it is no surprise to find musicians visible mid-scene at that venue. In Middleton's *A Mad World, my Masters* (PB, 1604–1607, Paul's), Sir Bounteous Progress speaks repeatedly of a wonderful organ installed at his house and valued at 'some hundred and fifty pound', and a performance shortly follows in one of the theatre's 'musick houses'.[37] Perhaps this was a meta-theatrical advert for a recent addition to the company's musical resources, or perhaps Middleton simply found overzealous organ enthusiasts as ripe a target for satire as Puritans. In any case, the scene indicates that musicians could be seen from the stage below, for Sir Bounteous points out 'My Organist' to his guest immediately before '*The Organs play*'. This is presumably the 'Walloon' who 'plaies vpon e'm', rather than the 'Welchman' who 'blowes wind in their breech', as Sir Bounteous describes them through typically Middletonian *double entendres*. Austern sees it as exceptional that 'the curtains of the music room have been drawn back so that it becomes the musicians' gallery of a banqueting hall' here.[38] Certainly, the scene echoes the design features of such a venue, but in the light of Beaumont's stagecraft at Blackfriars and Dekker's repeated references to music rooms as spaces for the display of musicians as well as their music, it seems likely that a visible organist mid-scene was as conventional to indoor playhouse practice in the earlier Jacobean period as it was to the diegetic world of this particular play.

---

[35] T. Dekker, *The Magnificent Entertainment* (London, 1604), G1v.

[36] Austern, *Children's Drama*, 28.

[37] T. Middleton, *A Mad World, my Masters* (London, 1608), B4v–C1r; Marston, *Antonios Reuenge*, K1v.

[38] Austern, *Children's Drama*, 74.

Performers in the music room could nonetheless be concealed, presumably by curtains, when necessary for particular dramatic purposes. Such concealment is required in Fletcher's *The Captain* (KM, 1609–1612, Blackfriars & Globe) when characters on the lower stage hear but cannot see music emanating from an upper 'chamber', before two more characters '*Enter at the window*' and sing a duet in full sight.[39] Likewise, the previously considered 'instruments' playing for the '*Song aboue*' in *The Fatal Dowry* are explicitly hidden from the sight of Charalois below. However, our assumption that musicians were hidden *by default* in music rooms requires rethinking, at least in relation to earlier years of the Jacobean period, given that playhouse musicians at Blackfriars and Paul's, not to mention Dekker's viol consort and beautifully warbling birds, are all noted for their visibility in both literal and figurative music rooms of the 1600s. The music room, like the stage, appears to have been a space for the visual display of musicians, as well as a significant location for musical performance.

This essay has explored many musical performance spaces at Jacobean indoor playhouses, taking in whole groups of musicians on the lower stage, music both afar off and within inches of playgoers, and swift transitions between tiring house music above and below. Instrumentalists appeared ostentatiously on the stage and, it seems, were often on display in the music room as well. Clearly, unseen performance in the music room was just one of many sorts of music heard and seen indoors. What might this investigation suggest, then, about the role of music in Jacobean dramatic performance, including in the work of Shakespeare and the King's Men after 1609? Certainly, musical locations often serve important dramatic purposes, offstage flourishes creating imagined worlds of military conflict, or serenades below recasting the upper tiring house as a dwelling. Moreover, musicians appear as strikingly dynamic playhouse presences, not altogether different from the actors making their exits and their entrances. Their visual contribution to the experience of playgoing is both significant and easily overlooked when a music room curtain becomes the symbol of music indoors. Yet these musicians occupy a liminal place within diegetic worlds, sometimes appearing as characters, sometimes unseen, and at other times visible mid-scene above the stage yet outside of the dramatic world, as 'necessary attendantes' of the playing company.[40] In their very appearance, then, musicians draw attention to the Jacobean

---

[39] J. Fletcher, '*The Captaine*', in *Comedies and Tragedies*, 2G4r.

[40] Bawcutt, ed., *Control and Censorship*, 158.

indoor playhouse's fluid boundary between diegetic world and social event, serving as a reminder that Shakespeare and his contemporaries wrote for theatres in which the relationships amongst playgoers, musicians and actors had different configurations from those of our contemporary dramatic performances.

CHAPTER 3

In Practice I

Original Practices and Historical Music in the Globe's London and Broadway Productions of Twelfth Night and Richard III

Claire van Kampen

Introduction: Establishing the Stage

One of the principal reasons why Sam Wanamaker dedicated himself to the recreation of Shakespeare's Globe theatre on Bankside was to explore Shakespeare's working practices in a Playhouse amphitheatre of the 1600s. The major dynamic of this open-aired circular playhouse is a standing yard audience surrounded entirely by galleried seating. There were to be no microphones and no lighting rigs. The music is live and acoustic and, for the most part, visible; actors take their own cues to enter the stage, and take responsibility for their own focus as storytellers. When combined with period clothing and musical instruments and arrangements of music of the sixteenth and early-seventeenth century, we have developed a playing style that we term 'Original Practices'.[1]

Original Practices: Its Derivation

From 1997, a consensus about clothing, music and the use of the stage has been derived from references and sources available to the creative teams dedicated to creating a world onstage, both visually and musically, that Shakespeare would have recognised. The arrangements of music are not 'pastiche' but reconstructions from extant sixteenth and seventeenth century tunes, consort books and keyboard music.

Musically, there are some factors that weigh against us when we use the term 'authenticity'. Shakespeare wrote for actors dressed in the same period

---

[1] Recordings of the music for these productions are now available digitally and on CD from Globe Music, the Globe's record label. See GlobePlayer.tv for links and information.

as those in the audience. Music was performed on instruments that were current, not historical. The tunes the audience came to hear changed frequently to keep pace with fashion. The meaning and importance of these instruments was culturally known – especially trumpet calls and street music – as was the signification of specific instruments accompanying supernatural elements of the story, the appearances of ghosts, or the descent of gods. However, there are few in the audience of the newly-recreated Globe theatre who will have previously heard a shawm or 'hoboy', or who will recognise references to 'antique song' in *Twelfth Night* (2.4.4), or understand the specific command of a trumpet call. Likewise, names of dances current in 1600 such as 'coranto', 'sink-a-pace' and 'galliard' are specific to the dance fashions of the 1590s, and their forms would be largely unknown now. Furthermore, actors and entertainers such as the company fool, Robert Armin, had to battle for attention in an amphitheatre holding up to 3000 people, all of whom were as interested in seeing each other as they were the play. Understanding the size of this sound world helped me to realise that loud instruments such as the shawm, sackbut, trumpet, and drum are vital in alerting the audience. In this regard, Shakespeare's textual references to flourishes, fanfares and tuckets, drums afar off or getting nearer, are signals to a standing audience to pay close attention to the story.

Our 'Original Practices' approach was to work closely with Shakespeare's musical stage directions. He rarely specifies any kind of musical underscore, partly because it is very difficult to underscore text with live and acoustic period instruments; music generally pulls aural focus from text. Unless the text is being underscored by an instrument as quiet as a lute, it is impossible to achieve low enough sound levels for the music to perform the function we are so used to hearing on film and in modern theatre, where sound is 'cheated' under voice electronically. It is clear from the play-texts that music did not perform the emotional narrative function that it carries today. On stripping away all modern techniques of using musical underscore and its mood-illustrative functions, music played on period instruments with Shakespeare's texts acquires different functions: it can serve to re-locate characters; it can also 'change gears' textually – a technique found more often now in the stage musical than in new theatre writing. Played visibly from the central gallery above the stage music carries a strong iconographic statement. Balanced between heavenly and earthly worlds, it expresses the influence of the Muses, and therefore consolidates the 'great Globe itself' as a stylised and microcosmic representation of the Elizabethan world view.

Twelfth Night: The Original Practices Rubric

Possibly the most well-known of the Globe's 'Original Practice' productions is *Twelfth Night*, which has enjoyed a remarkable longevity from its birth in 2002 through to its extraordinary success in the 2013–14 Broadway season in the USA, where it played in The Belasco, a proscenium theatre.

Invited by Middle Temple Hall's Master of the Revels, Anthony Arlidge, QC, The Globe's *Twelfth Night* was initially created to play on the 400th anniversary of its first recorded performance by Shakespeare's Company in Middle Temple Hall on the 2nd of February 1602. There is little information about the nature of this performance but we know that it had been requested by the Inns of Court, and was performed, according to Manningham's diary,[2] at a feast at Candlemas to an audience who were largely lawyers and members of the Inns. In other words, this performance was not for the 'common people', the groundlings and prostitutes of Bankside, but to a highly educated and privileged group of men. Creating a production of *Twelfth Night* in the very hall where Shakespeare's company played meant, in 2002, that this particular incarnation of Original Practices served to highlight courtly references. Though open to the general public at a premium ticket price, the audience also consisted of lawyers, politicians and even princes (Prince Charles attended on the anniversary itself).

Seated and partly visible behind the screens of the musicians' gallery in Middle Temple Hall, the band consisted of a consort of flute/recorder, violin, lute, cittern, bandora and bass viol.[3] The Elizabethan mixed consort is very useful for all kinds of entertainment: its wide variance of tonal spacing offers room for lute divisions; flute and violin carry melodies supported by the viol on the bass line; the bandora provides the rhythm section needed for dancing.[4] I was initially concerned that we would need to add a drum for the 'jig' at the end of the play, but the three strumming instruments with the bandora holding it all together gave a wonderful percussive basis for any dance figure.

For the pre-show of Middle Temple's *Twelfth Night*, the six musicians were placed around a table in the middle of the hall as the audience entered. They played off part-books propped up on stands on the actual

---

[2] Manningham, J., *Diary of John Manningham, of the Middle Temple, and of Bradbourne, Kent, barrister-at-law, 1602–1603* (Westminster: Printed by J.B. Nichols and sons, 1868).

[3] Keith McGowan arranged the music, and also played in the band.

[4] See William Lyons's discussion of the repertoire of the Elizabethan Mixed consort above.

table, very much as the Henry Unton painting (*c.* 1596) suggests. When given the nod by stage management in preparation for the start of the actual show to begin, the band moved upstairs to the gallery in the Hall, necessitating a short break in the continuance of music while they retuned their instruments and stood by to play the first music 'cue' – in the actual show itself.

In terms of the music used and referenced below, all would have been known to the audience in 1602. 'If music be the food of love, play on' (1.1.1) was called out to the consort playing 'Lachrymae' by Dowland. 'The Funeralls' by Holborne introduced the arrival of Viola; Morley's 'Can she excuse' and 'The Frog galliard' were associated with the household of Olivia, and her obsessive love for 'Cesario' (Viola disguised as a young man). This offered a musical panoply of leitmotifs rich in dance-style structure.

Musically, *Twelfth Night* moves from extreme melancholy to the reflective sanguinity embodied by Feste's epilogue song, 'When that I was.'[5] It seems to have been a commonplace – certainly in the 'people's theatre' of the Globe and other amphitheatres – for songs to adapt and change their melodies to both be 'in fashion' and topical. Instrumental music is also important in *Twelfth Night*, and not only in its opening with a call for music. Act 2.4.1 also begins with a command from Orsino: 'Give me some music.' There is no indication in the Folio text whether or not the instrumentalists begin to play here; but they certainly do respond to the direct request 11 lines later to 'play the tune the while', where the Folio has the direction 'music plays', and presumably it continues, as underscore – a rare effect – until Feste is ready to sing 'Come away death.'

Further difficulty arises since, though the beginning of each music cue is carefully noted by the author, there is no 'out point' for the first cue. Does this mean that with the appearance of the Fool, the music just stops? It would seem that the instruction '*music*' as the Fool sings implies accompaniment to the song, and not that he is required to sing unaccompanied. Does he accompany himself on the cittern?[6] If Robert Armin did so, then this would establish a reason for the courtly musician (lute) to give way to the music of the world of the Fool. In the play, he forms a clear bridge between 'the people' – soldiers, tavern life, 'spinsters and knitters in

---

[5] The original melody of this final song is lost to us; the most commonly known melody is in fact ascribed to Joseph Vernon in a 1772 songbook entitled *The New Songs in the Pantomime of the Witches, the Celebrated Epilogue in the Comedy of Twelfth Night*.

[6] Similar examples of the absence of clear instruction as to when music stops are *R II*, 5.5 and *H IV2*, 2.4.

the sun', and the worlds of Orsino and Olivia, the pale-faced and genteel aristocracy.

In our production in 2002, we did not – as most contemporary Shakespeare productions also do not – have a Feste who was expert enough on a historical plucked instrument to be able to accompany himself. Modern circumstance therefore distanced us from what Shakespeare would have routinely expected. Feste is a difficult role; it requires an actor of experience and technique who can sing well enough – this was felt to be paramount. In all our incarnations of this production of *Twelfth Night*, Feste's 'Come Away Death' was accompanied by the lutenist on a theorbo from the gallery,[7] who seamlessly moved from underscore to accompaniment during the scene. No contemporary music for the song survives. I chose James Lauder's 'My Lord of Marche Pavan' as the musical basis for the song; the piece had been played in the pre-show, and its melancholic and sombre nature fitted the words well.

Drawn from the masque culture of courtly music, Lauder's tune and the song style was quite a departure for Feste from other songs he leads in the play. Songs such as 'Three merry men be we' and 'Hold thy peace' (2.3.67, 57) are catches and rounds common to taverns and alehouses. Sir Toby Belch demonstrates his familiarity with the tavern world as he sings snatches of popular ballads such as 'There Dwelt a Man in Babylon' or 'O the Twelfth Day of December' (2.3.69, 73).

The use of 'Hey Robin' is intriguing.[8] The Fool sings it 'at' the imprisoned Malvolio in 4.2.58-65, who, from his vantage point, is unable to see the singer. Yet he recognises the Fool immediately by the song; is it the material, or the voice of the Fool, which gives him the clue? This is indeed a very 'antique song' by Elizabethan standards, and would have been perceived by the audience as very 'out of joint' with fashion. Is there a point being made here about the character of Malvolio being similarly 'out of joint' in imagining that a humble steward could entertain ideas of being married to a countess? Certainly the Fool has played his part in Maria's plot to teach Malvolio the simple lesson that the servant classes must never think they are socially equal to their 'masters'.

The text of *Twelfth Night* ends with a song by Feste. Given that it is possible, even probable, that the performance concluded with a dance, I felt that Morley's 'Lavolto' (a play on the popular courtly dance 'la Volta')

---

[7] From a strict 'Original Practices' perspective, our use of the theorbo in this production was knowingly anachronistic; the theorbo (the lute's large cousin) arrived in England at a later date, possibly around 1610. But the theorbo gave us a fuller resonance in the Globe.

[8] From a catch by William Cornyshe (1465–1523).

could serve for both song and segue dance, as Morley was undoubtedly known to the Inns of Court and the melody of Lavolto worked extraordinarily well with the words of the song. To suit the baritone voice of the actor, the song, accompanied only by theorbo, was in one key, but then, to suit the mixed consort, it was reprised a sixth higher for the dance. The effect of this key change gave the dance a definition without changing to another piece of music. A galliard was choreographed (by Siân Williams) for the company, and this courtly dance did not have the sense of robust storytelling motifs that were found in later Globe and ensuing theatrical performances of this production.

From the courtly and exclusive setting of Middle Temple Hall we moved the production, for the 2002 Summer Season, to the Globe theatre. Suddenly there were questions of suitability for the open-air acoustics. The delicacy of the Elizabethan mixed consort was exchanged for a consort of reed and brass instruments: shawms, sackbuts and curtals. The theorbo player doubled with drum for the jig. A consort of the bassoon-like curtal was used to define the character of Toby Belch. Recorders and a theorbo were used for the opening 'Lachrymae'. There was still a pre-show of music, but played from the musicians' gallery; the music consisted of very much the same masque tunes as had been played in the Middle Temple Hall, but this time arranged for 'loud' instruments. Players were dressed fully as Elizabethans, complete with hats and wearing theatre 'livery' from the 1600s. The jig was re-choreographed to include 'vignettes' of various characters combining both dance and story.

When *Twelfth Night* returned to the Globe in September 2012, in a production where all the music was sourced and arranged by me, the Globe's acoustics had already changed their nature; during the intervening ten years the green oak had hardened to such an extent that it was possible to explore the use of historical instruments which exhibited a more delicate aural palate and a wider dynamic range. It was thus possible to create effective arrangements based around a cornett and sackbut ensemble, plus drum – again 'doubled' by the theorbo player. The cornetts doubled on recorders[9] allowing us a variety of different textural sounds; 'Lachrymae', for example, remained for recorders and theorbo. The use of the recorder to an Elizabethan audience was significant. Iconographically, the instrument often represents the melancholy of death, or the world between heaven and earth; it is an instrument which carries a spiritual significance. The use of a consort of recorders at the opening, where all the conversation

---

[9] Not a usual double for the modern cornett player, though common in the earlier period.

is of melancholy, and then again at the top of Act 5 in 'The Frog Galliard' just as Olivia and Sebastian become secretly married, to signify the heavenly union and blessing of the angels, would not have been without meaning to a Globe audience of the 1600s. An instrument beloved of the Tudor court, the velvety sound of the cornett behaved like the human voice; it could be both soft and loud – unusual for most Elizabethan melodic instruments of a high tessitura which usually had little dynamic control. The sackbut (the ancestor of the modern trombone) also falls into this category, able to play pianissimo but also able to make a loud and defined noise when required.

The 2012 production of *Twelfth Night* was transferred from the Globe into the very different environment of the proscenium-arch Apollo Theatre in the West End. Interestingly, the cornetts sounded a little smaller in that indoor space, despite not having to compete with the outdoor ambient sounds of planes and distant London traffic. In spite of it being an open-air theatre, the Globe is built as a cylinder or drum; its galleries are vertiginous, and the box-like music gallery together with the roof over the stage creates near-perfect acoustics which are satisfying for both voice and music.

To create that 'Globe-like-feel' in the Apollo, we used a wide, angled sound baffle above the music gallery to help project the music naturally the way the Globe's gallery does. We used real candlelight over the stage, with subtle enhancement by a steady electric lighting state. We also created a twelve-minute musical pre-show, with three musicians playing from memory onstage joined by the actor playing Feste – who had learned the pipe and tabor very effectively. Some of the audience elected to be seated onstage in specially constructed 'standings' and the design (by Jenny Tiramani, who has designed all incarnations of this production), attempted to create an 'inclusiveness' among the audience, whilst not actually having any standing audience. In this sense, it was a hybrid of the Globe and Middle Temple Hall. A vigorous *Springtanz* was the entr'acte before the second half – without house-lights dimming, the audience needs their ears and eyes to be focused back to the stage after the social interaction of the interval. In the Globe, this function in an 'Original Practices' production is performed by a trumpet surge from the music gallery followed either by speech or music. It was remarkable how many elements of the production successfully transported themselves to a nineteenth-century proscenium arch theatre, and received a response very comparable to that of audiences within the Globe's architecture.

Illustration 3 Peter Hamilton Dyer Playing Pipe and Tabor as Feste in *Twelfth Night*
(Globe 2012). Photograph by Simon Annand © Shakespeare's Globe

In the Apollo Theatre, the *Twelfth Night* company played in repertory
with another 'Original Practices' production, *Richard III*, which had also
played at the Globe from July, 2012.

Richard III

Richard III's musical score was shawm-based, partly to differentiate it
from *Twelfth Night*, but mainly because the shawm and sackbut ensemble
(with baroque timpani, for which I can find no musical reference, except

Illustration 4 Musicians Playing Period Instruments in the 'Original Practices'
Richard III (Globe 2012). Photograph by Simon Annand © Shakespeare's Globe

pictorially on horseback!), lent itself to a more strident and military world.
The shawm (or 'hoboy') is an instrument that Shakespeare uses significantly in his texts; it appears as 'hoboys under the stage' in *Anthony and
Cleopatra*, taken as a presage of doom to the watchmen on guard on the eve
of the Battle of Actium. The shawm is an interesting instrument in
Shakespeare's world: once the iconographic painted image to be found in
the hands of angels and the instrument of religious music, by 1600 it was
being played secularly and on street corners in the hands of the city waits as
they played for civic functions, memorably described by Edward Ward in
the early eighteenth century:

> We heard a Noise so dreadful and surprizing that we thought the Devil
> was riding on Hunting thro' the City, with a Pack of deep-mouth'd
> Hellhounds ... At last bolted out from the corner of a Street ... a parcel of
> strange *Hobgoblins* ... Of a sudden they Clap'd [their instruments] to their
> Mouths and made such a frightful Yelling, that I thought the world had been
> Dissolving, and the Terrible Sound of the last Trumpet to be within an Inch of
> my Ears.
>   Under these amazing Apprehensions I ask'd my friend what was the
> meaning of this *Infernal outcry*? ... Why, what, says he, ... these are the

topping tooters of the town, and have *Gowns, Silver Chains*, and *Sallaries*, for playing *Lilla Burlera* to my Lord Mayor's horse thro' the city.[10]

The use of the shawm is entirely appropriate for a story concerned with the malevolent and politically astute character of the King. The natural double for shawm players is the recorder, which becomes very significant around the visitation of the ghosts to Richard on the eve of the battle of Bosworth. To sustain the illusion of ghostliness, I broke the rule here of no underscore by using a sustained and looped trio for recorders offstage, playing *'Une Jeune fillette'* by Jean Chardevoine (1537–1580).

Little of the music and effects used in productions in Shakespeare's own period found their way into the First Folio, though there must have been a great variety of choices even within sixteenth and seventeenth century parameters. In other 'Original Practices' productions – *Hamlet* in 2000, *Julius Caesar* in 2014 – I have used offstage recorders and/or sustained offstage sound to support the illusion of the ghostly apparition. When the Ghost of Hamlet's father appeared in full armour in a brightly lit matinée, and without offstage music, the audience laughed. They were not convinced. The next day, with the inclusion of offstage sustained sound, there was no laughter and the illusion was complete. We clearly need sound in the twenty-first century to support the illusion of the supernatural, but the question remains whether a sixteenth-century audience also needed such a device for the suspension of disbelief. The closing sequence of Richard III's fight with Richmond, leading to the former's death, tied in this production with the return of the ghostly apparitions interfering with Richard's vision on the battlefield. The bagpipe played the tune 'music for the battel' from *'My Lady Nevill's keyboard book'* across a volley of trumpet and drum calls to represent the battle that was raging beyond the veil of the *frons scenae* (the back wall of the stage) – referred to and heard about, but never visually depicted in full.

A word about trumpet and drum calls here: there have been reconstructions of drum signals by sixteenth-century re-enactors, but there do not seem to have been written calls specifically for drums and the infantry as we have them for the trumpet, and the cavalry, by Arbeau and Mersenne (French), Thomsen (Danish), and Bendinelli (Italian). The calls range through a variety of commands such as 'clap on your saddles', 'retreat', 'alarum', and 'parley'. We use extant commands such as those described

---

[10] *E. Ward, *The London Spy Compleat* (1703), I. 34–5. See Lyons' essay above for more on the waits.

above in all 'Original Practices' productions. The audience in the Globe has begun to understand and recognise these – particularly 'alarum' and 'parley'. Elizabethan audiences were very likely to have known a great variety of them.

Original Practices on Broadway

When the *Twelfth Night* and *Richard III* company took both these productions to Broadway in 2013, it became clear for both budgetary and acoustic reasons that we could use only one set of musicians to perform both shows. I decided to adapt the score for *Twelfth Night* to fit shawms and recorders (and theorbo doubling lute). It was interesting how little I had to change, musically. The *Twelfth Night* pre-show was always predominantly onstage, and was supplemented by a shawm entr'acte from the gallery of a similar pre-show set as before, with the addition of 'Clement Woodcock's Hackney' (1575) which was played to enable the final lighting of candelabra onstage when the stage-seated audience were in their places. The entr'acte piece '*Springtanz*', which had worked so well on cornetts and drum, now sat equally well on shawms; though it lacked the 'trumpety' feel of cornetts, it had the precision and pointedness of the reed instrument. Curtals were used together with sackbuts to very good effect in Holborne's 'New Years Gift' at the end of 1.3 as a leitmotif for Sir Toby Belch. The curtal, being a double reed instrument, is extremely versatile; it has the capability of providing a firm bass line, like a bassoon, in a mixed ensemble of cornetts, shawm and sackbuts. The shorter tenor/alto curtals have a mellower sound which can blend very well with softer instruments. Though they were used in the 1600s as part of a waits ensemble there is no direct evidence of a consort of curtals being used in the original performance of Shakespeare plays. But yet, as a consort they are sublime, and like the cornett they sit well with the human-speaking voice.

Discovery through Recovery

It was one of the hallmarks of a player in the 1600s, whether playing in the waits, theatres or taverns, that they could 'double' on other instruments.[11] This is very much the case with many of the early music players at today's Globe, and it is one of the features of an 'Original Practices' production

---

[11] See Lyons, 21 above.

that audiences will see and hear. Today, these musicians have often come out of conservatoires abroad where they have specialised in one instrument only. They realise quickly, through playing in Shakespeare productions at the Globe, that by learning a variety of period instruments, they are increasing their chances of steady employment (in the theatre at any rate). I would venture that this is a very similar situation to that of a London musician 400 years ago: the more instruments you can play, the more bread you can put on your table. In this sense, the 'Original Practices' work is not only generating a consensus about what music may have sounded like in Shakespeare's theatre 400 years ago, but is also replicating patterns of work and opportunity in the twenty-first century – including performing for various functions as offshoots around the theatre season. This 'Third Globe' is therefore musically synergised with the First Globe.

Having access to the recreation of Shakespeare's theatre in London has enabled me, and many others, to begin to understand how a particular form of architecture shaped this playwright and his contemporaries. The process of experimenting with acoustic early modern instruments in the Globe theatre, and realising Shakespeare's sound world alongside the performance of his plays in this unique amphitheatre space has been an epiphany to me as a theatre composer. It has been a journey which has required me to learn and understand new techniques, and the limitations of sixteenth- and seventeenth-century instrumentation; but above all, to understand music and play-texts from an Elizabethan and Jacobean world view.

It is a mark of the greatness of Sam Wanamaker's vision that the performance of Shakespeare all over the world has, by 2015, been most decidedly affected by the playing style of performances at Shakespeare's Globe. It is now a regular occurrence to see 'jigs' – or dances – at the end of Shakespeare productions in theatre spaces which were not created with any sense of 'original working practices' – including the National Theatre, Royal Shakespeare Theatre and the Barbican. This year, I noted that Shakespeare in the Park's *Cymbeline* in New York likewise adopted a jig, and there was indeed an actor from the founding 1997 Globe company in that production.

Cynics would say that 'jigs' are 'claptraps' and therefore a 'must' for any director to stick on the end of a production as a juiced-up curtain call. This is to misunderstand the nature of 'jigs'. In 2015, in the Globe, every Shakespeare – and even non-Shakespeare – production ended with a jig, even following a tragedy like *Hamlet*, or *King Lear*. The audience now expects it. It is also something that they do not necessarily clap their way through; it has been a challenge to find a way to tell the story of the particular jig in such a way that the audience will want to watch and listen, and not simply clap along with the music from the start. Sometimes the musical challenge is successful, sometimes it is not; if we want the audience to focus on the jig and not their applause, this has worked best when the jig is clearly a piece of danced-story (as in both *Twelfth Night* and *Richard III*, in which the dance featured a very serious pavan-type choral movement interspersed with cadenzas from company members gifted with movement and dance.

I feel that the work of discovering the possibilities of period music that could be employed with productions is giving the audience an opportunity of 'recovering through discovery.' Whilst the 'Original Practices' rubric cannot claim to be providing 'authenticity' there is, however, something essentially 'Shakespearean' about this approach. It is the result that could be described as 'authentically authentic': the audience's physical attention, their understanding, focus and special connection to a production in which period music has played a key role.

List and Description of Music in the Globe's Productions of *Twelfth Night* 2012–14 and *Richard III* 2012–14:

Twelfth Night

All arranged by Claire van Kampen for recorders, cornetts, sackbuts or Rauschpfeifen, plus lute/theorbo/cittern and percussion.
'All Creatures Now' – John Bennet (c. 1575–1614)
> A madrigal from the collection *The Triumphs of Oriana*, compiled by Thomas Morley in 1601, issued in 1603.

'Mrs Winter's Jump' – John Dowland (1563–1626)
> Most of Dowland's music is for his own instrument, the lute. The poet Richard Barnfield wrote that Dowland's 'heavenly touch upon the lute doth ravish human sense'.

'Hollis Berrie' – Anonymous
> A popular (and possibly country) tune in the 1590s, here played by cornetts and sackbuts in a somewhat nobler rendition such as would fit the Candlemas festivities of households such as Olivia's or Orsino's.

'Michills Galliard' – Anonymous
From *Erster Theil au Berlesemer Paduanen und Galliarden*, published 1607 in Hamburg by Ratsmusik members Zachariah Fullsack and Christian Hildebrand. This slower meditative Galliard presages the melancholy of Olivia and Orsino.

'Wanton' No. 61, from *Pavans, galliards, almains* – Anthony Holborne (c.1545–1602)
This collection, published in 1599, is the largest of its kind. Holborne had links with the Inns of Court and was held in the highest regard as a composer by contemporaries.

'Lachrimae Antiquae' – Dowland
The famed Elizabethan lutenist was so closely associated with this, his most popular composition, that he was already signing his name 'Jo: dolandi di Lachrimae.'

'The Funeralls' from *Pavans, galliards, almains* – Holborne
Here arranged for recorder consort with theorbo.

'Come Hither Rowland/Lord Willoughby' – William Wigthorpe, (1570–1610)
This piece retained its popularity by virtue of the flexibility of its arrangements and its jolly tune.

'Can she excuse my Wrongs' ('The Earl of Essex's Galliard') – Dowland
From Dowland's first collection of music, The *First Booke of Songes or Ayres* (1597). Reprinted at least four times, and groundbreaking in its 'table layout', this first book of lute songs enabled performance in different settings and consorts.

'The New-yeeres Gift' No. 6 from *Pavans, galliards, Almains* – Holborne
Twelfth Night's performance at Candlemas on February 2nd, 1602 (see above) actually presaged the real New Year (March 25th). England didn't adopt the 'popish' Gregorian calendar until 1752.

'Springtanz' (from *Terpsichore*) – Michael Praetorius (1571–1621)
Terpsichore (1612), a compendium of more than 300 instrumental dances, was very popular at the Elizabethan court, where dancing was a favourite pastime. Praetorius, a German composer, organist and music theorist, was the greatest musical academic of his day. His meticulous documentation of seventeenth-century practice

was of inestimable value to the early-music revival of the twentieth century.

'Hey Robin' (Ah Robyn) – William Corneyshe (1465–1523)

Sung by Feste in the text of *Twelfth Night*, it is clear that this Round for 3 or 4 voices was still in common currency in 1602, a remarkable accomplishment for a piece some eighty-years old from the time of Henry VIII.

'The Frog Galliard' – Dowland

Nobody is sure how John Dowland's Frog Galliard earned its curious title, but it may have something to do with one of Queen Elizabeth I's suitors, the Duc d'Alençon (later, Duc d'Anjou), whom the Queen referred to as her 'frog'. It was one of Dowland's most popular pieces, so ubiquitous that it was arranged by Morley for an ensemble in *The First Booke of Consort Lessons* (1599) without giving Dowland credit.

'Lavolto' – Thomas Morley (1557–1602)

Lavolto (Anon.) is found arranged by Thomas Morley in his 1599 and 1611 consort books. It is also found in the Fitzwilliam Virginals Book where it was arranged by William Byrd, Morley's teacher. Morley was an English composer, theorist, editor and organist, and the foremost member of the English Madrigal School. He was the most famous composer of secular music in Elizabethan England and an organist at St Paul's Cathedral. He and Robert Johnson are the composers of the only surviving contemporary settings of verse by Shakespeare. It is tempting to imagine that Morley's Lavolto was used as the base tune for this song and developed into the jig, a traditional dance at the end of the play. At the Globe in 2012 it was played on Rauschpfeifen, sackbuts and drum – instruments for the open air.

Richard III

All arranged by Claire van Kampen for shawms and sackbuts, recorder consort, Renaissance timpani and percussion.

'Tantara Cries Mars' – Thomas Weelkes (1576–1623)

Originally a three-part madrigal but arranged here for five (three shawms, two sackbuts), plus Renaissance timpani, its counterpoint and cross rhythms provided an unusual and arresting extended fanfare.

'In Midst of Woods' – John Mundy (1550–1630)

I was attracted to this wonderful madrigal in 5 parts by the words 'In midst of woods or pleasant grove, where all sweet birds do sing' which struck me as a very appropriate way to welcome in the Globe's audience to an amphitheatre made entirely from a thousand oak trees.

'Three Galliards' (from *Erster Theil au Berlesemer Paduanen und Galliarden*) – Benedict Greebe (?–1619)

Greebe's galliard became the signature piece for this production of *Richard III*. Though relatively little known to the early music world, this galliard displays a secure grasp of both dance structure and harmonic line; unlike many galliards written primarily for lute, this piece fits the character of classic shawm and sackbut tessitura.

'Galliard' – Jacob Praetorius or Schultz (1586–1651)

'Bransle de Champagne' – Claude Gervaise (1540–1560)

The branle or bransle was a dance that was less exotic than the favoured galliards and voltas of the 1580s. In contrast to *Twelfth Night*, which is a late Elizabethan play and featuring an unprecedented amount of musical reference so prominently as part of its text, I considered the humble bransle as a dance form that recaptured an earlier period in Tudor history, placing it very much in the realm of a Tudor version of the reign of Richard III.

'Une Jeune Fillette' – Jean Chardevoine (1537–1580)

This beautiful French melody from 1576, originally for voice and keyboard or lute has such a unique and innocent flavour that I thought it perfect to score it for recorders and make it the signature of imminent death, for Clarence in the Tower and Richard's dream on the eve of Battle, where he is visited by the apparitions of those he has murdered.

'Deux Bransles Simples' – Gervaise

From *Sixieme Livre de Danceries* (Paris, 1555), arranged here for recorders as a gesture to the innocence and imminent murder of the young Duke of York.

'Hunting – A Hunt's Up' – Bennet, from *A Brief Discourse* (1614)

Bennet was known chiefly for his madrigals, which ranged from light and festive in character to serious and even solemn. This piece, arranged for shawms and sackbuts with drum, sets the scene for

Richard in his avid and crafty fox-like pursuit of the crown for his own.

'**Music for the battle**' – Arranged for bagpipe with trumpet calls in the field from *My Lady Neville's Book*

My Ladye Nevells Booke (British Library MS Mus. 1591) is a music manuscript containing keyboard pieces by the English composer William Byrd, and, together with the *Fitzwilliam Virginal Book*, one of the most important collections of keyboard music of the renaissance. The origins of the manuscript are obscure. Not even the exact identity of the dedicatee is clear, but Lady Neville was presumably a pupil or patron of Byrd.

Finally, two dances found in the *Sixieme Livre de Danceries* (Paris, 1555):

'**Pavanne d'Angleterre**' – Anonymous, arranged for recorders, and

'**Fin de Gaillard**' – Gervaise, arranged with an additional part for the final jig.

CHAPTER 4

Ophelia's Songspace: Élite Female Musical Performance and Propriety on the Elizabethan and Jacobean Stage

Paul L. Faber

In his essay 'Music in Shakespeare' W. H. Auden remarks of Ophelia's mad scene: 'we are meant to be horrified' not only by the bawdy nature of the songs she sings, but also by 'the fact that she sings at all'.[1] Frederick W. Sternfeld concurs, describing Ophelia's singing before the court of Denmark as 'contrary to all sense of propriety for an Elizabethan gentlewoman'.[2] The belief that Shakespeare's audience would have been shocked simply by the 'public' nature of Ophelia's performance, naughty lyrics aside, prevails today.[3] Yet despite its widespread currency, this view is ultimately misguided, enduring into the twenty-first century because of a scholarly predilection for contemporary conduct manuals and the arguments of polemicists and apologists for music. Such works, while vital, ultimately distort perceptions of musical decorum in elite social spheres if they are not tempered with more pedestrian evidence such as accounts of, and references to, the common musical practices of actual people. Such evidence, admittedly, is scarce. Yet there is enough to suggest strongly that parents and peers proactively encouraged young ladies to perform regularly before mixed company within social spaces that, while exclusive, were hardly private. Incorporating this evidence into a revised model of contemporary musical decorum affords us crucial insights not only into

---

[1] W. H. Auden, 'Music in Shakespeare', in *The Dyer's Hand and Other Essays* (1948) (New York: Random House, 1989), 500–27 (522–3).

[2] F. W. Sternfeld, *Music in Shakespearean Tragedy* (London: Routledge, 1963), 54.

[3] 'Ophelia sings before an assortment of courtiers only because she is unhinged; Gertrude would never perform in so public a setting.' S. Gillespie, 'Shakespeare and Popular Song', in *Shakespeare and Elizabethan Popular Culture* (London: Bloomsbury, 2006), 174–92 (175). See also D. Lindley, *Shakespeare and Music* (London: Bloomsbury, 2006), 158; and A. E. Winkler, *O Let Us Howle Some Heavy Note: Music for Witches, the Melancholic, and the Mad on the Seventeenth-Century English Stage* (Bloomington: Indiana University Press, 2006) among others.

Shakespeare's vision of Ophelia but any contemporary dramatic representation of female musical performance.

Conduct manuals, or 'courtesy books', were all the rage in late sixteenth-and early seventeenth-century England, and they are essential to our understanding of normative behaviour in polite society. It is prudent to keep in mind, however, that the exemplars and prescriptions in books such as Baldassare Castiglione's *The Book of the Courtier* were perfections to which many no doubt aspired but few probably achieved.[4] Nevertheless, within such texts one finds three consistent messages with regard to music and manners: first, the cultivation of musical skill is a worthwhile endeavour;[5] second, musical activities should not distract from more important duties;[6] third, and crucially to this discussion, musical performance of any kind should be a strictly private business. Castiglione's champion, Count Lodovico da Canossa, would never perform music 'in the presence of persons of low birth or where there is a crowd'.[7] Such activity, warns Henry Peacham, 'eclipse[s] State and Majesty, and by consequence contempt with the meanest'.[8] Ordinary people, writes Thomas Elyot, forget 'reverence whan they behold [a gentleman] in symilitude of a common servant or mynstrel', and thus such performances are best avoided.[9] With such consistent warnings, it is reasonable to assume that most gentlemen took the advice to some degree.[10] And if eschewing public performance was the common caution to elite men in the sixteenth and seventeenth centuries, surely performance restrictions governing elite women and girls were more severe. We get a hint of this in one of the few conduct manuals written expressly for ladies, Richard Brathwaite's *The English Gentlewoman* (1630–1), where the author, while generally supportive of recreational music, spends substantial energy warning against 'immodest' musical expression. Those 'sensuall *Curtezans*' who revel too much in the delight of 'songs, pipes, earthly melody', and the 'Compliment' they represent, shall howl miserably in hell, 'crying, as it is

---

[4] The authors often make this explicit. 'I am content,' declares Castiglione's surrogate, 'to have erred with Plato ... there is the Idea of the perfect Republic, the perfect King, and the perfect Orator so likewise is that of the perfect Courtier.'Baldesarre Castiglione, *The Book of the Courtier*, trans. C. S. Singleton, ed. D. Javitch (New York: Norton, 2002), 7.

[5] See Castiglione, 55–7; T. Elyot, *The Boke Named the Governor* (London, 1537), 20^v–23^r; H. Peacham, *The Complete Gentleman* (London, 1622), 98, 104; and R. Brathwaite, *The English Gentlewoman* (London, 1631), 167. See also W. Higford, *The Institution of a Gentleman* (London, 1660), 77.

[6] See Castiglione, 77; Elyot, 21^v–22^r; Peacham, 98–9; and Brathwaite, 171–3.   [7] Castiglione, 76.

[8] Peacham, 100.   [9] Elyot, 22^v–23^r.

[10] Most conduct manuals are male-to-male discourses and rarely speak directly to female musical activities.

in the Apocalips ... *Woe is me that euer I was borne*'.[11] Clearly we are well beyond 'eclipsing State and Majesty'.

The often-quoted diatribes against music found in the writings of Puritan polemicists such as Phillip Stubbes and William Prynne prescribe female musical abstinence with predictable vigour. 'And if you would have your daughter whoorish bawdie, and uncleane, and a filthie speaker', Stubbes snarls, 'bring her up in musick'.[12] 'What a miserable Spectacle is it to chaste and wel-mannered eyes,' laments Prynne,

> to see a woman, not to follow her needle or distaffe, but to sing to a Lute. Not to be known by her owne husband, but to be often viewed by others as a publicke whore: not to modulate or sing a Psalme or confession, but to sing songs inticing unto lust: not to supplicate to God, but willingly to hasten unto Hell.[13]

Defenders of music offer little to counter Puritan polemic. John Case, the most often-quoted apologist, pauses in his defence of liturgical music only to caution 'noble' readers to practice music rather 'for their priuate solace, than publike ostentation'.[14] Among those speaking directly to musical decorum, then, the prevailing opinion seems clear: elite musical activity should be reserved for private entertainment only, and to approach the boundaries of decorum, especially when it comes to ladies, is to court immodesty and from there shaming and shunning.

In the wider literary world, this model appears to hold true. Comments on recreational music from prominent educators such as Richard Mulcaster and Roger Ascham and in the writings of authors such as Robert Burton and Francis Bacon offer little to contradict the prescription of privacy.[15] In the drama itself, elite female characters who sing almost always do so from behind some form of barrier. Desdemona, for example, sings in the confines of her bedchamber; the Welsh Gentlewoman in Middleton's *A Chaste Maid In Cheapside* performs behind closed doors in the home of a wealthy goldsmith; and the Countess of Arrain sings with daughter Ida from their private balcony in Robert Green's *James IV*.[16]

---

[11] Brathwaite, 77.   [12] P. Stubbes, *The Anatomie of Abuses* (London, 1583), sig. D5^r.

[13] W. Prynne, *Histriomastix The Players Scourge* (London, 1633), 277.

[14] J. Case, *The Praise of Musicke* (Oxford, 1586), 68–9.

[15] See R. Ascham, *Toxophilus the Schole of Shootinge* (London, 1545) 9–12^v; R. Mulcaster, *Positions* (London, 1581), 37–40 and *Elementarie* (London, 1582), 5, 9 and 25–7; and R. Burton, *The Anatomy of Melancholy* (London, 1621), 580–1, 586; and F. Bacon, *Sylva Sylvarium* (London, 1627), 35–57.

[16] See Shakespeare, *Othello*, 4.3.38–55. T. Middleton, *A Chast Maid in Cheape-side* (1613), ed. V. Wayne in *Thomas Middleton: The Collected Works* (Oxford: Clarendon Press, 2010), 167–193, 4.1; and R. Greene, *The Scotish Historie of James the Fourth* (1594?) (London, 1598), sig. D^v, 2.1, SD.

Moreover, when musical boundaries appear to be tested or breached one commonly finds allusions to wantonness and ultimately to prostitution. Maria in Beaumont and Fletcher's *The Woman's Prize* barricades herself in her chambers and with the help of 'city' and 'country' wives sings a gender-bending song clearly audible to all in the vicinity. Referring to the performance, husband Petruchio labels her 'Lady Green-Sleeves', alluding to the courtesan of the popular ballad.[17] Similarly in Fletcher's *The Chances*, two Constantina's, one a chaste gentlewoman and one a courtesan, are heard singing from beyond their chambers by men a number of times during the play, with the prevailing implication being that female musical performance beyond its proper place can invite dangerous associations.[18] Ophelia then, singing her racy song fragments from beneath a shroud of madness before at least some of the court at Elsinore, in *Hamlet*, 4.5, seems merely another example of this sort of dynamic, especially if she carries a lute, as she does in Q1, which David Lindley suggests would associate her still more 'perilously with the prostitute'.[19] Indeed her spectacle would have probably evoked in the minds of some audience members the figure of the *cortigiana*, the eminently cultured, celebrity courtesan of sixteenth- and early-seventeenth-century Venice whose representations, while already popular in the contemporary literature through the works of Italian writers such as Pietro Aretino,[20] were beginning to appear fully fleshed on the public stage around 1599.

The *cortigiana*, however, is only one component of Shakespeare's complex conflation of musical allusions in his presentation of Ophelia. Traditional reliance on conduct authors, polemicists and apologists has, unfortunately, dulled scholarly perception of her equally prominent counterpart, an archetype which emerges clearly as one reads records from the

---

[17] See F. Beaumont and J. Fletcher, *The Woman's Prize, or The Tamer Tamed* (1611?), ed. F. Bowers, in *The Dramatic Works in the Beaumont and Fletcher Canon*, 10 vols (Cambridge University Press, 1979–96), iv, 2.6.36–57 and 3.4.106, respectively.

[18] Fletcher, *The Chances* (1617?), 3.2.1–50; and 4.3.1–147. Since the lyrics to each woman's song appear to have been inserted into the 1679 folio, it is unclear precisely what was sung in the early performances.

[19] Lindley, 158.

[20] See for example *Quattro comedie del diuino Pietro Aretino* (London, 1588) and *La terza, et vltima parte de Ragionamenti del diuino Pietro Aretino* (London, 1589). Probably the best-known travel narrative featuring the *cortigiana* was T. Coryate's *Coryate's Crudities* (London, 1611). D. Salkeld traces the emergence of the Italian courtesan in early modern drama in *Shakespeare Among the Courtesans* (Farnham: Ashgate, 2012), Ch. 5. See also M. Feldman and B. Gordon, eds., *The Courtesan's Arts: Cross-Cultural Perspectives* (Oxford University Press, 2006), Introduction and chapters 4, 5, 6, 9, 10, and 15.

royal court, elite households, and the incidental remarks of music teachers, diarists, and other writers. She is the chaste, young gentlewoman display-ing her marriageability through a musical performance to a select group of social equals in an exclusive but hardly private space. In Ophelia's perfor-mance, then, Shakespeare conjures not only the singing courtesan but also, simultaneously, the musical would-be bride, whose signification would no doubt have reminded contemporary audience members of a performance someone like Ophelia might well have given had not things gone so terribly wrong. Such performances were commonplace in elite circles, and their representation on the Globe stage, with appropriate music of course, would have offended few and shocked no one.

Female musical skill was a sign of erudition, worldliness and wealth in the age of the Tudors and Stuarts, and it was cultivated at the highest social levels as much for display as for entertainment. In the court of Henry VII, musicality was among the requirements for the queen's Maids-of-Honour, who performed not only in the queen's private chambers but also during ceremonies and other events at court.[21] Elizabeth Blount and Anne Boleyn both performed songs regularly before mixed company in the court of Henry VIII,[22] and musical training appears to have been important enough to Henry, himself an avid musician and composer, that Nicholas Watton, while prospecting for the king's fourth wife, thought it wise to report its absence from the schooling of Anne of Cleves.[23] There is record of Henry's daughter Mary performing on the lute and virginals before a group of elite guests,[24] and considering the well-documented musical inclinations of Henry's second daughter, Elizabeth, it is hard to imagine Mary's as the only performance of this kind.[25] One finds further hint of this from her childhood tutor, Roger Ascham, as he suggests that 'minstrelsie of lutes, pipes, [and] harpes ... is farre more fitte for the womannishness of it to dwell in the courte among ladies'.[26]

The musical proclivities displayed by royalty generated a demand for musical brides in proximal social spheres. Aspiring young gentlemen training to mingle with their betters sought young ladies whose musical

---

[21] See B. J. Harris, *English Aristocratic Women 1450–1550* (Oxford University Press, 2002), 231.

[22] Ibid.

[23] See M. C. Boyd, *Elizabethan Musical Criticism*, 2nd edn (Philadelphia: University of Pennsylvania Press, 1962), 17.

[24] According to the contemporary account, Mary for her performance 'was of all folk there greatly praised'. See Boyd, 6.

[25] Elizabeth loved to dance, composed songs, and was proficient on both the lute and virginals. For contemporary accounts, see Boyd, 6.

[26] Ascham, 10[v].

abilities would augment their social capital. Conversely, musical daughters represented opportunities for parents to cultivate financial and political alliances through marriage. One finds ample suggestion of this in the financial records of wealthy houses, many of which record significant expenditures for the musical education of young women and girls.[27] More explicit evidence can be found in the writings of prominent tutors. In his *First Book of Ayres* (1622), John Attey recounts his service in the household of the Earl of Bridgewater,

> where I had the happiness to attend the Seruice of those worthy and incomparable young LADIES your Daughters, who (by Gods fauour) shall one day repay vnto you a plentiful Haruest, of that Noble and Vertuous education you now bestow upon them.[28]

By 'harvest' Attey implies not only an abundance of grandchildren but also profits engendered from land or other resources gained through the marriage of the girls whose 'Noble and Vertuous' education will surely attract suitors from prominent families. Thomas Whythorne in his discussion of a patron competing for his services remarks,

> I do think that she was the more earnest to have me to continue at her house continually, because her eldest daughter had then a suitor and wooer, who should see how willing they were to have their children brought up gentle-woman-like.[29]

Forty-five years later Robert Burton, while not a music tutor himself, comments at some length on the musical training of potential brides in his *Anatomie of Melancholy*, where he writes, 'To heare a faire young gentlewoman to play upon the Virginalls, Lute, Viall, and sing to it must need be a great entisement',[30] and while Burton frets that singing women might drive male 'spectators mad', he admits that musical performance is,

> [a] thing nevertheless frequently used, and part of a Gentlewomans bringing up, to sing, and dance, and play on the Lute, or some such instrument, before she can say her *Pater noster*, or ten Comandements, 'tis the next way their parents think to get them husbands.[31]

---

[27] See D. C. Price, *Patrons and Musicians of the English Renaissance* (Cambridge University Press, 1981), Ch. 3; C. Marsh, *Music and Society in Early Modern England* (Cambridge University Press, 2010), 198–208; *The Autobiography of Thomas Whythorne* (1576), ed. J. M. Osborne (Oxford University Press, 1962), passim; and V. Larminie, *Wealth, Kinship and Culture: The Seventeenth-Century Newdigates of Arbury and Their World* (Suffolk: Boydell Press, 1995), 120.

[28] J. Attey, *The First Book of Ayres of Fovre Parts* (London, 1622), sig. A2ʳ. For similar, if more subtle dialogue, see T. Robinson, *The Schoole of Mvsicke* (London, 1603), sig. Bʳ⁻ᵛ.

[29] Whythorne, 84.   [30] Burton, *Anatomy*, 580–1.   [31] Ibid., 586.

The custom of cultivating musical daughters to attract eligible young men thus appears to have been widespread and enduring. Yet if this was so, it is difficult to reconcile the phenomenon with the model of musical decorum as conceived by Auden, Sternfeld and so many others. If to play music in any forum beyond one's 'private recreation' was to court shame, or worse, damnation, how would gentle parents, after all the preparation and expense, have gone about advertising talented female children to other prominent families? For surely they engaged in such manoeuvres, and surely there were more effective means of showcasing daughters to desirable sons-in-law than through some prescriptively chaperoned and inevitably stilted encounter. If one returns to the conduct manuals armed now with evidence of actual rather than exemplary behaviour, a more probable model emerges. Clearly 'private recreational' music to Castiglione, Peacham, and to most Elizabethans, did not refer strictly to isolated or sequestered activity but to musical production within one's private *circle*. This makes far more practical sense: for the Prince, the Justice, and the gentleman, recitals in the alehouse were out – and doubly so for wives and daughters. But performances in the *manor* house audited by family, friends, peers and associates – not to mention private servants-[32] *this* sort of activity was perfectly proper. In the dedication of Henry Lichfield's *First Set of Madrigals*, the writer speaks of his patron, the Lady Cheney, listening contentedly as his music is presented 'by the Instruments and voyces of your owne familie'.[33] 'It is difficult to believe', writes David Price of the depiction, 'that the entertainment of other elite families did not include similar performances' for relatives and friends. 'Such a careful display of musical taste', Price argues, 'would have been expected'.[34] A compelling glimpse of this sort of dynamic can be found in John Danyel's *Songs for the Lvte Viol and Voice* where the author addresses his former student, Anne Grene, daughter to Sir William Grene of Great Milton manor:

> That which was onely priuately compos'd
> For your delight, Faire Ornament of Worth,
> Is here, come, to bee publikely disclosed:
> And to an vniuersal view put forth.
> Which hauing been but yours and mine before
> (Or but of few besides) is made hereby

---

[32] The vast majority of music teachers in early modern England were of lower social status than their pupils. For a discussion of this liminal existence see Marsh, 154–72.

[33] H. Lichfield, *First Set of Madrigals of 5 Parts* (London, 1613), sig A2ʳ.   [34] Price, *Patrons*, 109.

> To bee the worlds: and yours and mine no more
> So that in this sort giuing it to you,
> I giue it from you, and therein doe wrong,
> To make that, which in priuate was your due:
> Thus to the common world to belong.

Here Danyel refers almost certainly to music composed for, or even during, Anne's private lessons, and indeed in his description one detects a mild distress, as if the tutor fears his former student, now perhaps married, might think it improper that he offers this product of their extensive association to the 'common world'. His allusions seem almost dangerous until one reads his apology that begins,

> ... why had it not been ynow
> That Milton onely heard our melodie?
> Where *Baucis* and *Phileomon* only show
> To Gods and men their hospitalitie:
> And thereunto a ioyfull eare afford,
> In mid'st of their well welcom'd company:
> Where wee (as Birds doe to themselves record)
> Might entertaine our priuate harmonie

'Baucis and Phileomon' are the pious old couple in Ovid's *Metamorphoses* who welcome two travellers into their home when others in the surrounding community will not. The men reveal themselves to be Jove and Mercury, and they reward Baucis and Philemon handsomely for maintaining classical traditions of hospitality.[35] Danyel's reference to the myth thus firstly dispels any suggestion of impropriety one might perceive earlier in the dedication.[36] Second, and more importantly, Danyel's linking the myth to 'our melodie' surely alludes to musical performances by Anne and, at the least, Danyel before visiting guests in keeping with traditional notions of 'hospitalitie'. The line 'To Gods and men' suggests strongly that these guests were people of various social ranks; in other words, nobles and citizens, family and friends. Moreover, rereading Danyel's description of his madrigals 'hauing been but yours and mine before (*Or but of few besides*)',[37] one gets the sense that some of the visitors enjoyed the performances so much that they requested

---

[35] Ovid, *Metamorphoses*, trans. by A. Golding (1565), ed. M. Forey (New York: Penguin Books, 2002), 257.

[36] 'Baucis and Phileomon' is one of the few stories in *Metamorphoses* that Ovid imbues with platonic love rather than sexual energy.

[37] Italics mine.

manuscript copies of the music. Jonson illustrates the dynamic, if satirically, in *Poetaster* where, in 4.3, Crispinus sings an 'odiferous' song before an elite audience after which Gallus asks if he may have a copy.[38] Indeed 'Gods and men' at Greater Milton may have traded for music, offering in exchange works penned by *their* tutors. Price notes numerous occasions when elite English families undertook large-scale visits to wealthy neighbours, taking along household musicians in a kind of protracted 'cultural exchange'.[39] The dissemination of music would surely have been a feature of such events.

This then is the sphere in which 'private harmonies' like those of Anne and Danyel, were regularly performed: an exclusive but hardly private social space where wealthy families, taking cues from royals, performed music for each other as an everyday part of 'the good life'. It is only natural that parents seeking matches for their children would utilise such occasions of cultural exchange to advertise a daughter's social value. There would simply be no better circumstances where the right people could casually witness a talented daughter first hand and subsequently extol within the best circles her worthiness as a bride. Indeed, it would be naïve to think this dynamic of calculated female performance was not cultivated in manor houses, at court, and elsewhere. The aristocracy danced with their guests, and they surely played music with them and for them as well, and their music shaped and mediated their association as it does, and has done, in all societies. Ironically, perhaps the clearest evidence of musical performance wielded to catch a man comes from Puritan circles where, despite the rhetoric of Stubbes and Prynne, music was practised and enjoyed almost as much as it was in less socially conservative communities.[40] James Melvill recalls in his diary frequent visits as a young man to the home of John Durie, a radical Presbyterian minister[41] and music lover who regularly 'entertained expert singers and players' and brought up all his children, including his eldest daughter, Elizabeth, 'in music'.[42] Melvill, also a Presbyterian minister, and also a lover of music, recounts how at Durie's he was 'lovingle and hartlie interteined' by Elizabeth, and in the

---

[38] B. Jonson, *Poetaster* (1600?), ed. G. B. Jackson in *The Cambridge Edition of the Works of Ben Jonson*, 7 vols (Cambridge University Press, 2012), vol. ii., 4.3.74.

[39] Price, *Patrons*, 70, 79, 80, 90, and 143.

[40] See J. T. Cliffe. *The Puritan Gentry* (London: Routledge & Kegan Paul, 1984), 141–5.

[41] J. Kirk, 'Melville, James (1556–1614)', *Oxford Dictionary of National Biography*, Oxford University Press, 2004.

[42] J. Melvill, *The Autobiography and Diary of Mr. James Melvill*, ed. R. Pitcairn (Edinburgh: The Wodrow Society, 1842), 79.

very next line he begins the story of how an 'affection enterit verie extreamlie' between himself and this musical young lady who would later become his wife.[43]

The knowledge that well-to-do women and girls commonly performed before what we might term 'exclusive publics' alters, often to a significant degree, appreciation of associated representations in the drama. The clearest depiction of elite female performance before a prospective husband occurs in Thomas Middleton's *Women Beware Women* where Isabella, a young gentlewoman, sings before a large audience at a banquet given by the Duke of Florence. The play, as a whole, is a censure of the aristocracy, and all characters in this scene offer either direct or ironic comments upon the corruption of marriage for the sake of socio-political gain. Isabella's father, for example, speaks of her as one might speak of livestock, and the prospective groom is a crass fool. Under the traditional model of musical decorum, one might perceive Isabella's performance itself as merely further evidence of a prevalent depravity. Yet we can now understand that Middleton presents here not a shockingly public display but merely a component of traditional social practice that has been corrupted along with everything else.[44]

In Middleton and Dekker's *The Patient Man and the Honest Whore*, we can now more fully perceive the implications of Bellafront's opening scene in which we find the courtesan singing before her mirror while preparing for guests.[45] Her first lines are from an unknown wanton ditty: 'Cupid is a god, / as naked as my nail / I'll whip him with a rod / if he my true love fail'. These are shortly followed by the final lines of a popular lute song by John Dowland which read, 'Down, down, down, down, I fall / Down, and arise I never shall'.[46] The two songs, the two Bellafronts (the character and the image in the mirror), and the two spaces they occupy suggest her inner torment: Every day the courtesan gazes into her mirror and 'sees' the gentlewoman she could have been had things gone differently. Recognition, however, that musical performance commonly occurred beyond the private chamber amplifies the

---

[43] Melvill, 80.

[44] Middleton, *Women Beware Women* (1621), ed. J. Jowett in *The Collected Works*, 3.2.

[45] See Thomas Middleton and Thomas Dekker, *The Patient Man and the Honest Whore* (1604), ed. P. Mulholland, in *The Collected Works*, 280–327 (280).

[46] For the scene, see Middleton and Dekker, *Patient Man* Sc. 6 (1–42). For discussion of Dowland's works and their popularity, see D. Poulton, *John Dowland*, 2nd edn (London: Faber and Faber, 1982). For the complete song, see Dowland, *The Second Booke of Songs or Ayers* (London, 1600), sig. C^v-C2^r.

potential significance and indeed the pathos of the scene: singing back to Bellafront then, is not merely the woman she could have been, but the image of her lost self preparing to show her quality in a world of privilege, where she is loved and accepted, a world into which the courtesan can gaze but never truly step.

Turning back to Ophelia, there is no question that of the many archetypes she conjures as she sings on the floor of the court the musical *cortigiana* is one.[47] Yet if we now balance with this the figure of the chaste, cultivated, elite female playing and singing for the delight of all and, perhaps, a particular young man, we illuminate with startling clarity just *how* Ophelia's musical performance is, like her, a 'mad' one. She does not play and sing as she would normally, at a family dinner or celebration, but effectively at a family funeral; she is not the object of healthy male attention, but of toxic, male abandonment; her songs, at first the ayres one might expect from Elizabeth Blount, Anne Grene or Elizabeth Durie, are madly, angrily blotted out by inappropriate street song; and, crucially, Ophelia's performance will not help two families (who have effectively, from behind the scenes, engendered it) to a harvest of grandchildren; instead it will inspire their mutual destruction. 'Hadst thou thy wits, and didst persuade revenge', declares Laertes in response to his sister's song, 'It could not move thus' (4.5.168–9).

It is a rich irony indeed that while the moralisations surrounding women and music published by the likes of Stubbes and Prynne appear to have found little purchase in the households of the sixteenth and seventeenth-centuries, they did manage to engender at least seventy-five years of confirmation bias in the academies of the twentieth and twenty-first. Perhaps with less focus on Puritan rhetoric and more attention to accounts of actual activity, scholars might have fashioned from the rest of the informing literature a model of female musical decorum more reflective of the contemporary common sense. It is time to revise our notions of the lute and its relation to the lascivious, time to take our eyes and ears away – at least for a moment – from the song of the courtesan and properly recognise, in the drama and elsewhere, the ordinary yet iconic figure she ultimately performs: the early modern gentlewoman, the 'original'

---

[47] One of these relating to music probably comes from Virgil's *Aeneid*. One cannot help but note the striking resemblance between Ophelia's mad scene, with its numerous snippets of popular ballads fluttering cryptically in and out of her speech, and the depictions of the Cumaen Sybil in Books III and VI. See Virgil, *Aeneid*, trans. R. Fagles (London: Penguin Books, 2006), III.518–37 and 55–92.

construction of beauty, chastity and erudition whose music in polite, public society projected not wantonness but worthiness. Numerous mixtures of women and music appear in the corpus, and it will be fruitful to visit each of these moments now mindful of real female musicians and their proper place in English life.[48]

---

[48] Among many examples, see J. Phillip, *The Commodye of Pacient and Meeke Grissill* [1565?] (London, 1565?), 6.840–75; J. Lyly, *Mother Bombie* (Manchester: Manchester University Press, 2010), 3.3.1–14; Jonson, *Every Man Out of His Humour* [1598], ed. by Randal Martin, in *The Cambridge Edition* i, 233–428, 3.3.66–109; T. Heywood, *A Woman Killed with Kindness* [1603] (London, 1607) sig. E2ʳ (See also Q1617, E4ʳ); and Shakespeare, *Pericles* [1607?], 4.0, 4.5.160–6, and esp. 5.0.1–3 and Marina's song in 5.1.

CHAPTER 5

Jangling Bells Inside and Outside the Playhouse

Katherine Hunt

Of all the man-made sounds that intruded into the aural territory of the outdoor playhouses, church bells were among the loudest and most common. These sonic interlopers sounded alongside the bells that would have been rung on or above the stage, forming a concert of theatrical and extra-theatrical noise that blurred the boundaries of dramatic space.[1] In a book about music and performance, what place can we assign to bells, the sounds of which were almost, but not quite, musical? In fact, around the turn of the seventeenth century, bells were becoming thought of as more musical than ever before; innovations in their ringing meant, too, that bells were now sounded in a kind of performance that competed aurally with those going on within the theatres' walls.

Bells ring through the plays of Shakespeare and his contemporaries, both literally and as metaphor. As well as the bells that ring on the stage in *Hamlet*, disorderly ringing is invoked by Ophelia to describe Hamlet's madness: his 'sovereign reason' is 'Like sweet bells jangled out of tune and harsh' (3.1.159).[2] This essay considers the resonances of ringing bells in this play in particular – beginning with Ophelia's speech. Her words contain traces of sound and of performance, and the term 'jangling' signals the way in which bells straddled the division between musical and non-musical sound. At the same time as Ophelia invokes the newly tuneful sounds of

---

[1] These ideas owe much to Bruce Smith's work on the soundscape of early modern England, and the development of the discipline of sound studies more generally. Studies of sound in Shakespeare include B. Smith, *The Acoustic World of Early Modern England* (University of Chicago Press, 1999); W. Folkerth, *The Sound of Shakespeare* (London: Routledge, 2002); K. Gross, *Shakespeare's Noise* (University of Chicago Press, 2001); on music as indecipherable sound in the plays see J. Ortiz, *Broken Harmony: Shakespeare and the Politics of Music* (Ithaca and London: Cornell University Press, 2011).

[2] The second Quarto reads 'time' (3.1.157). All references to the second Quarto are to *Hamlet*, ed. A. Thompson and N. Taylor (London: Arden Shakespeare, 2006). All references to the Folio text are to the same editors' *Hamlet: The Texts of 1603 and 1623* (London: Arden Shakespeare, 2006) and are given parenthetically in the body of the essay. All other Shakespeare references are to the New Cambridge Shakespeare editions.

71

bells, she suggests that they can be misused to become the jangling opposite; the fact that 'sweet bells' have been violently misused in this way, out of tune and time, suggests that their proper sound is not horrid noise but harmonious music.

Bells provided an unusual aural continuity between the pre- and post-Reformation soundscapes and Ophelia's speech reflects the new ways in which bells were rung and heard in England around 1600. The jangling she describes also has a confessional aspect. Jangling – as sound and as metaphor – brought together the sounds of disagreement in speech and disorder in bell-ringing; it was a sound that was used metaphorically by people of all confessional dispositions to suggest the chaos and the falsity of their opponents' opinions. The actual sounds of bells in and outside the playhouse jingled and jangled alongside the metaphorical resonances of these instruments in the words of the plays. In a play of such profound, and deliberate, religious ambiguity, I suggest some ways in which Ophelia's lines here might make use of familiar parts of the soundscape to encode another aspect of the confessional dimensions of *Hamlet*.

Bells In and Out of Tune and Time

Ophelia's lamentation over Hamlet's muddled mind hinges on the metaphor of sound, disordered and made unmusical:

> I, of ladies most deject and wretched,
> That sucked the honey of his music vows,
> Now see that noble and most sovereign reason
> Like sweet bells jangled out of tune and harsh –
> That unmatched form and feature of blown youth
> Blasted with ecstasy.   (3.1.156–61)

Here the reasonable is the musical. It was Hamlet's 'sovereign reason' that promised those 'music vows', and which Ophelia likens to sweet bells, then in tune. Madness, on the other hand, is discordant, as though harmonious instruments have been used in a performance so 'harsh' that their very tuning has come undone; these words of hers will be echoed in descriptions of her own madness later on. Music, and its disordered opposite, is placed within a frame of looking: first at Hamlet, 'Th'observed of all observers' in the 'glass of fashion'; then through Ophelia's own weary eyes 'T'have seen what I have seen, see what I see' (3.1.154–5;162). Moving from the visual to the aural and back again, Ophelia's description of madness is rooted in sound; something easier heard than seen. Indeed, her very speech is one of many that are overheard: it ends as Claudius and Polonius step forward from where they have been listening, behind the arras.

The textual variants of the 'sweet bells' line reflect the sounds on which it draws, and their meanings and resonances. The line doesn't appear at all in Q1, but in Q2 the sweet bells jangle out of *time*, not tune. The difference is usually explained as a minim error, made at some point when composing the type from manuscript, or even when composing F partly from Q2; modern editors are evenly split when it comes to deciding which is to be preferred.

The confusion of time and tune is present in other plays too: 'This time goes manly' in the Folio edition of *Macbeth* (4.2.238), for example, which – despite the lack of other textual evidence – editors often change to 'tune'; elsewhere the words are swapped the other way round, so that 'I will fit it with some better tune' in the Folio text of *King John* (3.2.26), sometimes becomes 'time'. In a long note to his Arden second series edition of *Hamlet*, Harold Jenkins examines such potential (mis)readings of tune/time in the corpus. Because Shakespeare uses 'tune' elsewhere to describe confused senses (when Cordelia speaks of Lear's 'untuned and jarring senses' [4.6.16], for example) and, perhaps even more persuasively, because in two other places Shakespeare associates being out of tune with harshness,[3] Jenkins himself ultimately – and rightly, I think – chooses F's 'tune' for Ophelia's line.

The choice between tune and time is so difficult because both are essential for musical performance – and both seem equally (if differently) to apply to bells. The connections between bells and time are fundamental; bells operate as makers and markers of time throughout *Hamlet*, from the striking of clock time – the first time Barnardo sees the ghost, the 'bell' was 'beating one' – to the signalling, or creation, of the symbolic time of funeral rites with Ophelia's 'bell and burial' (1.1.38; 5.1.231). I want to suggest, though, that around 1600 bells were becoming more associated with tune, and musical sound, than ever before.

Objects of the old religion, bells survived in remarkable numbers into and beyond the seventeenth century. In the Roman Catholic church bells had called people to church; announced the transformation of the host; commemorated births, deaths, victories, and coronations; marked curfew, and the canonical hours; warned about a fire; or driven away demons and

---

[3] *Romeo and Juliet*, 'It is the lark that sings so out of tune/ Straining harsh discords' (3.5.27–8); *Othello*, 'Murder's out of tune,/ And sweet revenge grows harsh' (5.2.116–7). See *Hamlet* ed. H. Jenkins (London: Routledge, 1982), 498.

thunder that might be hovering in the air around the steeple. They were often dedicated to saints, baptised by a bishop and given godparents. They were hallowed objects, part of the sensory experience of the pre-Reformation church. Their tunefulness was not unimportant, but their principal functions were to mark and create time, whether of celebration, regular prayer, or alarm. Their uses changed over the course of the sixteenth century, but the story of bells' survival is not straightforwardly one of desacralisation: rather it is one of accommodation into post-Reformation liturgical and communal life.[4] Many functions persisted into the new religious climate – indeed, certain types of ringing, such as that on All Hallows' Eve, were done long after they were officially outlawed.[5] Others continued under a different cover, incorporated into what David Cressy has called 'a new national, secular and dynastic calendar centring on the anniversaries of the Protestant monarch'.[6] Bells were much loved by the communities over which they sounded, and the enthusiasm for communal ringing helped bells not only to survive, but to be augmented in the seventeenth century.[7]

For this communal, often recreational ringing, the tunefulness of the bells became more important than ever before. When visiting London in 1602, as the secretary to the Duke of Stettin-Pomerania, Frederic Gerschow remarked that '[p]arishes spend much money in harmoniously sounding bells, that one being preferred which has the best bells'.[8] An example from St Michael, Cornhill shows just how far Londoners wanted to make their bells not only harmonious in themselves, but actually in tune with music that would be heard outside the church. In 1587, the parish recast one of their favourite bells, known as Rus. Despite the considerable expense of this new bell, its sound was 'not lyked of'. It had to be replaced the following year, when a new bellfounder melted down the bell and re-cast it. The churchwardens' accounts show several payments to musicians to check that the sound of the replacement bell was tuneful enough: on 1 December 1588 a musician was paid 13d to sound the bell; soon after, the parish paid 18d to 'ye Waytes of the Cittie that took paynes to take the

[4] R. Whiting, *The Reformation of the English Parish Church* (Cambridge University Press, 2010), 171–181.

[5] On this, see P. Marshall, *Beliefs and the Dead in Reformation England* (Oxford University Press, 2002), 128–132; D. Cressy, *Bonfires and Bells* (London: Weidenfeld and Nicolson, 1989), 28–30.

[6] Cressy, *Bonfires and Bells*, xii.

[7] On communal ringing see C. Marsh, *Music and Society in Early Modern England* (Cambridge University Press, 2010), 454–504.

[8] Frederic Gerschow, 'Diary of the journey of Philip Julius, Duke of Stettin-Pomerania, through England in the Year 1602', *Transactions of the Royal Historical Society*, n.s., 6 (1892), 7.

note of o[r] belles & . . . of the newe bell then cast'; another company of musicians was further engaged to check the sound.[9] The churchwardens of Cornhill were committed to ensuring the soundness of the instrument, its harmony in musical terms with the other bells in the ring it was joining, and even its compatibility with other musical systems that could be heard in the city.

Around the time that the parishioners of Cornhill were recasting their bell, and indeed when *Hamlet* was first performed, bells began to be rung in a new, and almost musical, way. This ringing, which later in the seventeenth century became known as 'ringing changes', and eventually as change-ringing, sounds the bells in series of mathematical permutation, in which the object is to exhaust all possible orders in which a given number of bells can be rung. Its complicated system was based more on mathematics than on melody but timing and tuning were both essential. In *Tintinnalogia* (1668), the first book published on change-ringing, Richard Duckworth emphasises that the ringer must know how to keep good, regular time; he must also understand, he writes, 'the *Tuning of Bells*; for what is a *Musitian*, unless he can *Tune* his *Instrument*, although he plays never so well?'[10] In fact, of course, bell-ringers actually couldn't tune their instrument: bells were out of both reach and sight in the bell tower. Nevertheless, the understanding of their tuning was important, and the ringers had to work together to ensure a timely and pleasing peal. This practice, in its nascent form, may have been what Frederic Gerschow described as 'a great ringing of bells in almost all the churches going on very late in the evening, also on the following days until 7 or 8 o'clock in the evening': a new aural performance in the London soundscape.[11]

The practice was very new in 1600, so it's unlikely that Ophelia's speech refers directly to change-ringing. But her lines do seem to be responding to the new ways in which bells were being attended to, including the fact of their increased 'sweetness' and tunefulness, and their use for performance and practice outside their customary liturgical and communal functions.

Overlapping Performances: Hearing Bells Inside the Playhouse

Would the sound of sweet bells in tune – or jangled out of it – have been audible within the outdoor playhouses? There is no question that bells

---

[9] W. Overall, ed., *The Accounts of the Churchwardens of the Parish of St Michael Cornhill* (London: Alfred James Waterlow, 1869), 176–9.

[10] R. Duckworth, *Tintinnalogia* (London, 1668), 3. [11] Gerschow, 'Diary', 7.

from nearby parish churches would have been overheard. Tiffany Stern has identified the closest tower bells to the theatres: St Mary Overy, now Southwark Cathedral, for the playhouses at Southwark, and the clock of St Ann for Blackfriars.[12] Other church bells would also have been within hearing range of the outdoor playhouses, providing a concert, if not a jangle, of variously loud sounds to punctuate the play.[13] The clock time and service time signalled by these bells was laid over the time of the plays and provided, Stern argues, the only fixed method of time-telling for those within the two-hours' traffic of the theatre's stage. Even in today's much louder soundscape the bells of St Paul's, directly over the water from Shakespeare's Globe, can be heard during performances.

So the bells ringing clock time would have been heard, but what about more performative kinds of ringing? Gerschow describes the ringing happening 'until very late in the evening'; indeed, a late seventeenth-century London ringing society, the Western Green Caps, met every week at 6 pm in summer and an hour earlier in winter to practise, and numerous reports survive of recreational ringing being done at night-time, to the annoyance of the clergy and those living near the church.[14] Bruce Smith is probably right, then, to argue that 'congregation at the play houses was an event of the afternoon; recreational bell-ringing, an event of the evening'.[15] The sounds of recreational ringing and the plays in performance wouldn't overlap but they would share an acoustic space, if not time.

There were bells on, as well as near, the early modern stage: their ringing is mentioned throughout the plays, and Henslowe's inventory of the Admiral's Men's goods of 1598 includes '2 steples, & 1 chime of bells, & 1 beacon', which probably refer to different sizes of bells. A 'chime' of small hand-bells or cymbals, tuned in a set, might have made incidental or musical bell sounds, but the other two were more like the loud bells

---

[12] T. Stern, 'Time for Shakespeare: Hourglasses, sundials, clocks, and early modern theatre', *Journal of the British Academy* 3 (2015), 22.

[13] It is difficult to estimate how many nearby church bells would have been audible, given the vast changes in the cityscape and the soundscape. Bells at St Mary Overy are likely to have been heard and perhaps also those at St Olave, further east in Southwark. Stow lists more than a dozen churches directly over the river from the Rose and Globe whose bells may well have been audible; the largest and closest was St Martin Vintry. The Map of Early Modern London resource uses the sixteenth-century Agas map, annotated to show playhouses and churches mentioned by Stow, to give an idea of the potential cacophony of the many bells within aural range of the outdoor playhouses (https://mapoflondon.uvic.ca/index.htm).

[14] Rule book of the Western Green Caps, London 1683. Bodleian Library, Rawlinson MS D1089, f.12r; Marsh, *Music and Society*, 487–9.

[15] Smith, *Acoustic World*, 55.

heard from nearby churches: a 'steple' was a large bell that approximated the rich sound of a tower bell, and a 'becon' was a bell specifically for alarm.[16]

These real onstage sounds could have multiple meanings within the world of the play. In *Macbeth*, the bell rung publicly to signal that Macbeth's drink is ready, is the sound that privately 'invites' him to kill Duncan (2.1.62); the alarm bell rung two scenes later (perhaps using a 'becon') marks the discovery of the body (2.3.68). As Tiffany Stern points out, these two bell sounds are misremembered by Lady Macbeth as consecutive strikes, marking 2 am: collapsing the time in which the murder took place and inventing this ringing of clock time when in fact the clock 'goes down at twelve' (2.1.3).[17] The very real sounds of these stage properties were interpreted variously and recalled (sometimes erroneously) within the play as signal, symbol, or abstract time.

Indeed, such slippery interpretation of sounds made on stage could conduct a conversation with the noise happening outside the playhouse. In Dekker's *The Shoemaker's Holiday* (1600), bells operate on several dramatic and extra-theatrical levels. Erika Lin shows how the soundscape outside intrudes into the world of the play when, for example, the jingle of coins is compared to the nearby bells of St Mary Overy. When the pancake bell rings in the play to mark Shrove Tuesday festivities it has to be signalled within the play's dialogue, so that the audience can interpret the onstage sound correctly, but this bell then operates as though it is the *real* pancake bell, giving an aural signal that helps to collapse real time with the time of the play. As Lin argues, 'in the playhouse ... every day is Shrove Tuesday',[18] despite *The Shoemaker's Holiday* being first performed in the more sombre autumn season. By attending to the sounds heard outside the theatre, and signalling the meanings of those made within it, actors and playgoers were incorporated into the world outside and London was brought into the playhouse.

As the examples from *Macbeth* and *The Shoemaker's Holiday* suggest, bell sounds were encoded within the plays not as straightforward aural cues and signals but as complex networks of resonance and meaning; they were also used richly as metaphor. I want now to suggest the ways in which Ophelia's lines tapped in not just to real sounds overheard in London, sounds

---

[16] R. A. Foakes, ed., *Henslowe's Diary*, 2nd edn (Cambridge University Press, 2002), 319; see also Smith, *Acoustic World*, 219–20.

[17] Stern, 'Time', 20.

[18] E. T. Lin, 'Festivity', in H. S. Turner, ed., *Early Modern Theatricality* (Oxford University Press, 2013), 220.

unavoidable in the outdoor playhouses, but also into the metaphorical resonances of these sounds and the words used to describe them, particularly the sound of jangling.

The Jangle

What kind of sound was a jangle? For Ophelia, bells jangling together signalled a disordered individual mind: one which, with the loss of its 'sovereign reason', had implications for the health of the state. In a short piece, 'Upon a ring of Bels' (before 1631) Joseph Hall, Bishop of Exeter, provides a comparison to Ophelia's metaphor, using bells in a similar way to suggest both actual sound and implied social discord. For Hall, 'wee testifie our publike reioycing by an orderly and well-tuned peale', but 'when wee would signifie that the Towne is on fire wee ring confusedly'. The first sound is 'sweet & harmonious' but the latter, in which bells are 'iangling together, or striking preposterously', is 'harsh and vnpleasing'.[19] Hall extrapolates the sounds that he describes in order to portray the social body. As with bells, he writes, as with 'Church and Common-wealth':

> when euery one knowes and keepes their due rancks, there is a melodious consort of Peace and contentment; but when distances, and proportions of respects are not mutually obserued; when eyther States or persons will bee clashing with each other, the discord is grieuous, and extreamely preiudiciall.[20]

Hall's metaphor works because people knew that the aural signal of a jangle signified confusion and alarm, and he taps into a common understanding of the nomenclature of sounds and a shared aural memory to make these sounds have meaning metaphorically. For Hall, as for Ophelia, the jangle is at once a recognisable noise, and a suggestion of dangerous disorder.

This sense of the word 'jangle' was, however, relatively new when Shakespeare and Hall were writing. Before the middle of the sixteenth century it wasn't bells that jangled, but people. To jangle was to prate, to quarrel; a loud clash of words and opinions. Indeed, before *Hamlet*, Shakespeare himself used only this sense of the word: 'Good wits will be jangling,' warns the Princess in *Love's Labour's Lost* – that is, they squabble,

---

[19] J. Hall, *Occasionall Meditations by Ios. Exon*, 2nd edn (London, 1631), 198–9.
[20] Ibid., 199–200.

to no use – and she implores her auditors to do the opposite, and 'agree' (2.1.221); Puck, observing the confusion he's wrought among the Athenian youths, remarks that 'this their jangling I esteem a sport' (3.2.343). Ophelia's speech marks Shakespeare's first use of 'jangle' to refer to bells; Shakespeare never uses the word again, although George Wilkins has one of the fishermen talk of the 'jangling of the bells' in scene 5 of *Pericles* (2.1.38). These four examples show the progression of the word in microcosm: from disorderly speech to a disordered non-verbal sound.

It's perhaps not surprising that bells began to jangle, to make a noise more usually associated with speech, because they were long thought to have voices: common inscriptions on their bodies were often given in the first person, such as 'vivas voco' (I call the living), or 'funera plango' (I wail at the funeral).[21] In jangling, however, they took on a particularly antagonistic strain of voice, becoming angry speaking subjects. This change coincided with the changing functions of bells during and after the Reformation, and the wording of successive visitation articles highlights these new voices that bells took on. In 1547, jangling was still associated with unwanted chatter: the visitation articles of Edward VI ask 'whether any doo vse to common, Iangle or talke in the Churche, at the tyme of the diuine seruice'. In 1561 John Parkhurst, Bishop of Norwich, issued articles asking whether clerks 'vse to ring oft or longe peales at the buryall of the dead or vse muche iangling in festiuall daies in ringing none or curphew'. In an early association of the word with bells, jangling here describes excessive ringing which could be a sign of recusancy in the parish. By 1571 Thomas Cooper, Bishop of Lincoln, incorporated both kinds of jangling in his articles. The laity were to be asked whether there were 'any walkers, Janglers, or Talkers, that disturbeth the minister in the time of diuine seruice'. And in the injunctions that follow, jangling of *bells* is forbidden: Cooper orders that 'no man shall enterprise nor presume to ring nor Iangle any Belles vppon all Halowe[e]n daie, or in the night of the same day, superstitiously or Popishly, as they haue bene accustomed to do, otherwaies then to call the people to Diuine Seruice'.[22] Jangling was always an annoyance or a potentially godless kind of a sound, either signifying not enough, or the wrong kind of, reverence for the church. Over the course of

---

[21] P. Price, *Bells and Man* (Oxford University Press, 1983), 275.

[22] *Articles to be enquired of, in the Kynges Maiesties visitacion* (London, 1547), sig.B1v; *Iniunctions exhibited by Iohn . . . Bishop of Norwich* (London, 1561), sig.B3r; *Articles to be inquired of the clergie set foorth by . . . Thomas Bishop of Lincoln* (London, 1571), sigs.A3r, A4r.

the sixteenth century the source of this sound shifted: now it could also describe not only the human voice, but the sonorous metal of the bells.

Indeed, just as bells began to jangle, the jangling of speech took on particular weight in Reformation battles over liturgy and doctrine. For writers on both sides of the confessional divide, jangling described what those on the other side did. Gregory Martin, a Jesuit Englishman at the College at Rheims who translated parts of the Bible into English, included in his 1582 refutation of the Protestant Bible a rant against the way that 'they [Protestants] dispute and iangle', or permit the 'iangling of Gods word'.[23] In his retort, William Fulke returns the sound back to Martin, complaining that it was rather the latter and his co-religionists who 'dispute and iangle', with a 'iangle of grosse & false translations'.[24] Indeed, the Jesuits came under particular criticism for jangling, perhaps because of the alliterative potential of the insult.

The use of jangling as an anti-Catholic metaphor began to incorporate the sound and significance of bells into the jibe. William Tyndale, writing on the doctrine of purgatory, famously derided the existence of 'such a Iayle as they Iangle': using the weight of the bells, rung for so many purposes in the rites of death and burial, along with the word's association with idle chatter as a way of deriding the doctrine of purgatory itself.[25] In a poem (c.1618–1625[26]) by William Browne, it is specifically Roman Catholic bells that jangle. Browne attends both to the sounds Ophelia describes, and to the metaphorical extrapolation of these sounds: bells jangling out of tune and time and, their opposite, bells being rung in ordered performance.

The poem was, the title states, *Occasioned by the most intolerable jangling of the Papists' bells on All Saints' Night, the eve of All Souls' Day, being then used to be rung all night (and all as if the town were on fire) for the souls of those in Purgatory.* Written when he was in north-west France, in the poem Browne satirises the Catholic practice of ringing bells on All Souls Eve to

[23] G. Martin, *A discouerie of the manifold corruptions of the Holy Scriptures* (Rheims, 1582), sig.P2r; Martin, *The New Testament of Iesus Christ, translated faithfully into English* (Rheims, 1582), sig.B1r.

[24] W. Fulke, *A defense of the sincere and true translations of the holie Scriptures into the English tong* (London, 1583), sigs.Bb7r, K1r.

[25] W. Tyndale, in *The whole workes of W. Tyndall, Iohn Frith, and Doct. Barnes* (London, 1573), sig. AA6r. On this passage, see S. Greenblatt, *Hamlet in Purgatory* (Princeton University Press, 2001), 33.

[26] Cedric Brown and Margherita Piva suggest a date of 1624 in 'William Browne, Marino, France, and the Third Book of Britannia's Pastorals', *Review of English Studies*, n.s., 29:116 (1978), 388, 403. Gillian Wright prefers 1618–9, see 'A commentary on and edition of the shorter poems of William Browne of Tavistock in British Library MS Lansdowne 777', unpublished PhD thesis, University of Glasgow (1998), 201.

help the passage of souls in Purgatory. This pre-Reformation practice holds none of its old meanings for him; in his ears it is something both doctrinally ridiculous and aurally annoying.[27] Browne can't help but to listen closely to the unordered sound he hears coming from the bell towers of the town:

> For I am sure all this long night to hear
> Such a charyvary, that if there were
> All the Tom Tinkers since the world began,
> . . .
> I think all those together would not make
> Such a curs'd noise as these for all souls' sake.[28]   (ll.30–3, 37–8)

The 'intolerable jangling' that Browne hears as he writes is an impossible charivari; these are bells that are out of tune and out of time, making a cacophony in the service of a lost and misguided cause. As Gillian Wright points out, this is mild anti-Catholic satire from a man often considered a rather staunch Puritan,[29] but Browne nevertheless makes clear that the 'curs'd noise' that he can't not hear has no spiritual value.

Browne proposes an alternative to the jangling: this noise could be resolved into something in tune and in time if it is put into order by an experienced, English, performer:

> Honest John Helmes, now by my troth I wish,
> Although my popish hostess hath with fish
> Fed me these three days, that thou wert here with speed,
> And some more of thy crew, not without need,
> To teach their bells some rhyme or tune in swinging,
> For sure they have no reason in their ringing.   (ll.39–44)

John Helmes, on whom Browne has provided a note in the margin ('A good ringer'), perhaps performs the methodical proto-change-ringing with which Browne was familiar in England. The 'rhyme or tune' that Helmes and his 'crew' ring provides the counterpoint to the jangling, noisy, and pointedly Popish cacophony that Browne hears in France. The immanent, sacred time of All Souls Eve could be broken by

---

[27] Because this bell-ringing was a way to speed the soul through purgatory, this practice has a particular importance for *Hamlet*. See Greenblatt, *Hamlet in Purgatory* 43–4, 246. Peter McCullough notes that the murder of Old Hamlet is placed 'with remarkable precision in All Hallowstide, the feasts of All Souls and All Saints' ('Christmas at Elsinore', *Essays in Criticism* 58:4 (2008), 315).

[28] Gordon Goodwin, ed., *The Poems of William Browne of Tavistock*, 2 vols (London: Lawrence and Bullen, 1894), II, 229–32. Line numbers given here refer to this edition of the poem. The only extant MS copy of the poem is British Library Lansdowne MS 777, f.19v.

[29] Wright, 'Commentary', 201.

a patterned, ordered kind of ringing, one done by a group of men in concert, and one which shares characteristics not with abstract timekeeping but with 'rhyme or tune' – with poetry, or music. Indeed, it is only in this patterned sound that Browne locates any kind of 'reason'. Tune, like Hamlet's 'music vows', provides the aural as well as semantic counterpoint to noisy, meaningless jangle.

For Browne, as for Tyndale, jangling was a particularly Catholic sound, but Ophelia's lines do not necessarily suggest a Protestant inflection to *Hamlet*. Peter McCullough is right to warn against 'the impulse to define the play as either broadly Catholic or broadly Protestant [which] flies in the face of its own relentless effort to assert both possibilities in a dramaturgical process that cancels the signifying power of each'.[30] As we have seen, bells in the play display the deliberate ambiguity that McCullough asserts: they sound for secular clock time as for sacred, and for acceptable Protestant time as for now-outlawed Catholic funeral rites. The resonances of Ophelia's use of 'jangling' similarly avoid such a stark confessional determination and, rather than asserting a single position, the word signals disorder and discord.

Indeed, the jangle echoes what Michael Neill has described as the play's (and its characters'), 'intense narrative and interpretative desire':[31] the search for order in a disordered world. Nowhere is this impulse stronger than in the description (given by Horatio in F, and an unnamed gentleman in Q2) of Ophelia's own madness:

> Her speech is nothing,
> Yet the unshaped use of it doth move
> The hearers to collection. They aim at it,
> And botch the words up to fit their own thoughts   (4.1.7–10)

Her speech is confused, unshaped: its listeners have to impose their own interpretations onto it, 'botch[ing] the words up', in order for it to make sense. Ophelia lamented Hamlet's confused speech, but it is now her words that jangle out of all reason.

In the years around *Hamlet*'s composition and performance the use and the sound of bells were changing, as were the words used to describe their ringing. As bells started to be not just of time but in tune, they also became increasingly capable of being out of both: they could be used for musical performance, but they could also jangle noisily. Jangling bells had to be

---

[30] McCullough, 'Christmas', 311.
[31] Michael Neill, *Issues of Death: Mortality and Identity in English Renaissance Tragedy* (Oxford University Press, 1997), 218.

interpreted, even if the meaning of jangling was meaninglessness itself. They could signify confusion, as Hall suggested, when the town was on fire; they could refer to a sound that was judged pointless or plain wrong, as in the insults in religious polemics, or Browne's take on the All Souls bells. In the post-Reformation years, as the new religion took hold, bells were the sonic sites of intricate debates and subtle shiftings in religious and secular practice and performance. They were also ubiquitous, intruding upon and mixing with the sounds of the playhouses. By using bells to describe the confusion and the disorder of Hamlet's musical reason Shakespeare signals the new varieties of music, and also of confessional commotion, that these sounds meant to their listeners in a changing, bewildering, noisy world.

CHAPTER 6

Music, Its Histories, and Shakespearean (Inter-) Theatricality in Beaumont's Knight of the Burning Pestle

Linda Phyllis Austern

Music and musical taste are among many targets of theatrical satire in Francis Beaumont's *Knight of the Burning Pestle*. Extant tunes have been matched to a number of the play's song-texts since the mid-nineteenth century, and several widely-circulating editions of the work include notation and partial histories for at least some of these.[1] Likewise, *The Knight* is referenced in such seminal collections of early modern English song and music as Thomas Percy's *Reliques of English Poetry*, William Chappell's *Ballad Literature and Popular Music of the Olden Times*, and Claude M. Simpson's *The British Broadside Ballad and Its Music*.[2] Scholars have long discussed the use of music in the work, especially Old Merrythought's frequent quotation of pre-existing songs.[3] What has gone unremarked are the ways in which songs and instrumental music performed and mentioned in this play form polyvalent connections to that circulating through the early seventeenth-century English theatre and the

---

[1] F. Beaumont, *Knight of the Burning Pestle*, ed. J. Doebler (Lincoln: University of Nebraska Press, 1967), 111–35; Ibid., ed. A. Gurr (University of California Press, 1968), 115–123; Ibid., ed. S. P. Zitner (Manchester University Press, 1984), 173–83 (all future references are to this edition); W. Chappell, *The Ballad Literature and Popular Music of the Olden Times* (London, 1855–59; reprint ed., New York: Dover Books, 1965), vol. 1, 122–23, 140–41, 162, 170, and 172; and E. S. Lindsey, 'The Original Music for Beaumont's Play 'The Knight of the Burning Pestle', *Studies in Philology* 26 (1929), 425–443.

[2] For example Chappell, *Ballad Literature*, vol. 1, 122, 140–41, 162, 170, and 172; T. Percy, *Reliques of Ancient English Poetry*, vol. 3 (Dublin: P. Wilson and E. Watts, 1766), 102; and C. M. Simpson, *The British Broadside Ballad and Its Music* (Rutgers University Press, 1966), 284 and 742.

[3] M. Bauer, 'Doolittle's Father(s): Master Merrythought in *The Knight of the Burning Pestle*', in *Plotting Early Modern London*, ed. D. Mehl et al. (Ashgate, 2004), 41–54 on 48–50; D. Bonneau, 'On Merrythought's Singing, with a Glance at Sir Toby', *Bulletin de la Société d'Études Anglo-Américaines des XVIIe et XVIIIe siècles, Colloque 'The Sister Arts' 25 et 26 Novembre 1994*, pp. 7–26; P. J. Finkelpearl, *Court and Country Politics in the Plays of Beaumont and Fletcher* (Princeton University Press, 1990). 81 and 84; and K. Wong, 'A Dramaturgical Study of Merrythought's Songs in *The Knight of the Burning Pestle*', *Early Theatre*, 12 (2009), 91–116.

culture(s) from which the audience was drawn. Just as *The Knight* blends multiple forms of drama, speech, and performance in ways that challenge distinctions between them, so does its music. Most tellingly, the music in the play recalls with a parodic edge the histories of many genres as they appeared in London theatres, other entertainment venues, and as marketed accoutrements for social status and self-fashioning in Shakespeare's era.

It is generally agreed that Beaumont's play was first performed by the Children of the Revels in the Blackfriars Theatre in 1607.[4] It is also agreed that, as its first printer claimed, the original audience 'utterly rejected it', perhaps due to 'want of judgement, or not understanding the privy marke of Ironie about it'.[5] Modern scholars have offered further explanations, including the young playwright's misjudgement of audience expectations at the Blackfriars, the work's uncomfortable blurring of the line between performance and spectatorship, failed generic experiment, and being ahead of its time.[6] Why and however it failed, its theatrical self-consciousness was especially appropriate to conditions of playgoing the year of its premier. In 1607, the fashion of attending plays was at its height in London. No fewer than six play-houses were in operation in and around the city, competing with each other for shares of a live entertainment market that also offered non-theatrical pleasures. Each house presented its own repertory and promised a specific experience. Audiences and playwrights seemed especially aware of distinctions between the offerings and ambience in the public and private playhouses that were situated in different neigh-bourhoods, and charged different rates for admission into contrasting spaces in which to see, and be seen.[7] Financially, the period between James's accession and the closure of the theatres in 1608 was healthier for

---

[4] J. S. Smith, 'Reading Between the Acts: Satire and the Interludes in *The Knight of the Burning Pestle*', *Studies in Philology*, 109 (2012), 474–95, on 477.

[5] *Knight of the Burning Pestle* (London: Walter Burre, 1613), sigs. A2–A2v.

[6] D. M. Bergeron, 'Paratexts in Francis Beaumont's *The Knight of the Burning Pestle*', *Studies in Philology* 106 (2009), 456–67, on 459–60; R. J. Booth, '"Down with Your Title, Boy!" Beaumont's *The Knight of the Burning Pestle* and Its Insurgent Audience', *Q/W/E/R/T/Y* 5 (1995), 51–58, on 57; R. Madelaine, 'Apprentice Interventions: Boy Actors, The Burning Pestle and the Privy Mark of Irony', *Q/W/E/R/T/Y* 5 (1995), 73–78, on 77; L. Munro, '*The Knight of the Burning Pestle* and Generic Experimentation', in *Early Modern English Drama*, ed. G. A. Sullivan et al. (Oxford University Press, 2006), 189–199; Smith, 'Reading' p. 477; and B. E. Whitted, 'Staging Exchange: Why *The Knight of the Burning Pestle* Flopped at Blackfriars in 1607', *Early Theatre* 15 (2012), 111–130.

[7] Booth, '"Down with Your Title"', p. 52; A. Gurr, *Playgoing in Shakespeare's London*, 3rd edn (Cambridge University Press, 1987), 85–94; A. Leggatt, 'The Audience as Patron: *The Knight of the Burning Pestle*', in *Shakespeare, and Theatrical Patronage in Early Modern England*, ed. P. Whitfield White and S. R. Westfall (Cambridge University Press, 2002), 295–315 on 296–99 and 306; and Smith, 'Reading Between the Acts', 478.

the public theatres than the pricier private ones including Blackfriars.[8] The latter, with its relative intimacy, ambient lighting, slightly smoky interior, sumptuous decorations, and affable if sometimes daringly satiric fare, was a place to show off the latest costumes, jewels, and plumed accessories worn by audience members, as well as actors, in an ongoing performance of taste and status. Some of the spectators sat on the stage from which they could be seen while watching more scripted action. In fact, plays written for the Blackfriars feature a striking number of showpieces in which one set of characters watches another perform, presumably reflecting concentric rings of spectatorship in the same visual field.[9] *The Knight of the Burning Pestle* toys with this metatheatricality at the expense of at least part of its audience. The play is comprised of three overlapping narratives that constantly threaten to collide: a fashionable city comedy that ends in marriage, an antiquated chivalric romance that ends in death (and owes more than a little to Cervantes's *Don Quixote*),[10] and a burlesque of playgoing and theatrical commerce that ends as it begins, with running commentary and redirection by a couple of voluble spectators who are actually part of the cast.

Whether Blackfriars or Red Bull, Globe or St. Paul's, the Shakespearean-era theatre was as much a place for music as for speech and action. Over a quarter-century before Beaumont's play premiered, Stephen Gosson railed against the affective allure of the 'straunge consortes of melody' that one found in the theatre along with equally seductive 'costly apparel', 'effeminate gesture', and 'wanton speache'.[11] As the two spectator-characters repeatedly remind the actual audience of *The Knight*, instrumental music accompanied the movements of characters in featured plays and, at least in the enclosed 'private' theatres such as the Blackfriars, the conventional inter-act entertainment. Elizabethan and Jacobean actors routinely received training in song, dance, and sometimes instrumental music. Even for those whose musical ears or singing voices were not outstanding, such training complemented other abilities. 'Player hath many times, many excellent qualities', claims commonplace compiler Thomas Gainesford in 1616,

---

[8] A. Gurr and M. Ichikawa, *Staging in Shakespeare's Theatres* (Oxford University Press, 2000), 18.

[9] T. Stern, 'Taking Part: Actors and Audience on the Stage at Blackfriars', *Inside Shakespeare*, ed. P. Menzer (Selinsgrove: Susquehanna University Press, 2006), 35–53, on 47.

[10] S. H. Gale, 'The Relationship Between Beaumont's *The Knight of the Burning Pestle* and Cervantes's *Don Quixote*', *Anales Cervantinos* 11 (1972), 87–96; and Gurr, ed., *Knight of the Burning Pestle* 2–4.

[11] S. Gosson, *Schoole of Abuse* (London: T. Woodcocke, 1579), 14.

as dancing, activitie, musicke, song, elloqution, ability of body, memory, vigilancy, skill of weapon, pregnancy of wit, and such like: in all which hee resembleth an excellent spring of water, which growes the more sweeter, and the more plentiful by the often drawing out of it: so are all these the more perfect and plausible by the often practise.[12]

To supplement musical troupe members, Jacobean theatres employed additional instrumentalists as needed. At the larger semi-open amphitheatres on the south bank of the Thames, these might include the town waits, while the smaller, enclosed theatres in London proper on the north bank probably maintained their own proprietary ensembles, supplemented on occasion by professional musicians.[13] The ensemble at the Blackfriars was famous by the early years of the seventeenth century for its pre-play concerts, as the comments of German visitor Frederic Gerschow attest.[14] Blackfriars plays called principally for the softer 'indoor' instruments instead of the strident trumpets and hautboys associated with the open-roofed theatres on the south bank. The more subtle and elegant cornett was generally used in place of the hautboy in the Blackfriars and St. Paul's theatres.[15] The Citizen's requests for 'shawms' (Induction, 100–103) and 'the waits of South-warke' (Induction, 105–6), and his later complaint that he 'gave the whoreson gallowes money, and I thinke hee has not got mee the waits of South-warke' (Interact II, 5–6), are therefore all the more amusing, since they reveal the character's lack of musical discrimination and misunderstanding of London theatrical practice in which said waits played in a different sort of house in a different part of the landscape.[16] As we shall see, Citizen George and his wife, Nell, know titles of current repertory available for purchase, but their use of musical terminology underscores their outsider status. George, for instance, uses the more antiquated term 'shawm' while printed play texts almost invariably refer to the same instruments as 'hoboys' or 'hautboys', although both terms remained in current English usage well into the seventeenth century.[17]

---

[12] T. Gainesford, *Rich Cabinet* (London: Roger Jackson, 1616), 118.

[13] See W. Lyons's essay in this volume.   [14] See p. 17 above.

[15] The company at Blackfriars occasionally used trumpets although none of its extant plays call for shawms or hautbois; see L. P. Austern, *Music in English Children's Drama of the Later Renaissance* (Philadelphia: Gordon and Breach, 1992), 63–68.

[16] Smith, 'Reading Between the Acts', 483.

[17] See, for instance, J. A. Comenius, *Orbis Sensualium Pictus*, transl. C. Hoole (London : J. Kirton, 1659), 'Musical Instruments', p. 204; and F. North, *A Philosophical Essay of Musick* (London : John Martyn, 1677), 15. German musician Michael Praetorius reminds readers that the instrument known in England as the 'hoboy' was more widely called a shawm, *Syntagma Musicum*, band 2: *De Organographia* (Wolfenbuttel, 1619; Faksimile-Nachdruk, Basel: Barenreiter Kassel, 1958), 36.

The instrument by any name was so closely connected with municipal bands that it was also known by non-connoisseurs as the 'wait'.[18]

Music in Elizabethan and Jacobean playhouses was used not only to entertain before, during, after, and between the acts of featured dramas. It also added verisimilitude to scenes whose non-theatrical equivalents included musical activity, characterised individuals and groups, created atmosphere, defined genre, emphasised scene changes, guided audience emotion, and, when necessary, covered the sound of stage machines. Early modern English theatrical music was assembled specifically for each play, and, like today's cinematic soundtracks, often combined original compositions with pre-existing works that carried significance for listeners. Songs and instrumental pieces floated freely in and out of dramatic works. Some originated from, or were subsumed by, repertories of orally transmitted song and dance. Others were maintained by musicians employed by theatre companies, court, or the municipalities of London or Southwark, from which they could pass from play to play, or between plays, masques, and other non-theatrical entertainments. Music also found its way into the theatre from broadsides and printed music-books. Songs, dances, and ballad-tunes used in plays were included in anthologies for domestic recreation or pedagogical purposes, much like show tunes and soundtrack theme songs today. Then, as now, stock dramatic situations, characters, and locations were associated with specific sorts of music, which could be used literally or with irony. Just as *The Knight* is a pastiche of dramatic customs and cultural clichés, so is its music. The era's play whose generic range and dramatic use of music most closely resembles that in *The Knight* is Chapman, Jonson, and Marston's *Eastward Ho*. The only other one that provides such detailed information about its inter-act music is Marston's *Sophonisba*. Not coincidentally, both of these were presented by the same company not long before Beaumont's work.

For the early modern era as for our own, music was of the essence of memory and self-fashioning. Music moves through time and affects the listener, yet lacks material form. Music can help to suggest objects of sight, smell, taste, and touch through synaesthetic pathways or through association from previous hearings.[19] 'That strain again', exclaims Orsino as a passage recurs, 'O, it came o'er my ear like the sweet sound/ That breathes

---

[18] For example, C. Butler, *Principles of Musik*, 94; and F. W. Galpin, *Old English Instruments of Music*, 2nd edn (London: Methuen & Co., Ltd., 1911), 161–62.

[19] L. P. Austern, *Music, Sensation, and Sensuality* (New York and London: Routledge, 2002), Introduction, 2 and 7; and T. DeNora, 'Music and Self-Identity', *Popular Music Studies Reader*, ed. A. Bennett et al. (London and New York: Routledge, 2006), 144.

upon a bank of violets,/ Stealing and giving odour' (*Twelfth Night*, 1.1.4–7). The temporality of music links it closely to recalled experience and provides parameters for reliving events; even a brief phrase can induce yearning for past times and poignant emotional states.[20] 'That song tonight/ Will not go from my mind', muses Desdemona as she remembers the tragedy of her mother's maid Barbary just before her own reiteration of both melody and circumstance (*Othello* 4.3.29–30). Emilia's dying repetition of the work's refrain not long thereafter (*Othello* 5.2.246) adds Desdemona's performance and subsequent murder to a growing chain of recollection that unites audience and characters through fragments of a single song.

In Shakespeare's and Beaumont's era as in ours, many musical genres relied on repetition and audience recognition of familiar patterns, as Orsino and Emilia remind us. Western musical practice also has a long tradition of associating specific works, styles, and even instruments with particular times, places, performers, and performance practices. Music of any sort is a powerful referent for personal experience and provides a template for elaborating self-identity.[21] On stage (or screen) it therefore signifies important aspects of character and situation. Once in circulation, musical genres and styles cannot be associated with social status, for they accrue significance through use. Such labels as 'popular', 'high art', 'courtly', and 'folk' lose meaning as works pass from musician to musician, venue to venue, and context to context.[22] This means that dramatic music may paradoxically represent status through contextually recognisable codes. Orsino attends at his command to instrumental ensemble music befitting his noble status, and Desdemona sings to herself a servant's ballad. The staged performance of each piece suggests contrasting genesis and cultural significance, and audience members from different backgrounds may have had deeper personal acquaintance with one sort over the other. Yet both have become aspects of a common theatrical repertory of sound.

The music in *The Knight* relies for its full effect on these capacities of music, as well as recognition of the theatrical convention, cultural

---

[20] DeNora, 'Music and Self-Identity', 144; and J. Starobinski, 'On Nostalgia', transl. Kristen Gray Jaffin, in *The Emotional Power of Music*, ed. Tom Cochrane et al. (Oxford University Press, 2013), 329–35.

[21] DeNora, 'Music and Self-Identity', 144–45.

[22] Bennett et al., *Popular Music Studies Reader*, Introduction, 2–4; R. Middleton, 'Articulating Musical Meaning/Reconstructing Musical History/Locating the Popular', *Musical Belongings* (Ashgate, 2009), 6–7.

custom, and, in several cases, recall of the larger work or prior performance context from which a segment has been borrowed. Most importantly, as even the uncultured George recognises when he asks the Prologue for the shawms he should have known were not in use at the Blackfriars, the music in the play underscores character by type and provides clues to identity, self- or otherwise. 'What stately music have you? You have shawms?', asks the Citizen before insisting that his apprentice must be accompanied on stage by these strident reeds because 'he plays a stately part' (Induction, 98–101).

If conscious attention is first drawn to the music on stage through George and Nell's voluble dilettantism, the same joke returns in variant form with each interact. The Citizens' comments not only reveal their greater familiarity with conventions of the public theatre and lack of musical discrimination, they also reflect on multiple levels of musical connoisseurship and especially the circulation of repertory in early seventeenth-century London. These rely, in turn, on varying degrees of musical training and memory. Far from being a mere grocer, George is a citizen and merchant, affiliated with one of London's prominent livery companies and successful enough to engage at least one apprentice.[23] He is therefore a man of substantial civic and economic position. In order for Beaumont's running gag to succeed, he and Nell must be dressed and groomed at least as sumptuously as those seated around them. George belongs to the same class as the 'Gentlemen and Merchants of good accompt', who, at least since the 1580s, had played a significant role in the development of native musical taste and commerce.[24] Such persons were the targeted consumers of many printed music books, including self-tutorials for singing and for playing fashionable instruments. The decade leading up to 1607 had seen a veritable explosion of mass-market works on the fundamentals of music as well as some of the most reprinted music books of the entire era. Conduct manuals and commonplace books emphasised the need for gentlemen – and women – to be able to perform and discuss music. George and Nell may have the outward signifiers of wealth and status, but they have not learned music, or even its critical vocabulary, in ways that would confirm them as members of the leisured classes.

As the first interact begins, following directions that a 'BOY danceth. Musicke', Nell refers to the instruments she hears and praises as 'fiddles'

---

[23] Smith, 'Reading Between the Acts', 479–80.
[24] N. Yonge, *Musica Transalpina* (London: Thomas East, 1588), cantus partbook, sig. Aii.

and 'Rebeckes'. The former was early modern English slang for any (stringed) instrument, especially bowed.[25] Randle Cotgrave's 1611 *Dictionarie of the French and English Tongues*, defines 'Fidler' as a 'common Musition, that playes on a violin'.[26] Whatever instruments Nell heard or saw in the Blackfriars were probably not played by the kind of common 'fiddlers' decried by the likes of Gosson.[27] Furthermore, by 1607, the bowed, arm-held rebec had fallen into disrepute among elite connoisseurs, though still used by lower-status oral entertainers especially in rural areas. The smallest member of the seventeenth-century violin family, 'the little, narrow and long violin', known in England as the kit or poche[tte], was morphologically an updated rebec associated with kinds of practice unlikely in the exclusive Blackfriars.[28] 'Rebec' was already considered an 'old and obscure word' by 1598, and a 'hard word' by 1661.[29] Nell thus lacks the proper discriminatory faculties and critical vocabulary to describe whatever she – and the audience – actually heard.

Her husband is no more discerning. By the second interact, when George finally realises that he isn't hearing the Waits of Southwark, he disparages the famous Blackfriars ensemble in the timeless manner of a pop-music aficionado confronted with unfamiliar repertory. 'You musicians, play "Baloo"', he calls, requesting a widely-circulating lullaby-ballad (Interact II, 8). 'No, good George', says his wife, 'let's ha' "Lachrimae"', an intricate and melancholy pavan by John Dowland, full of hidden philosophical and numerological symbolism. 'Why, this is it, cony', replies George (Interact II, 9–10). Presumably, it isn't – but musically literate members of the audience, especially recreational lutenists and viol-players who could have bought, played, or copied many

---

[25] Austern, *Music in English Children's Drama*, 70–71.

[26] R. Cotgrave, *Dictionarie of the French and English Tongues*, sig. Mmmm.

[27] Gosson, *Abuse*, sig. B4v; and P. Stubbes, *Anatomie of Abuses* (London: Richard Jones, 1583), sigs. O3v-O6v. See also C. Marsh, *Music and Society in Early Modern England* (Cambridge University Press, 2010), 79–82.

[28] John Florio equates fiddle, kit, and violin in *A World of Wordes* (London: Edw[ard] Blount, 1598), sigs. N2v and Mm4. Frenchman Marin Mersenne presents the 'poche' as the smallest 'violon', *Harmonie Universelle*, Livre second (Paris: Sebastien Cramoisy, 1636), 177–178. M. Remnant. 'Kit.' *Grove Music Online*, Oxford University Press. <www.oxfordmusiconline.com.turing.library .northwestern.edu/subscriber/article/grove/music/15075> (accessed 9 August 2015).

[29] T. Speght, ed., *The Works of . . . Jeffrey (sic) Chaucer* (London: Geor[ge] Bishop, 1598), Table of 'old and obscure words', n.p.; T. Blount, *Glossographia* (London: George Sawbridge, 1661), sig. Kk3v. Mersenne no longer acknowledges the instrument in 1636; *Harmonie Universelle*, 176–79. See also Galpin, *Old English Instruments of Music*, 3rd edn, revised (London: Methuen, 1932), 84; and M. Remnant 'Rebec', *Grove Music Online* (accessed 9 August 2015).

available arrangements of the piece – would be in on the acoustic jest.[30] A cursory examination of mass-market sources of both tunes available in 1607 gives greater dimension to the joke, which may fall on even further segments of the audience. John Dowland's *Lachrimae, or Seaven Teares Figured in Seaven Passionate Pavans ... set forth for the lute, viols, or violins*, had been printed three years prior and was eminently suitable for the kind of ensemble resident at the Blackfriars as well as for domestic use. Like other elite lutenist-composers of the time, Dowland lived and sold his printed works in the same part of London as the private theatres.[31] *Lachrimae* was dedicated 'To The Most Gracious and Sacred Princesse ANNA QUEENE of England, Scotland, France, and Ireland', sometime patron of the troupe that presented *The Knight*. On the title page, the composer had styled himself 'lutenist to the most royall and magnificent, Christian the fourth, King of Denmarke', the 'deare and worthiest Brother' to the same Queen.[32] Members of the audience who had ever perused or purchased the book would know this. Even those who had heard or discussed any of its contents might recall its double court cachet. Other connoisseurs or collectors of music would be familiar with the tune from the same composer's 'Flow My Tears', included in his *Second Booke of Songes or Ayres* in 1600. However, both 'Lachrimae' and 'Baloo' had been printed together even earlier by an arranger who may have had a connection to Shakespeare and the public theatre.[33] They appear in Thomas Morley's *Firste Booke of Consort Lessons* of 1599 and 1611, arranged for almost exactly the ensemble described at the Blackfriars by Gerschow and used in wealthy homes: 'the Treble Lute, the Pandora, the Cittern, the base-Violl, the Flute & Treble-Violl'.[34] The music in *The Knight* was almost certainly not provided by the waits of Southwark, but may have been played on instruments associated with those of London for their more intimate engagements – which were certainly in use at the Blackfriars. Repertory

---

[30] See P. Holman, *Dowland Lachrimae (1604)* (Cambridge University Press, 1999), xiii and 36–46. For 'Baloo' (also 'Balow') see Simpson, *British Broadside Ballad*, 31–34.

[31] M. Spring, *The Lute in Britain* (Oxford University Press, 2001), 105.

[32] J. Dowland, *Lachrimae* (London: John Windet, [1604]), title page and sig. A2.

[33] S. Beck, 'The Case of "O Mistresss Mine"', *Renaissance News*, 6 (1953), 19–23; E. Brennecke, 'Shakespeare's Musical Collaboration with Morley', *PMLA* 54 (1939), 139–52; V. Duckles, 'New Light on "O Mistresse Mine"', *Renaissance News*, 6 (1953) 19–23; and J. H. Long, 'Shakespeare and Thomas Morley', *Modern Language Notes*, 65 (1950), 17–22.

[34] T. Morley, *First Booke of Consort Lessons* (London: William Barley, 1599), title page. Also see Beck, ed., *Consort Lessons*. 1–9; and W. Edwards, ed., *Music for Mixed Consort* (London: Musica Britannica Trust, 1977), xiii–xiv.

at least offered to the Waits of London therefore included two of the pieces whose names George and Nell drop in this interact. The same tunes circulated to even further venues arranged for other performing forces, and variants may have been associated with the public theatre with whose traditions the couple seems more familiar.[35]

Most of the more directly musical characters also seem to have transferred performance choices from other (meta)theatrical realms. Rafe, the apprentice-hero of the title romance, moves to the beat of martial drums (5.5.79–89). Old (Charles) Merrythought, prodigal father to the apprentice-hero of the parallel play *The London Merchant*, appears to have learned at least one example of every secular vocal musical genre that was readily available in London in 1607. His repertory includes not only the ballads to which most commentators refer, but also newly-composed theatrical songs, rounds and catches, an Italian madrigal with translated text, and the lute-ayres that were all the rage among discerning consumers during the first decade of the seventeenth century. Merrythought borrows from oral and written repertories, and from genres associated with performance venues including alehouse, domicile, and public thoroughfare, as well multiple theatrical traditions. Merrythought seldom speaks if he can sing; instead, he inserts textually appropriate snatches of song into conversation. He also sings with his equally merry mates and directly to the audience. In several cases, memory of either a larger section of the song itself or its other performance contexts helps increase its impact.

What has gone largely unremarked about Merrythought, with his obsessive and indiscriminate performance of song, is that he is quite literally following a prescription for music therapy.[36] From Galen through such early modern English guardians of body and soul as physician Timothy Bright and priest Thomas Wright, music was acknowledged as a powerful agent for dispelling dark humours and infusing the body with life-affirming blood. 'Many and sundry are the meanes, which Philosophers and Physitians have prescribed to exhilarate a sorrowfull heart', writes Robert Burton most famously in a work that was still in progress when *The Knight* premiered. '[B]ut', he continues, 'in my judgement none so present, none so powerfull, none so apposite as a cup of

---

[35] Beck, ed., *Consort Lessons*, 1–9; and R. T. Dart, 'Morley's Consort Lessons of 1599', *Proceedings of the Royal Musical Association* 74 (1947–48), 1–9 on 5–7.

[36] Bonneau recognises that Merrythought's singing is largely sanguinary, 'functional[,] and not decorative', 'On Merrythought's Singing', 9–11.

strong drinke, mirth, musicke, and merry company'.[37] Burton might as well be describing the aptly named Merrythought, especially in Acts 3 and 4. The character's harmonious habit is therefore not just a massive overdose of 'pills to purge melancholy'.[38] It also belongs to a metatheatrical tradition of therapeutic performance practice. '*Musica est mentis medicina maestro*, a roaring-meg against melancholy' adds Burton, 'to ereare and revive the languishing Soule, yt affecting not only the eares, but the very arteries, the vitall and animall spirits, it erects the minde, and makes it nimble. . . This it will effect in the most dull, severe, and sorowfull Soules, [and] expel griefe with mirth[.][39]

Although early modern England inherited a longstanding tradition of treating melancholy with music, no Western commentator ever pre-scribed any particular genre. Merrythought demonstrates a range of possibilities, mostly chosen either for text that reminds the audience of how and why he is presented as a 'humorous songster', or because short quotations work as dialogue with other characters. Ironically, by virtue of his status as an 'old man' (1.4.52; 2.9.39) and a 'gray-beard' (3.4.74), he is in the stage of life most often associated by physicians, philosophers, and other learned writers with the very melancholy that his music has more than completely eradicated. He even explains that 'this [mirth] is the Philosophers stone. . . that keeps a man ever yong' (4.5.16–17). Part of the joke is doubtless the youthful voice that issued from the character; as Shakespeare reminds us in *As You Like It*, the 'lean and slippered pantaloon' of the sixth age of life has 'a big manly voice/Turning again toward childish treble' (2.7.158–61).

As Burton implies would be the most effective 'roaring-meg against melancholy', Merrythought joins 'strong drinke, mirth, musicke, and merry company' several times. When his wife and son Michael attempt to return home in 3.4, they find that he has filled their domicile with 'mangy companions' whom she asks him to 'turn out' (17). At least some of these are instrumentalists from whom Old Merrythought requests 'some light musicke, and more wine' (46), to 'Strike up lively lads' (61), and 'a light *Lavolto*'(81). When his wife berates him to let her in, he sends her away with two stanzas from the song 'Go From My Window' (24–27 and 42–46). This tune, with and without words, circulated in multiple

---

[37] Burton, *Anatomy*.

[38] Phrase borrowed from the later, much-reprinted *Wit and Mirth [or] Pills to Purge Melancholy* (London: Henry Playford, 1682), title page.

[39] Burton, *Anatomy*, 294.

arrangements for performers ranging from elite keyboardists, to beginning cittern students, to ballad singers. Morley's *First Book of Consort Lessons* includes an arrangement by Richard Allison.[40] The song was also used in several other plays, including Heywood's *The Rape of Lucrece*, whose story is also referenced in *The Knight* by the Citizen's Wife in Interact II.[41] Whether Merrythought's musicians 'struck up lively' to accompany him, or whether he sang alone, virtually every member of the audience would have known some version of the song and associated it with some other circumstance and venue – perhaps even another play. Mistress Merrythought finally gets the message that she's not welcome unless she, too, joins the musical merriment (85) when her husband dismisses her yet again with two lines from the traditional ballad 'Lady Margaret and Sweet William'. Audience members familiar with this song of supernatural vengeance and love from beyond the grave would have recognised his lines of 'You are no love for me Marg'ret/ I am no love for you' (87) as those with which William dismisses Margaret and causes her death from sorrow. The tune and full narrative context had already been recalled for the audience as Merrythought sang a few lines referring to Margaret's ghost in 2.9.1–4.

In 4.5, when two boys successively remind Merrythought that he is out of bread and money, he replies 'Hang bread and supper! Let's preserve our mirth, and we shall never feel hunger, I'll warrant you. Let's have a catch; boy follow me'. The two youngsters do follow him immediately in the lively three-voice catch 'Ho, Ho Nobody at Home' with its circumstan-tially-appropriate reference to 'Meat, nor drink, nor money ha' we none' (lines 36–40). This work had been circulating in manuscript, if not orally, for some years before the play premiered, and would therefore likely have been familiar to at least some catch-singers in the audience.[42] From *Twelfth Night* through *The Tempest* and well into the Restoration, this simple canonic genre, associated on and off stage with drink and merry (male homosocial) company, was used in plays to convey a mood of boisterous buffoonery and boyish hijinks. As Maria and Malvolio remind us in *Twelfth Night*, catches were not seemly repertory for high-born men, especially as late-night entertainment in 'my lady's house'. They most strongly suggested the alehouse, the barber-surgeon's shop, or, later in

---

[40] Beck, ed., *Consort Lessons*, 117–126; and Dart, 'Morley's Consort Lessons', 8–9.
[41] See Simpson, *Broadside Ballad*, 257–58.
[42] The catch first appeared in print after the play premiered, T. Ravenscroft, *Pammelia* (London: William Barley, 1609), 41.

the century, the sort of gentlemen's club frequented by the likes of Samuel Pepys. In *Twelfth Night* and *The Tempest*, Shakespeare uses catches not only as a means of separating comical sub-plot from the main romance, but also to enable characters with one set of musical taste to serve as foil for another.[43] Merrythought erases these boundaries through his indiscriminate use of musical genres and his paradoxical position as both buffoon and hero's father.

Merrythought and his sanguinary music also exemplify humoral self-fashioning and performance. By the late 1590s, the deliberate cultivation of an air of melancholy had become fashionable among a certain sort of young man, lampooned in the theatre and catered to commercially with the publication of sorrowful song and lute music by such composers as Dowland. 'Many men are melancholy by hearing musicke', says Burton, 'but it is a pleasing melancholy that it causeth'. There was quite a market for such indulgent and paradoxical pleasure on and off stage. 'More, more, I prithee, more', begs Jacques after Amiens has sung 'Under the Greenwood Tree' in *As You Like It*. 'It will make you melancholy, Monsieur Jacques', replies the singer, to which Jacques responds 'I thank it. More, I prithee, more. I can suck melancholy out of a song as a weasel sucks eggs. More, I prithee more' (2.5.10–12).

In 2.10 of *The Knight*, after already singing part of a stanza from 'Lady Margaret and Sweet William', another from 'The Knight and the Shepherd's Daughter', a snatch of the ballad 'Walsingham' (also quoted by Ophelia in *Hamlet*), melodic lines from a couple of catches, and what is evidently a newly composed theatre song, Old Merrythought (slightly mis-)quotes from one of the era's most famous and widely circulating musical vehicles for emulating, if not stimulating, melancholy: the exquisite 'Sorrow Stay' from Dowland's *Second Book of Songs or Ayres*. When Merchant Venturewell is distraught by the elopement of his daughter with Merrythought's son Jasper, and even more upset by the old man's indifference to his loss, Merrythought suggests that Venturewell 'Let her goe, thinke no more on her, but sing lowd', which would actually be effective, if callously prescribed, physick for the Merchant's misery. He also tells him that, if both of his 'sons were on the gallows, I would sing '*Downe, down, downe:* they fall,/ Downe, and arise they never shall' (64–66). On one hand, this is a nasty bit of literal gallows humour. On the other, those familiar with Dowland's darkly melancholy song would recall these

---

[43] P.T. Dircks, 'Shakespeare's Use of the Catch as Dramatic Metaphor', *Shakespeare Quarterly* 24 (1973), 88–90.

as the last two lines of a text of utter despair, with music full of clashing dissonance and unexpected turns, belonging to a genre associated with interiority and personalised confession.[44] As printed in the *Second Book* with its multiple voices, the lines Merrythought sings are truly anguished, with the melody set over a descending bass that forms an ironic counterpart to the elongated attempt of the narrator to 'arise' impossibly.[45] When Venturewell is finally coerced to sing (5.3.75–77), what he selects is a better-known, less elite song also associated with melancholy, especially in the theatre: '*Fortune my foe, &c.*' (line 77). This ballad tune is one of the most familiar from the period between the late Elizabethan era and the Restoration, used for endless broadsides of hangings, murders, natural disasters, pacts with the Devil, and similarly dark deeds. It also served as the basis of numerous instrumental arrangements in manuscript, and at least one theatrical parody (in Fletcher's *The Wild Goose Chase*, 3.1).[46]

No Jacobean romance or romantic comedy would be complete without a love song. Neither could there be a funeral without sombre instrumental music or plaintive lament. It is a tribute to Beaumont's satiric vision that the title Knight never comes across vocal music during his quest, as would be expected especially when he encounters the King of Cracovia's daughter (4.2), or remembers the 'lady' for whose sake he took arms (3.3.6–8). Since his death is presented retrospectively by his ghost, there is no chance for so much as a dead march. However, the romantic heroine of *The London Merchant* plot, Venturewell's daughter, Luce, does not disappoint. The sweetest and most charming of the extant songs from the play, composed by Robert Johnson at the beginning of his long and fruitful connection to the Blackfriars, is a duet between her and her true love, Merrythought's son Jasper (3.1.31–44). It unifies theatrical conventions of the lullaby, music for enchanted sleep, siren seduction through song, and the early modern metaperformative notion of the vocal duet as an exchange of souls. Like so much else in this play, it is at once a parody that dashes audience expectations and an opportunity to dissolve the line between performance and belief.

At the start of Act 3, the lovers have run away from London and become lost in the woods at night. Luce is sleepless and frightened, while Jasper is vigilant and protective. His lines emphasise his bold masculinity and her innocent femininity. When he suggests that they sing, the expectation is a tender love duet to reaffirm their bond and emphasise their gender roles.

[44] D. Fischlin, *In Small Proportions* (Wayne State University Press, 1998), 263–66.
[45] Dowland, *Second Book*, sig. cv–cii.   [46] Simpson, *Broadside Ballad*, 225–235.

However, Jasper's flirtatious directives remind us of the potential for music to inflame the passions through sensory channels, and of the dangerously seductive potential of women's voice in song. He and Luce seem to be performing two different scenes:

JASPER. Why then wee'l sing,/ And try to see how that will worke upon our
    sences.
LUCE. I'le sing, or say, or any thing but sleepe.
JASPER. Come little Mer-maid, rob me of my heart/With that inchanting voice.
LUCE. You mocke me Jasper. (3.1.26–31)

He begins the duet, and, as is proper, she follows. But their voices never join. She draws out her answers to his questions, rising higher and higher in increasing excitement, strikes him with a musical flash of lightening, and wavers between tonal areas instead of settling on one. His music becomes more agitated as he wrests the song back from her. The text belongs to the era's ongoing literary controversy about women, with Luce gaining the upper hand both verbally and musically.[47] Jasper, believing the performance above her dialogue and action, blames her for his ill fortune and tries to murder her for inconstancy. She is rescued by her father's pursuing search party, if not by Nell's attempt to raise the watch at Ludgate to prevent 'man-slaughter upon the harmlesse Gentlewoman' (3.1.99–103).

Later in *The Knight,* when confronted with a coffin bearing Jasper's supposedly dead body, Luce follows the theatrical convention of a woman privately lamenting the unexpected death of her beloved, first in speech, and then in a song whose music has not yet been located (4.4.28–65; see for comparison Chapman, *The Revenge of Bussy D'Ambois*, 2.1; and Jonson, *Cynthia's Revels*, 1.2). As she plans to join him in death, to 'fill one Coffin and one grave together' (4.4.48), he rises alive and the two are joyously reunited.

Space does not permit exploration of even more ways in which Beaumont's play makes use of musical materials, conventions, gestures, and expectations from his era's theatres and other performance venues. *The Knight of the Burning Pestle* uses music to recall and reflect on the multiple institutions in which it was practiced and the varied sources from which it was known by members of its audience. It also raises issues concerning musical taste and knowledge, the polyvalency of musical memory, and the histories of genres and specific pieces it presents.

---

[47] C. A. Henze, 'How Music Matters: Some Songs of Robert Johnson in the Plays of Beaumont and Fletcher', *Comparative Drama*, 34 (2000), 18–21.

CHAPTER 7

Changing Musical Practices in the Shakespearean Playhouse, 1620–42

Lucy Munro

One of the most famous musical moments in Shakespeare involves an instrument that need not actually be played. In the aftermath of the performance of the 'Mousetrap' in *Hamlet*, the exhilarated prince repeatedly calls for music:

> Ah ha! – Come, some music! Come, the recorders!
> For if the king like not the comedy,
> Why then – belike he likes it not, perdy.
> Come, some music! (3.2.265–8)

Brought the recorders by the visiting actors, he uses one to provoke Rosencranz and Guildenstern, the erstwhile friends who are trying to probe his intentions and sanity:

HAMLET. Will you play upon this pipe?
GUILDENSTERN. My lord, I cannot.
HAMLET. I pray you.
GUILDENSTERN. Believe me I cannot.
HAMLET. I do beseech you.
GUILDENSTERN. I know no touch of it my lord.
HAMLET. 'Tis as easy as lying. Govern these ventages with your fingers and thumb, give it breath with your mouth, and it will discourse most eloquent music. Look you, these are the stops.
GUILDENSTERN. But these cannot I command to any utterance of harmony. I have not the skill.
HAMLET. Why look you now how unworthy a thing you make of me. You would play upon me, you would seem to know my stops, you would pluck out the heart of my mystery, you would sound me from my lowest note to the top of my compass – and there is much music, excellent voice in this little organ, yet cannot you make it speak. 'Sblood, do you think I am easier to be played on than a pipe? Call me what instrument you will, though you can fret me, you cannot play upon me. (3.2.318–36)

Giving Guildenstern (accurate) instruction in how to use the recorder, Hamlet also exploits the idea that the instrument was easy to learn yet capable of complex expression, drawing an analogy between his companion's inability to play the recorder and his clumsy attempts to 'play' Hamlet himself. As Christopher Wilson observes, 'If Guildenstern does not know the basics how can he play a difficult piece?'[1] The musical analogy, vividly evoked through the physical presence of the recorder, gives focus and expression to Hamlet's growing irritation, allowing him briefly to pull intellectual and artistic rank on Guildenstern before the exchange is broken up by the entrance of Polonius.

What interests me here, however, is not so much the complexity of Hamlet's interaction with the recorder but a more basic question: why does this instrument appears on the Globe stage at all? Recorders and similar wind instruments such as flutes did not routinely appear in outdoor playhouses in the Elizabethan and early Jacobean periods: in fact, this appears to be the only appearance of a recorder in the stage directions of surviving plays associated with these theatres and the only play in which dialogue requires that one be present. Hamlet's recorder is, therefore, perhaps an intruder from another musical world. While the visiting players within the play's fiction clearly have the instruments to hand for their performance before Claudius's court, the late-Elizabethan Chamberlain's Men, who play them, seem to have had less use for this instrument.

The recorder points to issues that will be at the heart of this essay, which explores the ways in which Shakespeare's plays helped to facilitate new trends in playhouse music in the later Jacobean and Caroline periods. Before the second decade of the seventeenth century, there appear to have been conventions governing the use of music in indoor and outdoor playhouses.[2] Softer instruments such as recorders, flutes and cornetts rarely, if ever, appeared in plays performed outdoors at the Curtain, Globe, Fortune, Red Bull and Rose theatres; conversely, trumpets and drums hardly ever featured in the repertories of the indoor playhouses.[3]

[1] C. R. Wilson, 'Shakespeare and Early Modern Music', in *The Edinburgh Companion to Shakespeare and the Arts*, ed. M. Thornton Burnett, A. Streete and R. Wray (Edinburgh University Press, 2011), 119–41 (134).

[2] See L. P. Austern, *Music in English Children's Drama of the Renaissance* (Philadelphia: Gordon and Breach, 1992), 61–77; D. Lindley, *Shakespeare and Music* (London: Thomson Learning, 2006), 93–100; B. R. Smith, *The Acoustic World of Early Modern England: Attending to the O-Factor* (University of Chicago Press, 1999), 245; L. Munro, 'Music and Sound', in *The Oxford Handbook of Early Modern Theatre*, ed. R. Dutton (Oxford University Press, 2009), 543–59.

[3] See C. R. Wilson and M. Calore, *Music in Shakespeare: A Dictionary* (London: Continuum, 2005), *s.v.* cornett, drum, recorder, flute, trumpet; Austern, *Music*, 67. See also essays by Lyons and Austern in this volume.

Both kinds of playhouses featured extra-dramatic music, but at the out-door playhouses this took the form of jigs and dances at the end of a play, whereas the indoor playhouses prefaced their plays with instrumental music and inserted it into the act breaks that were not employed outdoors. Stereotypically, such distinctions between indoor and outdoor playing persisted. As late as 1671, Edward Howard could comment on the – to his eyes – incongruous success of popular theatres such as the Red Bull in the period before the Civil War by using their soundscapes as a shorthand for their other perceived aesthetic failings: 'remember that the Red Bull writers, with their Drums, Trumpets, Battels, and Hero's, have had this success formerly, and perhaps have been able to number as many Audiences as our Theatres'.[4] Quoted by scholars, these lines have helped to give an impression of remarkable continuity across the Elizabethan, Jacobean and Caroline periods, in which outdoor playhouses are marked out for their louder, harsher, less sophisticated soundscapes.[5]

The only problem with this vision of aesthetic continuity is that it does not wholly fit the evidence. A Red Bull play such as Thomas Heywood's *The Rape of Lucrece* (Queen Anna's Men, *c.* 1607), uses sound, music and song in ways that are crucial to the company's aesthetic and generic project, as Richard Rowland and Eva Griffith have recently argued.[6] Furthermore, a closer examination of the surviving plays also suggests that the musical landscape of the later Jacobean and Caroline periods was remarkably fluid. When the King's Men took over the Blackfriars playhouse around 1609, they began to play indoors during the winter months, maintaining the Globe for summer performances, and they appear not to have developed separate repertories for the Blackfriars and Globe until the later 1630s. Perhaps as a result, indoor practices bled into outdoor plays, and vice versa. The outdoor playhouses quickly picked up the custom of act-breaks from the indoor playhouses, meaning that commercial plays settled more squarely on a five-act structure than they had hitherto, and they also experimented with cornetts and recorders; simultaneously, plays written for the indoor playhouses began to test the effects of trumpets and drums.[7] Peter Holman

[4] *The Six Days Adventure, or, The New Utopia* (London, 1671), A4v.

[5] See, for example, A. Gurr, *Playgoing in Shakespeare's London*, 3rd edn (Cambridge University Press, 2004), 92.

[6] See R. Rowland, *Thomas Heywood's Theatre, 1599–1639: Locations, Translations, and Conflict* (Farnham: Ashgate, 2010), 4–15; E. Griffith, *A Jacobean Company and its Playhouse: The Queen's Servants at the Red Bull* (Cambridge University Press, 2013), 160–70.

[7] On the introduction of act-breaks see G. Taylor, 'The Structure of Performance: Act-Intervals in the London Theatres, 1576–1642', in *Shakespeare Reshaped 1606–1623*, ed. G. Taylor and J. Jowett (Oxford: Clarendon Press, 1993), 3–50.

notes that companies such as the King's Men began to commission composers and employ dedicated musicians during the later Jacobean period, while in the most detailed study of Caroline theatre music to date, Julia K. Wood sees little evidence to distinguish between the instrumentation in indoor and outdoor theatres in this period.[8] Therefore, if revivals of *Hamlet* by the King's Men in 1619–20 and 1637 included performances at both the Globe and Blackfriars, as seems likely, Hamlet's recorder would have seemed less out of place at the Globe than it had on the play's earliest performances.[9]

This essay explores this shifting soundscape, arguing that the plays of the King's Men – and those of Shakespeare in particular – had a lasting impact on the musical environments of both indoor and outdoor playhouses. Considering instrumentation, the combination of visual and musical elements of performance, and the use of song, it focuses on two sets of interactions, one from the early 1620s and the other from the early 1630s. It first examines the uses to which musical and dramaturgical allusions to *The Tempest* were put in the early 1620s, focusing on a largely overlooked play, *The Two Noble Ladies*, performed at the Red Bull by the Company of the Revels around 1619–22, which embodies some of the opportunities that indoor practices offered the outdoor playhouses at that time. It then looks at the uses of music in the Caroline history play, in the shape of John Ford's *Perkin Warbeck*, performed by Queen Henrietta Maria's Men around 1632–3, and Robert Davenport's *King John and Matilda*, performed by the same company around 1634. Exploring these plays in the context of Caroline revivals of *Richard II, Richard III, Henry IV* and Shakespeare and Fletcher's *Henry VIII*, I argue that they deliberately fuse aspects of earlier practice with the more elaborate song effects of the Caroline playhouse, creating a hybrid variation on the history play that was both nostalgic and contemporary.

***

The rapid reconstruction of the Fortune playhouse, after its destruction by fire in December 1621, argues as much as does the rebuilding of the Globe

[8] P. Holman, 'Music for the Stage I: Before the Civil War', in *Music in Britain: The Seventeenth Century*, ed. I. Spink (Oxford: Blackwell, 1992), 297–300; J. K. Wood, 'Music in Caroline Plays', unpublished PhD thesis, University of Edinburgh (1991), 89–90.

[9] *Hamlet* was apparently being considered for court performance in 1619–20, and it was performed at Hampton Court on 24 January 1637. See F. Marcham, *The King's Office of the Revels 1610–1622: Fragments of Documents in the Department of Manuscripts, British Museum* (London: Frank Marcham, 1925) 10–15, 32–3; G.E. Bentley, *The Jacobean and Caroline Stage*, 7 vols (Oxford: Clarendon Press, 1941–68), 1: 51.

in 1613–14 for the continued value of the outdoor playhouse within the late-Jacobean theatrical marketplace.[10] Moreover, the King's Men did not treat the Globe theatre as an aesthetic backwater. Two plays drawing on *The Tempest* and written by the King's Men's leading dramatist, John Fletcher, appear to have been licensed for initial performance at the Globe in 1622. *The Prophetess* was licensed by the Master of the Revels, Sir John Astley, on 14 May 1622; it was performed again at the Globe a few years later, when Astley's successor, Sir Henry Herbert, recorded a payment from the King's Men, '[t]he benefitt of the summers day . . . upon the play of The Prophetess', on 21 July 1629.[11] Fletcher and Massinger's *The Sea Voyage* was licensed by Astley on 22 June 1622, meaning that it was almost certainly intended for initial performance at the Globe.[12] These were probably not isolated occurrences: as Roslyn L. Knutson has pointed out, '[t]he status of the Blackfriars as the [King's Men's] premier playhouse came later than 1619, perhaps later than 1625'.[13]

A similar attention to the capacity of the amphitheatre can be seen in the contemporaneous history of the Red Bull. A surviving prologue for *The Two Merry Milkmaids*, performed there around 1619–20, sets out an agenda for the playhouse, one that focuses to an intriguing degree on its soundscape:

> This Day we entreat All that are hither come,
> To expect no noyse of Guns, Trumpets, nor Drum,
> Nor Sword and Targuet; but to heare Sence and Words,
> Fitting the Matter that the Scene affords.
> So that the Stage being reform'd, and free
> From the lowd Clamors it was wont to bee,
> Turmoyl'd with Battailes; you I hope will cease
> Your dayly Tumults, and with vs wish Peace.[14]

The prologue promises a fresh aural environment, one that prizes verbal play above martial noise, and it appears to address head-on a reputation that the Red Bull had for noisy spectacle. Recent criticism has begun to push against the idea that Red Bull spectators were

---

[10] On the fire and rebuilding see G. Wickham, H. Berry and W. Ingram, eds., *English Professional Theatre, 1530–1660* (Cambridge University Press, 2000), 638–41.

[11] N.W. Bawcutt, ed., *The Control and Censorship of Caroline Drama: The Records of Sir Henry Herbert, Master of the Revels 1623–73* (Oxford: Clarendon Press, 1996), 168.

[12] Bawcutt, 137.

[13] 'Two Playhouses, Both Alike in Dignity', *Shakespeare Studies* 30 (2002), 111–17 (116).

[14] *A Pleasant Comedie, Called The Two Merry Milke-maids. Or, The Best Words Weare the Garland* (London, 1620), A2v.

necessarily crude or ill-informed. As Rowland argues, if we accept the idea they were 'semi-literate fools, addicted only to fireworks, noisy spectacle and gratuitous sexual comedy, and prone to vociferous and violent protest when their appetites were disappointed, we buy into a shameless advertising campaign mounted by their rivals'. Moreover, as the prologue to *The Two Merry Milkmaids* suggests, this was 'a campaign of which the purveyors of entertainment at the Red Bull were themselves increasingly and amusingly aware'.[15] The outdoor playhouse was reappraising itself and its own capabilities.

The aesthetic project of the Company of the Revels at the Red Bull, the rebuilding of the Fortune and the writing of new plays for the Globe by the King's Men's leading dramatist all argue that the amphitheatres were in good artistic and commercial health. In this context, the use of *The Tempest* in plays written for the Globe and Red Bull is especially intriguing. Despite its reputation as an archetypal Blackfriars play, *The Tempest* has distinct connections with outdoor techniques and traditions. As Andrew Gurr observes, the opening storm sequence appears to employ a technique more suited to an outdoor, rather than an indoor playhouse. However, Gurr pulls back from this position when he argues that Miranda's first two lines – 'If by your art, my dearest father, you have / Put the wild waters in this roar, allay them' (1.2. 1–2) – confirm to spectators that this is a magical rather than a 'real' storm, and '[i]t is not after all going to be a rough-and-tumble amphitheatre play of the kind Heywood was writing for the Red Bull'.[16] While he acknowledges connections between *The Tempest* and outdoor playhouse practice, Gurr is also keen to maintain an aesthetic and, perhaps, social distance between the Blackfriars and the Red Bull.

In contrast, Jonathan Bate sees an interaction with the Red Bull at the heart of the entertainment that Prospero stages for Miranda and Ferdinand – a sequence that is more often linked with the elite form of the court masque – in the shape of *The Tempest*'s inter-theatrical dialogue with Heywood's *The Silver Age*, a play that was actually performed before Queen Anna, on 12 January 1612, by a combined company of the King's and Queen's Men.[17] These plays are quite different in their narrative construction: where Shakespeare presents a single story, uncharacteristically conforming to the unities of time and place, Heywood ranges

[15] Rowland, *Heywood's Theatre*, 15.
[16] '*The Tempest*'s Tempest at Blackfriars', *Shakespeare Survey* 41 (1989), 91–102 (102).
[17] See E.K. Chambers, *The Elizabethan Stage*, 4 vols (Oxford: Clarendon Press, 1923), 3: 344–5; W.R. Streitberger, ed., 'Jacobean and Caroline Revels Accounts 1603-1642', *Malone Society Collections* 13 (1986), 49.

the cosmos in a set of interwoven stories from Homeric myth. However, they share certain techniques: songs, dumb-shows, noisy sound effects recreating thunder and lightning, and descents from the stage's heavens. As Bate puts it, 'Mercury flames amazement like Ariel; Juno and Iris work in tandem, descending from the heavens on several occasions' and at the centre of *The Silver Age* is a pastoral song to Ceres, 'which represents the closest analogue in all Jacobean drama to the agricultural benison of Prospero's masque'.[18] Neither play can be safely viewed as a 'source' for the other, as they are so close in date, but their similarities in technique and effect suggest the ways in which the practices of the outdoor and indoor playhouses were starting mutually to inform each other.

By the early 1620s, this process had advanced further. *The Prophetess* and *The Sea Voyage* reinforce the connection between *The Tempest*'s dramaturgical strategies and the Globe, and techniques associated with indoor and outdoor traditions are similarly fused in *The Two Noble Ladies*. The play opens with the noise typically associated with the earlier generation of outdoor theatre plays: an '*Alarm*', a '*Flourish*', a '*Shout within*', and a whirl of movement, as the '*flying*' Justina and the wounded soldier Doron meet onstage in the aftermath of the sack of Antioch by the forces of the Souldan of Egypt.[19] However, as the play progresses, it begins to fuse Justina's story with that of the enchanter Cyprian, in a process that will eventually lead to Cyprian's conversion to Christianity. The moment of crisis and conversion is dramatised in ways that draw on indoor playhouse convention in general, and on *The Tempest* in particular. Cyprian lusts after Justina and, when she resists all of his attempts to persuade her, enlists the help of the spirit Cantharides, who significantly takes his name from an aphrodisiac. The sequence that follows, which flirts repeatedly with sexual violence, combines visual and aural effects. Justina '*is discovered in a chaire asleep, in her hands a prayer book, divells about her*' (ll. 1752-4SD), and Cyprian uses song to try to soften his transgression, commenting,

> if such violence
> must be the end yet the beginning shall
> be milde, and I will steale into my roughnesse
> by soft gradations. Let sweet musicke plead
> with ravishing notes to winne her maidenhead. (ll. 1766-70)

---

[18] *Shakespeare and Ovid* (Oxford: Clarendon Press, 1993), 260.
[19] *The Two Noble Ladies*, ed. R. G. Rhoads (Oxford: Malone Society, 1930), l. 0SD. All references are to this edition; I have omitted the deleted text that Rhoads includes in square brackets.

Stage directions call for '*Musique*' and '*Musick. A song*'. The song is
a 'blank', with no lyric or instrumentation specified, but it probably
involves the recorders used in an earlier moment of magical spectacle
when an Angel appeared to Cyprian and foretold that he would eventually 'renounce Magicke, and turne Christian' (l. 1114). If so, the
moment at which Cyprian plans to force Justina combines various
forms of transgression and the perversion of music from its earlier,
heavenly purpose.

At length, Cyprian is moved by Justina's prayers and their impact on
the devils, which retreat when she takes up her Bible, and the sequence
that follows deploys a powerful mixture of visual and aural effects. He
'*kneels*' to her (l. 1817SD), and the emotional and spiritual impact of this
gesture intensifies as he apparently continues to kneel for at least the next
thirty lines. Visual and aural stimuli then follow thick and fast at the
moment at which she hands him the Bible. '*The feinds roare and fly back*'
(l. 1846SD), and music plays, the manuscript playbook showing that
a direction for '*Soft musicke*' was replaced by a more specific one for
'*Recorders*' (l. 1856SD).[20] The aural dissonance of the devils' roaring is
converted into heavenly music, and a '*patriarch-like Angell*' enters '*with
his crossier staffe in one hand, and a book in the other*' (ll. 1856-7SD).
Cantharides screams and the devils roar as they sink through the stage's
trapdoor, '*a flame of fier riseth after them*' (ll. 1860-1SD), the aural impact
of the screaming and roaring working in tandem with the carefully
managed stage spectacle of the satanic inferno. The Angel then '*gives
[Cyprian] the Booke*' (l. 1866SD) and '*Toucheth his breast with his crosse*'
(ll. 1869-70SD), converting the conjurer's 'carnall lust ... to loue of
heau'n' (1869-70); the angelic visitor brings a moment of calm to the
stage, and a touch of harmony to the dialogue as he moves into verse to
tell Justina,

> And thou Iustina happie Christian maide,
> Bee not hereafter of this man affrayde.
> his hart is changed now, thy company
>   shall strengthen him in Christianitie.
>   (ll. 1871-4)

He then prophesies that the pair will return to Antioch: 'There shall you
both (ere long) in Martyrdome / Mayntayne your faith, and meet the ioys

---

[20] For the iconography of the recorder see also Austern, Lyons, above.

to come'. Visual and acoustic technologies combine with the performances of the actors to create an overwhelmingly emotional aesthetic experience.

The dramaturgy of this sequence strongly recalls that of other saints' plays performed at the Red Bull in the early 1620s, such as *A Shoemaker a Gentleman, The Martyred Soldier* and *The Virgin Martyr* – in which music is repeatedly used to reinforce the appearance of angels on stage – while its roaring devils also rework the techniques of *Doctor Faustus*, an outdoor playhouse classic that was itself current onstage around 1620.[21] To some extent, *The Two Noble Ladies* also counters the association of music with Prospero's magic in *The Tempest*: Cyprian's magic is usually accompanied by thunder, and his only use of music comes when he attempts to seduce Justina. The sequence is capped, however, with another allusion to *The Tempest*, one that capitalises on Shakespeare's play rather than critiquing it. Concluding his affirmation of his new faith, Cyprian declares,

> And now in token of my loue to heau'n,
> This Arte wch heretofore I so esteem'd
> Thus I abandon,
>   *Throws his charmed rod, and his books [under]*[22] *the stage. a flame riseth.*[23]
> and these curious bookes thus sacrifice.
> This sacred trueth alone –   *The Angells booke.*
> shall be my studdy, and my ill spent yeares
> I expiate with pænitentiall teares.   (ll. 1897–1904)

As Elizabeth Williams notes, *The Two Noble Ladies* at this moment recalls both Marlowe and Shakespeare: 'Rather than being dragged under the stage by devils as Faustus is, [Cyprian] throws his necromantic books down after them in a gesture reminiscent of Prospero's promise to drown his entire library'.[24] Furthermore, the stage effect used to signal the devils' return to hell earlier in the scene here becomes a cleansing fire that destroys Cyprian's suspect magical tools.

As these scenes suggest, *The Two Noble Ladies* uses *The Tempest* as a means of negotiating a theatrical environment in which the soundscapes previously associated with indoor and outdoor playhouses were becoming

---

[21] On *The Two Noble Ladies* and the Red Bull plays, see J.H. Degenhardt, *Islamic Conversion and Christian Resistance on the Early Modern Stage* (Edinburgh University Press, 2010), 73–120.

[22] The words 'into a' have been erased and the word 'vnder' interlined here.

[23] In the manuscript and Rhoads's edition, this direction appears in the margins of ll. 1899–1901.

[24] E. Williams, *The Materiality of Religion in Early Modern English Drama* (Farnham: Ashgate, 2013), 152.

fused. Its soft recorders invoke heavenly power and influence, while its military soundscapes, roaring devils and thunder create the wordly and infernal contexts against which they are opposed. *The Two Noble Ladies* is a smart piece of popular theatre, attuned to the ways in which aural and visual stimuli might be combined. It points to the fact that the outdoor playhouse was a site of renewed experimentation in the early 1620s, a period during which indoor practices of act breaks and 'soft' music had consolidated their position within outdoor practice, and at which a 'Blackfriars' play like *The Tempest* might have a broader theatrical resonance.

***

Plays such as *The Two Noble Ladies* demonstrate the ways in which the musical practices of the indoor playhouses had begun to inform those of the outdoor playhouses by the 1620s. A form of reverse traffic can be seen in plays performed at the indoor Blackfriars, Cockpit and Salisbury Court playhouses in the 1630s and early 1640s, which return to instrumentation and musical strategies earlier associated with the outdoor playhouses. This process is especially clear in Caroline re-workings of genres such as the history play, a mode strongly associated with the Elizabethan and early Jacobean outdoor playhouses, which created works such as Ford's *Perkin Warbeck*, printed in 1634 with the title-page claim 'Acted (some-times) by the Queenes *Maiesties* Servants at the *Phoenix* in *Drurie* lane', and Davenport's *King John and Matilda*, performed by the same company in 1634 and published in 1655 'As it was Acted with great Applause by her *Majesties* Servants at the Cock-pit in *Drury-Lane*'.[25] Although Caroline history plays are often perceived as anomalies, they appear to have been in dialogue with revivals of Shakespeare's histories. The Duke of Buckingham attended a performance of *Henry VIII* at the Globe in early August 1628; *Richard II* was performed at the Globe on 12 June 1631, when Herbert took his share of the second day's profits; and *Richard III* was performed by the King's Men at court on 17 November 1633.[26] Plays referred to as 'Oldcastle' (the original name apparently given to Falstaff) were performed by the King's Men at court on 6 January 1631 and 29 May 1638,

---

[25] On the dates of these plays see Bentley, *Jacobean and Caroline Stage*, 2: 679–80, 3: 455–6; P. Ure, 'A Pointer to the Date of Ford's *Perkin Warbeck*', *Notes and Queries*, n.s. 17 (1970), 215–17.

[26] See G. McMullan, ed., *King Henry VIII*, Arden Shakespeare Third Series (London: Thomson Learning, 2000), 16; E.K. Chambers, *William Shakespeare: A Study of Facts and Problems*, 2 vols. (Oxford: Clarendon Press, 1930), 2: 348; Bawcutt, 173, 184.

and John Greene saw 'ffalstaffe' at the Blackfriars on 9 April 1635: these references are probably to the first or second parts of *Henry IV*, although it is possible that the King's Men had somehow acquired the Admiral's Men's *Sir John Oldcastle*, first performed in 1599.[27] In this way, Shakespeare's histories retained a living presence on the stage long after their first performances, and their uses of music continued to resonate, from the ceremonial and military music of *Richard II* to the royal masquers and the '*Sad and solemn music*' (4.2.80 SD) of Queen Katherine's vision in *Henry VIII*.[28]

Plays such as *Perkin Warbeck* and *King John and Matilda* revisit the aural strategies of earlier history plays, featuring extensive use of military and ceremonial music. *King John and Matilda* includes direction for a flourish when John's readmission to the Church is celebrated and, later, the sound of an offstage battle, signalled with the direction '*A Charge afar off*'.[29] In a similar fashion, most of the directions in *Perkin Warbeck* do not call for specific instruments, but in Act 4, Scene 1 Surrey and his forces enter '*with Drummes and Collors*' before a '*Trumpet*' is called for, a sound that Surrey describes as 'a Heralds sound'.[30] Here, the sound of the trumpet seems to be used specifically to invoke the authentic sound of the battlefield. Elsewhere, flourishes are associated with the royal authority of King Henry VII and King James of Scotland, and James self-consciously plays on this association when he calls for music at the point at which he meets Warbeck for the first time: 'sound sprightly Musique, / Whilst Majestie encounters Majestie' (C4v). The word '*Hoboyes*' then appears in the margin, and the music apparently continues throughout the entrance of Warbeck and his ceremonial greeting by the King, the sequence concluding with the direction '*Salutations ended: cease Musique*' (C4v). Music here has a powerful ambivalence, potentially suggesting both the plausibility of Warbeck's imposture and the desire of King James to believe in his cause. Using ceremonial music both to signal and call into question royal status, *Perkin Warbeck* appears to draw on *Richard II*, often regarded as one of Ford's main sources for his play.[31] In *Richard II*, as David Lindley

[27] See Bentley, *Jacobean and Caroline Stage*, 1: 28; Chambers, *William Shakespeare*, 2: 353; J. R. Elliott, Jr., 'Four Caroline Playgoers', *Medieval and Renaissance Drama in England* 6 [1993], 179–93 (192).

[28] For accounts of music in *Richard II* and *Henry VIII* see Lindley, *Shakespeare and Music*, 115–16, 122–4, and McMullan, ed., Henry VIII, 458–61.

[29] *King John and Matilda, A Tragedy* (London, 1655), D3v, E4r.

[30] *The Chronicle Historie of Perkin Warbeck. A Strange Truth* (London, 1634), G2r-v.

[31] See, for example, D.K. Anderson, Jr., '*Richard II* and *Perkin Warbeck*', *Shakespeare Quarterly* 13 (1962), 260–3; A. Leggatt, 'A Double Reign: *Richard II* and *Perkin Warbeck*', in *Shakespeare and his*

notes, a flourish signalling the king's appearance '*on the Walls*' (3.3.61SD)
is 'given a bitter irony as Richard appears on the walls clutching to
himself the empty signifiers of his kingship'.[32] His entrance temporarily
has an overwhelming impact: Bullingbrook compares him with 'the
blushing discontented sun [. . .] When he perceives the envious clouds
are bent / To dim his glory' (3.3.63, 65–6), and York cries 'Behold,
his eye, / As bright as is the eagle's, lightens forth / Controlling majesty'
(68–70). But neither his appearance nor the sound of the flourish can
maintain Richard's royal status: like Warbeck, he is better at playing the
role of king than embodying it fully.

Both *Perkin Warbeck* and *King John and Matilda* also include
representations of festivities in the royal household, in which music
accompanies a masque and dance. Music thus has the potential to create
or help to create two different expressions of royal authority: the ceremonial music of the medieval and early modern periods and the masque
entertainments of the Tudor and Stuart courts. However, the use of the
masque in both plays is complex. In *Perkin Warbeck*, the masque of '*Scotch
Antickes*' and '*wilde Irish*' (F2v) is performed for the marriage of Warbeck
and Katherine, in a sequence preceded by a long conversation between
Huntley and Daliell in which they lament that the pair have married and
look forward to civil strife instead of the harmony often projected by the
Stuart masque. In *King John and Matilda*, masquers appear at the house of
Matilda's father, Fitzwater, their arrival announced by Richmond:

> A Barge with divers youthfull Citizens,
> Apparell'd rich like Masquers, is now land'd
> Upon the Stairs, hearing the Queen was here,
> Withall this meeting of their noble friends,
> Proffer their loves and duties to conclude
>   And grace the evening with their Revels.
>
> (F2 v-F3 r)

Davenport appears here to recall the scene in *Henry VIII* in which King
Henry arrives in disguise at Wolsey's banquet with a group of masquers
'*habited like shepherds*' (1.4.63SD) and first meets Anne Bullen. However,
King John does not appear as one of the richly dressed masquers, and he
does not approach Matilda openly; instead he is disguised as a torch-bearer
and abruptly '*takes*' Matilda, forcing his intentions on her and eventually

---

Contemporaries: Essays in Comparison, ed. E.A.J. Honigmann (Manchester University Press, 1986),
    129–39.
[32] *Shakespeare and Music*, 116.

having her abducted from her father's house. The misuse of the masque is made explicit by Fitzwater:

> *John, John,* now I speak out;
> You made your Masque for this, a Masque indeed,
> And wel-aday! that it should prove a Cover
> For such a night of Tempests, such wilde affections,
> Such an ill-favour'd night.   (F4 r)

Like Henry, John uses the masque as an opportunity to commit adultery; unlike Henry, he does not even put a courtly veneer on his abuse of royal power. It is thus appropriate that he should appear in the liminal figure of the torch-bearer rather than being a performer himself.

The most elaborate use of music in either play occurs in *King John and Matilda*, in the display of Matilda's corpse in the final scene:

> Hoboyes sound, whilst the *Barrons* descend, each on his knee kissing the Kings hand, both Parties joyfully embrace; suddenly the Hoboyes cease: and a sad Musick of Flutes heard. Enter to the *King* and *Lords*, the Lady *Abbess*, Ushering *Matilda's* Herse, born by Virgins, this Motto fastned unto it—*To Piety and Chastity.* The Body of *Matilda* lying on the Herse, and attended by the *Queene*, bearing in her hand a Garland, compos'd of Roses and Lillies; after her, young *Bruce, Hubert, Chester*, and other Gentlemen, all in mourning habites.

> ### The Song in parts.
> 1. *Looke* what Death hath done! here laid
>   (In one) a Martyr, and a Maid.
>
> 2. Angels Crown Those with just applause.
>   Dye in defence of Vertues Lawes.
>
> Chorus *Such was her cause! Death! boast not of thy hands*
> *Cruelty, since the uanquish'd victor stands.*
>
> 2. Her Chastity, to Time shall last
>   Like Laurel, which no lightning can blast.
>
> 1. Sweet Maids, with Roses deck her Herse,
>   Whose Vertue stands above the reach of Verse.
>
> Chorus *Heaven hath her pure part, whil'st on Earth, her Name*
> *Moves in the Spheare of a refulgent Fame.*   (I3 v-I4 r)

The sequence is structured around changes in its aural texture. First, the ceremonial hoboys are replaced by mournful flutes, and finally the voices are introduced, in a song that probably featured a chorus following alternating voices.[33] We might compare the direction for a song 'in parts' with a similar moment in Nathanael Richards's contemporaneous *Messallina*, performed at Salisbury Court around the same time as *King John and Matilda* was performed at the Cockpit. A stage direction requires that '*Two Spirits dreadfully enter and (to the Treble Violin and Lute) sing a song of despaire, during which Lepida sits weeping*', but Richards comments, in a direction immediately after the song, that it '*was left out of the Play in regard there was none could sing in Parts*'.[34] The provision of elaborate songs in parts may have been newly fashionable in plays in the mid-1630s, and some playing companies found it difficult to keep up. Where the sequence in *King John and Matilda* differs from that in *Messallina*, however, is in its combination of aural and visual effects, a technique to which Davenport deliberately draws his spectators' attention. When the song is complete, John says '*Hubert* interpret this Apparition', and Hubert concludes his account with the words 'Look here King *John*, and with a trembling eye, / Read your sad act, *Matilda's* Tragedy' (I4 r). The impact of Matilda's death depends upon the ability of the audience – on-stage and off-stage – to 'read' spectacle, in a technique often employed by Caroline dramatists such as Ford and Richard Brome.

Instead of an epilogue, the play concludes with another song, again sung in parts with a chorus:

> 1. *Matilda! Now goe take thy Bed,*
> *In the darke dwellings of the dead.*
>
> 2. *And rise in the great Waking-day,*
> *Sweet as Incense, fresh as May.*
>
> 1. *Rest thou chaste soule, (fixt in thy proper spheare,)*
> *Amongst heauens faire Ones; All are fair ones there.*
>
> Cho. *Rest there chaste soul, whilst we (here troubl'd) say,*
> *Time gives us Griefs, Death takes our joyes away.*

King John and Matilda thus departs far more than *Perkin Warbeck* from the pattern of the uses of sound in Elizabethan history plays. Davenport's play features greater use of song and is far more emblematic in its treatment of

---

[33] See Wood, 'Music in Caroline Plays', 75.
[34] *The Tragedy of Messallina the Roman Emperesse* (London, 1640), F6r-v.

stage spectacle; song helps to bridge the distance between past and present, as up-to-date song structures and settings help to make Matilda's death an overcharged emotional experience for spectators. The use of music to focus attention on Matilda also signals the ways in which Davenport re-orientates the history play so that it pays far greater attention to female subjectivity and experience, a characteristic that scholars such as Sophie Tomlinson have noted in Caroline theatre more broadly.[35] In these ways, Ford and Davenport adopt the techniques that reanimated historical narratives for Elizabethan and early-Jacobean audiences in the outdoor playhouses, fusing them with conventions of instrumentation and song that had previously been more strongly associated with the indoor playhouses. The Caroline history play emerges as a dramaturgical and aural hybrid, drawing its strength from different theatrical traditions.

***

In the early 1620s, *The Tempest* provided a useful model for playwrights attempting to reconceive outdoor playhouse dramaturgy. Its soft music and crashing thunder suggested ways in which practices that had pre-viously been associated with disparate traditions might be reconciled. In the 1630s, in contrast, plays such as *Richard II* and *Henry VIII* offered techniques that Ford and Davenport could adapt for the indoor play-houses, and ways of redeploying history play conventions for their own uses. If Bart Van Es is right to argue that Shakespeare had 'a protracted and changing relationship with the Blackfriars, stretching from early hostility, through accommodation, to absorption',[36] the musical afterlives of Shakespeare's plays suggest that they swung through new cycles of chan-ging relationships with both Blackfriars and Globe, indoor and outdoor playhouses.

---

[35] S. Tomlinson, *Women on Stage in Stuart Drama* (Cambridge University Press, 2005).

[36] B. van Es, 'Reviving the Legacy of Indoor Performance', in *Moving Shakespeare Indoors: Performance and Repertoire in the Jacobean Playhouse*, ed. Andrew Gurr and Farah Karim-Cooper (Cambridge University Press, 2014), 237–51 (251).

CHAPTER 8

In Practice II
Adapting a Restoration Adaptation – The Tempest, *or* the Enchanted Island
Elizabeth Kenny

Restoration adaptations of Shakespeare were famously uninhibited: plot and characters were changed, machines, scenery, court-influenced music and singing actresses were added in order to captivate audiences with recent developments in spectacle and variety. Derided by nineteenth-century scholars, in recent years Restoration Shakespeare has been rehabilitated as a viable performance and audience experience rather than as Shakespeare lost in translation. Music historians have also revised their thinking on the 'semi-operatic' production style, a tradition rooted in the Caroline masque and revived in the Restoration, no longer treating it as an evolutionary step on the way to through-composed opera but as a genre in itself. It is almost exclusively associated now with Henry Purcell, whose music can be presented successfully in concerts and occasionally in staged productions (such as the 2009 Glyndebourne production of *The Fairy Queen*, based on *A Midsummer Night's Dream*). Lesser-known figures such as the team of leading composers of the pre-Purcell era who worked on *The Tempest* – Matthew Locke, John Banister, Pelham Humfrey and Pietro Reggio – are more difficult to 'place' in current performance contexts. This chapter will discuss the 1674 production of *The Tempest, or the Enchanted Island* and the process of adapting it for semi-staged performance in the Sam Wanamaker Playhouse in 2015.

Sir William Davenant introduced the idea of spoken drama 'operatized' during the 1650s as a creative solution to the Commonwealth restrictions on 'straight' theatre. He was much influenced by court masque practice, and his own experience as masque scriptwriter to Charles I. Keeping the novel formula when the theatres re-opened after the Restoration in 1660, Davenant passed it on to his creative successor Thomas Betterton for further development in the 1670s, 80s and 90s. Betterton visited Paris to watch French *comédies-ballets;* back home he followed their success in his specially equipped London theatre, producing a series of French-inspired 'semi-operas' for which English playwrights supplied words and London-based composers supplied music. Our Betterton tribute was part of the Wanamaker's Candlelit Concert series with musicians and singers from the Orchestra of the Age of Enlightenment, and script, direction and actors from the Globe. Conventional concert hall norms were easy to suspend thanks to the Wanamaker space. On entering, audiences discover that they are nose to nose with musicians and actors, not separated from them by distance and staging; this was crucial in opening up a context for a convincing representation of a relatively little-known work from which familiar Shakespearean dialogue and music by Henry Purcell were largely absent. The title of this essay reflects the contingent circumstances in which *The Enchanted Island* was hastily produced in 1674. It also points towards one of the most interesting trains of thought pursued by the current generation of the historical performance practice community: that 'authentic' musical experiences, using historical instruments and sources, derive partly from imaginative reconstruction of carefully-examined evidence and partly from the sense – demanding equal imagination – that modern audiences encounter these works in a modern context and listen to them in a modern way. Both text and music speak in a number of different voices, none of them 'authentically' Shakespearean but all working together under the Brand of the Bard.

It's worth noting some of the major changes to which Shakespeare's play was subject.[1] It endured two rounds of revision, the first in 1667, preparing it for production in Davenant's original Lincoln's Inn Fields theatre, the second in 1674, adding more music and spectacle to take full advantage of facilities available in the company's new Dorset Garden theatre, which had opened in 1671. Davenant himself died in 1668, and Betterton had taken over as company manager.

With John Dryden assisting, Davenant modernised the language of Shakespeare's *Tempest* line by line, stripping out poetic magic – or padding, depending on your point of view – in favour of clarity of expression and coherence of motive. Extra characters were added, reflecting an Augustan desire for symmetry. Miranda, the woman who has never seen a man, was provided both with a sister-confidante (Belinda to her Dido) named Dorinda, and a male counterpart, a man who has never seen

---

[1] These changes are analysed in detail in M. Raddadi, *Davenant's Adaptations of Shakespeare* (Stockholm: Almqvist & Wiksell, 1979).

a woman, Hippolito. This foursome expanded the original Ferdinand-Miranda love story into a double plot à la *Midsummer Night's Dream*. Caliban acquired a twin sister, Sycorax (confusingly named the same as their mother); Ariel also had a partner, Milcha, whose main function was to sing a song. The parts of Trinculo (spelled Trincalo in the 1670 published text) and Stephano were enlarged as they fight – and fail – to set up a plausible Republic with new comic characters Mustacho and Ventoso. Davenant the former Navy man expanded the depiction and importance to the plot of the storm itself. As well as new characters being added, existing characters changed somewhat: Miranda became a more ordinary girl, Prospero less of a magical artist-sage and more of a vexed father, and a responder to rather than omnipotent controller of events. Two masques were added at strategic moments. The 'Masque of Devils' in Act II underlines the importance of retribution for the disloyalty and ambition of Alonzo and Antonio. The grand concluding masque in Act V ties up the action with the subduing of the wind and the waves by Neptune and Amphitrite, rather than by Prospero abjuring his magic arts. This last was added in 1674, together with a new song slightly extending the 'Masque of Devils': Thomas Shadwell supplied words for both. In our adaptation Milcha and Sycorax were excised to fit a concert-length evening, but we resisted the urge to use cuts to 'normalise' the adaptation, retaining as many as possible of the changes to which lovers of the original might reasonably object.

There are in fact two violently opposed reception histories of Restoration Shakespeare. *The Tempest* joins many other plays that were altered and augmented to enhance their immediate audience appeal. Until well into the nineteenth-century adaptations like *The Enchanted Island* continued to be revived (further adapted) as practicable stage vehicles. On the other hand, increasingly learned multi-volume Shakespeare editions catered separately for scholarly consumers. The critical assault on Shakespeare-as-currently-staged was a later nineteenth-century phenomenon, ushering in a new era of experimentation with Globe replicas, Elizabethan costume, 'early music' (for which the Dolmetsch family did much of the work in those pioneering days), and aggressive fidelity to 'authentic', i.e. unaltered texts. Conceiving a Restoration Shakespeare performance today involves encountering, and then strategically ignoring, both these approaches, in search of a *raison d'être* for attempting to give a twenty-first century audience a meaningful theatrical experience. As a starting point, the recognition that, for the London audience post-1660 a theatrical experience was also a musical one, helps in negotiating the modern performance spectrum from play to concert. When the plays are largely seen as literature, the loss of the poetical depths of Shakespearean language is indeed catastrophic. But Restoration theatre-goers were interested in events and experiences rather than psychological complexity. *The Tempest, or The Enchanted Island* delivered handsomely: it was entertaining, frequently very funny, full of music and spectacle and engaged with the politics of its own era, confronting the very 'live' issues of regicide and usurpation. I shall return to the politics later.

Modern scholars prefer Dryden's coinage 'dramatic opera' to its implicitly apologetic alternative 'semi-opera' – the former suggesting improvement over insufficiently dramatic 'pure' (all-sung?) opera while the latter hints at a compromise or watering down.[2] Semi-opera scores by Henry Purcell are now often performed in concert halls around the world. Familiarity with Purcell's plots – now much better known than they used to be – helps negotiate the emotional journey of the music. Full stagings tend to happen in opera houses rather than concert halls: Purcell can then be positioned as John the Baptist to Benjamin Britten, the true Messiah of opera in English, and a three-hour evening, normal in opera but longer than most concerts, can accommodate both play and music.[3] Despite early eighteenth-century commentator Roger North's caveat that 'Some come for the play and hate the musick, others come onely for the musick, and the drama is penance to them',[4] semi-opera productions can be satisfying events for performers and for audiences thanks to the strength of the music and – unexpectedly – the plays, and thanks also to the sense of occasion sparked by their comparative rarity.

But when it is Shakespeare, rather than the less-revered Sir Robert Howard (*The Indian Queen*) or even Dryden (*The Indian Queen, King Arthur*), who is implicated as posthumous author of a semi-opera text, and the site chosen for experiment is the hallowed space of Shakespeare's Globe, audience familiarity is a double-edged sword. The shadow of Shakespearean loss can hang over the enterprise. The 2009 Glyndebourne production of *The Fairy Queen* confronted this head on, opening with the whole first scene of the original *A Midsummer Night's Dream* – material deliberately, perhaps brutally, excised when *The Fairy Queen* was created in 1692 in order to pass quickly on to the main business of the Restoration show,

---

[2] 'Semi-opera' was first coined by Roger North in his *Essay of Musicall Ayre* (British Library Add. MS 32,536, ff. 1–90).
[3] As a continuo player I have been involved in a number of these stagings, including the landmark Purcell anniversary *King Arthur* at Royal Opera in 1995, and Glyndebourne's *The Fairy Queen*, 2009.
[4] J. Wilson ed., *Roger North on Music* (London: Novello and Company, 1959), 307.

music and knock-about comedy. Director Jonathan Kent was addressing a modern problem: our preference for 'proper' Shakespeare and reluctance to depart from an academically approved, learned-at-school Shakespeare text. The problem worsens when 'proper' Shakespeare is exchanged for music by lesser-known and lesser-loved composers, as with *The Tempest, or the Enchanted Island*. Understanding the priorities and decisions taken by Davenant and Dryden was, for us, less an exercise in historical accuracy and more an urgent means of renegotiating the gains and losses *vis à vis* Shakespeare and music, in order to present an evening memorable for positive reasons.

Sir William Davenant had succeeded Ben Jonson as Charles I's poet laureate, in that capacity collaborating with Inigo Jones on the last of the great Caroline masques. During the unpromising climate of the 1650s, Davenant put on masque-like entertainments at his London home, Rutland House, evading the ban on public play performances and setting a precedent of performance-adapted-to-context.[5] The first version of Davenant's *The Siege of Rhodes*, 1656, counts as the earliest all-sung English opera (its music is no longer extant); but when theatres reopened soon after the Restoration in 1660, Davenant restaged it purely as a play (lines sung in recitative in 1656 were spoken instead) adding extra scenes to pad it out to full-play length. Significantly, although music skills were at a low ebb thanks to the cessation of professional opportunities during the Civil War and its aftermath, the team of composers and performers who worked on *The Siege of Rhodes* in 1656 provided an element of continuity with the next generation. In the scramble for monopoly privilege that accompanied the relicensing of the London theatres Davenant did not come out as well as he might have hoped. His Duke's Company was allowed to trade but had to surrender much of the best pre-war play repertory to the King's Company run by Thomas Killigrew. Davenant retained the rights to plays that he himself had written and acquired adaptation rights to nine named Shakespeare plays. It is worth remembering the legal constraints under which Davenant had to operate: he had to rewrite his own, as well as Shakespeare's plays, to be within the legal terms of his patent.[6]

---

[5] The literature on the masque is too large for a full bibliography here, but of especial value in reflecting on the relationship between text and music, and containing extensive bibliographical material is P. Walls, *Music in the English Courtly Masque 1604–1640* (Oxford: Clarendon Press, 1996).

[6] *The Siege of Rhodes* and the theatre culture of the 1650s–90s are discussed by Andrew Pinnock in R. Herrissone, ed., *The Ashgate Research Companion to Henry Purcell* (Farnham: Ashgate Publishing, 2012), 175–80.

While some of the changes were the result of legal issues, others were to do with aesthetics and catered to the taste of audiences intrigued by the new possibility of female performers. Actresses played female roles and one of the new male ones in *The Enchanted Island*, a titillating feature to which Dryden referred in his 1667 prologue:

> [We] . . . by our dearth of youths are forc'd t'employ
> One of our Women to present a Boy . . .
> What e're she was before the Play began,
> All you shall see of her is perfect Man.
> Or if your fancy will be farther led
> To find her Woman, it must be abed.[7]

These lines fell embarrassingly flat when tried out in rehearsal in the Wanamaker and so we cut them, but kept a female actor to play Hippolito.[8] Mary Davies played Ariel in the 1667 *Tempest:* she had caught Charles II's eye on stage and soon afterwards embarked on a career as both a royal mistress and a royally-sponsored opera singer, appearing in the 1675 court masque *Calisto* and as Venus in John Blow's 1683 court opera *Venus and Adonis* (her daughter by Charles II, Lady Mary Tudor, sang Cupid). The role of Dido in Purcell's *Dido and Aeneas* may well have been created with Davies in mind.[9]

Davies's performance in the 1667 *Tempest* underpinned the success of the whole enterprise. She was, as her later achievements attest, a compelling and remarkably versatile artist. When she retired from the commercial stage in 1668 and Winifred Gosnell replaced her as Ariel, Samuel Pepys noticed the difference: Gosnell was not as good. Pepys went to see the 1667 *Tempest* again and again. His diary mentions the 'old play' only glancingly; he preferred to focus on new costumes, new songs and their more or less charismatic singers.

Because London's theatre audience in the later seventeenth century was by modern standards very small, even the most popular productions ran for only a short time continuously – occasional one-off revivals satisfied residual demand from then on. After Davenant's death in 1668, interest in his *Tempest* died down. The Duke's Company – taken over by

---

[7] This and all subsequent references to the 1674 play-text are taken from the facsimile edition of *The Tempest, or The Enchanted Island* published by the Cornmarket Press (London, 1969).

[8] Molly Logan, in our version, partnering Dickon Tyrell.

[9] See A. Pinnock, 'Deus ex machina: a royal witness to the court origin of Purcell's *Dido and Aeneas*' and 'Which Genial Day? more on the court origin of Purcell's *Dido and Aeneas*, with a shortlist of dates for its possible performance before King Charles II', *Early Music*, 40/2 (2012), 265–78 and *Early Music*, 43/2 (2015), 199–212.

Davenant's widow and managed on her behalf by Betterton and Henry Harris (Betterton clearly the ideas man) – pressed ahead with Davenant's development plans and in 1671 opened a new, purpose-built theatre in Dorset Garden. To show it off to best advantage Betterton commissioned a sumptuous English-language version of the Lully-Molière *comedie-ballet, Psyché,* the Paris opera hit of 1671. London's*Psyche* was a monumental undertaking subject to delay after delay, opening eventually in 1675. To satisfy his increasingly impatient audience Betterton threw together a stop-gap the year before, in 1674 – a hurriedly-conceived restaging of the 1667 Davenant-Dryden *Tempest* – to which all the composers working (slowly) on *Psyche* contributed fresh material. Matthew Locke wrote the overtures and act tunes; John Battista Draghi wrote the dance tunes (now lost); John Banister's 1667 'Ariel's Songs' were recycled; 1667 music for the Act II 'Masque of Devils' was very probably recycled, with the addition of an extra devil's song for Shadwell's words and Pietro Reggio's music. The Chapel Royal singer James Hart supplied another new song, 'Adieu to the pleasures and follies of love'. Shadwell's text for a brand-new Masque of Neptune and Amphitrite, the 1674 *Tempest*'s grand finale, was set to music by Pelham Humfrey. The whole was a loosely co-ordinated committee effort but, against the odds, a runaway hit. It was revived repeatedly over the next 150 years, subject to occasional musical re-fits and further textual modernisation.[10] As the Duke's company prompter, John Downes, ruefully remarked in his memoirs, 'not any succeeding opera got more money' – certainly not *Psyche*, not even the Purcell operas which Betterton went on to produce in the early 1690s. *The Tempest* was a one-off: an accidental triumph to which audiences responded far more favourably than they did to 'higher' forms of operatic art. Charles II's interest in the project got it off to a good start: for the first performances in 1674 he released the entire Chapel Royal choir and his 24-piece string orchestra to appear in Dorset Garden. The choir filled the music room above the proscenium arch and the orchestra was crammed in front of the stage. Later performances would have been more modest, but the magic hung around.

Dryden wrote in his preface to *The Tempest, or the Enchanted Island* (1670; reprinted practically verbatim in 1674) that there were three essential ingredients to Shakespeare's original design, treating it – as we did – as a resource to be mined rather than a complete work to be revived: the

---

[10] An early eighteenth-century setting formerly attributed to Henry Purcell is now thought to be the work of John Weldon. See John Cunningham's essay for the music of Thomas Arne.

storm, the desert island, and the love story of the woman (Miranda) who has never seen a man (Ferdinand). I will treat each of these in turn, showing how music helps to define the changes made by Davenant and Dryden.

The Storm

The storm had topical relevance in 1667 with the successful revival of John Fletcher's *Sea Voyage* and news of the loss at sea of the governor-in-chief of the English Colonies in the Caribbean, Captain Willoughby; his ship was destroyed by a hurricane off Barbados.[11] Davenant added suitably technical and zesty terminology from his early experiences in the navy. We used his scripted interjections to intensify Locke's musical depiction of the storm:

TRINCALO. Is the Anchor a Peek?
STEPHANO. Is a weigh! Is a weigh!
TRINC. Up aloft, my Lads, upon the Fore-Castle! Cut the Anchor, cut him . . . [etc.]

These words are not Shakespeare's but they do convey a sense of drive and urgency that perfectly complements the music.

The stage direction for the sinking of the ship is deservedly well known both for its advertising of the Stuarts and for its close descriptive correspondence with Matthew Locke's musical programme. It also introduces the monsters and devils who are already plaguing the corrupt sailors and who will return in the 'Masque of Devils' in Act II.

> *The Front of the Stage is open'd, and the Band of 24 Violins, with the Harpsichals and Theorbo's which accompany the Voices, are plac'd between the Pit and the Stage. While the Overture is playing, the Curtain rises and discovers a new Frontispiece, joyn'd to the great Pylasters, on each side of the Stage ... A little further on the same Cornice, on each side of a Compass-pediment, lie a Lion and a Unicorn, the Supporters of the Royal Arms of England. In the middle of the Arch are several Angles, holding the Kings Arms, as if they were placing them in the midst of that Compass-pediment. Behind this is the Scene, which represents a thick Cloudy Sky, a very Rocky Coast, and a Tempestuous Sea in perpetual Agitation. This Tempest (suppos'd to be rais'd by Magick) has many dreadful Objects in it, as several Spirits, in horrid shapes flying down amongst the Sailers, then rising in the Air. And when the Ship is sinking, the whole House is darken'd, and a shower of Fire falls upon 'em. This is accompanied with Lightning, and several Claps of Thunder, to the end of the Storm.*

---

[11] See A.M. Taylor, 'Dryden's "Enchanted Isle" and Shadwell's "Dominion"', *Studies in Philology*, Extra Series, 4 (1967), 39–53.

While a 'real' (i.e. staged) shipwreck can happen only once, Locke's extraordinary 'Curtain Tune' bears its notated repeat. We played it twice, the first time purely as music, the second time with the added shouting, noise and confusion of the text signalling the start of the action. Musical wind-and-wave imagery in the 'Curtain Tune' anticipates the non-Shakespearean appearance of 'subterranean winds' in Act II and in the final masque of Neptune and Amphitrite. Locke's opening music allows both characters and audience to experience a foretaste of the calming of the wind and waves that concludes the play. The choice of Pelham Humfrey to compose the music to the final Masque of Neptune and Amphitrite was strategic: he, like many musicians with court ambitions, had been to France for training, coming back, according to Pepys an 'absolute monsieur'. Neptune and Amphitrite are not especially engaging characters, nor are they meant to be: their vocal display is what conjures their power as forces of nature. This use of pure vocal sound to create mood effects had been an essential ingredient of the *comédie-ballet* since its inception: Balthazar de Beaujoyeulx' *Le Balet Comique de la Royne* of 1581 contains a showcase dialogue between Tethys, goddess of the sea and wife-sister to Oceanus, and Glaucus the fisherman who is transformed into a merman. This was written as a vehicle for the vocal talents of the leading singer-couple at court, Genoese soprano Violante Doria and her husband Girard de Beaulieu.[12]

The concluding masques of Purcell-Betterton's *The Fairy Queen* and Purcell-Betterton's *Dioclesian* have the same effect: the task is to lead the audience from a forward-moving plot to a more static concert-feel. Stylised choreography and spectacular scenic effects signalled this change of gear in Dorset Gardens. We used an improvising bass violin and a large dose of Reggio-style ornamentation on top of Humfrey's French style *agréments* to translate the gear-change into musical terms. The music as written is rather plain, the expectation being that the performers would customise it to showcase their skill in ornamentation in order to encourage the audience to respond to them as performers as well as characters.

There is a tension between this sort of vocal artifice and the highly individual manner of Locke's instrumental pieces that simultaneously pull towards and away from the drama. Locke's 'Conclusion' is a grave canon which does exemplify coming back to where we started, but there is also

---

[12] An extract of the music along with biographies of its original performers can be found in J. Brooks, *Courtly Song in Late Sixteenth-Century France* (London: University of Chicago Press, 2000), pp. 200–1 and 245.

a sense that writing to serve the drama was not necessarily Locke's priority here: the movement is stark, beautiful yet mathematically sombre – a 'Canon 4 in 2'. It functions as an alternative ending to Humfrey's evocation of the triumph of natural order, evoking dark thoughts that have been banished from the text. Caroline Williams' staging emphasised this by gradually extinguishing the Wanamaker Playhouse candles until the musicians were illuminated only by the small distant light of Ariel, finally set free.

The Desert Island and the Rebellion Sub-Plot

The comedy of the sailors and their efforts to set up a republic were added by Davenant and Dryden, expanding the Caliban-Stephano-Trinculo plot in Shakespeare's play. This and the third element, the love story, brought us up against the Restoration habit of converting Shakespearean drama to tragi-comedy.[13]

Robert Appelbaum has convincingly argued that the execution of Charles I in 1649, and restoration of Charles II in 1660, were recent enough for plays like *The Tempest* to evoke trauma in a deeply unsettling way. Onstage representations of sedition and usurping rulers without their humiliation and reformation were impossible.[14] While Prospero decreases in complexity to become a character preoccupied with revenge and with control – a diminution compared to his Shakespearean predecessor – the minor characters increase in importance. This can be seen as a gain when linked with music. The extended scenes where Stephano, Trinculo, Mustacho and Ventoso compete for leadership of their government, based around access to 'Peace, and the Butt [barrel of wine]' were an opportunity to harness the talents of Edward Angel and Cave Underhill, the Duke's Company's specialist comic actors.[15] In our version, their quicksilver exchanges and physical comedy were linked with interplay between the musicians and the actors: musicians punctuated their attempts to style themselves rulers of the island with quasi-military fanfares on the hurdy-gurdy, and musicians took charge of the Butt, which passed between

[13] Nahum Tate's *King Lear* with its new happy ending is the most notorious example. Though Tate was the librettist of, on the face of it, the unequivocally tragic *Dido and Aeneas*, performances which recognise *Dido*'s intermittent comic strain as well as sinister aspects of the witches have the capacity to throw an audience into interesting, unexpected and jarring emotions.

[14] See R. Appelbaum, *Literature and Utopian Politics* (Cambridge: Cambridge University Press, 2002), 210–17.

[15] See M. Raddadi, *Davenant's Adaptations*, 41.

them and the actors in their roles of sailors and Caliban. (Musicians as bodies to be addressed were useful too when the number of characters referred to exceeded those actually on stage.) Stephano thinks he has concluded the business, daringly invoking the ghost of the real war behind the words:

STEPHANO. Hold, loving Subjects: we will have no Civil War during our Reign:
 I do hereby appoint you both to be my ViceRoys over the whole Island.

But Trincalo appears, having escaped the flood on a 'Butt of Sack', sings his 'Sailor's Song' and disputes their claims, then meets Caliban and decides to marry Caliban's twin sister Sycorax. By Act 2 Scene 3 the rest of the sailors are hungry and thirsty enough to agree to call him the Duke. Music and dance cement the alliance but Mustacho tries to get Sycorax on his side, something which Trincalo interprets as treason, and their subsequent fight interrupts the fragile harmony.

VENTOSO. Who took up arms first, the Prince or the People? . . .
MUSTACHO. I'm against Rebels! *Ventoso*, obey your ViceRoy!

That being rather close to the bone, the scene returns to the less controversial theme of gender-related cynicism with Trincalo deciding to 'be rid of my Lady Trincalo, she will be in the fashion else; first, Cuckold her husband, and then sue for a separation, to get alimony'.

The parallel story of aristocratic usurpers Antonio and Alonzo, their repentance and punishment, was played out on the opening night in 1674 in front of Charles II: crown-sponsored revenge for the events of 1649.[16] The Act 2 'Masque of Devils' is an extended reflection on the dangers of ambition. There is a tendency towards abstraction in the nature of masque texts which has been addressed by literary historians in a largely successful effort to exonerate them from the charge of being poor drama – i.e. non-urgent, non-forward-moving and plot-driven. In this case simplifying and dramatising the nature of Ambition, Murder, Rapine and Pride was an urgent topical necessity.

GONZALO. Musick! And in the air! Sure we are Shipwrack'd on the Dominions of
 some merry Devil! . . . What horrid Masque will the dire Fiends present?

Disconcertingly, in 1674 the fearsome Devils were cast as boy trebles: charming, funny, but not remotely terrifying. We used boy trebles too. This tricky combination of humour and moralism was helped by the

---

[16] For more on this see P. Holman, *Four and Twenty Fiddlers: The Violin at the English Court 1540–1690* (Oxford: Clarendon Press, 1993), pp. 251–389.

character of the Sam Wanamaker Playhouse itself, as they emerged through the trapdoor from Hell and hurdy-gurdy improvisations added strangeness to Pelham Humfrey's rather up-beat, dance-like music. Here again the unstable relationship between performer and character needs the responses both of the concert-hall and the stage.[17] It also needs performers – both actors and singers – with large personalities unsuppressed by the disguise of character. In the 'Song of the Fifth Devil', 'Arise ye subterranean winds', the bravura tenor is both Devil and celebrity singer: Pietro Reggio brought Italian flair and charisma to court singing and published the rigorous *The Art of Singing* in 1677. A copy recently came to light which amply confirms his skill in the art of florid song.[18]

The tricky part for the audience is then to switch back to responding to the actors as characters. Making a virtue of economic necessity – our smaller cast associated with an enhanced concert rather than a cut-down play – our actor-performers revealed just a touch of their sense of the absurdity of being terrorised by people half their size, and used physical and verbal agility to evoke scenes of horror and disturbance on a much larger scale. Restoration audiences relished the pleasure of virtuosity revealed – (performance) – as well as concealed (the suspension of disbelief that comes with involvement in the drama). A nice example of how this worked is given by Pepys in his diary: for him Ferdinand's Echo Song with Ariel (Moll Davies) was a particular highlight. He tried to note down the song as he liked it so much, but failed despite repeated visits to the theatre; eventually he collared the Ferdinand-actor Henry Harris at the stage door and asked him to repeat the words slowly so that he could write them down in daylight instead of the half-light of candles. The music he got from John Banister himself.[19]

The other notable scene was the imaginary banquet (2.3) with which Ariel and his sweetheart Milcha torment Alonzo, Antonio and Gonzalo after singing 'Dry those eyes which are o'er flowing'. (The stage direction here reads: 'Dance of fantastick Spirits, after the Dance, a Table furnish'd with Meat and Fruit is brought in'.) Missing from a semi-staged production is of course the magic of large-scale scenic effects such as

---

[17] See Stephen Orgel's comment: 'a masquer's disguise is a representation of the courtier beneath. He retains his personality, and hence his position in the social hierarchy'. *The Jonsonian Masque* (Cambridge, MA: Harvard University Press, 1965), 117.

[18] British Library Music Collections D.621.s. The title is instructive, underlining the need for the performer to add to what they find on the page: *The Art of Singing or, a Treatise, Wherein is Shown How to Sing Well Any Song Whatsoever: and also How to Apply the Best Graces with a Collection of Cadences Plain, and then Graced, for All Lovers of Musick.*

[19] Pepys: Diary entries for 7 November 1667, 7 and 11 May 1668.

these; however, the smaller-scale and the porous nature of the divide between stage and pit in the Playhouse allowed actors to move easily around the audience, offering them the real food – fruit pointedly denied to the shipwrecked sailors while a long violin solo was played. Two layers of reaction were invited: ears relishing the sound and eyes (occasionally even mouths) appreciating simultaneous on- and off-stage action.

The Love Story

Dryden said, in his preface to the play, that although he had written many of the scenes it was Davenant's idea to introduce Hippolito, a man who has never seen a woman, in order to balance the woman who has never seen a man – the Shakespearean Miranda. In a piece of Augustan symmetry Miranda also acquired a sister (Dorinda), who falls in love with Hippolito. Most commentators have sighed despairingly as Shakespeare's symbol of sublime innocence morphs into two fairly air-headed girls, with Prospero as their fussy, overprotective father. While listing what is lost in Restoration Shakespeare is tempting but ultimately self-defeating, justifying the adaptations comparatively by what is gained falls into the same trap. Instead, thinking simply of creating a new show was the attitude we attempted to adopt. The dialogues between two men and two women allow the play to examine the development of 'natural' love from its first indiscriminate polyamorous phase to Ferdinand's 'you are made for one, and one for you' (4.1).

Ferdinand and Hippolito engage in some quasi-primitivistic banter:

HIPPOLITO.   I know I'm made for twenty hundred
                            Women
    (I mean if there so many be I'th world)
    So that if once I see her, I shall love her . . .
FERDINAND.   I find I must not let you see her then.
HIPPOLITO.   How will you hinder me?
FERD.   By force of arms
HIP.   By force of Arms?
    My Arms perhaps may be as strong as yours.
FERD.   He's still so ignorant that I pity him . . .

The language is unadorned and fast-paced. One actor played both parts at breakneck speed, embodying the bizarre speed at which things escalate into a duel during which Ferdinand thinks he has killed Hippolito.

FERDINAND. He's gone! He's gone! O stay, sweet, lovely Youth! Help!
   Help!

Prospero's response is equally extreme, as the murder shows his and Ariel's lack of control over the situation. A Jacobean revenger lurks beneath his scholarly exterior: Prospero sends for Alonzo to witness his son's execution:

PROSPERO. And I, in bitterness have sent for you,
   To have the sudden joy of seeing him alive,
   And then the greater grief to see him die.

Just as we are adapting to this combustible mix of humour and violence, Dorinda stumbles upon Hippolito's body and sings 'Adieu to the pleasures and follies of love'. James Hart – one of the Court singers loaned to Dorset Garden for the opening run of *The Enchanted Island* in 1674 – set it to a beautiful and simple tune, and it is unexpectedly, jarringly real in its heartbreak. As with Locke's music, the song suggests emotional depths which a text-only assessment of the play would miss. The nature of music as emotional reflection is part of Shakespeare's *The Tempest*, but it is there more exclusively associated with the sense of magic about the island – the 'thousand twangling instruments' – and the singing of Ariel. Robert Johnson's Jacobean settings of Ariel's songs were replaced in a more up-to-date style by John Banister. Banister led Charles II's Twenty Four violins for a while, and like Pelham Humfrey had been to France.[20] His Ariel's songs have dance-inspired French rhythmic fluidity – and are graced with French-style ornaments which makes them sound quite different to the bravura virtuosity of Reggio's and the angularity of Locke's contributions.

   In general it is believed that there was little, if any underscoring of the text until the late eighteenth century, but for our purposes, given especially the tendency of the spoken language to dispense with emotional complexity or evocative imagery, underscoring was a useful tool in connecting the text with moments of heightened importance or emotion:

ARIEL. Harsh discord reigns through this fatal Isle,
   At which good Angels mourn, ill spirits smile.

(The underscore was an echo of *Full Fathom Five*):

---

[20] See Holman, *Four and Twenty Fiddlers*, p. 291.

Music Example 1 – 'Full fathom five': the graceful sarabande metre, subtle
chromaticism and dark G minor tonality conjure both consolation and ambiguity
for Ferdinand reflecting on the death of his father.[21]

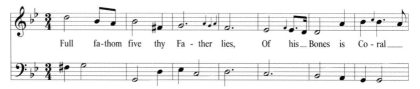

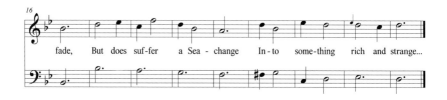

ARIEL. When I was chidden by my mighty Lord for my
    Neglect of young Hippolito, I went to view
    His Body and soon found his Soul was but retir'd,
    Not sallyd out . . .

Here improvised music from a dark to a joyful mode underlined the
change as Ariel applies healing herbs to Hippolito's wounds, signalling
the start of the resolution of the plot which will lead to the final
Masque.

We used an archlute for this: the Playhouse acoustics respond to
quiet sounds, drawing people into closer listening rather than amplify-
ing the volume of the text. Improvised music could either provide
a suggestion of rhythm in counterpoint to that of the text, or be more
ambiguous in order to let the metre of the speech dominate, and

---

[21] The 1674 text has it sung by Milcha but in our abbreviated production this was a complication too
far: we reassigned it to Ariel.

provide a sonic contrast to the more extrovert and dance-inspired music of Matthew Locke.

Restoration theatre companies adapted works to their players, rebalancing singing and acting requirements from production to production. Our Wanamaker version of *The Tempest, or the Enchanted Island* used smaller forces than Dorset Garden had in 1674: two or three actors, string quartet and continuo, with soprano, trebles, tenor and bass singers. But the Wanamaker is a smaller venue. Modern productions tend to enforce a clear divide between singers – especially opera singers – and actors, though there is of course potential for considerable overlap between the two. The negotiation between actor-character and singer-character can be an opportunity for theatrical sleight-of-hand, as when in our production acting Ariel became singing Ariel with the use of some fancy footwork and the cover of candle half-light.

Conclusions

There is merit in recognising and harnessing strong reactions to Restoration Shakespeare. If sub-Shakespearean language distances us from the inner lives of famously complex characters, music filling the emotional gap is even more important: singers and instrumentalists move into the aural spotlight and point to deeper problems and emotions around the edges of the words. The actors also have a different and equally virtuosic task, that of embodying and responding to the dizzying changes of pace allowed by the momentum of the text. Caroline Williams's staging used constant changes of mood and audience perspective, challenging them to respond to performance as well as to plot and character. The added scenes with the sailors and the pairs of 'innocent' lovers made for an evening with many more laughs than one expects from *The Tempest* with its magic and mystery. Productions in the Restoration theatre reinvented Shakespeare as unabashed entertainment, something that the comedy, and the variety of musical voices, helped us to discover. A routine concert performance of Restoration 'Shakespeare' music on its own would lack coherence and engagement with the story, as well as the close connection between performers and audience colluding in an affectionate – and irreverent – take on *The Tempest*. Classical concerts and humour do not always go together, and it seemed to be a surprise for the audience that they did on this occasion. In the Wanamaker, paradoxically, candle-lit 'concert' conditions – while setting limits on how fully staged the evening would (or could afford to) be – helped to negotiate the push-pull of actor-performer. Strong personalities – of actors, singers and players – were needed to project this dual focus, as well as an environment whose magic is susceptible to a director's imagination.[22]

---

[22] Andrew Pinnock's programme note summarising the production history of the Restoration *Tempest* can be accessed and downloaded via the University of Southampton's ePrints Soton website.

CHAPTER 9

The Reception and Re-Use of Thomas Arne's Shakespeare Songs of 1740–1

John Cunningham

On the evening of Monday 25 April 1864, Sims Reeves took to the stage in Stratford-Upon-Avon for his second appearance in the Shakespeare tercentenary celebrations. He had spent the afternoon performing in Handel's *Messiah* and, with his fellow soloists, had also been enlisted to participate in 'A Grand Miscellaneous Concert of Music Associated with the Words of Shakespeare'. The concert was a curious mélange of instrumental and vocal music, much of which had been composed at least fifty years earlier. Reeves sang 'Blow, blow, thou wintry [*sic*] wind' from *As You Like It*, as set by Thomas Augustine Arne (1710–78). Enthusiastically received, he responded positively to calls of '*encore*'.[1] Three days later, the song was heard again at the Tercentenary, now restored to its original dramatic context and delivered by W. H. Cummings as Amiens. Today Cummings is best remembered as custodian of the last great Victorian music library, but after his stage debut at the Tercentenary – during which his renditions of 'Blow, blow, thou winter wind' and 'Under the greenwood tree' were encored – he was hailed by one pun-happy critic as '"the coming man" for English opera'.[2] Although these songs were some of the oldest musical items heard at the Tercentenary, they were neither novelties nor curiosities to Victorian audiences. They were among a handful of settings written by Arne for Shakespearean revivals at Drury Lane in the 1740–1 season, most of which continued to be performed in stage productions into the nineteenth century. This was part of a wider trend. Indeed, David Lindley rightly identified 'the tenaciousness with which familiar settings held the stage' as one of the main musical trends observable in

[1] *Jackson's Oxford Journal* (30 April 1864). See J. Cunningham, '"Solemn and appropriate Shakespearean music": The Stratford Tercentenary of 1864', in C. Jansohn and D. Mehl, eds., *Shakespeare Jubilees: 1769–2014* (Münster: LIT Verlag, 2015), 57–78.
[2] *Sheffield & Rotherham Independent* (2 May 1864). The reviewer rendered his surname as 'Cumming', greatly facilitating the pun.

Shakespearean performance history of the eighteenth and nineteenth centuries.[3]

By focussing primarily on the songs for the 1740–1 revival of *As You Like It*, this essay offers a preliminary examination of the contemporary reception of Arne's songs and the circumstances that facilitated their continued re-use in Shakespearean stage productions. In doing so it also seeks to explore the implications for the performance history of the play as these songs became part of the theatrical – and ultimately the Shakespearean – canon.

The 1740–1 Revivals

With the restoration of the theatres in 1660, Shakespeare's plays were divided between the two patent companies – Covent Garden and Drury Lane. However, when they were performed it was typically as adaptations (some more heavily adapted than others), with the language modernised, sexual themes emphasised and – in light of neo-classical fashion – with perceived dramatic infelicities ironed out.[4] There was somewhat of a revival of interest in Shakespeare's (unadapted) works in the wake of Tonson's 'Rowe' edition of 1709. However, as Robert Hume has shown, they 'were expensive volumes aimed at a premium market' and, in terms of the dissemination of Shakespeare's works, made little impact on the London stage.[5] In fact, before about 1730 London's theatre audiences had little contact with, or knowledge of, Shakespeare's original plays as literary texts. It was not until the availability of affordable single plays in the 1730s (thanks to a price war between Tonson and Robert Walker) that the modern 'Shakespeare' began to take shape.[6] This trend was given impetus by the 1737 Licensing Act, which gave the Crown further control over the works produced in the theatres through increased powers of censorship.[7]

---

[3] D. Lindley, '"Sounds and sweet airs": Music in Shakespearian Performance History', *Shakespeare Survey*, 64 (2011), 60.

[4] For more detailed accounts, see C. Price, *Music in the Restoration Theatre* (Ann Arbor: UMI Research Press, 1979); R. Neighbarger, *An Outward Show: Music for Shakespeare on the London Stage, 1660–1830* (Westport: Greenwood Press, 1992); R. Hume, 'Theatre and Repertory', in J. Donohue, ed., *The Cambridge History of British Theatre: 1660 to 1895* (Cambridge University Press, 2004), 53–70.

[5] R. Hume, 'The Economics of Culture in London, 1660–1740', *Huntington Library Quarterly*, 69 (2006), 487–533. See also G. Taylor, *Reinventing Shakespeare* (London: Hogarth Press, 1989), 52–99; R. Hume 'The Value of Money in Eighteenth-Century England', *Huntington Library Quarterly*, 77 (2014), 373–416.

[6] R. Hume, 'Before the Bard: "Shakespeare" in Early Eighteenth-Century London', *English Literary History*, 64 (1997), 41–75.

[7] See J. Milhous, 'Theatre Companies and Regulation', in Donohue, ed. *Cambridge History*, 108–25.

The Act also forced the closure of theatres that had offered illegal competition to the patent houses. While the most damaging result of the Act was a decline in the number of new plays, one corollary was a substantial increase in Shakespearean productions which, in turn, coincided with rise of Charles Macklin and David Garrick, as well as actresses such as Kitty Clive.[8]

On 28 November 1740, the Shadwell/Dryden adaptation of *The Tempest* (1674) was revived at Drury Lane.[9] Few details are known, though Thomas Arne contributed two new song settings; one of which was presumably the famous 'Where the bee sucks'.[10] This adaptation was followed in quick succession by productions of three long dormant plays, presented 'as written': *As You Like It* (20 December 1740), *Twelfth Night* (15 January 1741), and *The Merchant of Venice* (14 February 1741). They were clearly popular, given twenty-eight, nine and twenty times respectively in the season. A full assessment is difficult, as the earliest acting editions published in London were *Bell's Edition of Shakespeare's Plays* (1773–4).[11] Bell's editions may be a fair representation of performances earlier in the century; or more accurately, they may reflect an accumulation of well-established performance practices in the period 1740–70. We know that Arne wrote most, if not all, of the vocal music for these revivals. Indeed, much of our knowledge of the music used in these plays comes from two of his song collections, published in 1741:[12] (1) *The Songs in the Comedies called As You Like It, and Twelfth Night. . . .* and (2) *The Songs and Duetto, in the Blind Beggar of Bethnal Green. . . . With the Favourite Songs . . . in The Merchant of Venice.*

As You Like It

As You Like It met with 'extraordinary applause' and was given a remarkable twenty-eight times in the 1740-1 season.[13] The play remained

[8] F. Ritchie, 'Shakespeare and the Eighteenth-Century Actress', *Borrowers and Lenders*, 2 (2006) www.borrowers.uga.edu.

[9] See Kenny's essay above. The most detailed account of the musical stage histories of Shakespeare's plays is I. Cholij, 'Music in Eighteenth-Century London Shakespeare Productions', unpublished PhD thesis, King's College, London (1995). See also C. B. Hogan, *Shakespeare in the Theatre, 1701–1800* (Oxford: Clarendon Press, 2 vols., 1952, 1957).

[10] As an example of the tune's enduring popularity and familiarity, Julius Benedict used it as the theme for a set of piano variations published in 1859; the 'fantasia' was performed at the 1864 Tercentenary by Arabella Goddard (1836–1922), immediately before Sims Reeves sang 'Blow, blow, thou winter wind'.

[11] See Cholij, 'Music', 20–3, 42–4, 92–3.

[12] Transcriptions may be found in T. Gilman, *The Theatre Career of Thomas Arne* (Newark: University of Delaware Press, 2013).

[13] *Daily Advertiser* (22 December 1740).

a favourite, and was given at least once at Drury Lane and/or Covent Garden each year to 1800, with the exception of 1749, 1765, 1766, and 1781.[14] Given eighteenth-century theatre audiences' thirst for music, *As You Like It* was perhaps an obvious choice for revival: it calls for more songs than any of Shakespeare's other plays except *The Tempest* (five songs and a popular ballad), though not all appear to have made it onto the stage in 1740–1.

Arne included three songs from the play in *Songs in the Comedies*: 'Blow, blow thou winter wind', 'Under the greenwood tree' (one stanza) and 'When daisies pied' (an interloper from *Love's Labour's Lost*, better known as the 'Cuckoo song'). Whether this represents all of the music heard is not known, though there seems little reason to doubt it. It is perhaps worth noting that the play was advertised with 'The Songs new set by Mr. Arne',[15] and that Arne similarly used the definite article in the published collection (*The Songs in . . .*) but he was careful to note that *The Blind Beggar* included only a selection (*the Favourite Songs . . .*). The 1773 Bell edition generally follows Shakespeare's text but with some omissions.[16] Bell included texts for the three songs published by Arne. Omitted are: the snatch from the ballad 'Sweet Oliver' (Touchstone, 3.4.75–81); 'What shall he have killed the deer' (Jaques, 4.2.8–17); 'It was a lover and his lass' (two Pages, 5.3.12–43); 'Wedding is great Juno's crown' (Hymen, 5.4.125–30). Hymen's lines beginning 'There is mirth in heaven' in 5.4.93 are indicated as being sung in the Bell edition, though it seems that originally they were recited over the 'still music' for which the stage direction calls. The only known setting of these lines was attributed to Arne in the eighteenth century, though this is now thought to be dubious. One suspects that these lines were not sung in 1740-1 productions and that the surviving setting was written for a slightly later revival of the play: it has therefore been excluded from the following discussion.

Audiences and the Nature of Song Performance

Song performance in the eighteenth century differed from that of the early modern theatre.[17] In Shakespeare's theatre, songs were generally accompanied, if at all, by a lute or perhaps viol. Thus, even the so-called 'formal'

---

[14] See Hogan, *Shakespeare in the Theatre*, I, 89–98 and II, 117–49; *London Stage*, passim.
[15] *London Daily Post and General Advertiser* (30 December 1740).
[16] Hogan, *Shakespeare in the Theatre*, vol. I, 90 and vol. II, 117.
[17] See C. R. Wilson, 'Shakespeare and Early Modern Music', in M. Thornton Burnett et al., eds., *The Edinburgh Companion to Shakespeare and the Arts* (Edinburgh University Press, 2011), 119–41.

songs would have been quite organic, often arising from the dramatic context without too much disjuncture. By contrast, eighteenth-century theatre songs were generally accompanied by a modest orchestral ensemble.[18] The instrumental introduction (however short) would serve as an aural sign to the audience as well as to the actor(s). This also ensured an element of precognition as the tune of the singer was often anticipated by the orchestra. It also seems likely that the singer(s) would have faced the audience during a song regardless of the dramatic situation. Moreover, as David Lindley has pointed out, it is important to understand that any incidental music heard on the early modern stage was 'always part of the world of the play itself, heard and responded to by the characters on-stage'.[19] Eighteenth-century audiences, however, would have been unperturbed by the aural presence of an orchestra in, say, a forest. In effect, the music was more for the audience and the actors than for the characters. Indeed, eighteenth-century London theatres were audience-driven – aggressively so. Patrons were active participants and flexed their critical muscles with growing confidence.[20] Emotion, approbation and displeasure could be shared with the players immediately, both physically and verbally. Plays and players could be brought to a sudden stop by catcalls, missiles or even riots. Contrariwise it was common for popular songs to receive encores.

These basic conventions naturally meant a greater demarcation of songs from the dramatic context than in the early modern theatre. Songs were entertainments within the entertainment, easily divorced from, and replicated beyond, their original context: such recreations were particularly enabled by the availability of popular songs in printed form. In addition to the possibility of private recreation, the most popular songs could also be heard publicly as entr'acte entertainments or in concerts. This meant greater association of specific songs with individual performers. Actors, becoming ever-more identifiable as public personae, tended to play the same roles in revivals (regardless of whether they were age-appropriate). We see this particularly in musical sources, and even in collections of song texts with no music, where the name of the singer was typically given but the name of the composer and/or lyricist/dramatist was often omitted.

---

[18] See R. Fiske, *English Theatre Music in the Eighteenth Century* (Oxford University Press, 1986), ch. 7.
[19] D. Lindley, *Shakespeare and Music* (London: Thomson Learning, 2005), 112.
[20] See L. Hughes, *The Drama's Patrons: A Study of the Eighteenth-Century London Audience* (Austin: University of Texas Press, 1971); J. W. Fisher, 'Audience Participation in the Eighteenth-Century London Theatre', in S. Kattwinkel, ed., *Audience Participation* (Westport and London: Praeger, 2003), 55–69.

The *As You Like It* Music: Reception

In the absence of theatrical reviews of the 1740-1 Drury Lane revivals, we can gauge some measure of the popularity of Arne's songs through advertisements of their re-performance beyond the parent plays. Of the *As You Like It* songs, 'Blow, blow, thou winter wind' proved particularly popular, and remained so. Emancipated from character and context, the song was also heard between the acts of Ben Jonson's *Volpone*, sung by Arne's wife Celia (née Young; 1712–89), the finest female English soprano of the day.[21] It was also heard as part of a concert of Italian and English music at Hickford's Rooms in April 1741, given by the renowned bass singer Henry Reinhold (d.1751) who had sung in Arne's first theatrical success, the opera *Rosamond* (1733).[22] In *As You Like It*, 'Blow, blow, thou winter wind' was sung (as was 'Under the greenwood tree'), by Thomas Lowe (c.1719–83) as Amiens. Lowe was another associate of Arne.[23] The first record of him singing professionally (as a tenor) is in Arne's masque *Alfred*, given in August 1740 at Cliveden, then a residence of the Prince of Wales. Lowe also sang 'Blow, blow, thou winter wind' between the acts of no fewer than fourteen other works in the 1740-1 season alone.[24] (It seems that even his son, Halifax, later became associated with the song, since among the various entertainments on offer as part of a benefit for himself and Mr Huntley at Sadler's Wells on 28 September 1786, he was to sing 'that admired Air, called "BLOW, BLOW, THOU WINTER WIND"' in the otherwise unknown *The Oxfordshire Miller*, one of two 'favourite musical Pieces'.[25]) There are further tantalising references in the 1740-1 season to the independent performance of the *As You Like It* music. Two revivals of *Rosamond* (25 February and 24 March 1741) ended with 'the Songs and Chorusses in *As You Like It*'; advertisements for the first concert noted that they were 'as intended originally to be performed'.[26] The songs had another outing the following month at a benefit concert for Mrs Steele, which included 'the Songs in *As You Like It*, by Mrs Dunstall',[27] and they were performed again at Cuper's Pleasure Gardens, Lambeth, in July.

---

[21] *London Stage*, part 3, vol. II, 906.

[22] *London Stage*, part 3, vol. II, 911. According to an undated single-sheet folio print (British Library, Music Collections H.1601.b.(110.)) it was also sung by Kitty Clive, though it is not known in what context.

[23] For a detailed biographical account, see P. H. Highfill et al., eds., *A Biographical Dictionary of Actors, Actresses, Musicians, Dancers, Managers, and Other Stage Personnel in London, 1660–1800*, 16 vols (Carbondale: Southern Illinois Press, 1973–93) vol. IX, 372–5.

[24] *London Stage*, part 3, vol. II, 908, 911, 913, 914 (2), 915, 916 (3), 918 (4), 919 (2).

[25] *General Advertiser* (28 September 1786).   [26] *London Stage*, part 3, vol. II, 892 and 900.

[27] *London Stage*, part 3, vol. II, 905.

A concert of 'Several curious Pieces of Musick' with fireworks was advertised several times and drew specific attention to 'the Songs in As you like it, Blow, blow, the Cuckow, with the Chorus's, &c.'.[28]

Arne's choruses were not included in the published settings of the songs and are not known to have survived. However, the wording of the advertisement: 'as intended originally to be performed', may suggest that they were composed for the play but did not appear in the stage production. The pleasure gardens concerts suggest that at least two, and probably all three, of the published songs originally had choruses. The only song not to be mentioned is dramatically the most obvious place for a chorus: 'Under the greenwood tree'. In the original play (2.5.1), Amiens, Jaques and the other Lords enter, with Amiens singing. He sings the first stanza, which is then followed by some dialogue with Jaques. The next stanza is given as 'All together here' (2.5.29 SD), implying a chorus. There is then further dialogue, followed by the final stanza offered by Jaques, which may or may not have been intended to be sung (it is given in roman type, rather than italics, in the 1623 Folio and in later editions). The 1773 Bell edition omits much of the scene: only the first stanza of the song and the next five lines of dialogue remain.[29] It seems to be no coincidence that Arne also only set the first stanza. The most likely explanation is that a more complete (and reasonably faithful) rendering of the scene was first intended, and that Arne was given the two stanzas to be set as a solo for Thomas Lowe and a chorus, respectively. It was evidently decided that the chorus would not (or could not) be sung and so was omitted from performances: the easiest solution was to cut most of the scene after the first stanza.

It is less clear what form the choruses could have taken in Arne's other two songs from *As You Like It*. In 'Blow, blow, thou winter wind', he omitted the final two lines of each stanza, perhaps because they were originally set as a chorus. The second half of 'When daisies pied' is also repeated in both stanzas and seem the most likely lines to be set for a chorus.[30] In all three scenes there are enough characters onstage to deliver a chorus, though only in the first is one explicitly called for in Shakespeare's text. It may be that there simply were not enough able singers to carry it off in 1740-1. (Of the relevant 1740 cast only James

---

[28] *London Daily Post and General Advertiser* (18, 23, 24, 28 July 1741).
[29] Hogan, *Shakespeare in the Theatre*, vol. I, 117.
[30] This interloping song usually replaced 4.1.157–67 in eighteenth- and nineteenth-century productions; see, *As You Like It*, ed. J. Dusinberre (London: Arden, 2006), 296.

Quin (Jaques) and Hannah Pritchard (Rosalind) are known as singers.) The popularity of Arne's settings ensured that these omissions would become theatrical traditions.

'When daisies pied' (the Cuckoo song) remained particularly popular, both in stage revivals and independently, well into the nineteenth century. Inserted into 4.1., the text was taken from *Love's Labour's Lost*, the only play in the Shakespeare canon not to have been staged in the eighteenth century.[31] Dramatically the song is not entirely out of place given Rosalind's characterisation of married women (e.g. 4.1.133–43), but it is by no means necessary. One assumes that the actual reason for the inclusion of 'When daisies pied' in 1740 was to give Kitty Clive an appropriate song to sing. Clive, who took the role of Celia, was one of the most talented and well-known actresses of the day. Having joined the Drury Lane company in 1728, she made her name in a series of ballad operas. By 1740, Clive was a star soprano; Berta Joncus has described her as 'perhaps the first female "pop" star'.[32] Unlike many of her female colleagues in the theatre, Clive enjoyed a respectable reputation. She married the lawyer George Clive in 1733, but the union was short-lived; the couple separated in 1735, though they did not divorce. Chastity became part of Clive's reputation/persona. Thus the Cuckoo song (a song about cuckolding) must have been layered in irony for the audience.

Most, if not all, members of the Drury Lane audience in 1740-1 would not have missed the omitted lines and scenes in *As You Like It* or have recognised the interpolation of songs from other works; nor would it have mattered to them if they did. However, as audiences became more knowledgeable of the plays as literary texts these small changes created a tension between the plays as performed and the plays as read. But traditions can be hard to break. 'When daisies pied', for example, continued to be sung in performances of *As You Like It* into the nineteenth century, even as it was recognised as an interloper. In his 1816 anthology *Shakespeare's Dramatic Songs*, William Linley (1771–1835) noted that 'The song at the end of the play [*Love's Labour's Lost*] is usually introduced in "As you like it", and is sung by Rosalind; there is no reason, however, why it should be misplaced

---

[31] Presumably hoping to capitalise on the song's popularity, Arne published a setting of the companion stanzas in *The Blind Beggar*: 'The Owl. Written by Shakespeare in (*Love's labour lost*) it is a description of Winter as the Cuckow Song is of the Spring'.

[32] B. Joncus, '"A Likeness Where One Was to Be Found": Imagining Kitty Clive', *Music in Art*, 34 (2009), 89–106.

here'.[33] Although Celia was originally to have the song, in the 1773 Bell edition it is given to Rosalind. Its inclusion appears to have depended on the availability of an able singer, whichever character she played. So ingrained was Arne's setting in the play's performance history, that a production in the Theatre-Royal, Edinburgh, on 14 March 1807 advertised a Miss Benson as Celia 'with the *original* Cuckow Song in character' (emphasis added).[34]

In short, musical decisions taken in the 1740 revival of *As You Like It* – apparently for practical reasons – had a significant impact on how the play was performed for the rest of the century and beyond. The same is true of the two other 'as written' revivals of the 1740-1 season. *Twelfth Night* opened on 15 January 1741 on the back of the success of *As You Like It*. Arne published two songs from the performance with the *As You Like It* songs. The text of one, 'Tell me where is fancy bred', was introduced from *The Merchant of Venice*. Again, we may assume it was interpolated to give Kitty Clive (Olivia) a suitable song.[35] Yet when *The Merchant of Venice* was itself revived 'as written' on 14 February, this, the only original song, was omitted (even though it can be interpreted as helping to guide Bassanio to the correct choice of casket). Indeed, this new association of 'Tell me where' with *Twelfth Night* became so strong that, even at the end of the century, it was still omitted in theatrical performances of its original play.[36] But having lost 'Tell me where is fancy bred' *The Merchant of Venice* acquired at least two new (non-Shakespearean) songs in the 1741 revival, which in turn became part of the performance tradition of the play. Arne published two songs in *The Blind Beggar*, the title of which describes them as '*the Favourite Songs*', as sung by Thomas Lowe.[37] The 1773 Bell edition also includes a song for Jessica at the end of 2.3.[38] (In 1741, Jessica was played by a Miss Woodman; Kitty Clive played Portia, but it seems that no

[33] Vol. I, 8. Almost a decade later, a copy of the song printed in *The Harmonicon*, 3/2 (1825), 14–15 was titled 'When Daisies pied. Song, in Love's Labour lost, but now sung in As you like it'.

[34] *Caledonian Mercury* (14 March 1807); Amiens is listed as 'with a Song'.

[35] Arne did not set lines 3.2.70–2. The last lines of both stanzas are given as choruses in the original play. His other song was Feste's 'Come away death', sung by Lowe as the Duke; the character of Feste was cut in the 1773 Bell edition and evidently also in 1741. Arne composed another setting several years later, probably for another revival: see Cholij, 'Music in Eighteenth-Century London Shakespeare Productions', 93–4.

[36] See also Cholij 'Music', 40–4. It is perhaps suggestive that Linley makes no mention of Arne's setting in *Shakespeare's Dramatic Songs*.

[37] Further advertisements suggest that more songs were added to performances of the play over the second half of the century, though they are generally not possible to identify: see Cholij, 'Music', 40–4.

[38] The text is given in Cholij, Ibid., 273. The only surviving setting, by Joseph Baildon, appears to have been written for a 1751 Covent Garden revival.

new song was introduced for her on this occasion.) The first of Arne's songs, 'My bliss too long my bride denies' was inserted in 2.4 before Lorenzo calls to Jessica at her window. According to Irena Cholij, a late-eighteenth-century prompt book suggests that the song was added to allow Jessica more time for a costume change.[39] The second song, 'To keep my gentle Jesse', was added to 5.1 instead of background music; it is a simple love song allowing Lorenzo to express his devotion to Jessica.[40] Its only function was musical entertainment. We know from prompt books that both of these new songs remained in the theatrical repertoire at least until the end of the century.

Publication and Popularity

The song settings written by Arne for the 1740–1 revivals had many opportunities to enter public consciousness simply because the plays themselves were well received and given many times during the season. The songs clearly met with approbation, demonstrated by the fact that Arne sought to capitalise through publication of them. He published the collection himself (as he had done several times previously), thus retaining copyright (which would otherwise have been sold to a bookseller) and maximising profits. This also meant that he absorbed the initial costs of engraving, paper, printing and advertising. It is difficult to estimate these costs, and we have no way of knowing how many copies were printed, though in the eighteenth century an average print run from engraved plates was usually 200–250; the potential market was often gauged by issuing batches of twenty to fifty copies.[41] *Songs in the Comedies* sold for 3s 6d: reasonable value for eight songs with settings also for flute (the amateur gentleman's instrument of choice) and bass, though still fairly expensive for the average consumer.[42]

As the publisher, Arne also had to be mindful of the threat to his profits from pirated editions of the songs, which tended to appear either as single-sheet folios or within larger anthologies. Around the time of the *As You Like It* revival Arne pursued a royal privilege protecting his music from being printed without his permission for fourteen years: the privilege was granted on 29 January 1741 and was included in *Songs in the Comedies* and *The Blind Beggar*. Henry Roberts included five songs from *Comus* (1738), as well as

[39] Ibid., 42.   [40] The texts for both are given in Ibid., 272–3.
[41] See A. Devriès-Lesure, 'Technological Aspects', in R. Rasch, ed. *Music Publishing in Europe 1600–1900* (Berliner Wissenchafts-Verlag, 2005), 63–88.
[42] See Hume, 'The Value of Money'.

'When daisies pied', in his two-volume collection *Calliope or English Harmony* (August 1739; January 1741), and continued to sell copies of the books after Arne's privilege was invoked. John Johnson also continued to sell songs from *Comus* and 'Blow, blow, thou winter wind' as single sheets.[43] The affair ended in legal action, with Arne's bill of complaint presented in the court of chancery on 12 November 1741. The case did not proceed in the court, suggesting that the parties reached an out-of-court settlement. Roberts and Johnson thereafter respected Arne's copyright; they continued to include the lyrics of his songs in their printed collections but omitted the music. Arne's litigious streak seems also to have successfully dissuaded other booksellers from ignoring his privilege. For example, Thomas Kitchin included 'When daisies pied' in *The English Orpheus* (1743); but he merely included the unacknowledged song text with a note saying that 'The musick can't be put to this song, Mr. Arne having a patent for it'.[44] The suit for copyright tells us something not only about Arne's vested interests and how he sought to protect them, but about the popularity of these play-songs which is further testified to by the number of reprints of single songs that appeared throughout the century.

The Machinery of Prosperity

In the case of the *As You Like It* songs, it could be argued that popularity led to publication, motivated by commerce; publication in turn reinforced the songs' popularity, or at least made them more readily accessible to the machinery of cultural memory, thus ensuring their re-use in later productions. But at this point we may ask: why were these songs so popular in the first place and why did they continue to be so? 'Cultural selection' is a complex phenomenon,[45] but we may identify three principal contributing factors in relation to Arne's Shakespeare songs.

First, the songs work as aesthetic objects and are excellent examples of Arne's gift for melody; moreover, they are accessible in style. As with many of Arne's songs, they are written in a comfortable range, usually not exceeding a tenth; the melodic lines avoid large leaps, written-out embellishments and melismas. This style was reflective of – and partly imposed

---

[43] R. J. Rabin and S. Zohn, 'Arne, Handel, Walsh, and Music as Intellectual Property: Two Eighteenth-Century Lawsuits', *Journal of the Royal Musical Association*, 120 (1995), 112–45.

[44] Quoted in Ibid., 124. See also J. Small, 'The Development of Musical Copyright', in M. Kassler, ed. *The Music Trade in Georgian England* (Aldershot: Ashgate, 2011), 233–386.

[45] See G. Taylor, *Cultural Selection* (New York: Basic Books, 1996).

by – the capabilities of the performers. Many of Arne's Shakespeare songs were sung by Thomas Lowe. The composer Charles Dibdin later recalled that Lowe's voice was 'more even and mellow' than that of the famous tenor John Beard (*c.*1717–91), 'and, in mere love songs when little more than a melodious utterance was necessary, he might have been said to have exceeded him'. However, Dibdin qualified this by noting that while 'Lowe lost himself beyond the namby[-]pamby poetry of Vauxhall [Gardens]; Beard was at home ever[y]where'.[46] Charles Burney described Lowe as 'the finest tenor voice I have ever heard in my life, [but] for want of diligence and cultivation, he never could be safely trusted with any thing better than a ballad, which he constantly learned by his ear'.[47]

Second, the songs could be associated with recognisable individuals. We see the emerging world of celebrity in Arne's (by then conventional) titular inclusion of 'Mr Lowe' and 'Mrs Clive' on the pages of *Songs in the Comedies* and *The Blind Beggar*, and the prominent display of their names on the title page of the latter. Moreover, by the 1740s Arne was himself one of the leading musical figures in London; his name (as being responsible for the music) is often seen in advertisements of these plays. The composer was, however, at the mercy of performers in terms of delivering the songs. Arne had an interest in their communication of his songs in terms of his own reputation, but he also saw the public performance of his songs as advertisements for potential commercial ventures. We can see this in an incident recounted by Charles Burney, who never resisted an opportunity to denigrate his erstwhile teacher:

> When one night Mrs Clive having undertaken a song in wh^{ch} she was imperfect: as she was given to be out of time as well as tune; at a hitch, she calls out loud to the band, 'why dont the fellows mind what they are ab^t?' At the end of the Act Arne went upstairs to remonstrate against her insolence, when the only satisfaction he obtained, was a slap on the face. In return, he literally turned her over his knee and gave her such a manual flagellation as she probably had not received since she quitted the nursery.[48]

Clive consequently refused to sing Arne's songs for a Drury Lane revival of *The Tempest* (1746) and William de Fesch was drafted in to write new settings.[49] The amusing anecdote demonstrates the power that performers

[46] C. Dibdin, *Complete History of the English Stage*, (London: [n.p.], 1800) vol. V, 364.

[47] C. Burney, *A General History of Music*, F. Mercer ed., vol. II, 1010. Burney served his apprenticeship under Arne.

[48] Quoted in Cholij, 'Music', 78.

[49] See Ibid., 77–80. Although de Fesch's *Tempest* music is perfectly good, tellingly it was Arne's music that was re-used later in the century, especially his setting of 'Where the bee sucks'.

such as Clive could wield. More interesting, however, is the fact that Arne felt the need to remonstrate in the first place: a singer's 'insolence' could have commercial ramifications.

Third: theatrical conventions. Style, popularity and celebrity endorsement combined with the machinery of the theatre to ensure that these songs remained in use. The publication of Arne's songs enabled them to enjoy a level of permanence in the cultural memory of theatre audiences. Unlike many of Shakespeare's original songs, Arne's settings existed not just aurally but on the printed page. Many of the 1740–1 songs were printed as single-sheet folios throughout the century, some in arrangements. Reprinting tended to coincide with revivals of the plays and a new singer-actor becoming associated with them. When plays were revived in subsequent seasons there was little practical advantage to commissioning new settings, especially if the existing ones had already proved popular and even more so if the same actors were involved. Rival theatres in London could also use Arne's settings, as they were readily available in print. For the same reason they were also used in provincial theatres, which generally followed in the footsteps of the capital. Arne himself was active in the London theatres until his death in 1778, and while he could earn by being commissioned to make new settings there may well have been more commercial value in reprinting highly popular, and increasingly established, songs. Revivals of musical settings generally were not uncommon. Richard Leveridge's music for a 1702 adaptation of *Macbeth*, for example, continued to be popular and regularly performed into the second half of the nineteenth century (though mistakenly attributed to Matthew Locke after William Boyce's edition of 1770).[50]

Conclusions

The revivals of 1740-1 began performance traditions that were long-lasting, some the direct consequence of the music and its popularity. The tenacity with which Arne's Shakespeare songs held the stage at first appears remarkable. But upon closer inspection it speaks to the conservative tastes of eighteenth-century London audiences. Initial popularity, followed by the reasonably continuous stage presence of the plays, ensured an unusually long life for Arne's songs. This was in part symptomatic of Shakespeare's gradual emergence as the 'national poet',[51] underlain as it was by the same

[50] See A. Eubanks Winkler, ed., *Music for Macbeth* (Madison: A-R Editions, 2004), especially viii–ix.
[51] See M. Dobson, *The Making of the National Poet* (Oxford: Clarendon Press, 1994).

cultural nationalism that resounded in Arne's famous setting of *Alfred*, which included the song 'Rule Britannia', first performed at Clivedon and later revised for the London stage.[52] In any event, the practical decisions made in accommodating Arne's songs in 1740-1 directly impacted upon the performance history of the plays. Some alterations were more long-lasting than others. For example, when *As You Like It* was given at the 1864 Tercentenary, the Cuckoo song appears to have been omitted: at least, there was no mention of it in reviews. Only 'Blow, blow, thou winter wind' and 'Under the greenwood tree' as sung by W. H. Cummings are mentioned by critics. Although there is no concrete evidence, we can be certain that Cummings sang Arne's settings, not simply because Cummings owned copies of *Songs in the Comedies* and *The Blind Beggar*,[53] but rather because by 1864 theatrical tradition had ensured that these songs were as Shakespearean as David Garrick.

---

[52] *Alfred*, ed. A Scott, *Musica Britannica* 47 (London: Stainer and Bell, 1981); see also M. Burden, *Garrick, Arne, and the Masque of Alfred* (Lewiston: Edwin Mellen Press, 1994).

[53] *Catalogue of the Famous Musical Library . . . of the Late W.H. Cummings*, lots 51, 61, and 1538; he also owned 'Shakespeare Music. Manuscript Collection of rare and uncommon Pieces by Ancient Composers' (lot 1537). Cummings began collecting at a young age, though it is not known when he acquired these items.

CHAPTER 10

Processing with Shakespeare on the Eighteenth-Century London Stage

Michael Burden

Introduction

In 1779, the audience at the theatre in Drury Lane was treated to
a burlesque of the then-fashionable tragic drama. The play in question
was titled *The Critic; or, A Tragedy Rehearsed* and revolved around the
private rehearsal before the writer, Sir Fretful Plagiary, and the critics
Dangle and Sneer, of a drama by its ridiculous author, Mr Puff. When
trying to justify the mismatch of the play's title and its content, Puff
petulantly declares:

> Yes- Yes- you know my play is *called* the Spanish Armada, otherwise egad,
> I have no occasion for the battle at all. – Now then, for my magnificence! –
> My battle! – My noise! – and my Procession![1]

In other words, the procession is merely an addition of vacuous content,
aligned with magnificence, a battle and lots of noise. However, the
procession cannot always have been – and indeed, was not – viewed
with such derision, and in fact, from the stagings of *Romeo and Juliet* in
the 1750s until the 1769 Shakespeare Jubilee, it was regarded much more
favourably.

Before going further, a word about the sources for this subject. Apart
from the *Romeo and Juliet* processions just mentioned, for which both text
and scores survive, we find little extant music; what does survive has few,
if any, performance instructions; and titles such as 'March' tell us little
about what action took place during the performance of those particular
numbers. Moreover, the playbooks and librettos tend to indicate
a procession solely by the word 'Procession', and give us little further
enlightenment. Indeed, the majority of the material that describes what
went on in these devices is what appears in puffs and advertisements that

---

[1] *The Critic; or, A Tragedy Rehearsed* (London: T. Beckett, 1781), 97.

the newspapers often had a vested interest in carrying; but while not everything mentioned in puffs may have appeared in the actual procession, they do at least convey something of the show.

The types of procession in the eighteenth-century English theatre can be divided into three categories: those that were fundamental to the drama in which they appeared; those that were add-ons, with no dramatic contexts; and those that were free-standing events, added to the bill to spice up a promoter's offering. As far as the integrated type is concerned, one can scarcely get more integrated than the funeral processions added to *Romeo and Juliet*; dramatically apposite, musically attractive, and bringing in or keeping engaged, an audience. And in the lists of processions staged in the eighteenth-century London theatre, others of a similar sort can be found, more or less assisting the drama in which they occurred. In a piece like David Garrick's *The Institution of the Garter*, for example, the procession of knights to St George's Hall can hardly be called superfluous; it forms the climax of the second part of the play, and places the knights in St George's Hall for the third act institution.[2]

At a more superficial level, there was the much-criticised, but in fact popular, interlude *The Village Fete*, written by Richard Cumberland. The writer in the *True Briton*, felt that 'something better might have been expected from such a literary veteran', even though 'it was written on the spur of the occasion'. The dialogue was described as 'dull in the extreme' and the 'songs nearly as barren'. But the '*rural pageant*, consisting of *Villagers* with all the instruments of husbandry in procession', was considered an amusing spectacle.[3] Even this brief commentary shows the material of the procession was tied to the interlude. Perhaps the most interesting, integrated events are those processions that appear in the pantomime ballets of the last quarter of the century. These appear to have been mimed by the dancers, and were pieces whose inherently integrated nature made it difficult or impossible to move them from one work to another. One of these was 'The grand procession of Iphiginia into Aulide',[4] from *Iphiginia en Aulide*, which was choreographed by the great dancer and ballet master, Jean-Georges Noverre. Pantomimed ballets of this sort were Opera House pieces rather than for the playhouses, and most were therefore written for the King's Theatre and performed by the foreign ballet troupes employed there.

[2] D. Garrick, *The Institution of the Garter, or, Arthur's Round Table Restored* (London: T. Becket and P. A. de Hondt, 1771).
[3] *True Briton*, 19 May 1797.   [4] *Morning Herald*, 27 April 1793.

Tacked-on processions – those that appear to have been added merely for the sake of having a procession – include many of those in the pantomimes at Sadler's Wells and Astley's Circus. The give-away here is that many of the press descriptions noted a variation of the phrase 'and at the end of the piece, will be included a new grand procession'. Thematically, they tended to be occasional and allegorical, such as the procession tacked on to the *Allegorical Divertissment* in July, 1792. A careful reading of the advertisement in the *Oracle Newspaper* reveals that the procession *was* the divertissement, and its songs, choruses and other attributes were part of the whole. Processions on their own are, to some extent, a further enlargement of the procession added to the drama. One of the more interesting of these occurred during some private theatricals at Brandenburg House, for the Margravine of Anspach, described as having 'not very creditable taste'. The performers on this occasion – the Margravine, her son, Mr Wynn, Mr Wathen, and Mr Angelo – performed a comedy of Henry Carey's which was followed by a 'whimsical procession' which was ill-received, being described as 'tedious in the extreme'. In fact, the evening lasted from 10 pm to nearly 3 am, and was finally judged as being 'stale, flat, and unprofitable'.[5]

Apart from demonstrating the popularity of the genre, this private performance emphasises that to make a procession work well, it needed some context, some money, and a lot of theatrical expertise to ensure that what was only a light-hearted add-on would work. When a procession was prepared in the theatre, it was under the general supervision of the management, but clearly everyone was involved; especially towards the end of the century there are a number of cases where the ballet master appears to have been in charge.[6] Skill was needed to ensure success.

Romeo and Juliet and Shakespeare's Jubilee

The origins of the procession as a dramatic device in the London theatre are unclear; although the actual number included in dramas before 1750 seems to have been small,[7] it was certainly current by 1744, for Charles Burney, recording his apprenticeship in composition to the composer Thomas Arne, noted that he had been employed 'behind the scenes in serenade

---

[5] *True Briton*, 10 April 1797.
[6] R. Houlton, *A Review of the Musical Drama* ... (London: J. Abraham, 1801).
[7] These included those processions in *Henry VIII* (1727), *Aurora's Nuptials, a masque* (1734), *Papal tyranny in the reign of King John* (1745), and *Merope, a tragedy* (1749).

processions and other musical purposes for stage effect'.[8] But it came into its own when both Covent Garden and Drury Lane staged *Romeo and Juliet* on the same night in 1750. Thomas Arne at Covent Garden contributed a 'Solemn Dirge' to accompany Juliet's funeral procession; this was received with rapture by the audience, to the extent that William Boyce at Drury Lane found himself with a demand from Garrick for something similar.[9] Arne's opened with the instruction 'at the Beginning of the procession the Trumpets advance with the Kettle Drums and sound the following Solemn notes between which the Bell tolls, till they are off the Stage'; the closing instruction directs that the performers should 'Repeat the foregoing movement Viz. Hark, Hark, till the procession is Over'. The sequence of numbers began with an opening flourish, with the 2nd trumpet and kettle drums muffled; then followed the Solemn Dirge – Chorus: 'Hark, Hark' – Adagio chorus – Chorus: 'Hark, Hark'.[10] Boyce's was very similar in conception; his sparse opening was accompanied by a striking bell which continued to sound throughout the procession, with the musical structure involving a repeating chorus: Chorus: 'Rise, rise, heartbreaking sighs' – Trio: 'She's gone, the sweet flow'r of May' – Chorus: 'Rise, rise, heartbreaking sighs' – Trio: 'Thou spotless soul look here below' – Chorus 'Rise, rise, heartbreaking sighs'.[11] The *Memoirs of George Anne Bellamy* give us some insight into this particular affair:

> This season at Covent Garden, promised much success. The Theatre opened with *Romeo and Juliet*. Rich made it his boast, that he has the Juliet now as well as the Romeo. One night, Miss B. observed to him with pleasure, that the house was prodigiously crouded; when taking a pinch of snuff, and turning short upon his heel he replied, "Yes, Mistress, but it is owing to the procession."[12]

At the other theatre, the author went on:

---

[8] S. Klima, G. Bowers, and K. S. Grant, eds., *Memoirs of Charles Burney 1726–1769* (Lincoln: University of Nebraska Press, 1988), 45.

[9] See R. Fiske, *English Theatre Musician the Eighteenth Century*, 2nd edn (Oxford: Clarendon Press, 1986). 217; C. Haywood, 'William Boyce's "Solemn Dirge" in Garrick's *Romeo and Juliet* Production of 1750', *Shakespeare Quarterly*, 11: 2 (1960), 173–87; and R. J. Bruce, 'William Boyce: Some Manuscript Recoveries', *Music and Letters*, 55 (1974), 437–43.

[10] T. Arne, *A Complete Score of the Solemn Dirge in Romeo and Juliet* (London: Henry Thorowgood, *c.* 1767).

[11] Boyce, 'Dirge, for Romeo and Juliet', GB-Ob MS. Mus. c. 3, ff. 9ʳ–20ʳ.

[12] A gentleman of the Covent Garden Theatre, *Memoirs of George Anne Bellamy* (London: J. Walker, 1785), 115.

> Mr Garrick, to check [Rich's] run of *Romeo and Juliet*, was at the expense of a new bell; which not availing to the purpose for which it was purchased, he brought forward Venice preserved, where he and Cibber excelled beyond a possibility of competition.[13]

Garrick's version of *Romeo and Juliet* was, 'in compliance to the public opinion', postponed; if the public preferred *Venice Preserved*, then that is what they got. The author went on:

> Miss B's sarcasm on this occasion, was perfectly *à-propos*. She advised the Manager to introduce his procession into some other piece, as it had been hitherto so efficacious in producing a full house.[14]

Miss Bellamy was, of course, only a player as far as John Rich was concerned.

In fact, the procession in Shakespeare's *Romeo and Juliet* lays down a marker for a number of aspects of this theatrical phenomenon. Firstly, the dramatic and musical spectacle was a source of audience attention; it was a dramatic add-on which the theatre would use to promote the main piece, of whatever genre it might be. Secondly, we are introduced to the idea that a procession was detachable; if it was a hit with the public in one context, then that context could simply be abandoned, and it could be inserted elsewhere, and in turn, be used as a crowd-puller in its new context. Thirdly, it introduces the importance of theatrical competition when looking at the processions. If one theatre had success with it, then the other houses were likely to respond. And fourthly, we see the beginnings of the broader narrative that the procession dumbed down English drama, that it was of doubtful taste, and that it became more important to the theatre than the performances of the actors.

As spectacular as these events were, however, they paled into insignificance behind the theatre processions that emerged in the wake of the 1769 Jubilee in Stratford. The story of the Jubilee is well known and need not be revisited in detail here;[15] suffice it to say that, planned under Garrick for 6–8 September 1769, the three days' worth of entertainment struggled

---

[13] Ibid. [14] Ibid.
[15] See J. M. Stochholm, *Garrick's Folly* (London: Methuen & Cop, 1964); C. Deelman, *The Great Shakespeare Jubilee* (London: Joseph, 1964); L. Fox, *A Splendid Occasion: the Stratford Jubilee of 1769* (Oxford: Vivian Ridler, 1973); and P. Tankard, 'The Stratford *Jubilee*', in P. Tankard, ed., *Facts and Inventions: Selections from the Journalism of James Boswell* (New Haven: Yale University Press, 2014), 17–34.

through torrential rain, flooding and cancelled events, with among the casualties a procession 'of the principal characters in the inimitable Plays wrote by the *Immortal* Shakespeare'.[16] The putative procession was illustrated in two plates in the *Oxford Magazine; or University Museum*.[17] It is unclear what authority these images have, for the first appeared before the procession was to have taken place; the second, in the same style, appeared the next month. If it can be assumed that the cuts convey the essence of what was intended, then we have a series of figures from Shakespeare's plays costumed in character. For the sake of the reader, each one is identified with a balloon containing a quotation from the appropriate play. Whether the bedraggled and scraggy-looking figures would have impressed the public had they actually seen them is doubtful, but the circumstances of the Jubilee and the public curiosity that it aroused both before and after the event offered Garrick the possibility of recreating the 'pageant that never happened' as part of his stage show, *The Jubilee*, which premiered on 14 October 1769:

> With (never-performed before) an Entertainment of Singing, Dancing, and Dialogue, call'd The JUBILEE. In which is introduced the PAGEANT, as it was intended for Stratford upon Avon.[18]

A number of accounts of the show appeared in the press, including that in the *Gazetteer and New Daily Advertiser*:

> The last scene shews the principal characters of Shakespeare in an illuminated transparent view. The statue of the Poet is seen at the extremity of the stage, crowned by the Tragic and Comic Muses. The characters that had before passed in procession now fill the sides of the stage; and the whole concludes with chorus and dancing.[19]

Illustration 5 shows the 1770 Johnson and Payne engraving of the procession in progress.

But, as it happens, Garrick's inspiration for this undertaking was not the original events at Stratford, but the exploitation of those events by manager George Colman at Covent Garden, as he wrote: 'We are preparing to Jubilee it upon yᵉ Stage – Mʳ Colman Enters yᵉ list with Us, much to my

---

[16] From 'Shakespeare's Jubilee,' a later handbill in the British Library; reproduced in Stockholm, *Garrick's Folly*, 104.
[17] *Oxford Magazine; or University Museum*, 3 (1769), September, opposite 103, and October, opposite 137.
[18] *Whitehall Evening Post or London Intelligencer*, 12–14 October 1769.
[19] *Gazetteer and New Daily Advertiser*, 17 October 1769.

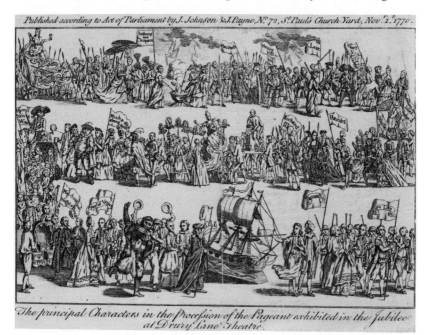

Illustration 5 Anonymous. The principal characters in the procession of the Pageant exhibited in the Jubilee at Drury Lane Theatre. Folger Shakespeare Library Shelfmark ART File G241.3 no. 5. Used by permission of the Folger Shakespeare Library.

Surprize.'[20] Such 'surprize' does, however, seem somewhat disingenuous, for others had also already laid claim to the material. Garrick himself had been reciting 'in the Manner it was performed at Stratford' the *Shakespeare Ode*, itself already published.[21] And if Edward Everard is to be believed, there was nothing accidental on either side about this particular piece of theatrical competition:

> It was said that Mr Garrick, hearing of Mr Colman's intention, wrote to him in a most candid manner, and declared that he would give up all thoughts of performing the "Jubilee" at his theatre, if he would drop the same. Mr Colman as candidly that he should not, and accordingly they both fell to work.[22]

[20] Letter to Joseph Craddock, 2 October 1769, in D. Little and G. Kahrl, eds., *The Letters of David Garrick*, 3 vols (Oxford University Press, 1963), II, 665–6.
[21] Garrick, *An Ode Upon Dedicating a Building, and Erecting a Statue, to Shakespeare, at Stratford upon Avon* (London: T. Becket and P. A. da Hondt, 1769).
[22] E. C. Everard, *Memoirs of an unfortunate son of Thespis* (Edinburgh: J. Ballantyne, 1818), 15.

Colman staged an altered version of his earlier matrimonial comedy, *Man and Wife*, a play that Vanessa Cunningham has described as 'routine': the play had its scene changed to Stratford, and now included a number of topical references to the Jubilee.[23] Colman's show duly appeared at Covent Garden and 'introduced a Pageant of the Characters of Shakespeare, concluding with a Masquerade'.[24]

Once again, it was Shakespearean processions which were the vehicle for theatrical competition between the two Theatres Royal. But it was also the case that the 1769 processions ushered in what we might call a 'new age', one in which the procession now truly had little to do with the drama in which it was inserted. In *Romeo and Juliet*, the procession grew out of the drama; it not only captured the dramatic moment in the play, but it also caught an audience response to the moment which made the procession meaningful. And both Boyce and Arne responded accordingly. Precisely the opposite pertained to the second pair of processions, those in *Man and Wife* and *The Jubilee*. Here, the drama was merely a peg on which to hang the Stratford processions, indeed – in the case of *Man and Wife* – not even cursorily tying the show to the drama. Both dramas were commercially successful: Colman's show only briefly, for it was overtaken by the success of Garrick's, but the latter ran for some ninety performances.

But neither Garrick nor Colman – both successful and skilled men of the theatre – were under the illusion that these pageants and the works that contained them were anything other than theatrical pap. And while Shakespeare's Jubilee may have been used by Garrick to cement his role as keeper of the Bard's flame, this particular theatrical flurry was followed by an increase in the use of the device in plays both newly written and already established, developments that were responsible for the subsequent, generally critical response, of commentators to the device and its employment in satirical plays such as the above-mentioned *Critic*; processions were 'extras', non-essential crowd-pleasers that could be put into any old show, and were there to be both parodied and exploited.

1789 and Beyond

Such was the situation until the end of the 1780s saw a new imperative in the writing and staging of processions, which moved the use of the device

[23] Vanessa Cunningham, *Shakespeare and Garrick* (Cambridge University Press, 2008), 113.
[24] *Whitehall Evening Post*, 12–14 October 1769.

decisively from the world of Shakespeare to its almost ubiquitous employment in a show with a concentration of musical events therein.[25] This
imperative was commercial, and was caused by the rebuilding of the
auditoria of the three main London theatres, new performing spaces
which required new strategies to attract and hold the audience's attention.
The Opera House was the first to be rebuilt; it was enlarged in 1782, and
then after a disastrous fire in 1789 it was rebuilt, with a seating capacity that
was increased from 1800 to 3300. Over at Covent Garden, Shepherd's 1732
auditorium was also rebuilt in 1782 and again ten years later; here the
increase in capacity was from 2200 to 3000. Drury Lane's rebuild by Henry
Holland in 1794 raised the capacity from 2300 to 3611. Naturally, com-
plaints followed. In 1792, Ann Larpent commented that in the evening 'we
all went to hear Mrs Siddons in *Macbeth*. The house is too large, attention
becomes a wearisome task to my eyes and ears.'[26] The Earl of Carlisle
remarked that both the playhouses were now too large for 'the gratification
of the eye and ear', and that 'more than half the verse [was] entombed in
the performer's stomach';[27] and in the supplement to his 1806 *Memoirs*,
Richard Cumberland wrote of the loss of theatrical effect resulting from
these modifications:

> Since the stages of Drury Lane and Covent Garden have been so enlarged in
> their dimensions as to be hence forward theatres for spectators rather than
> playhouses for hearers ... there can be nothing very gratifying in watching
> the movement of an actor's lips, when we cannot hear the words that
> proceed from them.[28]

Such problems could be addressed by increasing the amount of 'show':

> The splendour of the scenes, the ingenuity of the machinist and the rich
> display of dresses, aided by the captivating charms of the music, now in
> a great degree supersede the labours of the poet ... when the animating
> march strikes up, and the stage lays open its recesses to the depth of
> a hundred feet for the procession to advance, even the most distant spectator
> can enjoy his shillings' worth of show.[29]

[25] Michael Burden, 'The lure of aria, procession and spectacle: opera in 18th-century London', in
Simon Keefe, ed., *The Cambridge History of Eighteenth-Century Music* (Cambridge University Press,
2009), 385–401.

[26] Anna Larpent's Diary, US-Cn HM 301201, I, 20 March 1792.

[27] F. Carlisle, *Thoughts of the Present Condition of the Stage* ... (London: W. Clarke, 1808), 4–5.

[28] R. Cumberland, *Memoirs of Richard Cumberland* (London: Lackington, Allen, and Co., 1806,
supplement, 1807), 57–8.

[29] Ibid.

But the necessity of doing something larger to fill these larger theatrical spaces was urgent, and the processions – seen in the table – had become more frequent and more elaborate. The type of changes that took place can be seen in one of the more popular processions of the later eighteenth century, that in David Garrick's *Cymon*, which appeared in versions of the play in 1767 and in 1793. Originally staged in 1767, this was an adaptation of a play by John Dryden. The procession opened with a march of knights of the different orders of chivalry, with enchanters, who arrange themselves in a semi-circle around the back of the stage; Merlin, Cymon, and Sylvia are brought forward in triumph by the Loves. The procession was designed to be followed immediately by a chorus, and the piece closed with a series of solos and choruses. However, in 1793 – that is, after all the theatre altera- tions had been made – the play's procession was much expanded, possibly to retain its effectiveness in the now larger auditorium.[30] No longer was it simply a confirmation of the virtue of Cymon and of his fitness to rule; it now became a bombastic event of immense proportions. The procession – now accompanied by warlike instrumental music – also included a number of onstage bands dispersed throughout the procession: four heralds with trumpets; a 'warlike band' of 18 performers; a double drum and cymbals; and another onstage band, to play a 'grand march'. Throughout the procession, the pit orchestra was given directions, including 'orchestra silent', 'soft music in the orchestra', and so on. When the procession was assembled, there followed a series of 'combats' – including a joust between an Englishman and Spaniard on white horses – which were accompanied by 'both the Orchestra and the Martial Band introduced in the Procession'. A speech by Merlin, and a chorale finale closed the opera. The outcome of the joust – the Englishman won, naturally – serves to emphasise that it was impossible to divorce even such operatic extravaganzas from notions of being 'British'.

Technically, then, the elements of the procession became more varied, and the scenarios more elaborate in content and more grandiose in conception. Thematically, they also began to change, coming in a greater variety of guises, two of the most easily defined being those that represented recent history, and those that represented exotic locations. Those that represented recent history can also be seen as part of a dual thrust, on the one hand, for the staging of historical events, where historical subjects gradually replaced the use of classical stories, and on the other, the desire for correctness in the staging itself. When these two priorities met,

---

[30] David Garrick, *Cymon; an opera* (London: T. Beckt, 1792), 50–4.

declarations of veracity could be long and loud, as they were in the case of *Old England forever; or Lord Howe and the glorious 1st of June*, with its 'grand procession from the dockyards'.

> Mr ASTLEY, sen. Most humbly submits a NAVAL SPECTACLE, founded on the Glorious Victory obtained over the FRENCH FLEET, on the First of June – he having been present at Portsmouth for the arrival of the British Fleet; and the Prizes taken from the Enemy; and having visited several of the same, and obtained every information, and sketches of the above important event, so highly honourable to the British Nation, as well as to Earl HOWE, and the brave Officers, Seamen, and Mariners under his authority. Mr. ASTLEY, having completed the whole for public representation, flatters himself it will not be unacceptable for his numerous visitors.[31]

On the actual appearance of the procession, the *True Briton* remarked:

> The Procession of Naval Heroes at *Sadler's Wells* is a good idea, and is so managed by the ingenuity of that Theatre as to keep the Spectators in a continued buzz of approbation while it passes before them. The explanatory banners contain a neat compendium of English Naval History, very happily introduced, and easily read and remembered.[32]

In amongst the flummery, we can observe that the procession had to be managed; it had to be paced to keep the public happy and engaged until it was over. This particular procession was, others agreed, a success:

> OLD ASTLEY has wisely brought [the famous battle of Lord Howe] out on the stage, and not in a slight manner as some things have been brought out at the ROYAL SALOON, but in one which would do honour to the first Manager of the first Theatre of the town. To see a sea-fight on shore, conducted on the manner this is, is beautiful and extraordinary, surpassing both our expectation and that of others. The views of the shattered ships at anchor, the procession at Portsmouth, and many other things too numerous to mention here, have a happy effect, and tend to prove that ASTLEY has done more for the public in this piece than he could ever flatter himself to perform.[33]

In these cases, the public had to believe what they were told – or not, as the case may have been. There were other instances, though, where the public would have been able to judge for themselves. In the case of the

---

[31] *World*, 23 June 1794.   [32] *True Briton*, 15 July 1794.
[33] *Oracle and Public Advertiser*, 20 June 1794.

thanksgiving service at St Paul's in 1789, Sadler's Wells got up a Grand Spectacle called *Britannia's Relief; or The gift of Hygeia*:

> In which would be introduced A Complete and exact-Representation of the ROYAL PROCESSION to St. PAUL's, as it appeared on the 23rd of April 1789.[34]

There does not appear to be an illustration of the street procession itself to give us some idea of what the theatre might have put on stage, although the event appears in a number of caricatures which do convey the general look. The St Paul's part of the procession was the subject of an official engraving, although this section of the proceedings seems an unlikely subject for the theatre, which seemed to favour the processions moving on and off the stage, rather than coming to a halt in the manner suggested here. These were examples of recent history, but theatrical interest was also focused on the history of the middle ages. One of the results of this interest was the staging of a procession in a piece relating to the death of David Rizzio, the Italian secretary to Mary, Queen of Scots. As it happened, not only did it tap into early modern history, it also tapped into the relatively new obsession with the history of Scotland, which on the stage would show itself in the next forty years with the numerous plays and operas based on the novels of Walter Scott.

The use of the exotic in processions offers a different theatrical imperative to those staging history, recent or otherwise, and although these categories overlapped, the exotic offered processions a number of possibilities that mere history could not. The exotic procession could include a number of different races, exotic musical instruments, and exotic landscapes to pass through. In doing so, it offered the possibility that both the procession as an activity, and the business contained therein, could be justified; it could be seen to be natural within the context of the procession. One of the most popular of these was that which appeared in the play *The Widow of Malabar*, by Mariana Starke, which premiered in 1790, and which played against the 1790s stagings of *Romeo and Juliet*. The play was advertised as having been:

> built upon the barbarous customs of the East, which induces widows to sacrifice themselves on the funeral pile of departed husbands.[35]

The critic went on to congratulate himself that:

---

[34] *Diary or Woodfall's Register*, 28 April 1790.   [35] *Whitehall Evening Post*, 4–6 May 1790.

> In the present case, however, the timely interposition of British humanity rescues the intended victim from the devouring flames.[36]

While this might be read as an example of British imperialism, the critic dryly comments that the same humanity consigned her 'to the less terrific fires of an ardent lover'. The procession of the play was advertised as 'Representing the Ceremonies attending a Sacrifice of an INDIAN WOMAN on the Funeral Pyre of her deceased Husband'.[37] Another such procession is, after those in *Romeo and Juliet* and *The Jubilee*, one of the best-known on the eighteenth-century stage. This appeared in John O'Keefe's *Omai; or, A Trip Round the World*. This was a work that grew up out of the immense popularity of, and interest in, the voyages of James Cook, and was written after Cook's death on Hawaii. The piece concluded with a procession that had representatives of all those countries which Cook has visited on his voyages. And for once, the playbook prints details of the procession, although not much about the performance itself. O'Keefe commented on this procession in his 1826 *Recollections*:

> At Barnes, I composed a grand spectacle for Covent Garden, called *Omai*; the incident, characters, &c., appropriate to the newly-discovered island in the southern hemisphere, and closing with the apotheosis of Captain Cook. The effect of this piece was most happy. Shield's melodies were beautifully wild, as suiting his romantic theme; and the dresses and the scenery were done from the drawings of Mr Webber, the artist who had made the voyages with Cook.[38]

Here we can see that the desire for historical accuracy meeting the desire to indulge in the exotic; the result was acceptable because it was accurate enough to reflect what was known of the islands, but exotic enough to entertain the London audience. And we should note that the music joined in; O'Keefe describes William Shields's music as 'beautifully wild, as suiting his romantic theme', an important remark given the dearth of both musical and performance information in this context. The popularity of the Cook tale was also responsible for the tragic pantomime ballet, *The death of Captain Cook*, with its own procession of mourning, a show that was played on the same bill as *Romeo and Juliet* on at least one occasion at Covent Garden in 1789.[39] The public did not lack processions to attend and enjoy.

---

[36] Ibid.   [37] *World*, 5 May 1790.
[38] J. O'Keefe, *Recollections of the Life of John O'Keefe*, in *New Monthly Magazine*, 16 (1826, part 1), 566.
[39] *World*, 7 December 1789.

And all the strands discussed here came together in attempts by the London theatre promoters to put aspects of the French revolution on the London stage. One of these was called *The fugitives; or, France in an uproar*, which opened at Sadler's Wells on 23 July 1791, and was described as an 'entire, new, sketch'. As in the case of *Old England forever*, it bought into the notion of correctness in staging modern history, and like *Old England forever*, Mr Astley claimed to have been there:

> Mr. ASTLEY, Sen. being in Paris during the attempt made by their Majesties of France to escape, begs leave to lay before the public an entire new Sketch, consisting of Music and Dancing, &c.[40]

Astley does stop short of claiming to have sketched the events and collected eyewitness statements, but the immediacy of his presence on the scene is still paramount in the construction of *The World*'s puff.

The advertisement lists the events of the piece, divided into 13 scenes. The procession, which closed the piece, represented that which 'attended their Majesties of France, on their return to Paris'. Quite what the audience members then made of being offered 'a Grand Heroic and Historical Pantomime ... called *The Siege of Quebec; or, The Death of General Wolf*' is, sadly, not recorded. Another work with a similar aim was Covent Garden's new pantomime, *The picture of Paris, taken in the year 1790*. The 'picture' of the title can be taken literally; the work's scenes were advertised as having been taken 'from accurate Drawings made on the Spot', and to include 'an exact Representation of the Banners, &c., in The Grand Procession to the Champs de Mars'.[41] Even on the usual scale of London procession, this particular one appeared particularly grandiose. It included the provincial deputies each bearing a standard presented by the *garde nationale* of Paris; the choristers of Notre Dame to assist in the performance of the Grand Mass, and to celebrate the honours of the Fete; separate detachments of the Paris Guards from several districts; incense burners; Vicars-general carrying scared books; and on, and on.[42] The event it portrayed, the celebration of mass, was held on the Champs de Mars, the former site of the Bastille, and celebrated by Bishop Talleyrand. It was part of the *Fete de la Federation* held on 14 July 1790, to mark the first anniversary of the fall of the Bastille. The event had its own sense of theatre without doubt, and the events were widely reported in London.

---

[40] *World*, 26 July 1791.   [41] *World*, 20 December 1790.

[42] R. Merry, *Airs, Duetts, and Chorusses, Arrangement of Scenery, and Sketch of the Pantomime, Entitled The picture of Paris* (London: T. Cadell, 1790).

Table 1 *Processions in London Theatres after 1798*

Title of the drama	Author of the drama	1st date with procession?	The procession	Theatre
Britannia's relief; or, The Gift of Hygea	☐	1789: 9/1	A complete and exact representation of the Procession to St Paul's, 23 April 1789.	SW
Romeo and Juliet (5 performances)	**Shakespeare**	1789: 9/12	**Juliet's funeral procession with the Solemn Dirge.**	CG
The Jubilee	Garrick, David	1789: 10/5	A pageant, music by Mr Dibdin.	SW
The Bastille	☐	1789: 10/6	The procession of the citizens on the day of Unon.	SW
The picture of Paris. Taken in the year 1790	Moore, Robert	1790: 12/20	Procession of the several orders and descriptions of people who assist at the ceremony of the Grand Federation.	CG
The Mandarin	☐	1790: 4/5	A Chinese procession.	SW
All for Love	☐	1790: 5/24	Between Acts two and three, will be introduced a Grand Procession.	CG
Widow of Malabar	☐	1790: 5/5	A prcoession representing the ceremonies attending a sacrifice of an Indian Woman on the funeral pyre of her deceased hsuband.	DL
French Jubilee	☐	1790: 7/30	Procession	RC
Nootka Sound; or, Britain prepared	☐	1790: 7/30	To conclude with a Grand Procession.	TRR
The critic	David Garrick	1790: 8/27	With a Grand Procesion.	DL
Romeo and Juliet (2 performances)	**Shakespeare**	1790: 9/13	**Juliet's funeral procession with the Solemn Dirge.**	CG

Table 1 (cont.)

Title of the drama	Author of the drama	1st date with procession?	The procession	Theatre
The rival magic; or, Harelquin's victory	☐	1791: 4/25	With a Grand Procession of Neptune and Amphitrite.	AA
Neptune's Levee	☐	1791: 4/25	A Grand Naval Procession of British Admirals, Naval Commanders, and Eminent Seaman.	SW
Tippoo Saib; or British valor in India	☐	1791: 5/27	With Grand Procession (later an Indian and British Grand Martial Procession).	CG
The Royal fugitive; or France in an uproar	☐	1791: 7/23	… a procession that attended their Majesties on their return to Paris.	AA
Romeo and Juliet (3 performances)	Shakespeare	1791: 9/26	Juliet's funeral procession with the Solemn Dirge.	CG
A procession	☐	1791: 10/31	To conclude with the defeat of the Aramada and a Grand Procession.	KT
Cymon	Garrick, David	1791: 12/31	A grand procession iof all the Orders of Chivalry.	DL/KT
An Allegorical Procession	☐	1792: 6/29	… consisitng of Song, Dance, Procession and Decoration.	SW
Romeo and Juliet (5 performances)	Shakespeare	1792: 10/8	Juliet's funeral procession with the Solemn Dirge.	CG
Columbus; or, a world discovered. An historical play.	Morton, Thomas	1792: 12/1	Procession of priests and archers, conducting Cora with Solasco.	CG
An allegorical divertissement (Fourth of June?)	☐	1792: 6/29	A procession.	SW

Title	Author / Composer	Description	Date	Venue
Iphiginia en Aulide, or the sacrifice of Iphiginia	Procession by Jean-Georges Noverre	The grand procession of Iphiginia into Aulide.	1793: 4/274	KT
Hall of Augusta; or, The land we live in	[]	With a Grand Commercial Procession.	1793: 4/3	SW
The shipwreck; or, French ingratitude	[]	A naval and military procession.	1793: 5/27	CG
Romeo and Juliet (3 performances)	**Shakespeare**	**Juliet's funeral procession with the Solemn Dirge.**	1793:10/7	CG
Don Giovanni	Gazzinga	A Grand Funeral procession according to the ancient customs of Spain.	1794: 1/3	KT
Romeo and Juliet (5 performances)	**Shakespeare**	**Juliet's funeral procession with the Solemn Dirge.**	1794: 10/20	CG
Hercules and Omphale	Byrne, Mr; William Shield	A Grand Hyemnal Procession (13 Nov for 150 soliders).	1794: 11/17	CG
Henry VIII	Shakespeare	A grand procession to the christening of Princess Elizabeth.	1794: 5/14	DL
The Brussels ridotto	[]	A procession of masques.	1794: 6/19	AA
The sons of Britannia; or, George for England	[]	A procession.	1794: 6/20	SW
Old England forever	[]	A procession of officers, etc from the dockyards.	1794: 6/23	SW
Naval triumph; or, The tars of Old England	[]	Earl Howe attended by a characteristic procession.	1794: 7/29	SW
Rule Britannia, a new musical entertainment	[]	An appropriate procession.	1794: 8/18	TRH
The Glorious First of June	Sheridan, Richard	A naval procession.	1794: 8/19	SW
Romeo and Juliet (7 performances)	**Shakespeare**	**Juliet's funeral procession with the Solemn Dirge.**	1795: 9/21	CG/DL

Table 1 (cont.)

Title of the drama	Author of the drama	1st date with procession?	The procession	Theatre
Merry Sherwood; or, Harlequin Forrester	[]	1795: 12/21	The Procession of the Triumphs of Archery.	CG
Alexander the Great; or, The conquest of Persia	Lee, Nathaniel	1795: 2/12	A Grand Hyemnal Procession from Hercules and Omphale.	CG
Alexander the Great; or, The conquest of Persia	Lee, Nathaniel	1795: 2/12	A procession.	DL
Lee's tragedy of Alexander	Lee, Nathaniel rev. J. P. Kemble	1795: 3/12	Alexander's Triumphal entry into Babylon.	DL
The Prince of Candia; or, the Royal Nutpials	[]	1795: 4/21	An emblematic procession of the Princes of Wales.	RC
Bonduca, Queen of the Britons	Beaumont and Fletcher	1795: 4/24	Funeral procession of a Roman Commander.	CG
Peleus and Thetis (masque in Windsor Castle)	Salamon, Johann	1795: 4/6	Procession of Peleus and Thetis to the High Altar.	CG
The Lord of the Manor (Procession 1)	[]	1795: 4/6	Processional Spectacle in honour of the Nuptial Day of an English Harvest Home.	SW
The Fall of Rizzio	[]	1795: 5/30	A procession of the Scottish Court on receiving an ambassador from Queen Elizabeth.	SW
The Lord of the Manor (Procession 2)	[]	1795: 5/4	The procession of the Wool Trade.	SW
The Death of Captain Faulknor; or, British heroism	[]	1795: 5/6	Procession of interment: Dead March, firing over the grave, 'Rule Britannia'.	CG

Title	Author	Date	Description	Theatre
Olympus in an uproar	□	1796: 5/15	A procession to a sacrifice.	CG
Cato	Addison, Joseph	1796: 5/31	A martial procession with the body of Marcus.	CG
Alonzo and Imogen	□	1796: 8/18	A decorated procession of knights.	SW
Romeo and Juliet (5 performances)	Shakespeare	1796: 9/19	**Juliet's funeral procession with the Solemn Dirge.**	CG/HAY/DL
Romeo and Juliet (11 performances)	Shakespeare	1797: 11/2	**Juliet's funeral procession with the Solemn Dirge.**	CG/DL
[An exhibition]		1797: 12/20	An accurate and faithful representation of the Royal procession from St James's to St Paul's.	RT
Harlequin Quixotte; or, The Magic Arm	Cross, Mr	1797: 12/26	A Chinese and European procession with the exchange of presents in the grand hall of audience.	SW
Raymond and Agnes; or the Castle of Lindenbergh	Farley, Charles	1797: 3/16	Procession of Nuns and Friars.	CG
Sadak and Kalasrade; or, The Waters of Oblivion	□	1797: 3/6	A superb procession.	SW
Chrononhotonthologos	Carey, Henry	1797: 4/10	A whimsical procession.	BH
The Village Fete	□	1797: 5/17	A rural procession.	CG
The School for Wives	□	1797: 5/22	A rural procession (possilby from Village Fete).	CG
Blue Beard; or, Female curiosity	Colman, George	1798: 1/16	A magnificent and picturesque procession.	DL
Blue-Beard; or, female curiosity!	Colman, George	1798: 1/16	Procession of Abomelique.	DL
Romeo and Juliet (5 performances)	Shakespeare	1798: 10/8	**Juliet's funeral procession with the Solemn Dirge.**	CG

Table 1 (cont.)

Title of the drama	Author of the drama	1st date with procession?	The procession	Theatre
Ramah Droog	Mazzinghi	1798: 11/12	A grand procession of the return of the Rajah from hunting the tiger.	CG
The knights of Malta; or, The midnight bell	□	1798: 11/9	Procession and installation of the Grand Knight of Malta.	RC
Albert & Adelaide, or the victim of constancy	Birch, Samuel, with music by Steibelt and Attwood.	1798: 12/11	Procession of Villagers.	CG
Aurelio and Miranda: a drama.	Boaden, James, music by Michael Kelly	1798: 12/29	A Procession of Friars and Nuns.	DL
May Day; or, The little gipsey	□	1798: 5/1	A rural procession.	CG
Bacchus et Ariadne	Gallet, Mr	1798: 5/9	A grand procession . . . by the corps de ballet.	KT
Romeo and Juliet (performances)	**Shakespeare**	**1799: 10/7**	**Juliet's funeral procession with the Solemn Dirge.**	**CG**
The volcano; or, The rival Harlequins	□	1799: 12/23	An allegorcial procession of the seasons, months, and hours.	CG
Almoran and Hamet; or, The fair circassian	□	1799: 3/15	A grand procession of Persians.	RC
The Four Engagements; or, the Heros of the Sea	□	1799: 3/26	A charcateristic procession of the four quarters of the world.	AA

Title	Author	Date	Description	Theatre
Telasco and Amghi; or, The Peruvian Nuptials	[ ]	1799: 5/14	With their religious processions.	DL
Pizarro; a tragedy	Kotzebue, August von	1799: 5/24	A solemn procession from the recess of the Temple . . .	DL
Rolla and Cora; or, The Virgin of the Sun	Kotzebue, August von	1799: 7/13	The exact procession which preceded Ataliba, Inca of Quinto.	RA
Romeo and Juliet (performances)	**Shakespeare**	1800: 10/6	**Juliet's funeral procession with the Solemn Dirge.**	CG
The bridal spectre; or, Alonzo and Imogene	[ ]	1800: 11/3	A superb and decorated procession of the crusades of Palestine.	NR
Harlequin Amulet; or, The magic of Mona	[ ]	1800: 12/22	A grand procession in celebration of St David's Day.	DL
The Magic Flute; or, Harlequin Champion	[ ]	1800: 6/23	A splendid and appropriate procession of Equestrian Knights.	NRC
The Pirate; or, Harlequin Victor	Astley, Junior	1800: 8/25	A grand nautical procession.	AA

A Counterpoint with *Romeo and Juliet*

Romeo and Juliet – with its included procession – was wildly popular. With its procession, it appeared thereafter in every London theatrical season of the eighteenth century. And in its repeated success lay the seeds of the success of the procession; its different types and functions can be found at all venues, and in all shapes and sizes from the 1750s, and throughout that period, they ran in counterpoint, of course, to the procession in *Romeo and Juliet*, which, as the table shows, continued to be performed even after the larger events staged after 1789. But ultimately (and predictably) such grandiose theatrical events were seen as (yet another) example of the decline in the standards of opera and drama in England. Cumberland saw it in almost Jonsonian terms, a situation in which the poet's efforts were seen as entirely secondary to those of the scene builder and the machinist, while a despairing Richard Bacon Mackenzie complained that opera was being used as 'a vehicle for combats or processions', and the genre was never allowed to be 'a combination of the beauties of all the arts'.[43] Indeed, remarks made on 'Alexander's Triumphal entry into Babylon' in Kemble's revision of Lee's *Alexander* sum up a whole slew of commentary: 'we would recommend it to the manager to keep some of his horses in stable, for they take from, in place of adding to, the effect.'[44] In search of verisimilitude, the author did, though, go on to comment on the historically inaccurate reins and stirrups used in the show. But – as I have written elsewhere[45] – it would be a mistake to think that because of such criticism, the drama itself was worthless; as the critic writing in *The Theatrical Repertory* commented of Prince Hoare's *Chains of the Heart*, 'the opera before us, considered merely as the vehicle for song and spectacle, is far from wanting in its recommendations.'[46]

---

[43] R. B. Mackenzie, 'On the construction of operas', *Quarterly Musical Magazine*, 3 (1821), 177–85.
[44] *Sun*, 12 February 1795.   [45] Burden, 'The lure of aria, procession and spectacle', 399.
[46] *Theatrical Repertory*, 14 December 1801, 197.

CHAPTER II

The Music for Henry V in Victorian Productions by Kean and Calvert

Val Brodie

In the Victorian era, music was an indispensable ingredient of theatre. The orchestra in front of the stage framed the performance, focussed the audience's attention, and established the temperature of the drama with melodic and instrumental colouration. Frequently, at key moments, music whipped up intense audience response and reaction in short, mood-defining passages (often called *melos*); it underlined, with appropriate key choice and structure, the characterisation of the protagonists and magnified, with underscoring, the tonal delivery of the actors. Orchestral sound pervaded performance, counterbalancing pictorially-realistic scenery and providing the soundscape to feed the imagination and lead the emotional response. In a century when art music's classical restraints of form were broken by Beethoven, Liszt, Wagner and others in favour of poetic imagery, rhapsodic descriptive structures and romantic outpourings of feeling, theatre music drew on the same *zeitgeist*. In their influential productions of *Henry V*, both Charles Kean and Charles Calvert used free-flowing and ebullient music.

In a ragged musical history, where most scores of *Henry V* (even in the twentieth century) have been lost or fragmented, those of Kean and Calvert are the oldest in existence, and are the only scores to survive from the many Victorian productions of the play. Kean cut 1500, and Calvert 1200, lines from the text in order to introduce spectacle, dance, choral singing and song, which, together with omnipresent instrumental music, was not merely a fashionable accessory to an evening in the theatre, but was a dominating and interpretative aspect of performance. Both began with a substantial overture but otherwise the musical choices of the two actor-managers were radically different. Kean responded to the immediacy of the plot within a framework that had its roots in early nineteenth-century techniques, using classical tunes, neat marches, historically-sourced anthems, rushing passage work in entr'actes, melodramatic crisis chords and refined Mendelssohnian-style melody. Calvert rejected this style and instead enveloped his *Henry V* with the weightier orchestral and choral sound of fashionable Italian opera. This was an emotional coupling of a medieval patriotic English conquest on French soil with the idiom and fervour of nationalistically-influenced contemporary Italian opera. Both Kean's and Calvert's scores not only show the nature of the orchestral effects but, considered together with the prompt books and play bills, reveal the cut and interplay of music with the text, the dominance of the music in certain scenes and, most significantly, a powerful choral dimension that has frequently been overlooked by scholars.

Charles Kean's Music for *Henry V*

Kean's production of *Henry V* at the Princess's Theatre, London in 1859 was the culmination of a style he had introduced during his sequence of Shakespeare plays which began in 1850. In *Henry VIII* (1853) he introduced 'festivals, masquerades, processions, and dances [and] mythological tableaux and supernatural appearances' which was a new approach 'unimagined and unattempted by ... his predecessors'.[1] Kean chose spooky music, redolent of popular melodrama for his revival of *Hamlet* (1855) which was notable for the 'impressive and majestic ghost'.[2] Sheep and goats, borrowed from a zoo, inhabited *The Winter's Tale* (1856) together with Greek music and dancing at the banquet, sweet pastoral songs and dances, a wild procession of noisily-tramping peasants and maskers, and Hermione (Mrs Charles Kean) descended from the temple, as she said, to 'great effect – depending on the music'.[3] Theodor Fontane, who saw *Richard II* (1857) was impressed by a scene when the king was led into the city, which 'brought onstage ... genuine London life and bustle'.[4] Here Kean employed six hundred supers, dummy horses and pealing church bells in a long, music-led Episode, a theatrical device he would use again in *Henry V*. In *Macbeth* (1858) he used complex effects – the trio of witches vocalised grimly in *recitativo secco*, and a SATB choral group was placed high in the flies above the stage to achieve supernatural effects.[5]

[1] J. W. Cole, *The Life and Times of Charles Kean, F.R.S.*, 2 vols (London: Richard Bentley, 1859), II, 342.
[2] *The Illustrated London News*, 6 Jan 1855, 11a.
[3] M. Glen Wilson, Letter from Mrs Kean to Edward Saker in 'Edward Saker's Revivals and Charles Kean: An Addendum', *Theatre Notebook*, vol. 34 (1980), 18–21.
[4] T. Fontane, *Shakespeare in London Theatre: 1855–58*, trans. and ed., R. Jackson (London: Society for Theatre Research, 1999), 52.
[5] All of Kean's Shakespeare scores are in the Folger Shakespeare Library.

It becomes apparent that when he approached *Henry V*, at the peak of his career, Kean was accomplished, imaginative, innovative and versatile in his use of theatre music.

The methodology involved in nineteenth-century theatre-music research at times involves a forensic aural archaeology involving close examination of minutiae in the score to reveal details which may not be apparent from other sources. For example, as Act One ended the king urged: 'Let our proportions for these wars / Be soon collected ... We'll chide this Dauphin at his father's door' (1.2. 304–8); Kean added an extra scene, not in the prompt book, marked on the manuscript 'Scene 3rd March on Stage' which revealed the army massed with 'Drum on stage'. To the accompaniment of tub-thumping, militaristic wind music, his army of supers gave a marching display as a culmination to the act. When the music is performed it establishes the duration, aural flavour and dramatic dominance of the event. None of this is ever a precise science since speed can only be estimated, and the modish qualities of instrumental performance (*vibrato, portamento, rubato*) may only be guessed at, but revivifying the music allows us to begin to understand a production where music played a crucial and defining role.

Kean frequently used his orchestra for rushing entr'actes that covered scene changes but, on occasion, he used it as an interpretative tool. This is well illustrated in his treatment of the French. Whilst English fanfares in 2/4 were solid, predictable and militaristically reliable – *left right! left right!* – the French marched in 3/4 time – <u>*one*</u> *two three* / <u>*one*</u> *two three* – a timing more associated with dancing. It is an unflattering military portrait suggesting effeminacy. Equally, before the battle the French are witnessed complacently anticipating success with their monarch surrounded by gentle music (a 9/8 serenade, sweetly set on the flat side with delicate birdsong in the flutes), an atmosphere suggesting that the king had no appetite for war. In this portrait of an effete king, Kean engendered a xenophobic disdain towards the French that caught the contemporary mood of the British. Antipathy to the old enemy abounded in the 1850s, and Palmerston's government was brought down in 1858 by issues concerning French aristocratic émigrés and their plots. The musical portrait reaffirmed an English contempt for the French, an approach built on in later productions.

Playbills outlined the dramatic intentions of the actor managers and in the cut-throat, market-led, theatrical business that was the nineteenth-century commercial theatre, Kean's musical content was advertised with panache. Striving for authenticity, he claimed to use 'ancient airs . . . anterior to the date of Henry the Fifth' and, eager to reassure clients of the quality and splendour of the sound, he added: 'To give effect to the music, fifty singers have been engaged.'[6] Kean made dramatic use of his singers when, after the battle, the king called for religious rites; he made his interpretation explicit in the italicised stage directions:

> Let there be sung 'Non Nobis' and 'Te deum'
> The dead with charity enclosed in clay:
> We'll then to Calais; and to England then;
> Where ne'er from France arrived more happy men.
> *[Organ music; all kneel, and join in Song of Thanksgiving]*[7]

(4.8.120–124)

Eight bars of hymn-like wind music marked *Andante Religioso*, created an impression of organ music, before the kneeling cast sang *Alta Trinita Beata*, an ancient Italian hymn of praise to the Holy Trinity (Example 2).

This intense, meditative, four-part setting was sung unaccompanied and it created an extra-textual, vocal ending to the act: it was raw, quiet and manly, and within the artifice of theatricality, real. Kean focused on the religiosity and the severity of medieval Catholicism in the king's words, and he engaged his audience with how those men who survived the battle felt. There was no concluding burst of curtain music. It is a pause for thanksgiving rather than a celebration of victory and the slow, densely-harmonic setting of the old melody extended the emotional peak of the drama beyond the ending of the text. It was a strikingly expressive *coup de théâtre*.

Michael Burden's essay describes the origins of the introduction of spectacular processions. Kean turned ambitiously and imaginatively to this extra-textual device in what he termed The Episode which portrays the scene briefly described by the Chorus before Act Five: 'London doth pour forth her citizens . . . The Mayor and all his brethren . . . fetch their conquering Caesar in' (5.0.24–28). Kean's scenario is musically driven, and well constructed as the crowds noisily gathered on the streets to celebrate a national victory. An illustration from Kean's Episode showing King Henry, on a white horse centre stage surrounded by timbrell-waving ballet girls, has frequently been used by theatre historians to define and embody

---

[6] C. Kean, Playbill, *Henry V*, Princess's Theatre, London, 9 March 1859.
[7] C. Kean, *Henry V* (London: John K. Chapman, 1859), 74.

Music Example 2   Kean, 'Thanksgiving after the battle', transcribed from orchestral
score, Folger Shakespeare Library.

their concept of pictorial realism.[8] Here was music on a scale to equal the
grandeur of the scenery.

Kean's composer/musical director was Bernard Isaacson, an experienced orchestral leader and composer of melodrama in the theatre. He
created an imaginative score for the Episode, boldly experimenting with
instrumentation to create specific effects. The sequence is continuous
and begins with the sounds of low-life revels on the streets. First the
distinctive sound of a bagpiper (oboe above a drone of two bassoons in
open fifths, with 'gracing' appoggiaturas) in a lively 2/4 as he walked
around, next, a traditional one-man-band pipe and tabor (flute, double-
stopped pizzicato violin and drum) playing a simple 6/8 dance tune.
As the scene gathered momentum, a brilliant fanfare of four trumpets
signalled the arrival of civic dignitaries in glamorous robes, accompanied

---

[8] F. Lloyds, a watercolour from the stage designs of William Telbin (1859) reproduced in, amongst
many others, T.W. Craik, ed., *King Henry V* (London: Thompson, 2005), 85.

with all pomp and stateliness by a long and solid *maestoso* march, thickly
orchestrated with an abundance of percussion. A medieval chronicler,
who claimed to have been at Agincourt said: '[W]hen the wished-for
Saturday dawned, the citizens went forth to meet the King ... trumpets,
clarions, and horns, sounded in various melody ... behind the Tower
were innumerable boys, representing angels, arrayed in white ... at the
King's approach sang with melodious voices, and with organs, an English
anthem.'[9] Kean followed the essence of this description and, as the long
procession reached Tower Bridge, the fifteenth-century *Agincourt Song*
rang out, sung by twenty young choristers dressed as angels, situated high
on the archway.[10] The song had been included in William Chappell's
Popular Music of Olden Times (1858) which may have been Isaacson's
source. The lightly scored introduction and accompaniment for woodwind (oboe, clarinets, and bassoons) again gave an impression of 'organs'
and although the original melody is medieval in outline, Isaacson
used nineteenth-century harmonies, not Dorian modality, removing
the lowered leading notes. After three repeats a fuller orchestration
of strings and high flutes was added and mature voices joined in.
Here was a lively, bright and ancient anthem of welcome for the arrival
of the medieval king. Next, in light triple-time, winged ballet girls,
flimsily-clad with naked arms and showing their ankles, danced
before the king. Inclusion of ballet was not unusual; as a cartoonist in
The Day's Doings later observed: 'Shakespeare spells ruin but "legs" mean
dividends.'[11] The display was an overt appeal to popular taste.
The Episode came to a climax with a grandiose, choral rendering of
another old melody, *Chanson Roland*, accompanied by a throbbing full
orchestra. A prominent trumpet rang out over an orchestral *maestoso*
march as the hero of Agincourt received the keys of the city from the
Lord Mayor, and the complex scene ended with shouts of 'Long Live the
King'. Kean cited the words of the chronicler on his playbill: 'A greater
assembly, or a nobler spectacle, was not recollected to have been seen ever
before in London.' This extra-textual scene, lasting nearly half an hour,
was the climax of the show. Afterwards the diplomacy of Act Five was
briskly concluded and the performance ended with a short march to
bring the curtain down.

[9] Sir H. Nicolas, trans., *History of the Battle of Agincourt; And the Expedition of Henry The Fifth into France, in 1415* (London: Johnson, 1833), in C. Kean, *Henry V*, vii.
[10] C. Kean, *Promptbook* signed 'Edmunds' 1859, 84, Harvard Theatre Collection, reel 011.
[11] 'The Days' Doings' (1870) quoted in T. C. Davis, *Actresses as Working Women* (London: Routledge, 1991), 111.

Charles Calvert's Music for *Henry V*

Calvert's *Henry V* opened at Prince's Theatre, Manchester, in 1872 and transferred to Booth's Theatre, New York, in 1875 from which a score survives in the New York Public Library. A piano reduction also exists in a vast commemorative album of the production presented by Mrs Charles Calvert to the Shakespeare Memorial Library in 1903. It was a high-profile production and Calvert invested in a large cast of 'instrumentalists, singers, dancers and two hundred supers'.[12] His playbill advertised 'A powerful and well-selected chorus [and] numerous corps de ballet' and his musical choices impressed the press:

> The incidental music certainly adds very much to the general effect … selections calculated to intensify the interest of the various scenes, to heighten in several instances the local colouring … The illustrations are taken chiefly from the less familiar works of several well-known Italian composers … Mercadante's *Il Giuramente*, Donizetti's *Parisina*, Rossini's *Tancredi* and Verdi's *Macbeth*.[13]

Edward Williams, Calvert's original composer/director, re-orchestrated the operatic extracts, turning them from arias or lightly-accompanied ensembles into solid orchestral pieces or choruses with orchestra. The production toured internationally, with new conductors and cuts and changes, before returning to England in 1879, when George Rignold, by then heading the company, advertised a 'full and efficient London Company … as produced throughout the world'. When finally the production returned to the north and Williams again took up the baton, Mancunians, accustomed to high-quality music-making in their city, were assured that it contained 'the original music' suggesting that the infusion of opera pleased audiences.

Calvert drew knowledgeably and subtly on opera, adapting more than thirty extracts. At Harfleur, he used the march from Rossini's *Tancredi* (1813), 'Plaudite o Populo', which was an evergreen in Victorian home music-making. He introduced lesser-known, delicate serenades from Donizetti's *Parisina* (1833) to surround the Princess's lesson and demilitarised the persona of the king, when he came to woo, using tender music from Mercadante's *Il Giuramento* (1837). The genre of Italian opera with its tender, decorative settings, and big tunes with warm harmonies and

---

[12] Mrs C. Calvert, *Autobiography: Sixty-Eight Years in the Theatre* (London: Mills and Boon, 1911), 139.
[13] C. Calvert, *Opinions of the Press, Henry the Fifth as Produced under the Direction of Charles Calvert* (Manchester: A. Ireland, 1872), 9.

Music Example 3 Calvert, no. 14, 'Larghetto', transcribed from orchestral score,
New York Public Library.

surging rhythmical accompaniments, was at the time popular in the
theatre, the concert hall, the music hall and the home. Yet in Italian
opera, generally one style fitted all circumstances, and the music did not
evolve from the specifics of each particular drama. This saga of the English
medieval king was set in a musically similar vein to that which surrounded
the Jews in Verdi's *Nabucco* (1841) or the Swiss peasants in Rossini's
William Tell (1829).

Within this style, Calvert, like Kean, musically engendered an unflatter-
ing response to the French. Although he did not inflict 3/4 marching on his
French soldiers, he surrounded the French king with languid music.
Calvert went further than Kean and turned the pre-battle scene with the
Dauphin (4.2) into a male drinking den. The scene began with a drowsy
9/8 Italianate barcarolle (Example 3), adapted from an intimate female duet
'Dolce conforto al misero' in Mercadante's *Il Giuramento*. This was sung
by boy choristers in the Rococo surroundings of the Dauphin's pink-
encrusted tent, a venue more redolent of the Paris Opera House than
battle headquarters.

Next, manly glee-singing of 'Who is Sylvia?' (the only non-operatic
music in the score) with lyrics transplanted from *Two Gentlemen of Verona*
(4.2.38–53), was followed by lively ballet music and more sensuous singing
from the boys whilst the Dauphin, and his cronies, drank and played dice.
In sharp contrast to the muscular 4/4 marches and pre-battle prayers of the
English, it offered, musically, a critique of the French courtiers. It served to

Music Example 4 Calvert, no. 20, 'More will I do', transcribed from orchestral
score, New York Public Library.

underline the blasé indolence of the time-wasting French, who with their dubious pastimes suggested that there was little to be done to achieve success in battle. The scene offered the audience the gratuitous enjoyment of a night-club atmosphere which was developed further by directors after Calvert.

From the luxury of the French tent, the scene changed to the grim, war-scarred English lines. In a long stark scene, with the text uninterrupted by music, the king met Bates and company and debated with them the issues of kingship, before his long soliloquy 'Upon the king' (4.1.218–93). As Henry offered up remorseful prayers for the murder of Richard II, and finally determined on action, Calvert made a significant departure from traditional treatment of the moment. Actors from Kemble to Kean, stirred to action on the point 'More will I do', leapt up as a single trumpet sounded. Calvert dwelt on Henry's mental distress and used the frenetic murder music 'Fatal mia donna!' from Verdi's *Macbeth* (1847) to capture his state of mind. (Example 4)

In the opera, having committed the slaughter off-stage, Macbeth returns, terrified by his actions, to sing, with his wife, this frantic, fast and melodi-cally-tight duet in F minor. It is a musical portrayal of criminality and guilt with a repetitive figuration in the second violins wrapped chromatically around the dominant C, disturbing the tonality. Williams broadened Verdi's narrow orchestral tessitura and gave the agitated second-violin texture also to violas, cellos and low woodwind, transcribed the vocal lines for piercingly-high woodwind (including piccolo), trumpets and

Music Example 5 Calvert, no. 24, 'More happy men', transcribed from orchestral
score, New York Public Library.

first violins, and punctuated the whole with bass and percussion. It began
quietly under the last few lines of text and, growing in volume, surrounded
the king in a whirlwind of melodramatic, fear-inspiring sound, extending
the mood and emotional climate well after the speech had ended.

In contrast to Kean, Calvert's approach to the post-battle scene was
joyous, and celebratory. His music cast aside the weight of mourning and
emphasised not the 'dead . . . enclos'd in clay', nor the 'holy rites', but the
'happy men' who knelt to sing a romping, Italianate chorus accompanied
by full orchestra (Example 5). No words for the song survive, or any
definite indication if it was sung in parts, but scribbled on the margins of
the orchestral score is a note 'Chorus of Monks – to be harmonized' which
suggests that part-singing was planned.

This powerfully-arching, double-dotted melody over a turgid
triplet-driven accompaniment surges forward supported by strong
harmonies and a booming bass. This chorus arrested the dramatic
action, and any potential ambiguity of audience response to war and
of victory were suppressed by music of dominating, stirring but
monochromatic emotional character. This is one of several instances
where Calvert imposed the weight of an emotionally-charged operatic
chorus to close a scene.

Calvert's Episode structurally and visually copied Kean, but musically
it lacked the earlier actor-manager's subtlety and dramatic finesse.
Calvert grafted together four marches and it has the feeling, as in many
operas of the period, that the action drew to a halt to give time for dance

and spectacle before the dénouement. But in a significant contrast to Kean's climactic Episode, Calvert shaped the performance differently, building towards an Espousal scene, a structural innovation which was to be copied and developed by directors for the coming twenty-five years.

The text of *Henry V* is male-dominated but Calvert's cutting and reallocation of speeches in Act Five, and his extended Espousal scene, altered the emotional climate of the ending of the play so that women played an important role. Whereas Kean cut the princess's lesson and a crisp, military march concluded the peace negotiations, offering a straightforward portrait of kingly duty, Calvert opened Act Five with the princess's lesson followed by the wooing, and ended with a royal wedding and joyous music, in the surroundings of Troyes Cathedral. Royal nuptials were a regular feature of public life (six of Victoria's off-spring married between 1858 and 1879) and Calvert expressed the joining in matrimony of Henry and Katherine in contemporary terms. After a splendid, choral, royal entry procession, Calvert cut and reordered the dialogue to give a prominent role to the French Queen. She opened the final scene 'So happy be the issue ... this day/ Shall change all griefs and quarrels into love', welcomed her future son-in-law and optimistically emphasised the personal element in this international bargain (5.2. 12–20). Appealing to an audience which had been ruled by a strong matriarch for almost forty years, the foregrounding of the queen in the marital dénouement and the choice of warm affirmative vocal music, were key elements in Calvert's refashioning of this final scene. It was an empow-erment of the French queen, whose final speech became a valediction by a mother and a queen, emphasising both the religious and personal importance of matrimony in the joining of the kingdoms. After her final words: 'That English may as French, French Englishmen / Receive each other – God speak this Amen!' the whole assembly sang the uplifting chorus 'In exitu' from Mercadante's *Il Guiramente* as the Espousal took place (Example 6).

Shakespeare's epilogue was cut, and the harsh reality of warfare and arranged marriage was musically subsumed in a wash of luscious harmony and the affecting emotional climate generated by massed singing.

Kean developed Shakespearian performance to a new level of complexity and spectacle using music in a dominating and interpretative role. The soundscape has been overlooked by scholars who have focused on his pictorial realism. Calvert built on Kean's shaping of the text, adding an extended feminised ending. Calvert's interlacing of text with a weighty

Music Example 6 Calvert, no. 42, 'To end scene', transcribed from piano
reduction, Shakespeare Birthplace Library and Archive.

wash of Italian opera created a hybrid genre. It extended moments of
emotional response beyond the text and tilted the dramatic high points
towards the climaxes of the music. Like Calvert, later actor-managers used
grandiose music, but none copied his reliance on Italian opera.

The Legacy of Kean and Calvert

There are only fragmentary musical indicators, and no scores, from the following decades when the craze for the medieval king was pursued by, amongst others, John Coleman (1876), Osmond Tearle (1891), Frank Benson (1897), Lewis Waller (1900), Richard Mansfield (1900) and later John Martin Harvey (1916). There is no reason to suppose that, for most of this time, music played a lesser part, for the outward signs – programmes, reviews, photographs, contemporary comment and fragments of music – indicate that there was little deviation from the pursuit of a grand style, with pictorial settings, large numbers of actors, supers, dancers, singers, and substantial orchestras. The innovations of Kean and Calvert were copied and enthusiastically embroidered.

Coleman turned to Isaacson for music for his revival at the Queen's Theatre, London (1876). He added extracts of *2 Henry IV* as a 'Prologue' and included a cornet fantasia *Henry Prince of Wales*. Fashionable musically accompanied tableaux were a recurrent feature of Coleman's production and his final wedding setting was fancifully entitled 'The Lion of England and the Lily of France'. Osmond Tearle (touring in 1891) engaged Samuel Potter to compose and arrange music for the 'pageants and spectaculars', and a large chorus to sing 'chants, dirges, and triumphal hymns', and he too lists a grand procession for the added coronation scene. In his Theatre Royal, Manchester, programme he paid a generous tribute to Calvert's influence, then aggrandising his ending, he brought the princess into the Episode (as a trophy of victory or a romantic alliance?) and he joined the Episode and Espousal for what he hoped would be an even more spectacular 'grand and fitting climax'.

In New York, Mansfield's *Henry V* at the Garden Theatre (1900) resonated with the delights witnessed twenty-five years earlier in Calvert's production. The *New York Times* (4 October 1900) declared 'Mansfield triumphs as the Warlike Harry' and staging standards were likened to Meininger and Bayreuth. The score is lost but, according to Mansfield's published version of the text, the Episode echoed Kean's structure and the Espousal was an elaborate religious scene with chorally-accompanied processions and as the ceremony concluded, a 'Joyous Gloria' rang out.

In the same year, the eminent musician Raymond Rôze, who worked regularly with Herbert Beerbohm Tree, composed a new score for Waller's London production. All the music is lost except the grandiloquent, long, secular *Wedding March* which survives in organ transcription (Example 7).[14]

---

[14] Raymond Rôze, *Wedding March for Organ* (London: Boston Music, 1910),

Music Example 7 Waller, *Wedding March for organ* by Raymond Rôze, transcribed
from copy in British Library

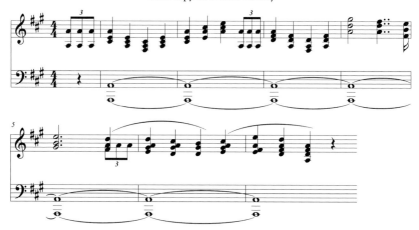

Rôze's music does not reverberate with the formality of a union arising
from diplomatic determinants or with the aura of military conquest but,
with a grand introduction, *cantabile* melodies, exaggerated climaxes and
allargando cadences, it speaks of the strength of a Victorian public appetite
for emotional expression in music, family values, marriage, and royalty.
It was ten years after Waller's première in 1900, whilst the production was
still being revived in London, that Rôze's *Wedding March* was published in
an organ arrangement underlining a public interest in the celebrity of both
the theatre and royal marriages.

There was an enduring popularity for a sexy French pre-battle scene;
it was an excuse for the inclusion of young, flimsily-dressed, female
performers which added a frisson of decadence and titillation. Coleman
made his intentions quite clear: 'Orgie [sic] in the Dauphin's tent'
although details are lost. Mansfield included ballet – 'Danse Antique' an
elegant and seductive French gavotte by the popular Broadway composer
Max S. Witt – which suggests that Mansfield too knew the commercial
value of 'legs'.[15] According to Mansfield's biographer, he knew the 'peculiar
value of music ... in association with the drama ... vocal and
instrumental ... arousing lively delight and winning wholehearted
applause'.[16] Mansfield's pre-battle French scene ended with a 'Night

[15] M. S. Witt, *Henry V: Danse Antique* (London: Joseph Stern, 1900). Max. S. Witt *Henry V: Dances
[sic] Antique* (New York: Jos. W. Stern, 1900).
[16] W. Winter, *Life and Art of Richard Mansfield* (New York: Moffat, 1910), 247.

Song' about whose expressive qualities, in the absence of a score, we may only guess.

Frank Benson's production (1897 touring until 1916) used less music than the earlier productions (no Episode or Espousal) although he did not stint in the French pre-battle scene where he introduced populist elements of music hall and operetta.[17] Casting soloists as French 'camp followers' a soprano sang a provocative waltz song about the pleasures of love and drink, and a scantily clad dancer performed an exotic Moorish dance. However, tastes change and Benson's touch of *la belle époque* was criticised by the Stratford Herald (28 July 1911) as 'dallying ... not consistent with Shakespearean precedent'.

Michael Pisani has pointed out that in the 1910s the grandiose style began to 'unravel'.[18] This is illustrated by productions of *Henry V* which used fewer extras, simpler scenery, and music of smaller dimensions that interacted eloquently and reflectively with the text. Adding lyrics by Charles Dalman, John Martin Harvey (1916) included a *Soldiers' Chorus*: 'Plenty of beef and plenty of ale/and maidens fair to see / never will fail/to please the likes of me', which democratised war and told of a soldier's earthly needs of food, drink and sex.[19] It brought the issue of conflict into the twentieth century and it would have resonated with an audience whose sons were fighting on French soil. The incomplete Benson score, and the tattered, much-adapted orchestral parts, show significant changes in his long-running production. Ralph Vaughan Williams, his musical director in 1912/13, replaced the seductive waltz song with French folk tunes, and altered the finale by removing a jingoistic, breezy march. Pasted onto the instrumental parts, in the composer's hand, is a meditative hymn-like ending which changed, aurally, the ethos of the ending.[20] This intimate, rich, soulful and harmonically-modal music placed in question any sense of triumphalism within the sorrow and strife of war. With European conflict on the horizon, this was a seismic shift from the euphoric finales of the turn of the century, and it ushered in the modern era.

---

[17] F. Benson, *Henry V*, 1897, incomplete scores and parts, SCLA.

[18] M. V. Pisani, *Music for the Melodramatic Theatre in Nineteenth-Century London and New York* (Iowa: University of Iowa press, 2014), 312.

[19] J. M. Harvey, *Soldiers' Chorus in Henry V* (words only), Bristol Theatre Collection.

[20] Val Brodie, *The Overlooked Evidence*, Unpublished PhD thesis, University of Birmingham, 2013, 212–27.

CHAPTER 12

In Practice III
Listening to the Pictures – an Interview with Composer Stephen Warbeck

Bill Barclay

Stephen Warbeck, winner of several awards, including an Oscar for Shakespeare In Love, *and notable for three decades of scores for all the major London theatres, speaks to co-editor Bill Barclay while in production for* The Tempest *in the Globe's Sam Wanamaker Playhouse.*

How did you get started writing music for plays?
I read French and Drama at Bristol, though I had mostly spent my time as an actor and a musician. Coming towards the end of university, Sue Lefton, a choreographer, asked me what I was going to do with myself, and I said, 'I'm going to write music for theatre.' Not really knowing how I was going to do that, she suggested I make some tapes. So I wrote some sad pieces, some slightly happier pieces, made four cassettes with three musicians, sent them off, and one person replied at Theatre Royal Stratford East and offered me a job as musical director and actor in a community tour. In the early bit of my career from 1977–85 I was asked to be in the plays as well, because a lot of the work I was doing for the regional theatres didn't have a budget for a composer. So you'd be the composer, music director and, say, the wicked landlord. I started to get quite an entertaining picture of what it's like to be an actor/musician. You play a few songs and you have to pop up from behind the piano and sing *When This Lousy War Is Over*, get shot, sit back down and keep playing. In 1985, I felt like I was getting slightly less quality music jobs and slightly less good acting jobs. I wasn't going to be Hamlet and I wanted to be more in control of the shape of my career and creative decisions.

Was there a moment when you simply decided not to act anymore?
At some point my agent said, 'What are you? I don't know how to sell you or advance your career. Are you an actor? A composer, or music director?' Slightly annoyingly in retrospect, he said I had to decide. Around that time

I had a very stressful job in Manchester with a lot of synthesisers and click tracks. I was the piano MD but had to start all the musicians and the recorded tracks together and keep everything in time. I noticed I had actually stopped enjoying being a music director and increasingly enjoyed sitting in the auditorium – or if it's film, in the control room – manipulating things, really seeing what effect your work is having. It was nice and sad at the same time – you get a better and more objective perspective but you're not a music director anymore and you miss actually making the work. The insight that performing as an actor had given me has been very useful however, because I feel as though I experience rehearsals from the inside. Composing for plays and being in them I think gives me a sort of visceral empathy with actors. In theatre you're so exposed to somebody's performance, and at its best that bypasses an intellectual thing and goes straight into some empathetic response that really helps me with the music.

Do you think that deeper sense of empathy from your experiences as an actor connects you to films you're working on as well?
It can and I think when it doesn't you're in very big trouble. Usually the pieces of my film or television work that I'm most proud of have triggered some sort of large emotional connection. Last year, Richard Eyre directed the Henry IVs as part of *The Hollow Crown* for the BBC, and there were a few very important facets of that collaboration to me. First of all, Richard Eyre is a remarkable director, slightly out of the mould of a lot of film and television directors in that he trusts you with a job so he values your contribution. Occasionally now there's a micro-management of every aspect of your work: 'Does that tune really have to go down there?' etc., and you're being questioned on every crochet and bar line, but Richard's not like that. I felt a wave of empathy for Falstaff played by Simon Russell Beale because I suddenly felt how needy and desperate Falstaff was and that gave me a genuine way into it because it made the music more about love and pain. The other very interesting thing about Richard was one of the guidelines he gave me for the battle music. I slightly dread battles because it's all so choreographed and they say, 'Could we have a crash when he does that sword there' etc., and you think, 'I've already done that, god how can I make another big impact on that moment,' etc., but Richard said 'No, let's do the beauty.' So in fact you're showing the other side of the coin. The battle becomes more about the emotion of what was lost in war, all those lives and families destroyed. That's what I could relate to emotionally.

In the case of *Shakespeare in Love* you had Gwyneth Paltrow speaking Shakespeare's verse on the stage for the first time and that moment the camera gets in close on Joe Fiennes' face, all the emotions between the characters suddenly begin to come alive. You don't literally start to feel exactly what the character feels but as soon as it touches that part in you, the music's fine. And the music starts to apparently write itself, but obviously it doesn't. Somewhere you've decided it's going to be D minor and of course fifty percent of film scores at the moment will then go to B flat. And that's what everybody would like it to do because it gives a little ray of hope. As in Spinal Tap, D minor was to be the saddest of all keys, yes?

So what happens when you accept a project based on a different factor, say it's a director you like but then the footage doesn't move you?
Recently a wonderful French director didn't like the first few tunes I did and that's quite tricky because your first response to a piece of work comes quite naturally and subsequent responses have to be dug out a little bit, then hopefully she accepts that new starting point and I'll get back into connecting with the work. If not, then you're falling back on an intellectual process of formulas and techniques; say a repeated snare drum and a muted trumpet will do something in an icy snowscape with men slicing each other to pieces. You know a very fast bass clarinet ostinato will do this and a trombone section will do that and you build up a vocabulary. They're not tricks but they can be shortcuts that allow you to simply get the thing done.

Do you find you have to reach for those shortcuts, let's say, more often than you'd like?
I don't want to be negative about the film industry but sometimes you think it's all solved then you get a reaction from somebody from another country who's one of the associate producers who says, 'We don't actually like the accordion because it sounds too French.' Well, who am I working for? If I get rid of the accordion then that upsets somebody else. So, then the job feels like a job. I made a list once, jobs that have been unhappy or that ended nastily and I try and think of the common things running through all those occasions and there are two: one is lack of preparation. So, if somebody says, 'What are we going to do for the dances?' and you haven't yet thought about it, that's bad – but the biggest one of all is when you're doing something that doesn't resonate with you in any way. It becomes about the whim of the director and there's no cross current between you and him or her, and you really are

just doing a job at that point and that makes everything much, much more difficult.

Do you have a preference composing for plays or films?
One of the reasons I like doing theatre so much is it's easier to have full creative input and to have a real ongoing dialogue with the people you're working with. In film so many decisions are made in post-production, after most of the hard work has been done, and you're not having creative input from the conception which might have helped build a connection to the story inside of you. So that makes theatre time consuming but also intriguing and rewarding. Generally, when you're scoring a film, it's not the same as polishing a table but it's a bit like the table's already constructed and you're doing a bit of decoration around the edges. There is a chemistry involved but it's a bit hard to explain. What you need to do is get inside the grain of it somehow and make the music seem like it was always there or always supposed to be there, or help lift the text off the page and into the screen, but you're slightly catching up in a way. In a battle, say, you can experiment, live as it were, playing things alongside it and you can examine the effect you're having on it. You hear something that's simply timpani, bass drum and four snare drums and then you say I'm not going to do that because the battle's already very percussive and instead you hear a long melodic line over it. It's not as intellectual as it sounds. You audition all your ideas against it by playing it or mocking it up in music software. And suddenly, hopefully, you find something that gets into the grain of it, and seems to live in it and make it work. Sadly or happily, I don't know which, the intellectual part of me is honestly not very engaged – it's much more an emotional response that requires you to identify with or to be moved by the characters.

Has composing music for the Globe influenced your other work?
All the bits of work influence each other. There's a stupid rule which I try to make for myself and which I don't manage to abide by, which is if I don't like the music I'm writing, it's a total waste of time. What helps me is to get to where I think the music's working for a scene and then you learn something new about it. What doesn't help is when you feel like your collaborators are pushing you in a direction that you don't want to go and you're trying to please other people. Somehow you have to make it a journey that's satisfying both for you and for them otherwise you're not doing your best work. What I like about the Globe is it teaches you to make your decisions simply because you can't hide behind effects. You have to make your statements overtly, in full view and on the front foot and that's quite a good discipline.

Broadly speaking, what changes when you score the same bit of Shakespeare to film versus in the theatre?

Well here at the Globe there are very different kinds of considerations because you don't typically amplify music here. For example, in *The Tempest* you have a storm at the top and the whole thing is a massive compromise. If it were a film you can have people thrashing away on timpani and thunder sheets at full volume but mixed so that you feel there's huge body of music in the left, right and surround speakers, meanwhile in your centre speaker you've got the dialogue, so you have a technical way of doing something huge while people are speaking. Now interestingly, in *The Tempest* here in 2014 there was a kind of unspoken compromise made to sacrifice some of the dialogue in order to get the whole effect across. The lords are making a terrible fuss but apparently the ship's sinking and they're frightened and the sailors are screaming to each other but there's not a massive amount of very important exposition. And there was a sort of silent agreement that that compromise helped tell the story.

How do the opportunities and dangers of underscoring change between films and plays?

I'm generally very hesitant to underscore in a play, especially with Shakespeare, as there seems to be such an implicit music in the language. In *The Tempest*, music is referred to on quite a number of occasions and equally in the masque sequence, which is a play within a play. Music gives that artificial context a little bit of help. In the case of the Jez Butterworth play, *Jerusalem*, you wouldn't know I was underscoring it because we're told there's a fairground about a mile or two away, and there's fairly constant music but it's at such a low level that you probably would think there wasn't any at all. I was once engaged to write the music for *The Weir* by Connor McPherson, a most intense, wonderful play set in a bar in Ireland, but I said to the director towards the end of rehearsals, 'I really can't think we can have any music in this.' The language was so musical in itself that anything else would detract from the music of the text. So I still worked on it but I didn't compose anything.

At the moment we're working on your score for *The Tempest* here in the Sam Wanamaker Playhouse directed by Dominic Dromgoole, but only two years ago I recall building several new instruments that you designed yourself for *The Tempest* in the Globe directed by Jeremy Herrin. Can you say briefly what your inspiration was for the original instruments?

Well in *The Tempest*, the characters arriving from Italy are having a strange experience. They keep referring to the noises on the island

and we had the idea that sound should come from all around the theatre. One of the instruments that made the strangest noises was metal plates wasn't it?

I believe we called it the strike, dunk, release machine. . .
That one, yes. Brass plates tied to a bar, and you pull a bar down and the plates drop into buckets of water that lower the pitch, and if you strike them gently enough you don't hear the attack, you just hear a falling noise. Another one was metal rods in a resonating box that you bow and it sounds a bit like a violin or cello but not quite, so the idea is you shouldn't be able to identify it as a conventional musical instrument. There was another one that had vertically strung piano strings with a box at the bottom for your feet. You press down on the box and change the tensions of the strings and then bow them while their tension is changing. We also bowed thunder sheets; again you get strange harmonics as it's a very irregular piece of metal. You can get some great sounds out of that and in the end I put in some conventional instruments just because I wanted to add some sounds that I could control a bit more like bass clarinet and a guitar to accompany the songs. Even some of those we used in unconventional ways, like bowing an acoustic guitar and I thought, 'I bet people don't know what he's doing.' Doing all this kind of bizarre stuff – 'What's he doing up there? On a kind of loom or something?'

Particularly in *The Tempest*, music is a sort of character and functions in a diegetic way – to borrow a word from film – heard by and affecting the characters onstage, which is typical of Shakespeare of course but extremely pronounced in this play. How do you incorporate into your music all of the characters' different reactions to it?
It is quite difficult isn't it, because there are lines in Shakespeare which really throw you, like 'That's the wrong tune,' and you think 'Should I write a tune which is wrong?' Stephano says, 'Oh, that's a scurvy tune to play at a man's funeral.' So 'Should I write a scurvy tune?' Or should I try and write a good tune that just he thinks is scurvy. Or has he sung it scurvily? When Trinculo and Stefano sing together, should you write a really nice piece of music that Caliban objects to, or should it be as rough and unruly as they are, or is the roughness the performance? In terms of Ariel's songs that the humans hear, I'm encouraged to get a bit theoretical by writing tunes that aren't completely predictable, that have some little surprises because Ariel can't be just of Ferdinand's world; he has to be bringing another quality to it.

I'm impressed that all seven of the songs are new this time.
That's because I couldn't remember them ...

Well I get to hear you set them all over again which is an enormous benefit to me, selfishly. Do you make any use of what academics say is the original source or function of the song, for example the style of the original Robert Johnson settings, or that the melody would have been known and popular but set to new lyrics by Shakespeare?
The songs that would have been used at the time of Shakespeare within his plays would have been popular songs. We can't do our own contemporary popular music because the language is still his language so you're in a bit of a pickle really. I probably ignore that and just say, 'What's going to serve the purpose in the scene? Why is Ariel pretending that Ferdinand's father is dead?' I'd go back to the basic function of it and ignore trying to get the cultural significance of popular song in that context, but that's because I wouldn't know how to do it. If I'd tried to use the vocabulary of a modern popular song, unless that was the nature of the particular production, I think it would stretch the frame a bit far or would sit somewhat uncomfortably. It's quite a complicated question, isn't it?

How do you collaborate with actors singing your songs and navigating their different levels of ability?
Well you'll recall two of the actors in *The Tempest* two years ago said, 'Could we sing the songs unaccompanied?' And you have to stay calm and say, 'Shakespeare wrote them as songs for a reason, he did not want them just to be subsumed into the text.' In the path of making these songs I like to accompany them in the rehearsal room because otherwise the actor falls into a kind of improvised approach and will change them rhythmically and then they lose the formality of a specially constructed song. I don't think you could ever really do this, but I've always wanted to do an experiment where you musically notate what the actors say. Sometimes you listen to a Sam Shepherd play and a lot of it sounds like music – the musicality in the speech is just as important as what's being said. Are we right to make divisions between music and text?

I've never thought so. I suppose as composers though we wouldn't. Yet Shakespeare so clearly intended the sounds of the words to mingle well with their meaning and you can't really address that facet of it with actors.
No you can't, strangely. They'd want to investigate the meaning and objective before and above everything and might begin to get a little

resentful the farther you stretch them from their intention. But it is about the tune and the melody of the speech at the same time.

Do you think that's because of a natural wariness or an inborn defensiveness against any discussion over how the text is ultimately going to sound?
It's such a sensitive thing. We did *The Lie of the Mind*, a Sam Shepherd play, ages ago at the Royal Court and there was one American actor and the rest were doing American accents. The American really understood how to do it in terms of the tune. He kept coming back to the same note – 'Her hair, her lips, her eyes . . . ' Rhythmically he knew just what the thing was, and the second word of each part of the list was the same note. Interestingly the passage was underscored, and I never said anything to him, but he did it in perfect harmony to the underscore. So he was actually working with the music. And although he was pretty open and it probably wouldn't have been an issue, speaking to actors is such a delicate thing that if I ever said 'I really like the way you're doing that' I'd risk destroying it. In Shakespeare, often you really want to talk about what the language is doing musically, what the song of the verse is doing, and I don't think you can.

In the 1930's, Schoenberg was once called in by MGM to score the film of Pearl S. Buck's *The Good Earth*. He was broke so he quoted $50,000 which was an obscene amount to compose for back then, but he also demanded complete control over all aspects of the sound: how the actors delivered their lines, the sound effects, and of course the music. Then he'd do it.
He didn't get the job presumably.

Sadly not.
No. It's never really like that for us. You admire it when an actor finds something that captures the musical essence rather than guiding them towards something. It's hard to imagine who in the room could engineer something like that. Schoenberg's point is really intriguing, but in a way wrong if you're a vaguely pragmatic person, which most of us are. If you're scoring a piece of Shakespeare for film, you've already got the pitch and the rhythm of what the actors are doing because it's already been shot. So you're not dictating to them but you are including their rhythms and voices in the score.

One thing you can do that's distinct from the theatre is what Richard Eyre did having Falstaff speaking to camera, closely mic'd and not using a lot of voice. He's confiding in you. And what's intriguing is though you couldn't do this in a theatre, you can put quite big music behind that in a film. So, you have Falstaff standing in front of a battle where people are being hacked to pieces, and you can work in counterpoint to the text in a way that you couldn't perhaps do in a play.

For someone that works with direct address at the Globe so much, in film I still find it so powerful, almost alarming. It seems to sharpen the relationship to the audience even more than in a play.
It unshakably confers on that character that the play or film is really about him. It means that against all the bravado and arrogance in Falstaff, we know the vulnerable other side to him, and as a composer that gives you access to serving his tragic side.

Are there film directors out there who prefer composers to work along-side them – writing and recording before or during filming?
I think quite a few directors, Anthony Minghella for one, liked to work with some pre-recorded music, music specially written for the film. Gabriel Yared, who used to compose for him would record the music, or some major themes, before filming and Minghella on some occasions, I believe, would actually play them during filming. There's certainly a case for it and I think what happens is a sort of cross-fertilisation between the director, design, and script. I like the fact that the two things grow up together as opposed to one imposed upon the other.

At what point in the rehearsal process of a play do you like to get engaged in composing?
Some directors want you to do stuff in advance; the choreographers definitely do. I find it very, very hard to write anything at least until I've seen the read-through and a couple of weeks of popping in and out of rehearsals, because you don't know what kind of Ariel you're writing for or what kind of *Tempest* it is – it's so different from production to production. If you were to write music in advance you'd be putting an artificial stamp on it that might not be true to the show. For example, you and I had a meeting about the show earlier today – well we had to think about what musicians we would have in advance for practical reasons because it starts very soon, but I like to imagine that I didn't have many preconceptions. You could say that I was completely unpre-pared for the meeting, or that I actually prefer to be unprepared, because then you can truly listen.

Then during the first week or so the choreographer will be saying, 'Please can we have some music?' After about three requests you have to give in, and then you leave it. You have to draw the line between giving the actor long enough to learn what they have to do and you getting into the spirit of the performance.

Is there a risk that by holding off you're then obliged to follow the decisions the designer and director have had to make before you've become fully engaged?
Sometimes you feel like the very way theatre's created in this country, those design decisions impose a heavy burden on all of us. The Globe is a bit of an exception to that because in a lot of cases, the design can't dominate.

It can't totally take over typically – although sometimes it threatens to.
That's rather good because everyone can still take that journey together and discover what the play needs for that particular version. Whereas sometimes I've worked on a play and it's an incredibly realistic version of a crumbling house and there's beautiful Russian tables or whatever it happens to be, an Irish fireplace, etc. and actually you think had we just done this on a mound of earth with a table and a solo trumpet player it would have been far more audacious. But because of the number of decisions you have to make in advance, you limit yourselves. So in that sense you say that theatre's a freer thing where you make the discoveries alongside everyone, but the reality is a great many imposing decisions are made already, so in that sense it's not so different than a film. But generally as a film composer you do feel outside of those conversations, and Schoenberg obviously didn't want to be – he required doing it all, and he didn't get the job.

Have you had experiences in film when you had to get more involved earlier in the process?
In *Captain Corelli's Mandolin* there's the main theme that Nicholas Cage plays in the square on the mandolin. The director, John Madden called a meeting a few weeks before so the actor could learn to do it. This is the case with some films; it's not for artistic reasons it's for practical ones. Anyway, he said, 'You'd better play me a tune.' And I thought to myself, 'I haven't written the tune.' And I must have looked a bit pale because he said, 'Are you hungry?' and I said, 'Yes.' And he went out to Marks and Spencer's and got some sandwiches and I wrote the tune while he was out. We ate the sandwiches and then I felt so guilty about it that I kept trying to rewrite it because it can't be right that I've written the theme tune in about ten minutes, but it was actually alright. Sometimes you can write something quickly and it's better than something you've spent weeks on.

On that film, again, we had ten minutes left of a recording session before filming and I said to the guitarist, 'Oh go on, just play the tunes for the mandolin on that.' He played it on a guitar, and the whole section of the film after the earthquake ended up cut to this music we'd created months beforehand. For me that's one of the most successful sequences because the music is sort of the lifeblood of the picture, and it pre-existed the visual.

You've composed many film scores set in a particular historic time and place. What kind of pressure is put upon you to convey historic period in the music?

In *Shakespeare In Love* we sat round and listened to a load of Elizabethan stuff which I used to love actually, but John Madden very much felt and I completely agree with him, that's it a film made now, it's not Elizabethan. It's our perspective. It's not even Shakespeare though it's got a lot of Shakespeare in it. The music needs to serve our perspective, our feeling about those people and about that story. I do get influenced by the location and the period but don't normally get hung up on it. In the end, we have to take our Shakespeare's-such-a-precious-commodity gloves off, so there's absolutely no reason to have a bunch of people squawking around on shawms, you might as well say 'let's do it all with analogue synthesizers' or whatever it happens to be.

Do you ever feel that composing at the Globe comes with a similarly abstract pressure to incorporate historical music?

I spend a lot of my life feeling guilty about all sorts of things I don't want to. I feel very uninspired about approaching period instruments, which is terrible because there's a load of people writing incredible music for them. Say if somebody says, 'You can only have a sackbut and rattler and a couple of baskets or something and you've got to do it all with that.' I say, 'Oh, all right then,' and then I quietly try to slip a clarinet in while nobody's looking and then I feel bad because I haven't really done it properly.

In this book Ramona Wray talks about music in Shakespearean film increasingly filling the void vacated by 'amputations' of language often in groundbreaking ways. Do you see that happening more and more in the last few decades, music having a bigger role as more text gets cut?

If large bits were taken out and you have a long passage of soldiers marching over the hill that you wouldn't have in the play, obviously that gives you an opportunity without being literal about it to be narrative in the music for the moment. You're not necessarily replacing something that's chopped out but you're given space in the text to do something interesting that wouldn't have been achievable in the theatre anyway.

Thinking about say, Ralph Fiennes's recent *Coriolanus* film, it seems that Shakespeare on film is starting to look more like other movies, and has forever evolved away from the old Olivier/Gielgud theatricalised versions. Does that makes the job of composing for Shakespeare on film more like writing music for other films?
I do think that. Also, which is a personal opinion, I don't like those old *Henry V*s. I mean I don't think they're bad films I just think there are other films from that period that survive much better, and there's something so innately theatrical about the delivery and the default settings of the smaller characters that I'm just not interested and I'd rather go to the theatre and see it. If it's going to be on film, I want it to use the strengths of that medium, not kind of flounder along despite being a film. And I think generalised, stirring big epic romantic scores for those films – this is a horrible generalisation – leave me a bit cold and I'd rather people to do something a bit more interesting.

So your predecessors in that lineage – Nino Rota, William Walton, even Patrick Doyle – do you take any inspiration from any of their work or are they not so relevant to what you do?
I don't think I ever consciously take inspiration from things like that, no. I might make a mental note that I don't like this or that. Nino Rota, there's virtually nothing he could do wrong for me, but whether he's inspired me in those scores, I wouldn't really know. I just feel more like a drain. Lots of different things drain in and it all sluices around a bit and then something else comes out. I suppose one thing I feel, and I suppose it also has to do with fashion, that very completed pieces of music don't feel right to me with Shakespeare, because it should be that the words complete the music, so that if it feels like it's too perfectly formed in terms of its harmonic development or its resolution or where it goes, it will often bother me somewhat. But coming back to the verse, you have to accept that the sound landscape – the words – are so powerful, and there are so many more of them in a film of Shakespeare, and you do have to leave room for them and you do have to operate in a different way. It would be vaguely interesting to know how many more words there were in a Shakespeare film than most films. There are easily 10 times the number of words said in *The Hollow Crown* than say . . .

. . .Mission Impossible 3.

Exactly. And you know the words in most things carry a small burden compared with what they carry in Shakespeare. So I suppose you have to watch out and let those words do their job, and not feel like you're following the path that the words have already notched out for themselves. Whereas if you see a Norwegian couple looking across the frozen wasteland in terrible paroxysms of pain because their marriage is finally over, unable to speak to each other, you can do a lot more musically perhaps than you can with Lear and the Fool in the stormy whatever it is. A lot of the work is done for you.

It makes the film of Peter Brook's *King Lear* with no music whatsoever – the only full-length film I can think of actually that has no music – incredibly brave and dynamic in that context.

It's very intriguing. About a week before we recorded the music for *Shakespeare In Love*, I watched it without music and it was a terrible couple of hours because I thought the film worked brilliantly without music. I thought 'Oh god, but I'm not going to tell anyone.'

Thankfully there was a dance so I had an excuse to get involved, and to your question earlier about needing to be vaguely historical, John Madden wanted music in the ball, which he said we should almost believe could be music of the time. It doesn't matter if it's harmonically slightly different from than what they would have done. I mean it did go from D minor to Bb major, like every other film. I promised myself that every job I do, I'm not allowed to go from D minor to Bb first inversion, but I still do. Directors often, now this is a terrible generalisation, they say 'I love that bit, what are you doing there, I love when you did that,' and you think, 'My god, have I got to do that again?' You play a tune and they don't quite like it but then you put a Bb in and it works out fine.

The whole Batman and James Bond franchises seem to be based on that little turn of the musical penknife.

Well, Schoenberg certainly wouldn't have done it.

CHAPTER 13

Film, Music and Shakespeare: Walton and Shostakovich

Peter Holland

Film Music: Two Ends of a Spectrum

At one end, a film with no music; at the other, film music with no film.

For the former, I turn to Peter Brook's film of *King Lear* (1971). It takes a moment for the viewer to realise and accept that it opens in complete silence, the camera dollying to and fro, as the credits roll, across a group of standing figures so immobile that only the occasional blink reassures us that the film is indeed rolling and the figures living. The shot changes to another space, an interior with a group of people clustered around a huge monolithic object (later seen as the phallic throne). There is still no sound, still no sign of movement. Then at the back of the scene, just to the right of the centre line, a door is seen to be closing and, as it completes its movement, there is the sound of its slamming shut.

I know of no other Shakespeare film (of the sound era) that opens in such absolute absence of sound and movement (other than of the camera). And throughout there will be no sounds that are not fully diegetic, firmly located within the activities seen in the image, except for some sound distortions in the midst of the storm, something that we hear imprecisely as though they may or may not be electronically generated noises accompanying Lear as he instructs the elements: 'Blow, winds, and crack your cheeks' (3.2.1). Perhaps these sounds were a throwback to those Brook himself had created as *musique concrète*, as it was then known, for his *Titus Andronicus* in Stratford in 1955 and his 1957 *Tempest* there. There are no film credits for sound in this *King Lear* other than that for the sound recordist, Robert Allen, then in the middle of his long career working on over 80 films. Unnervingly, because film-scoring is such a familiar, conventional facet of the films we watch that we do not usually notice it, only notice its stark absence, this film accommodates silence and refuses, that one scene apart, to argue that voices, action, event or narrative need music as underscoring to their screen presence. The non-diegetic presence of music as support and transition, indeed all the functions it could have in the practice of film-making, are abandoned in the unyielding world in which Brook's *Lear* takes place. In this world stripped bare, the film's sound is similarly stripped down to its 'real' sounds, the soundscape generating meaning in its meagreness, in its telling us what it is doing without, in its forms of representing the absence of the comforting familiarity, the reassuring quality of symphonic scoring to bolster what we watch and what else we hear.

For the latter, I turn to Arnold Schoenberg's *Begleitmusik zu einer Lichtspeilszene* (*Accompanying music for a film scene*, Op.34, composed in 1929–30, premiered in 1930), a score for a film that does not exist and that was never intended to exist. The eight minutes of its duration traverse what it identifies as three states, though there is no break between them, only something we are aware of, if we keep the work's subtitle in mind, as a movement across and between 'Threatening Danger, Fear, Catastrophe'. If there is a trace of narrative, it is the very familiarity of the three emotions as sequential: the danger that threatens producing fear and leading to catastrophe. But there is nothing more than the abstractions, no thought of locating the sequence in particularity, where film music in the sound era has always been composed for the specifics of the film's action. In 1929 Schoenberg had contacted the Society of German Film Composers to ask for 'advice and support for his interest in sound film'.[1] As early as the composition of his music-drama piece *Die Glückliche Hand* (1910–13), he had considered using film and there were subsequent unfulfilled flirtations with Hollywood studios, including a meeting with Irving Thalberg at MGM in November 1935 over his writing the music for the film of Pearl Buck's *The Good Earth*, negotiations that foundered when Schoenberg demanded a fee of $50,000.[2]

But, where composers like Saint-Saëns and Mascagni, Honegger and Satie wrote scores for silent film, Schoenberg did not. And at the point at which he wrote *Begleitmusik*, at the threshold of the sound era, he seems deliberately to have produced something of a throwback, a work that suggests the stock materials that were available to accompany silent films, the cheat-books of cue sheets for music defined and filed by emotional atmosphere. Indeed, Schoenberg's names of three states are all paralleled in

---

[1] S. M. Feisst, 'Arnold Schoenberg and the Cinematic Art', *Music Quarterly*, 83 (1999), 93–113, 96–7.
[2] Ibid., 93. I have long found it oddly pleasing that Schoenberg was living opposite Shirley Temple at the time, in the strange world of Hollywood and its emigrés.

such publications. For Schoenberg, it would seem that film music is simply a mode of emotional intensification: in film, danger becomes more disturbingly dangerous through the musical accompaniment. The notion that film music could do much more and achieve aims very different from such a purpose is not part of the project of *Begleitmusik*, a work which, for all its part in a radical approach to musical compositions, seems determinedly abstract.

Though Otto Klemperer intrigued the composer by suggesting that he ask Moholy to create a film to go with Schoenberg's score, nothing came of the idea, and, though a number of filmmakers have made films to match it, it has the odd effect of creating a film as an accompaniment to the score rather than a score to accompany the film. I shall return at the end to the disjunction between film music and film, in the context of the concert performance/recording of film music separated from its original purpose. For now, I want to emphasise the distance between the ends of the spectrum and the paradoxes the ends suggest: the emotional simplicity and strangely backward-looking intentions of Schoenberg's score and the powerful meaning generated by the absence of a score for Brook.

Another Door Closes

The first line of *Richard III* is probably the most famous opening in Shakespeare but Laurence Olivier's 1955 film delays it until more than eight minutes in. Before then, there has been a long credit sequence, placing the events between history and legend, the coronation of Edward IV, followed by a throne-room scene taken from the end of *3 Henry VI*, the king and his son setting off on triumphal progress through the city and much comic business with Richard's incompetent page who awkwardly shuts the door to the throne-room, ending with an extreme close-up of the door handle.

Then the door is nudged open again, as if by the camera, and the shot moves into the room to see Richard standing by the throne. As the camera travels, we hear the sound of the door closing and the pastiche early music that the soundtrack has been using for some time suddenly quietens, turning what we may have assumed to be simply atmospheric into something diegetic, the sound, presumably, of unseen musicians accompanying the procession, now fading into silence as Richard walks towards us, looking straight to camera, and begins to speak. The sudden shift of volume on the sound of the door closing redefines the function of the music, removing it from an ambiguity of location into a defined space, the space outside in the street, away from that powerful silent contact between Richard's eyes and our own, the conspiratorial space within which speech no longer needs musical support to define itself.

I want to align this definitional moment with one earlier in the film. From the first title, announcing that the film is 'in Vistavision with colour by Technicolor', William Walton's score is in his grandest vein, what James Brooks Kuykendall calls 'a portentous sample of the English cere-monial style', an 'expansive march' that 'seems incongruous, as it is anachronistic in the extreme, being unmistakably in the tradition of the 1953 coronation march *Orb and Sceptre*'. The 'reason for the *nobilmente* march is clear, and the anachronism intentional; the melody serves as a leitmotif not of a character but of the rightful succession to the crown.'[3] As Kuykendall points out, Walton's musical method in this, his fourth and last Shakespeare film score, is, unusually, to use a leitmotif technique as his 'primary mode of organization . . . with motifs assigned to every character, and quoted at even the slightest allusion in the text'.[4] So, here, the prelude's march theme is never used when Richard dominates. There had been traces of such effects in earlier scores, for instance, the one for Claudius's pangs of guilt in the play scene in Olivier's 1948 *Hamlet*, highly praised by Hans Keller in his entry on 'Film Music' in *Grove's Dictionary* (1954):

> Even the best Hollywood composer would just automatically have reused the music from the early backflash showing Claudius's murder, for underlining the corresponding 'murder' in the players' performance: the typical leitmotivic tautology . . . Walton, however, utilizes the backflash material . . . [for] Claudius's reactions to the poisoning of the actor-king, thus impressing upon us, more vividly than the picture itself could have done, that the king . . . is overwhelmed by the thought of his own deed.[5]

Orb and Sceptre, a successor to *Crown Imperial*, Walton's 1937 coronation piece, was first performed during the coronation itself and, unsurprisingly, given the huge impact of the event, stayed in Olivier's mind. Walton's widow recalled Olivier 'asking William to write a celebratory march for Richard III's coronation. He said that something like *Orb and Sceptre*

[3] J. B. Kuykendall, ed., *William Walton Edition, vol.22 Film Suites* (Oxford: Oxford University Press, 2010), ix.
[4] Ibid., x.
[5] Quoted by S. Lloyd, 'Film Music' in S. R. Craggs, *William Walton: Music and Literature* (Aldershot: Ashgate, 1999), 109–31, 124.

would do very nicely. William replied that maybe he could think of another such tune'.[6] But the film's 'Prelude' would also have functioned as an echo for the audience of the coronation two years earlier.

The march piece ends as the film transitions from the final words of the credits, 'Here now begins, one of the most famous, and at the same time, the most infamous of the legends that are attached to the Crown of England', to a shot of a crown, visibly suspended in mid-air on wires and soon, as the camera tilts down, shown to be hanging above the coronation chair as the archbishop raises the 'real' crown to be placed on Edward IV's head, again an echo of the impact of that moment in Queen Elizabeth II's coronation. But the music modulates as we see the hanging crown and, instead of ending with a strong resolution of the march, a key change and string trills emphasise the suspense, in both senses, that the crown here – and throughout the film – provokes. At the very end, the crown is held aloft by Lord Stanley and, as his hands vanish, it is left as an image suspended against the sky. Walton's music at the start, then, changes from the perhaps overly positive statement of the march to a hesitancy and doubt about the crown that prefigures the play's action with its recurrent questioning about who will wear it. What is crucial here is that this anxiety about succession is present only in the music. It is Walton's choice in scoring, presumably supported by Olivier, that makes the image carry such meaning. Watch it muted and one will not be able to gather any such provocation. It is both a clear demonstration of what film scoring can do, creating and limiting interpretation of the screen image, and of the power Walton's score has in this film.

Reflecting on Film Music

In 1956 Walton published an article on 'Music for Shakespearean Films' in the journal *Film/TV Music*, an expanded version of his 1948 essay in a collection of articles on the making of Olivier's *Hamlet*.[7] Walton identifies three principal areas for the 'value to a film of its musical score which rests chiefly in the creation of mood, atmosphere, and the sense of period. When the enormous task of reimagining a Shakespearean drama in terms of the screen has been achieved, these three qualities, which must be common to all film music, appear in high relief'.[8]

---

[6] S. Walton, *William Walton: Behind the Façade* (Oxford University Press, 1988), 143.
[7] Reprinted in S. Lloyd, *William Walton: Muse of Fire* (Woodbridge: Boydell Press, 2001), 276–8; see also B. Cross, ed., *The Film Hamlet* (London: Saturn Press, 1948), 61–2.
[8] Lloyd, 277.

Walton's examples for each are: for mood, 'the incidental musical effects in Hamlet's soliloquies which varied their orchestral colour according to the shifts of his thought'; for atmosphere, 'the music of rejoicing after the victory of Agincourt in *Henry V*, which also illustrates the power to evoke a sense of historical period . . ., for the contemporary Agincourt hymn . . . was adapted to my purpose'; and, for period, the entry of the players in *Hamlet* where he 'suggest[ed] the musical idiom of the time by using a small sub-section of the orchestra'.

Perhaps because of the context of its initial publication, Walton says nothing of his first Shakespeare film score, *As You Like It* (directed by Paul Czinner, 1936). Olivier had an unhappy experience playing Orlando in it, his first leading role in film, not least because he disliked both Elisabeth Bergner (Rosalind) and Czinner, and, though he met Walton on set, that may explain why he had forgotten Walton when his name came up as composer for *Henry V* (1944).[9] It was the second of four film-scores Walton would write for Paul Czinner and, though Walton's admirers praise it, the score was damned by the reviewer for *World Film News*, Benjamin Britten:

> There is, of course, the Grand Introduction . . . - pompous and heraldic in the traditional manner. There is a Grand Oratorio Finale with full orchestra, based on Elizabethan songs . . . Both these are written with great competence . . . But apart from suitable *Waldweben* noises at the beginning of each sequence, which tactfully fade out as the action starts, that is the whole of Walton's contributions to *As you like it*.[10]

The *Waldweben*, a reference to Wagner's 'Forest Murmurs' in *Siegfried*, are not quite all, for Walton provides frequent underscoring for soliloquies and, for instance, the quartet dialogue of Rosalind, Orlando, Phoebe and Silvius in 5.2. But, try as I might, I cannot find anything distinctive or impressive in the conventional scoring throughout. Compared with the virtuosity of Korngold's score for the Reinhardt-Dieterle film of *A Midsummer Night's Dream* for Warner Brothers (1935), one of the great examples of the symphonic score of the studio production system, out-doing Mendelssohn even as it elaborates on his incidental music,[11] Walton's is dully predictable and conventional.

---

[9] Lloyd, 'Film Music', 110. For Olivier's account of the meeting, see D. Lloyd-Jones, ed., *William Walton Edition, vol.23 Henry V* (Oxford University Press, 1999), vii.

[10] Quoted Craggs, 112.

[11] See N. Platte, 'Dream Analysis: Korngold, Mendelssohn and Musical Adaptations in Warner Bros' *A Midsummer Night's Dream* (1935)', *19th-Century Music*, 34 (2011), 211–36.

Walton's work on war films, especially *The First of the Few* (1942) and *Went the Day Well?* (1942), was far more impressive and began to stretch his technique and invention. Olivier took steps that went far beyond the normal procedures, even proposing that the music for the battle of Agincourt should be written and the film edited to fit it, rather than the other way round. In the event that version was not used and Walton had to start all over again. His letters were grumpy: 'our masterpiece went for nothing & no attempt whatsoever has been made to use it & I'm not surprised', he grumbled in December 1943.[12] In May 1943, the tensions with post-production were already evident: 'I've been working on the battle ... & luckily didn't get very far as all the footages were rearranged two days ago & they forgot to tell me! ... 10 mins of charging horses bows & arrows. How does one distinguish between a crossbow & a long bow musically speaking?'.[13]

The answer is, of course, that one does not, or at least Walton's score did not. Yet the concerns with mood, atmosphere and period remain central to the battle. Some of the period effects were derived from liberal use of sources: as well as the Agincourt song, which had been used by Vaughan Williams in his music for Frank Benson's 1913 Stratford-upon-Avon production of the play, Walton turned, for the battle, to a 15th century French battle-song, 'Réveillez-vous, Piccars', and, elsewhere in the score, to the Fitzwilliam Virginal Book and to three melodies from Canteloube's *Chants d'Auvergne*, this last a suggestion of Olivier's.[14] But Walton also built effects in the battle through reusing material from elsewhere in the score, like the Prologue's 'fanfare-like hymn of praise of – what? London Pride? Spirit of England? Grandeur and Glory?'[15] Most particularly there is mood and atmosphere created by the alignment of score and image, most obviously in the drum *ostinato* for the screen's line of French drummers, and most thrillingly in the famous tracking shot of the line of French knights, a lengthy *accelerando* as they move from walk to trot to gallop, to be met, at a moment of silence in the music, by the sound effect of the volley of arrows, matching the visual overlay of their flight. But there is also earlier in the sequence, for instance, the sudden switch to strings playing *sul ponticello* when, in the lead-up, we see water lying on the ground and the horses' hooves stepping through it.[16]

[12] M. Hayes, ed., *The Selected Letters of William Walton* (London: Faber and Faber, 2002), 147.
[13] Ibid., 145.
[14] C. Palmer in Lloyd-Jones, viii; on Olivier's suggesting Canteloube, see Lloyd, 197.   [15] Ibid.
[16] Part of the sequence is mapped with images and short-score in R. Manvell et al., eds., *The Technique of Film Music*, rev. ed. (London: Focal Press, 1975), 96–107, a structuring of shot and score analogous to the 'diagram of audio-visual correspondences' used by Eisenstein to represent part of the battle in

Brilliant and exhilarating, whatever the ordeal of writing it, Walton's score here is a perfect support for, mirroring of and intensifier for Olivier's equally brilliant and exhilarating filming.

The Sounds of Other Battles

But there are, as I shall explore below, other ways of creating music for a sequence of war, music that does not seek any effect of period or of atmosphere, but which offers, instead, a sustained and powerful commentary on the action from which its rhythms and style may be radically disjunct. The very emphasis on period in Walton's thinking about scoring for film was tightly intertwined with the costume-drama elements in Olivier's style in both *Henry V* and *Richard III*. The greater restraint in effects and choice of black-and-white for *Hamlet* as well as the emphasis on Hamlet's introspection seems to have freed Walton to find a markedly different relationship between speech and score, for the internal struggles of Hamlet's processes of thought can be, literally, underscored by the composer. Where Henry V's rousing speeches, like 'Once more unto the breach', are followed by music cues, not coloured by cues during Olivier's speaking, Hamlet's 'O that this too too solid flesh' becomes, in effect, part of the music. Christopher Palmer, who reworked Walton's *Hamlet* score as 'Hamlet: A Shakespeare Scenario', goes as far as to suggest that 'Walton scores for the speaking voice as if for a musical instrument' while Kuykendall argues that the speech gives 'the impression of . . . the calculated recitation over understated accompaniment of some of the early *Façade* numbers'.[17]

As the court disperses after Claudius's exit to the sound of bright trumpet fanfares while Hamlet remains slumped in his chair, Walton begins a fugal passage on cellos and basses in violent contrast to the echoes of the brass. The cut to an extreme close-up precedes the start of the speech and only after Hamlet stops looking after Claudius and Gertrude and stares vacantly at nothing in particular do we hear 'O that this too too solid flesh'. 'Hear' is the crucial feature for the audience cannot see the speech: the words are voice-over and are therefore even more firmly integrated into the soundscape of thought. In addition, the rhythm of entries in the fugal pattern do not muddy the act of listening to the speech since they are part

---

Alexander Nevsky (1938) with Prokofiev's music, a sequence that heavily influenced Olivier as director and, to a lesser extent, Walton; see S. Eisenstein, *The Film Sense* (New York: Harcourt Brace, 1975), following 175.

[17] Palmer, liner notes for recording by Marriner (CHAN10436X), 7; Kuykendall, ix.

of a known pattern. Looking minutely at a largely immobile face across which no trace of the thinking is moving enables extreme concentration on sound, both music and words.

Here, then, language is embedded in the music in a context in which there is no diegetic sound. But music can also serve deliberately to obliterate the sounds we extrapolate from what we see. In Gillo Pontecorvo's drama-documentary *The Battle of Algiers* (1966), scenes of terrorist bombings and of military torture of suspects are shown with the soundtrack limited to extracts from Bach's *St Matthew Passion*, just as Kurosawa's version of *King Lear, Ran* (1985), erases the sound of war and turns to music as he shows a terrifying montage of mutilation and death at the climax of the battle, fading back to the image's sounds at the end. Midway between these two films comes Grigori Kozintsev's *King Lear* (1971). Kozintsev's images of war – cannons firing, houses deliberately torched, hordes of people chaotically fleeing – are juxtaposed with two narratives: Edmund, delighting in the erotics of the battlefield, pursued by both Regan and Goneril, and Edgar, kneeling by his father's grave and then heading towards the battle, stopping to pick up a sword and armour from a dead soldier.

But what is the soundscape for this? Kozintsev outlined at length what he imagined in a letter to Shostakovich:

> The longest musical episode is the war. We tried to show madness, chaos and destruction on the screen. But I would like the theme of the music to be associated not with ruin or the raging power of destruction but rather with grief, human suffering, which has no limits. Not some individual complaint but the grief of the whole people. In Shakespearean dimensions it is the lament of the earth itself. A requiem perhaps? Only not with an orchestra but the chorus alone and without words. Grief has no words, there is nothing but weeping: the women, the children and the men all weep.[18]

At first, after Shostakovich refused to compose war music, Kozintsev's sound producer remixed some of the storm music and sound effects. But, the day after telling Kozintsev that he would try to write the chorus the director had described, Shostakovich delivered the score for 'Lament'. The film was re-edited to provide nine new shots of crowds to correspond to the nine segments of the piece. In a way unprecedented in Shakespeare film, the 'lament' became the commentary provided by a chorus both in the sense of a choir and that of Greek tragedy. As Kozinstev commented,

[18] G. Kozintsev, *King Lear: The Space of Tragedy* (Berkeley: University of California Press, 1977), 242.

> It was a tribal community raising its voice in lamentation for the dead. And
> so here in the film, in the very place where the powers of hatred and
> madness, the demonic element of tragedy had broken free and raged, this
> voice grew strong; grief brought people together, united them, the commu-
> nity grew and now it was enveloping mankind.[19]

But the placing of the start of the piece, as Edgar prays at his father's grave
surmounted by the rough cross of two sticks he has made for it, begins out
of personal tragedy, the death of Gloucester, a moment shot initially from
ground level but then from a crane shot. The lament takes on overtones of
Russian church choirs, its local and immediate meaning expanding as the
music continues and the vision of the consequences of aristocrats' war on
the local peasant population becomes the film's focus.

There is in this single piece – and it is echoed elsewhere in the score for
King Lear – a radical rejection of the conventions of film-scoring.
As Kozintsev outlined it, 'The music does not accompany the shots, but
transforms them ... The music should be the voice of the author.'[20] Far
beyond an effect such as the music for the suspended crown near the
opening of Walton's score for *Richard III*, Kozintsev and Shostakovich
set out to define film-music as analytic, not illustrative, and the resultant
score is full of cues that are titled to define meaning: at the start, as one of
the people gathering to hear Lear's decree sounds his horn, the piece is
'The call of life'; as, after Lear rejects Cordelia, he storms through the
palace selecting his retinue, the music is 'The beginning of the catastrophe';
as Cornwall dies, a brutal and brief brass snarl is 'The call of death'.

Shostakovich thought of the storm music as 'the voice of evil' and
wanted to balance it with 'the voice of goodness' but Kozintsev suggested
'the voice of truth',[21] a piece originally intended to accompany Edgar as
Poor Tom. The first edit simply could not make the music connect to the
images but, moved to a place to define Cordelia, it worked perfectly.
Though Kozintsev had wanted there to be no themes linked to characters
in *Lear*, Shostakovich had linked the director's abstraction for truth to
Cordelia and Kozintsev had to accept that the composer's 'voice of truth'
was effectively gendered female, not male.

Film Scores and Theatre Scores

The score for *King Lear* was Shostakovich's last film work and it may seem
odd that it was Kozinstev who was setting out the requirements for the

---

[19] Ibid., 251.   [20] Ibid., 243.   [21] Ibid., 246.

music, as if to a novice rather than to a great composer. But that would be to misunderstand the remarkable relationship between the two. They had, by the time they worked together on the film in 1970, been collaborators for over forty years. Shostakovich's first film-score was for *New Babylon* (1929), a silent directed by Kozintsev and Leonid Trauberg. Of the thirty-seven films for which he wrote the music, ten were directed by Kozintsev, including *Hamlet* (1964), the Soviet film contribution to the quatercentenary.[22] They first met through FEKS (the Factory of the Eccentric Actor), a theatre group established by Kozintsev and others in 1921 in the ferment of avant-garde art in Leningrad. Even as early as *New Babylon*, Shostakovich rejected the assumption that the task of the music was to illustrate the image, setting out his position in an article published before the premiere. Frequently he wrote music in deliberate contrast to the image so that, for example, a character's despair as the Paris Commune falls to the French army is counterpointed with music that 'becomes more and more cheerful, finally resolving into a giddy, almost "obscene" waltz reflecting the Versailles army's victory.'[23] At another point, Shostakovich set the 'Marseillaise' against Offenbach's can-can, an idea he probably derived from a passage in Dostoevsky's *The Devils*.

That many of the films Kozintsev and Shostakovich collaborated on were examples of the dull patriotic socialist realism permitted under Stalin was hardly surprising: no other kind of film could be made. Their two Shakespeare films, made under different political circumstances, were freer to subvert, as in *Lear*'s striking use of Christian imagery.

Their first Shakespeare collaboration was Shostakovich's 1941 score (Op.58a) for Kozintsev's stage production of *Lear* in Leningrad, music Kozintsev re-used for his stage *Hamlet* there in 1954. The recycling is unusual and suggests a kind of generalism in the score rather than something sufficiently particular to the play. For the programme Shostakovich wrote on Shakespeare:

> [Shakespeare] absolutely does not tolerate banality . . . [W]hen one speaks of the magnitude of Shakespeare then one needs to keep in mind the inner magnitude and the breadth of spirit, not the external pomp and circumstance.[24]

[22] This strand in Shostakovich's work is well surveyed by J. Riley, *Dmitri Shostakovich: A Life in Film* (London: I.B.Tauris, 2005).

[23] Quoted Riley, 9.

[24] G. McBurney, 'Shostakovich and the Theatre' in P. Fairclough and D. Fanning, eds., *The Cambridge Companion to Shostakovich* (Cambridge: Cambridge University Press, 2008), pp. 147–78, 173.

But some of it is banal, like the melodramatic storm of the Prelude and the 'folkish, Mahlerian' ballad for, of all people, Cordelia, using a non-Shakespearean text.[25] The superb best of the music is the ten brief songs for the Fool, quirky fragments that 'make up a miniature cycle of sourly absurd, almost expressionist outbursts'.[26] In their grotesque style they have no parallel in the dark, rather obvious music of the rest of the score.

Instead, the Fool's songs hark back to the hour of music that was his *Hamlet* score for Nikolai Akimov's provocative, almost parodic production at the Vakhtangov in 1932 (Op.32). Akimov had Hamlet as an obese glutton, delivering soliloquies in a deliberately boring monotone, Ophelia drunk in her madness and singing cabaret songs, and the ghost as a trick staged by Hamlet as part of his plan to take power. At one point, he added lines for Rosencrantz, complaining that 'when the critics see a satirical work, they say it is by far too much', and Shostakovich set it against a march which parodied a very popular song about the proletariat responding to oppression by Alexander Davidenko, a leader of the all-powerful Russian Association of Proletarian Musicians.[27] The score is throughout as bitingly sharp, abrasive and satirical as the director could have wished.

By comparison, Walton wrote only one score for a stage production of Shakespeare, for Sir John Gielgud's production of *Macbeth* in 1942, the whole score written in the week between Christmas and New Year and then recorded and played back during performances. To judge from the 'Fanfare and March', the only part of the score currently available, with its scotch snaps and fake bagpiping to represent location (if not period) and a heavy thumping bass line to point up the weight of tragic destiny, it lacks the acerbic daring of Shostakovich's best theatre work.

The Sound of Tragedy: Fool and Ophelia

Shostakovich reused none of his theatre music for the two Shakespeare film scores. Not only the distance between Akimov's *Hamlet* and Kozintsev's and between Kozintsev's two takes on *King Lear* but also the cultural shift in Russia between the earlier period and the 1960s meant there was nothing to be gained. Kozintsev tried to work out the central characteristics of Shostakovich's music for the films:

---

[25] Quoted McBurney, 174.   [26] G. McBurney, liner notes for recording by Elder (SIGCD052), 7.
[27] See E. Sheinberg, *Irony, Satire, Parody and the Grotesque in the Music of Shostakovich* (Aldershot: Ashgate, 2000), 104–6.

What is its main feature? A feeling for tragedy? Indeed, an important quality . . . Philosophy . . . ? Of course, how can one speak of *Lear* without Philosophy . . . But it's a different feature that is important, and one that's hard to describe in words. Goodness . . . virtue . . . compassion. But a particular goodness . . . In Shostakovich's music I hear a virulent hatred of cruelty, of the cult of power, of the persecution of truth.[28]

It is there in the astonishing music for the opening titles and the end of *Lear* (Op.437, no.8), not a statement by full orchestra but a haunting melody that seems almost wandering, built on octatonic scales,[29] played by a solo E-flat soprano clarinet, piercing (especially in the closely miked version on the soundtrack), plaintive and almost despairing, certainly not reassuring, its extreme contrast with the grandeur of, say, the opening of his *Hamlet* film score simply remarkable, its restraint a sign of the individual. By the film's end it will be defined as being and not being the sound of the pipe played by the Fool, 'not being' because he is plainly not playing a clarinet, his simple instrument not being the sound we hear. The Fool (Oleg Dal) crouches weeping in the way of the soldiers carrying the stretcher on which lie Lear and Cordelia's corpses; kicked by one of the bearers, he sits up to play. He is, for Kozintsev, a sign of '[a]rt in the grip of tyranny': 'He is the boy from Auschwitz whom they forced to play the violin in an orchestra of dead men . . . He has childlike, tormented eyes', with a 'mark of his profession . . . [in] the bells tied to his leg'.[30]

There is a similar effect in Ophelia's music. Before she is seen, we hear a harpsichord haltingly played but with a hint of something rather mechanical underneath (Op.116, no.7). The camera pans down to an old woman playing a lute as Ophelia practices her dancing, gracefully but impersonally, like a puppet. Again, it was a piece that Kozintsev asked for, at the point describing the 'instructress' as playing 'on an ancient little fiddle or clavecin': 'We want to show how they denaturalize the girl . . . a sweet girl, half child, whom they turn into a doll – a mechanical plaything with artificial movements, a memorized smile, and the like.'[31] The instrument the dance-teacher plays changed and so did Shostakovich's choice: initially he proposed a violin with a piano or guitar accompaniment, then as a violin solo, then a harpsichord.[32]

---

[28] Quoted in E. Wilson, *Shostakovich: A Life Remembered* (London: Faber and Faber, 1994), 371.
[29] See E. Heine, 'Shostakovich, *King Lear* and the Concert Hall', *DSCH Journal*, no. 26 (2007), 40–50, 41–2.
[30] Kozintsev, *King Lear*, 72.
[31] G. Kozintsev, *Shakespeare: Time and Conscience* (New York: Hill and Wang, 1966), 255–6.
[32] Ibid., p.256. Kozintsev or his translator says it is a celesta but I suspect this is an error, not a stage in the transition to harpsichord.

As with Walton, Kozinstev had a concern for period: 'the music would be in the spirit of the time, as though it were authentic'. But 'as though' is also a denial of period and the effect is rightly disjunct: we are not hearing what the teacher is playing but the music as a comment on it, a placing of the oppression of the lesson that defines her 'frailty, her artificiality, her tenderness, doomed to perish'.[33]

Later, after Polonius' death, when Ophelia has been strapped into a metal corset and massive skirts, the dress of mourning, with the veil seeming to suffocate her, she catches sight of the dancing teacher and reels back, recapitulating the dance steps, as if automatically from the stimulus of the confrontation, as the harpsichord piece is heard again. Later, now only in her shift, Ophelia wanders through Laertes' troops, with a harpsichord playing variations of the dance and strings expressing the infinite sadness of the sight of her (no.27). In sequences like these, as in the best of Walton's scores, the music begins to match the power of the play, making the film mean, demanding thought, not passive consumption, creating interpretation, not simply mood and atmosphere.

Walton's and Shostakovich's scores have been frequently recorded and performed in concerts but their origin vanishes. The numbers for Shostakovich's *King Lear* appear in recordings in the order of the published score, not their sequence in the film, so that the fanfares that Edgar calls for precede the music for the opening credits. The *Hamlet* score does not include the first version of Ophelia's dance music at all, only its return, eliminating the transformation across the expanse of the play. The fine OUP edition of Walton's music has the reworkings of the *Henry V* score by Christopher Palmer and the earlier suite by Muir Mathieson, the *Hamlet* 'Funeral March' and 'poem' by Mathieson, his version of the 'Prelude' to *Richard III* and his 'Shakespeare Suite' from the same score. But Walton's original scoring is not available. The concert versions and recordings have no place for the images that made Walton and Shostakovich create them. They become, like Schoenberg's *Begleitmusik*, film music without film.

---

[33] Kozintsev, *King Lear*, 247. See also Erik Heine, 'Controlling and Controlled: Ophelia and the Ghost as Defined by Music in Grigori Kozintsev's *Hamlet*', *Literature/Film Quarterly*, 37 (2009), 109–23.

CHAPTER 14

Music in Contemporary Shakespearean Cinema

Ramona Wray

Despite the commercial emphasis placed on Shakespearean film music, there has been little critical writing devoted to the subject. Work on Shakespeare and film has tended to concentrate on the fidelity of the adaptation and on the interpretative nature of the visuals, with limited attention being paid to the interactions between the Shakespearean text and the musical score.[1] What work there is has generally focused on the earlier – and the most popular – periods of Shakespearean music-making. In this collection, Peter Holland examines the films of Laurence Olivier and Grigori Kozintsev, scored by William Walton and Dmitri Shostakovich, respectively. Dmitri Shostakovich's scores for *Gamlet* (1964) and *Korol Lir* (1971) have been identified as significant supplements to Kozintsev's cinematography and directorial style, while other composers who have been singled out for treatment, such as Nino Rota (who wrote the rich and flamboyant music for Franco Zeffirelli's 1968 film adaptation of *Romeo and Juliet*), are considered in terms of the extra-filmic popularity of their creations.[2] And, if Patrick Doyle's scores for Kenneth Branagh's films have been recognised as characteristically sweeping and grandiloquent, then the innovative score for a film such as Baz Luhrmann's 1996 *William Shakespeare's Romeo + Juliet* has similarly stimulated comment.[3] In this latter instance, the film is rightly credited with changing the ways in which Shakespeare and film music interact, with Luhrmann's greatest achievement being seen as the 'compilation score' – the juxtaposition, alongside an original score, of

---

[1] The notable exceptions are M. Cooke, *A History of Film Music* (Cambridge University Press, 2010), 166–82; J. Sanders, *Shakespeare and Music: Afterlives and Borrowings* (Cambridge: Polity, 2007).

[2] See R. Shaughnessy, '*Romeo and Juliet*: the Rock and Roll Years', in P. Aebischer, E. J. Esche and N. Wheale, eds., *Remaking Shakespeare: Performance Across Media, Genres and Cultures* (Basingstoke: Palgrave, 2003), 172–189.

[3] M. Hattaway, 'The comedies on film', in Russell Jackson, ed., *The Cambridge Companion to Shakespeare on Film*, 2nd ed. (Cambridge University Press, 2007), 96.

pop and operatic 'musical selections culled from a variety of pre-existing sources'.[4] But, as this brief rehearsal suggests, criticism on Shakespeare and film music is confined to a handful of twentieth-century examples. As a result, an imperfect sense of how Shakespeare and music consort with each other across the filmic medium as a whole has been perpetuated.

In fact, in the late twentieth and the early twenty-first centuries, numerous new film scores have been inspired by Shakespeare's works and executed by some of the world's greatest living composers. In particular, as amputations of the Shakespearean text have become increasingly standard, music over the last twenty years has come increasingly to fill the void vacated by language, often in groundbreaking and avant-garde ways. This chapter brings the story of Shakespeare and music into the contemporary by considering the dynamic interaction between Shakespeare and music in a recent clutch of high-end, art-house Shakespeare films. It examines a group of living composers for whom the release of a soundtrack has become, in Jeff Smith's formulation, 'both an important tool of film promotion and ... an aesthetic and cultural phenomenon in its own right'.[5] In this particular assembly of Shakespeare films, music is forcefully a vehicle of narrative, a mediator of language and a surrogate for text, and it is able to perform in such a capacity because of the creative participation of both director and composer in the conception and execution of the score. All four subjects of this essay are exemplary of a highly collaborative mode of engagement. Hence, in Michael Almereyda's *Hamlet* (2000), Carter Burwell's 'original score' offers rhythmically looping minor key refrains that index Hamlet's predicament; it unfolds alongside a second compilation score in a way which points up the close relationship of director and composer. In *William Shakespeare's The Merchant of Venice* (2004), the composer-director relation is similarly underscored. But here the composer, Jocelyn Pook, produces a score quite different in its effects. Her period emphasis – in support of director Michael Radford's historical sense of intricately entangled Jewish and Christian worlds – combines Yiddish language chants, a choir singing plainsong and the prayers of a synagogue's cantors. In both cases, then, and to different ends, music complements and reinforces a distinct auteurial vision. The collaborative connection is extended in *Titus* (1999) and

[4] K. Kalinak, *Film Music: A Very Short Introduction* (Oxford University Press, 2010), 5.
[5] J. Smith, *The Sounds of Commerce: Marketing Popular Film Music* (New York: Columbia University Press, 1998), 1.

The Tempest (2010), in which the eclectic, visceral and minimalist scores of Eliot Goldenthal perfectly match the disquieting and *outré* nature of director Julie Taymor's visuals, and in *Coriolanus* (dir. Ralph Fiennes, 2012), in which a primal, angry and atavistic directorial take on the play is conjured in composer Ilan Eshkeri's experimental and martial sounds-cape. Eshkeri's score represents the most extreme instance of the ways in which sound and music produce new acoustic forms as well as fresh sonic experiences. As with all of the composers discussed in this essay, a focus on film music illuminates the extent to which Shakespeare's plays inspire talented and cutting-edge composers and musicians to new imaginative heights. In the process, text and narrative are reimagined in radical aural practices, and additional Shakespearean meanings are forged from musical experiment and exploration.

*

Distinctively, the soundtrack to Michael Almereyda's *Hamlet* was marketed in a dual manner, with two separate and genre-identified CDs being released. The first, an 'original score' written by Carter Burwell, trades on the composer's earlier association with the Coen brothers to offer minor key spiral-like refrains that, in a series of repeats and returns, not only index Hamlet's predicament (his circling and encircled state of mind) but also reinforce the filmic conceit of an imprisoning, circular environment (as suggested in the revolving drums of the laundromat or the Guggenheim Museum's swirling inner architecture). More subdued than scores by the likes of Walton and Doyle, Burwell's is an intimate confection played by a small ensemble, comprising woodwind (horn, clarinet and bassoon), strings (violin, viola, harp and cello) and keyboards. Its obsessive and contemplative acoustic realisation, symptomatic of the play's gloomy inwardness, is a dark mix perfectly in keeping with the alienated and alienating New York locale.

The circular score, with variations, sounds in the film's key moments. For example, an extended sequence concerning a failed meeting between Ophelia and Hamlet begins with a shot of Ophelia waiting by a waterfall in a downtown New York setting (the water turns and churns as part of an artificial cycle), moves on to Hamlet in his modern city apartment watching clips of his father on his video monitor (these are constantly replayed, as if the protagonist aims at bringing the deceased parent back via technology) and concludes with Ophelia still at the waterfall, her assignation having never materialised. The 'O that this too too solid flesh' (1.2.129) soliloquy sounds over the episode, and, crucially, it is supplemented by the

Burwell score. As if to accentuate the soliloquy's concern with the effort of remembering, the sonorous woodwind combines with an overlaid tick of a clock, all anchored by a *basso profundo* register that points up a funereal mood, wave-like articulations of yearning and scenarios distinguished by their capacity for repeating themselves.

Perhaps more strikingly, Burwell's score is elaborated as a series of signature musical motifs associated with Hamlet and Ophelia's suicidal tendencies and unresolved familial tensions. Hamlet, a perpetual student at odds with his corporate parents, encounters his spectral father only to find that he is threatened: the Ghost's aggressive and castigatory delivery of 'lend thy serious hearing' (1.5.5) seems particularly apposite here. Typically, and resonantly, the Burwell score swells the soundscape of the meeting, stressing the idea of a history – still playing itself out – of intimidation and infantilisation. Interestingly, Burwell's familiar loops are heard again in the scene in which Ophelia, embracing Hamlet in her grungy apartment, is interrupted by an angry Polonius: the suggestion, bolstered by the music, is that controlling parents are a constant. Further cementing links between Hamlet and Ophelia, the film elects to feature Burwell's score as an aural backdrop to the couple's shared preoccupations. As Ophelia is seen by the side of a swimming pool rehearsing the idea of drowning herself, so does Hamlet watch himself on his video screen practising the 'To be, or not to be' soliloquy. Common to each scene is the Burwell score, its recurring notes of foreboding, now slowed, affirming the deathly predilections of the protagonists. Reflecting on the film, Michael Almereyda describes the Burwell score as 'resolute music about irresolution ... chords describing a descent into madness, a man's mind resisting, and then riding, the sweep of fate', and his comments suggest a creative process where director and composer work in productive accord.[6]

Accompanying Burwell's score, the second – mainly pop – CD adds a counter-cultural flavouring to the film's aural elements. In each instance, snatches of pop in the film complement the thematics of a particular episode. Thus, when the camera cuts to Hamlet struggling over his stilted poem to Ophelia in a scruffy café we hear the thumping guitar accompaniment to the Michael Hurley song, 'Wildgeeses', played purposefully as an amateurish composition. Likewise, at the point where Hamlet approaches Claudius' limousine with murder in mind, the song, 'Hamlet Pow Pow Pow', as performed by The Birthday Party, dominates. An aggressively rendered electronic musical fusion, assisted by shouted lyrics that reference

---

[6] *'Hamlet': Music by Carter Burwell* (Nürnberg: Varèse Sarabande, 2000), sleeve notes.

the language of comic books, establishes a mood of threat and menace. Interestingly, this second CD to the film also includes the well-known classical music piece, 'Echoes of Ossian', by Niels Gade, an indication of the ways in which, in the film, classical music is deployed to signal differences in the social and generational register. By and large, classical music, such as Johannes Brahms's first symphony, Gustav Mahler's first symphony and Franz Liszt's symphonic poem on *Hamlet*, signify in the film an oppressive authority. Extracts from these works feature, then, over the opening credits, during the press conference, and in the scene where Claudius hatches his conspiracy. Sonorously and stereotypically Victorian, these constitute musical expressions of power against which Hamlet's counter-cultural musical tendencies are pitched. But the film simultaneously enlists classical music to suggest Hamlet's mockery – the ways in which a resistant appropriation of classical music is marshalled to challenge his superiors. Indicative is the use of Pyotr Tchaikovsky's overture to *Hamlet* during the film-within-a-film, Almereyda's witty conceptual translation of the play-within-a-play. The accusatory visuals of the film-within-a-film are wonderfully offset by the searing cellos, throbbing percussion and mournful lilt of the violins, pointing up how Hamlet is imagined as recuperating the cultures of his betters for his own critical ends.

   Julie Sanders notes that 'soundtracks ... do dual work in Shakespearean adaptations, contributing ... to a film's youth aesthetic, while also having deeper resonance at the level of punning reference or sustained analogy with the source-text'.[7] This is as true for *Hamlet* as for other film adaptations; for instance, the repeated use of the Morcheeba song, 'Let Me See', is exemplary, not least in its soulful aspiration towards clarity of vision in a cityscape characterised by glass surfaces that reflect frustratingly back on the viewer. Or, one might add the knowing introduction at salient points of 'Echoes of Ossian' by Niels Gade, the national composer of Denmark; the aural presence of Gade keeps alive, in the slick New York setting, the originary notion of a Nordic hinterland. Almereyda's eloquent transposition of *Hamlet* is facilitated by its score; it is also enriched by its heightened intertextuality and immersion in traditions of adapting the play, whether on screen (one clip appearing on the protagonist's monitor shows John Gielgud declaiming 'Alas, poor Yorick') or in the musical catalogue. As a result, the film stands both as a modern rewriting and as a contribution to the

---

[7] Sanders, *Shakespeare and Music*, 161.

history of adaptation, one that attests, via filmic music, to the play's continuing relevancies.

Excursions into the classical repertoire notwithstanding, Almereyda's *Hamlet* situates itself musically in the contemporary moment. By contrast, for the period-set *William Shakespeare's The Merchant of Venice* (dir. Michael Radford, 2004), an aural recreation of the early modern predominates. Unusual in the mainly male bastion of composers, Jocelyn Pook, who scored the film and had previously worked on productions such as Stanley Kubrick's *Eyes Wide Shut* (1999), visits on her interpretation a sense of period and regional detailing complemented by strains of lyricism and romance. Such emotional contours are vitally registered in, for example, 'Her Gentle Spirit', a theme associated with Portia. An introductory inset shows us an ethereal Belmont and the heroine's face framed by gold-red ringlets, the montage being nicely complemented by a score that, alternating between flute, harp and violins, conjures an idealised vision of womanhood. At the same time, because this particular theme recurs during the trial scenes, it accrues to itself suggestions of female empowerment. At other points, the score may be more pathetically realised. With Shylock's appearances, low-pitched strings, a stress on the bass register and strained, proximate notes create a sombre air, and this is given a specific Jewish detailing through the use of the *kinnor* lyre. The lyre is the signature instrument during Jessica's elopement and the trial scene, and it works in the *mise-en-bande* to elaborate a sense of a riven and embattled community. Instrumentation and the evocation of distinctive moods are central to the film's envisioning of different worlds and possibilities.

The 'standard operating procedure . . . is to bring the composer in after the film has been shot', yet Pook bucked this trend by beginning work early, composing the diegetic music for the dances and songs before and during the shoot.[8] Perhaps taking inspiration from the other comedies, in which onstage music is invariably part of the action, *The Merchant of Venice* incorporates musicians as performers into the narrative fabric. Hence, the Prince of Aragon, a particularly foppish suitor, bids two lutenists in an interpolated injunction to play '*musica*': their Elizabethan-style melody, with harshly plucked strings, accentuates the tension of the proceedings. On a further occasion, we witness a boy soprano (accompanied by another youth playing the lute) singing the refrain, 'Tell me where is fancy bred?' (3.2.63), as Bassanio begins his casket deliberations.

---

[8] Kalinak, *Film Music*, 93. See Stephen Warbeck's comments, 190–2, above.

The lifting octaves, up and down the scale, powerfully capture the complexions of imminent success or disappointment. A recurring musical theme, 'With wandering steps', as sung by counter-tenor Andreas Scholl, is first experienced as a diegetic performance by a minstrel accompanied by a violin and lutes. Introduced to mark the return to Belmont of Portia and Nerissa, the soaring performance is listened to by a feeling and attentive Jessica; the lyrics, for her, it is suggested, are particularly resonant. Diegetic music fills in for what a film cannot always execute. So, in the flyting scene between Jessica and Lorenzo, the song in the background, which is referred to by the couple, briefly features lyrics extracted from the play's disquisition on the 'moonlight' (5.1.53–56). Music fills in for much of the scene's language even as it provides an ironic counterpoint to the stated emphasis on 'sweet harmony' (5.1.56).

Thanks to her early involvement, when it came to writing the main score, Pook was wholly immersed in the motifs and styles she wished the film proper to deploy. But the instrumental sounds she privileges mostly point to the influence of Renaissance music rather than to an effort to recreate it authentically; this is a film that generally imagines as opposed to imitates. What emerges is a haunting, shimmering score that, utilising 'existing medieval or Renaissance themes' and 'various texts from the period', brings to mind, via lilting intervals and tossing arpeggios, the maritime situation of Shakespeare's Venice and the shifting fortunes of the central players.[9] Period-specific music is suggested in the theme, 'Bassanio's Palazzo'; here, a jaunty, Tudor-style madrigal, supported by a mandolin and pipe, nicely sets off a scene of mirth and merriment. Elsewhere, trumpets and drumrolls imply events of Renaissance magnitude: Bassanio's grand arrival in Belmont to begin his wooing is a case in point. Only on one occasion does Pook aim at a more fully-fledged authenticity. The film's comic rendition of the scene between Solanio and Salerio, which begins with the question, 'Now, what news on the Rialto?' (3.1.1), takes place in a brothel. In the midst of heaving bodies and glimpses of naked flesh, a young woman with a vihuela sings a ballad in Spanish, '*Paseavase el rey Moro*'. A secular fantasia by the sixteenth-century Spanish composer, Luiz de Narváez, the ballad reverberates at a number of levels. In its filmic contexts, the film's punning reference to a King of the Moors who strolls (rides) up and down indexes both one of Portia's suitors and the brothel's sexual activities. Because sung by a woman, the song also points

---

[9] *William Shakespeare's The Merchant of Venice: Music by Jocelyn Pook* (London: Decca, 2004), sleeve notes.

up an ideological conjunction of women, entertainment and prostitution, a nexus of operations from which Shylock (who is himself tauntingly addressed by the courtesans) is conspicuously excluded. The effect, to adopt Kendra Preston Leonard's formulation about periodisation in film, is to allow 'experients' to be 'engaged more fully in a film's complete cinematographic experience'.[10]

At its heart, Pook's 'Renaissance' auditory world captures a sense of potential collision and personal vicissitude. Thus, after an onscreen announcement about the marginalisation of the Jewish community, the 'Ghetto' theme (stringed crescendos weave in and out of the Yiddish language chants) establishes an empathetic place for Shylock; this is followed by a 'Blessing of the Boat' sequence sung by a boys' church choir (an organ and Latin plainsong suggest an ecclesiastical setting); and this, in turn, in rounded off by a diegetic 'Synagogue' theme characterised by the jarring harmonies of the cantors. Musically, then, the score stresses the proximity of Jewish and Christian worlds and, because occasionally ragged around its edges, hints at the prospect of conflicting destinies. If Shylock is identified in such moments, Jessica is a later focus of attention, as when she listens to 'Wandering Steps', a theme also linked to Antonio. Deploying as lyrics the final lines of Milton's *Paradise Lost*, the music implies that both characters have lost prelapsarian existences. And, as this theme gives way at the close to Pook's stately musical setting of Edgar Allen Poe's poem, 'Bridal Ballad', with its reflections on a 'sorely shaken . . . soul', the film moves outside its customary conjuration of the Renaissance to suggest, in Hayley Westenra's crystalline voice, the presence of Jessica and the dilemmas with which she, as a character, has been associated. It is at this point, more than any other, that *The Merchant of Venice* initiates a move beyond its period contexts so as to spotlight the purchase of the play on a more recent present.

A further, particularly fruitful collaboration in recent Shakespeare film is that shared by director Julie Taymor and composer Eliot Goldenthal. The latter's scores for Taymor's two films, *Titus* (1999) and *The Tempest* (2010), espouse a minimalist and eclectic approach. Uniquely, Goldenthal eschews the tried-and-trusted reliance on the classical/pop conjunction, preferring instead to develop wide-ranging musical realisations that chime with the somewhat *outré* modality of the director's highly visual interpretations. Having worked previously on films such as Ridley Scott's *Alien*

---

[10] K. P. Leonard, 'The Use of Early Modern Music in Film Scoring for Elizabeth I', in L. C. Dunn and K. R. Larson, eds., *Gender and Song in Early Modern England* (Aldershot: Ashgate, 2014), 171.

(1979) and Neil Jordan's *Interview with a Vampire* (1994), Goldenthal was well-equipped to bring to *Titus* a destabilising dimension, one that, in its discomforting combination of orchestral and electronic registers, and in its disquieting referencing of a number of styles, nicely complements the play's preoccupation with alterity, trauma and psychic breakdown. To a greater degree, the score weaves its particular magic because of its multivariate character, and, indeed, the music overall is characterised by a dizzying amalgam of (albeit muted) influences: hints of Mahler and Mussorgsky sound amidst fairground themes and 'boogie-cool jazz' numbers.[11] Indicative is the jazz number that announces the arrival of Saturninus' motor calvacade. Contrary to the verbal thrust of the soon-to-be emperor's speech ('And countrymen, my loving followers, / Plead my successive title' [1.1.3–4]), the cheeky and cacophonous blare of the clarinets and saxophones establish chaos and mayhem as dominant motifs, and this is clarified when the orgiastic and hysterical tone of the score finds its equivalent in the street riot sparked by the political elections. Another musical genre – this one suggestive of the circus – enters in the scene where a clown and his assistant invite Titus and his family to witness a performance (which, as it turns out, involves the showing in jars of the severed heads of the Roman general's sons). The preposterous musical intervals deployed for this episode's theme, as well as the skipping beat, suggest a comic mode, but all is grotesquely upset by the discovery of the heads, the score appropriately registering the shift in a major key refrain played over discordant minor chords. It is through such a *mélange* of musical styles that the film renders the mixed elements of Shakespeare's play and generates a unique cross-cultural and cross-temporal sonic experience.

If there is variety in the Goldenthal score, there is also a more streamlined approach to the film's aural dimensions. At the start, for example, the 'Victorious Titus' theme (we witness the mud-caked soldiers moving in robotic unison) suggests a thumping imperial primitivism, supported, as it is, by ecstatic woodwind, the clash of cymbals and a Latin chant that is itself a translation of the captain's valedictory address. Rather than staging Shakespeare's language directly, *Titus* elects to mediate it as part of a soundscape that is designed to prioritise an impression both of the grandiloquent and the antique. At the same time, as in this instance, the score can function in a powerfully stripped-back capacity: percussion alone mimes the clash of weaponry and, before the scene moves on, everything

[11] J. Taymor, *Titus: The Illustrated Screenplay* (New York: Newmarket, 2000), 182.

has been reduced to a solitary gust of wind. The film is able to contemplate the role of language in complementary ways, as when a scene of seeming pastoral bliss by a riverbank reveals the mutilated Lavinia, branches standing in for her hands, and a dreadful soundscape (made up of distorted moaning, laughing, weeping and birdsong) takes over. Paradoxically expressive is the way in which an unexpected surge of violins, playing a descending spiral of notes, illustrates the brute fact of Lavinia's tongueless silence. The rape of Lavinia paves the way for Titus' murder of Tamora's sons. In the scene where Titus serves up to his enemies the infamous human pie, Carlo Buti's well-known war-era populist song, 'Vivere!', plays as background. Clearly, a joyous anthem about life and living satirically draws attention to the mortal consumption in which the players unwittingly participate, a fact that the camera's focus on eating mouths serves only to reinforce. Even here, moreover, Goldenthal's minimalist tendencies announce themselves: the song is heard only in parts, extracts standing in for a larger whole, and the effect is designed to be associative. 'Vivere!', as Martha Nochinson notes, 'flourished on the radio in Fascist Italy the week before Mussolini died', and its echoing presence in *Titus* thereby equates histories of Roman despotism and twentieth-century political demagoguery.[12]

In *The Tempest*, too, Goldenthal's score tends towards the eclectic and the suggestive. Hence, if some parts of the film are symphonically orchestrated, others rely on single guitars or groups of guitars. More generally, the stark complexions of the score mirror the visceral appearances of the film's volcanic Hawaiian locations so as 'to create', in Taymor's words, 'a sense of timeless presentness'.[13] The 'Hell is Empty' theme is a case in point: it meshes tenor saxophones and unconventionally tuned guitars playing between three and five stabbing notes in such a way as to prioritise the cries of the drowning mariners and the orgiastic scream of Prospera with which the sequence climaxes. By contrast, a steel cello, nonwestern flutes and a glass harmonica (whose sound is akin to a fine glass played with the fingertips) are the instruments that represent Ariel's lightness and ethereality in passages capped by the *falsetto* vocals of Ben Whishaw himself. With surprising falls into alternate keys, Ariel's 'Full Fathom Five' is realised anti-romantically, with the combination of a blue filter, glimpses of a submerged body and a lyrical modification

[12] M. Nochinson, 'Home Video: *Titus*', *Cineaste*, 26 2 (2001), 49.
[13] J. Taymor, *The Tempest: Adapted from the Play by William Shakespeare* (New York: Abrams, 2010), 21.

('yellow' [1.2.378]) is changed to 'darkened') creating the impression of music emanating from a deep watery location. Breaking with tradition again, the film elects not only to include Prospera's epilogue but to instate it musically. Singer Beth Gibbons' echoing delivery of the farewell to magic and books is a husky-throated, elegiac affair full of pained, pleading sentiments. The slow-motion descent of the precious magic volumes into oceanic oblivion is replicated in the slow pace of the song; this is less a plea for audience indulgence than a woman's expression of grief and loss. *The Tempest*, the play, of course, is full of song, providing musical opportunities of which Goldenthal fully avails himself. 'O Mistress Mine', for example, borrowed from *Twelfth Night*, provides an additional context for the relationship of the young lovers and, in its unfussy orchestration, again highlights the significance of word and lyric. In other parts of the film, a song illustrates Goldenthal's predilection for streamlined scoring. ''Ban, 'ban, Cacaliban' (2.2.175), Caliban's celebratory song about his new dispensation, is without notes and entirely percussive, the banging beats of the drums enforcing the idea of an expression from below, about the below. Going beyond what many might see as a traditional film score, Goldenthal elaborates to impressive effect an acoustic aesthetic based on principles of minimalism, eclecticism and innovation.

Taking these ideas to an extreme, and perhaps representing an endpoint, is composer Ilan Eshkeri in his score for Ralph Fiennes' film adaptation of *Coriolanus* (2012). *Coriolanus* is a primal, angry and atavistic reading of the play that, by virtue of Belgrade shooting locations, extracts symbolic capital from 'fading communist constructions' and a generally 'denuded topography'.[14] Visually, the film announces chaos, disaffection and neglect. Underpasses gouged with graffiti testify to a sense of civic discontent; cratered streets represent everyday embodiments of a world in crisis; abandoned buildings underscore an impression of a city in decline; and piles of burning rubble suggest an apocalyptic scenario. When the action shifts to the Roman senate, and palatial, creamy interiors are substituted, the switch in location serves only to highlight unbridgeable social divisions between oligarchies and common people. Although the scene moves out of the urban when the exiled Coriolanus seeks Aufidius, there is no alleviating contrast, the *faux* pastoral of the protagonist's journey taking the form of a deserted road in a wintry, rubbish-strewn wasteland.

[14] M. Thornton Burnett, *Filming Shakespeare in the Global Marketplace*, 2nd ed. (Basingstoke: Palgrave, 2012), ix.

As befits a composer whose previous commissions include the gangster flick, *Layer Cake* (dir. Matthew Vaughn, 2004), and the television feature, *Colosseum: A Gladiator's Story*, Eshkeri matches this vision with an equivalently bleak, martial and raw soundscape. Score, indeed, may be too limiting a descriptor, for the film yields a cornucopia of non-conventional noises (gasps, guttural exclamations, handclaps and bangs) that are interwoven with music played on such avant-garde instruments as the taiko drum, tam tam, glass pad and bowed vibraphone. Percussion-loaded rhythms which underwrite scratchy strings and spiky single notes are the naturally disconcerting correlatives for a film that, as Mark Thornton Burnett remarks, gestures to 'recent conflicts – the war between Russia and Chechnya, the Arab Spring and the London riots – as part of its anatomization of a society in decline and disrepair'.[15] Consistently, then, the film's aural accoutrements make for unnerving effects. Unlike parts of the *Titus* score, there is no implication of an imperial theme here; rather, clanging, industrial and, above all, metallic auditory creations evoke a scarred, modern *habitus* in which the ruined factory or the soulless apartment block predominates. Electronic sounds – mostly keyboards complemented by some strings – often centre upon notes which, sustained over several bars in a trembling vibrato, conjure an idea of events of seismic consequence. Resembling Goldenthal in his predilection for percussion, but also developing in a unique fashion that composer's tendency, Eshkeri favours drums as forms of musical notation; typically, an eerie bass register punctuates the action, throbbing and pulsating with an unflinching bellicosity. The sound may rise suddenly in volume, refracting the unpredictability of the political milieu; alternatively, it may descend into apparently tuneless 'noise', itself symptomatic of a dystopian filmic imaginary.

Two 'scored' scenes stand out for particular comment. The first is the moment at which Coriolanus, now firmly ensconced with the warlike Volscians, is pleaded with by his mother to abandon the attack on Rome. Screenplay writer John Logan notes that, to 'allow linguistic explosions', we had 'to create moments of cinematic composure or stillness about them', a fact which Vanessa Redgrave, who plays Volumnia, seems to have ingested.[16] As Ralph Fiennes, who plays Coriolanus, observes of these encounters, 'She . . . came really close and put her hands on my knees.

[15] Burnett, *Filming*, ix.
[16] J. Logan, 'Introduction', in *'Coriolanus': Screenplay by John Logan* (New York: HarperCollins, 2011), ix.

With that physical proximity, it became very intimate.'[17] Not surprisingly, then, silence mostly characterises the meeting, yet Eshkeri's score still inserts itself to meaningful effect. As the episode begins, therefore, cymbals overlaid with wolf-whistles and a violin sliding tone-by-tone down the scale mark the moment as nervy, tense, expectant and volatile. The muted sounds are made to echo unsettlingly among the ruined factory walls, and they function in such a way as to offset the whispered yielding of Coriolanus to his mother's persuasions. The second is the climax – Coriolanus' death at Aufidius' hands. Once again, silence predominates. However, Eshkeri takes the opportunity to interweave the groans of the combatants with sounds of engines revving, a non-diegetic drum beating, and a high-pitched wail which, although not clearly identified as emanating from any on-screen source, nevertheless communicates an immediate experience of bodily affliction. As the scene closes, and we fade to black, the drop of Coriolanus' body on the floor of the lorry is picked up in a drum roll which sounds like a militaristic death knell. Intricately elaborated, and seamlessly integrated into the 'real-life' action of the narrative, the film's score vividly encapsulates the trials and tribulations of a nation-state in the throes of its own breakdown.

There is but one alleviating moment. This is in the song that plays over the final credits, 'Sta Pervolio', a Greek folk melody that evokes both a classical world and the film's Balkan/European conceptual template. Performed by female vocalist Lisa Zane, 'Sta Pervolio' reminds audiences of the power of women's speech in the drama we have just witnessed as this is incarnated in Volumnia's exhortatory address. Unaccompanied by any instrumentation, this solo suggests an effort to establish an individuated gendered identity even as it also, via demotic lyrical references to battle, drinking, gardens and death, brings to mind the fraught homoerotic relationship that obtains between Coriolanus and Aufidius (as this is represented in the film in a shot of their half-aggressive, half-loving embrace). As if in partial recognition that it is this triangulated relationship – between mother, son and war rival – that lies at the tragedy's core, the film is accompanied by a two-CD package, the one featuring music and the other showcasing speeches from the central players. This second CD includes rhetorical set pieces which are identifiable via titular tags, such as 'You Fragments' and 'What is thy name' and, most recognisably, 'O Mother'. But even here the words and the music frequently consort

[17] G. Crowdus and R. Porton, 'Shakespeare's Perennial Themes: An Interview with Ralph Fiennes', *Cineaste*, 37 2 (2012), 23.

with or dissolve into each other, pointing up a further level of experimentation – an initiative whereby Shakespearean language is reworked and reconceived as another sound effect. The concept marks a radical development in the marketing of Shakespeare film and, in particular, the 'music', and it suggests that auditors are granted a new set of engagement options and a fresh means of appreciating film as a holistic aural phenomenon. Its postmodern proclivities notwithstanding (the screen is rife with alienating devices of various kinds), *Coriolanus* demonstrates that the long-standing association between filmmakers and composers still admits of the Shakespearean word and that, in and through music, his language is alive and well. Responsive to the eddies and flows of trends in musical interpretation, the score to the film bears witness to the diversity and variety characterising the translation of Shakespeare's plays into the cinematic medium and, in so doing, announces the prospect of continuing acts of musical reinvention.

CHAPTER 15

The Politics of Popular Music in Contemporary Shakespearean Performance

Adam Hansen

Introduction

This chapter tries to reread, or to *hear again*, examples of the ways popular music has been used in some recent productions of Shakespeare. Given their number, this account can only be selective, suggesting ways of addressing what happens when popular music meets Shakespearean performance that go beyond the focus here on two different productions: one fairly faithful to an editorially established Shakespearean text, and one looser, more radical adaptation. In turn, this chapter contributes to a field of study developed by Stephen Purcell in his *Popular Shakespeare*, where he says 'an area . . . which remains as yet relatively unexplored is that of Shakespeare and 'the popular' in performance'.[1] We might note that there has been even less attention paid to Shakespeare and popular *music* in performance, and this silence continues. *Titus Andronicus*, directed by Pia Furtado in 2014 in a Peckham car park, featured 'beatboxing, breaking and more'.[2] One review praised the production's 'visual impact', while complaining it was 'full of loud music': this was the extent of the analysis of the staging's sonic aesthetic.[3]

This chapter's rereading, or rehearing, tries to address several questions, questions informed by research into the interactions between music and literature, as articulated by William E. Grim:

> The first way in which music may influence literature is on the **inspirational** level. . . . This is the case of music being the writer's muse. . . . Music can also

[1] S. Purcell, *Popular Shakespeare: Simulation and Subversion on the Modern Stage* (Basingstoke: Palgrave, 2009), 7. I'm grateful too, to audiences in London and Leeds for comments regarding earlier versions of this paper, especially Irene Morra, Richard Wilson, Varhsa Panjwani, and Susan Anderson.
[2] From the production's crowdfunding webpage: www.kickstarter.com/projects/thetoeco/titus-andronicus-at-bold-tendencies-car-park-peckh/posts/940029#description (accessed 26 August 2015).
[3] L. Gardner, www.theguardian.com/stage/2014/sep/05/titus-andronicus-review-visually-striking-but-flawed (accessed 26 August 2015).

influence literature at a **metaphorical** level. At this level, music serves as the subject matter, point of departure, or intertextual reference within the work of literature. ... The third type of influence that music may have on literature is at the **formal** level. At this level, the work of literature utilizes or attempts to imitate musical forms and/or compositional procedures within a literary context.[4]

On reading this, one might wonder what it has to do with popular music in recent Shakespearean performance. Grim focusses on what classical (not popular) music does to or for literature as text (not as performance), and on the creation of texts (not their consumption). Despite Christopher Ricks's playing with cultural hierarchies and chronologies to affirm Shakespeare was 'Dylanesque', and despite modern music's early modern roots, Shakespeare obviously hadn't heard twentieth-century popular music, so it would be hard to claim it 'inspired' him, or that he referenced or imitated it at a metaphorical or formal level.[5] But what Grim is saying still has relevance to this chapter, if we think of the Shakespearean text – like any drama – not simply as the words on the page, but also as their performance, and if we expand Grim's frame of reference to suggest that music can help audiences *interpret* the text and performances of it.

In other words, intertextuality is created by the ears of the audience and a particular production, not just by the pen of the author. If a short story cites music, or uses musical forms, this is an intertextual act that is meant to make readers put both writing and music text in new contexts. Comparably, a production's intertextuality – interaurality – can amplify resonances in a text, and condition interpretations of its performance.[6] David Lindley puts it like this: 'the majority of modern Shakespearian directors ... take advantage of the "enhancing" power of music.' Lindley goes on to characterise this 'enhancing' power as 'the affect and effect of the music':

> [I]t is possible to argue that music does not simply occupy a secondary role in endorsing dialogue or the visual qualities of the *mise-en-scène*, but that in important respects it may actively condition or even determine the way in which we see the action.[7]

---

[4] W. E. Grim, 'Musical Form as Problem in Literary Criticism', in W. Bernhart, S. P. Scher, and W. Wolf, eds., *Word and Music Studies: Defining the Field* (Amsterdam and Atlanta, GA: Rodopi, 1999), 237–48, 237–8.
[5] C. Ricks, *Dylan's Visions of Sin* (London: Penguin, 2003), 60.
[6] See Austern's essay for such effects in the seventeenth century.
[7] D. Lindley, '"Sounds and Sweet Airs": Music in Shakespearean Performance History', *Shakespeare Survey*, 64 (2011), 59–73, 59–61.

As Carol Rutter and Jonathan Trenchard's essay shows, this finds parallel in what some particular companies, like Propeller, try to do by using popular music, alongside other forms of music:

> There are many different types of musical styles in our production of *Henry V*. What unites them all is the earthy root of thirteen male actors performing it together to create an effect: to communicate something to the audience at a particular time. A Chorus both theatrical and musical.[8]

So, that's the first question: if popular music is meant to do something to people watching or hearing a Shakespeare performance that uses it, *what does it do*? What does it 'communicate'? This question is partially answered by, but also raises, another, which we can foreground by invoking one of the greatest writers on Shakespeare and music, W. H. Auden:

> Music is not only an art with its own laws and values; it is also a social fact. Composing, performing, listening to music are things which human beings do under certain circumstances just as they fight and make love.[9]

If music does something to audiences, it does so because it tells them something about their world. As Hanif Kureishi suggests, popular music is especially good at telling us about *our* world:

> The alternative history of our time [can be] told from the standpoint of popular music, which is as good a position as any to look from, since pop, intersecting with issues of class, race and particularly gender, has been at the centre of post-war culture.[10]

More recently, Irene Morra suggests that British popular music has become a particularly significant site for complex and contradictory expressions. To Morra, these expressions build upon, contest and reproduce fault lines like those Kureishi described, as well as others such as 'tradition' versus 'progress', and 'authenticity' as opposed to performativity. In this way, popular music both consolidates and queries collective and personal meaning:

> In the twentieth and twenty-first centuries, music . . . has gained a particular importance in the definition and assertion of British national identity . . . . Within this discourse, popular music is never just music: it claims

---

[8] N. Asbury 'The process of the Music for Henry V' (2011): propeller.org.uk/play/pocket-henry-v#/music/read (accessed 12 September 2012).

[9] W.H. Auden, 'Music in Shakespeare', in *The Dyer's Hand and other essays* (1948; New York: Vintage, 1989), 500–527, 502.

[10] H. Kureishi, "That's how good it was", in Hanif Kureishi and Jon Savage, eds., *The Faber Book of Pop* (London and Boston: Faber and Faber, 1995), xvii–xx, xix.

a dominant role in voicing an essential national identity, history and experience.[11]

Making and enjoying contemporary popular music, whether in a performance of Shakespeare or not, are inherently worldly acts. Lindley makes this point more broadly: 'The political significance of music should not be underestimated.'[12] But we might add: 'The political meaning of any music depends on its use.'[13] So we come to the second question: what are some of the (political) uses and meanings of popular music in recent productions of Shakespeare? To try to answer this question we could argue that the use of popular music creates what Josh Kun has called 'audiotopias':

> 'contact zones,' ... both sonic and social spaces where disparate identity-formations, cultures, *and* geographies historically kept and mapped separately are allowed to interact with each other.[14]

We might add different temporalities and cultural modes to Kun's list. The presence of popular music in a performance of Shakespeare connects past and present, an early modern play-text with a modern soundscape. But it also brings together cultural modes often still seen as 'high' and 'low', despite the evidence that Shakespeare can be conceived of as 'popular'. Is a theatrical performance, then, an 'audiotopia'? That is, not just a place of seeing and hearing, with spectators and audiences, but a place where 'sonic and social' differences manifest themselves in space, and, perhaps, where those differences are contested? Does popular music in Shakespearean productions create 'audiotopia'; not utopias, but spaces of contention, where things yet come together? To put these questions in very simple terms: in hearing pop do we hear the sounds of politics of Shakespeare's time, and our own? To answer this question, and with my previous questions in mind, I will begin with a discussion of Propeller's 2011–12 *Henry V*.

Henry V: 'Broken music . . . Broken English' (5.2.221–2)

Henry V emphasises the visual, even when the opportunity for aural metaphor seems obvious:

---

[11] I. Morra, *Britishness, Popular Music, and National Identity: The Making of Modern Britain* (Abingdon and New York: Routledge, 2014), ix, 11.

[12] D. Lindley, 'Literature and Music', in Martin Coyle, Peter Garside, Malcolm Kelsall, and John Peck, eds., *Encyclopedia of Literature and Criticism* (London: Routledge, 1991), 1004–14, 1008.

[13] R. Pratt, *Rhythm and Resistance: Explorations in the Political Uses of Popular Music* (New York, Westport, CT, London: Praeger, 1990), 1.

[14] J. Kun, *Audiotopia: Music, Race, and America* (Berkeley: University of California Press, 2005), 23.

CHORUS Think when we talk of horses that you see them
    Printing their proud hoofs i'th'receiving earth (Prologue, 26–7)

Here we're told to see, not hear, and there's even a hint at reading too, in that reference to 'print'. Despite this, and being required to 'sit and see' by the Chorus (4.52), we *are* also invited to hear at moments:

CHORUS Now entertain conjecture of a time
    When . . .
    Steed threatens steed . . .
    Piercing the night's dull ear . . .
    The country cocks do crow, the clocks do toll . . .   (Chorus, 4.1–15)

So the aural does have a part to play in the arsenal of our 'imaginary forces' (Prologue, 18), as we are petitioned 'Gently to hear' (Prologue, 34). Aurality is one of the tools that the play, especially the Chorus, uses to bond the soldiers to their king, and so to unite the 'nation', creating continuity between the action onstage and the people watching that action. Bruce Smith has observed of plays like *Henry V* that while 'divergent speech communities are brought together onstage just as they were in the arena and in the galleries', prologues use 'rhetorical power to counter this diversity', in 'oracular appeals to audience unanimity'.[15] Henry evokes harmony too, as described by someone who knows a thing or two about the power conferred by the celestial order:

CANTERBURY List his discourse of war, and you shall hear
    A fearful battle rendered you in music;   (1.1.43–4)

Henry's authority depends on this order and his ability to heed, represent and communicate it:

EXETER For government, though high and low and lower,
    Put into parts, doth keep in one consent,
    Congreeing in a full and natural close
    Like music.   (1.2.180–3)

So *Henry V* is a particularly useful play to discuss if we want to answer some of the questions raised at the start of this essay: sound, especially music, is political here. Controlling and conditioning what people hear, as well as what they see, equates to political power.

---

[15] B. R. Smith, *The Acoustic World of Early Modern England: Attending to the O-Factor* (Chicago and London: University of Chicago Press, 1999), 281–2.

But *Henry V* is also especially useful for the way it uses popular music. Such music functions in the play to counterpoint if not contradict author-itative aural positions:

BARDOLPH On, on, on, on, on, to the breach, to the breach!
NYM Pray thee, corporal, stay. The knocks are too hot, and for mine own part,
      I have not a case of lives. The humour of it is too hot, that is the very plain-
      song of it.
PISTOL 'The plain-song' is most just, for humours do abound.
      Knocks go and come, God's vassals drop and die,
(SINGS) And sword and shield,
      In bloody field,
      Doth win immortal fame.
BOY Would I were in an ale-house in London. I would give all my fame for a pot
      of ale and safety.   (3.2.1–11)

Bardolph's repetitions function as a mediated muddling of the King's seemingly stirring command: 'Once more unto the breach, dear friends' (3.1.1). As the King's resolute words dissolve into mimicry, and encounter only grudging assent, they are also countered in sound. Pistol sings a fragment of what is now an unknown popular tune, and his 'plain-song' not only generates complaint, but also invites the Boy's plainness, or plain-speaking. The truth of conflict undercuts the King's injunctions to fight as one.

These uses of music, and *popular* music, as mediums for both authority and complaint invite productions to amplify these tensions. Propeller's production did exactly that. To an extent, music, and popular music, in this production, preserved the distinctions and effected the unions the play realises. This production synthesised many styles of music, and was heard to do so by reviewers:

> Music is everywhere – from The Clash's 'London Calling' to a gorgeous
> *Te Deum*.[16]
>   It's very song-driven production – everything from a ravishing
> 'Te Deum' to Mahattan Transfer's 'Chanson d'Amour'.[17]

In her essay Carol Rutter reflects on how Propeller's productions work to create musical diversity as well as 'an ensemble identity'.[18] This production

---

[16] N. Norman, 'First Night Review: Henry V & The Winter's Tale', *Daily Express* (30 January 2012).
[17] P. Taylor, 'Henry V and The Winter's Tale', *The Independent* (30 January 2012).
[18] See 241, below.

thereby created a musical band of brothers from the all-male cast, with collective effort evident in the composition and execution of the music:

> We began to learn songs as a group ... Each man plays his part. To say I wrote the *Te Deum*, or did the arrangements for some of the songs, is true in one sense, but actually it came from us all.[19]

Yet for all these 'sonic and social' syntheses, music worked, as in the play, to reinforce distinctions (and not for the first time, as Val Brodie's discussion of Charles Kean's 1859 *Henry V* suggests). Scenes in the French court were soundtracked by the 1977 version of 'Chanson D'Amour' by the North American vocal group Manhattan Transfer. The 'English' troops, however, mingled football chants with The Clash's punkish 'London Calling', from two years later. Why counterpose these musical modes? Because in the play the French are cast as weak, soft and backwards-looking and this music 'underscores' that, according to reviewers like Paul Taylor; and because the 'English', driven ever 'On, on, on', outpace and beat them: 'with a blast of the Clash's 'London Calling' to put them in the mood, the hooligan band score a memorable away victory against the French'.[20]

This juxtaposed easy-versus-uneasy listening, vitality and vigour versus moribund middle-of-the-road schlock. Such juxtaposition evoked the play's conflicts, and endorsed its assumptions, but it did so by evoking musical and cultural conflicts from long after the play's conception, and the time of its content. Perhaps 'London Calling' was meant to create a sense of the now-ness, the situated-ness, that are so important to the play's articulation of a story from the past that mattered to its present, as it marshalled 'Englishmen' in London and beyond to support the Queen in her Irish ventures. For if The Clash sang about 'London Calling', impelled by a martial drumbeat, so does the play, obsessively, triumphantly:

CHORUS   So let him land
And solemnly see him set on to London. ....
But now behold, ...
How London doth pour out her citizens. ....
Now in London place him ...   (Chorus, 5.13–35)

Just as Shakespeare's 'now' sought to create continuities between English history and the 1590s, so this use of popular music sought to create continuities between Shakespeare's time and the present. *Henry V* can be

---

[19] Asbury 'The process of the Music'.
[20] A. Hickling, 'Henry V/The Winter's Tale' *The Guardian* (30 January 2012).

seen to celebrate what London can do, and so, perhaps, can The Clash's song:

> It's a powerful, instantly recognizable, highly memorable song about London by a (retrospectively) much-loved classic rock band from London ... so it's the perfect song to signify, evoke, celebrate or promote the capital.[21]

This certainly seemed to be the effect desired, or intuited, by reviewers like Neil Norman:

> Cry Oi! for England, Harry and St George! ... Visceral, intelligent and ironclad theatre, this isn't just Shakespeare – this is rock and roll.

Such comments conflate various things. Replacing 'Harry' with 'Oi!' remixes lines from the play (3.1.34) with references to a particularly 'visceral', if not intelligent, mutation of punk, in order to set up an analogy where 'rock and roll' both 'is' and surpasses 'Shakespeare', and where both are in service of 'England'.[22] But this account of triumphant English punks besting foppish French-speakers, and this reading of how the production's music endorses this victory, only tell half the story. The lyrics to 'London Calling' *are* a call to arms, but they are also a cry of, or for, contemporaneity opposed to the past.

In the late 1970s, this attention on the now and the future was set against the smooth nostalgic schmaltz of Manhattan Transfer, not least in Joe Strummer's eyes: 'Everyone's looking for yesterday because tomorrow's so shitty.'[23] As Gregory Colón Semenza has suggested, in his discussion of punk's appropriations of Shakespeare: 'Punk doesn't regard history or historical artefacts as sacred.'[24] The now and the future Strummer sings about are apocalyptic, as he describes a post-OPEC crisis world running out of oil, afflicted by climate change, water levels rising, and social alienation. 'London' may be 'Calling' but it doesn't do so in the measured tones used in BBC Overseas Service broadcasts from the capital during war-time.[25] The song's 'straight reportage from the Winter of Discontent'

---

[21] M. Gray, *Route 19 Revisited: The Clash and the making of London Calling* (London: Vintage Books, 2011), 486.

[22] For more on Oi! See M. Worley, 'Oi! Oi! Oi!: Class, Locality and British Punk', *Twentieth Century British History* (2013), 1–31.

[23] Joe Strummer interviewed by Charles Shaar Murray for *New Musical Express* (June 1979), cited in Gray, *Route 19*, 184.

[24] G. C. Semenza, 'God Save the Queene: Sex Pistols, Shakespeare, and Punk [Anti-] History', in Semenza, ed., *The English Renaissance in Popular Culture: An Age for All Time* (Basingstoke: Palgrave, 2010), 143–164, 151.

[25] Gray, *Route 19*, 190–92.

describes internal strife, not externalised crusades.[26] 'London Calling' is no hymn to Englishness: like other punks, The Clash 'were writing about the society they knew about: the tower blocks, the dole queues, the schisms in society about race and sex.'[27]

As their promotional materials indicate, Propeller had asked themselves the question: how to translate the conflict between French and English in *Henry V* into 'a more engaging way of expressing Shakespeare'?[28] One way, it seems, was by finding an aural parallel in the conflicts between late-1970s punk and what it set itself against. It helps that what is set against The Clash in this production sings in French accents, so to speak, but since punk began as a transatlantic rather than simply 'English' phenomenon, we might also observe that the focus of conflict has shifted, from one between nations to between generations and cultural forms. Or, more precisely, to conflicts within 'nations', and to conflicts that problematise what national identity might be.

Realising the discontinuity or break between Manhattan Transfer's smooth harmonies and The Clash's 'broken music' also realises what is 'broken' in the England, or 'Britain', evoked by Shakespeare's play, and by contemporary productions of it. Accordingly, 'London Calling' wasn't the only way in which Propeller's popular music complicated the play's apparent nationalistic fervour. Another song featured was The Pogues' 1985 'A Pair of Brown Eyes'. In the video to this song (directed by Alex Cox), many Londoners (and, by implication, many people in the country as a whole) have had their eyes removed or their vision swaddled in bandages. The song itself is full of violent imagery, akin to Williams' lines at *Henry V*, 4.1. In the words of James Fearnley, a founding member of the group, this was a 'nightmarish kaleidoscope . . . a landscape worthy of Wilfred Owen, full of dismemberment, with arms and legs scattered all around'.[29] If The Clash's Joe Strummer sang of impending apocalypse, Shane MacGowan evokes the then-ongoing conflicts in Northern Ireland, the recent Falklands War, and the equally recent Miners' Strike. He sings, in short, of a divided nation (or nations) which its rulers would seek to make stronger, or more integrated, through constructing and combating enemies

---

[26] Gray, *Route 19*, 182.
[27] C. Coon, interviewed by Jon Savage, *The England's Dreaming Tapes* (London: Faber and Faber, 2009), 471–79, 474.
[28] W. Wollen, 'About Propeller', in *Pocket Henry V: Education Pack* (Propeller Theatre Company, 2011).
[29] J. Fearnley, *Here Comes Everybody: The Story of the Pogues* (London: Faber and Faber, 2012), 143.

within and without. The Pogues have been seen to 'parody and interrogate aspects of Irishness in complex and confusing ways', but here they are questioning the condition of England or Britain in the mid-1980s.[30] Since The Pogues were comprised in part of second-generation Irish performers, and as their politics and poetics would 'coincide' with the 'emergence' of punk, they had good reason to maintain a sceptical, critical detachment from 'English' norms:

> As Shane MacGowan's English band-mates have explained, it was 'quite difficult' – and 'definitely not a good thing' – to be Irish in early-Eighties London. ... The early 1980s was a particularly 'polarized moment' (as Seamus Heaney would put it) in Anglo-Irish affairs.[31]

The Pogues' aesthetic, 'born of an expressly *inter*-cultural dynamic', represented a subversive ambivalence to the band identifying with only one nation: 'hyphenated Irish-Englishness ... is not reducible to either dimension ... which facilitates a flexible, fluctuating and (sometimes) fractious identification with both'.[32] What does it mean then, for 'English' troops in a production of *Henry V* to sing snatches of a Pogues' song of dissent and dislocation? Perhaps that through this the production could question the very status of 'Englishness', and the coherence of the 'nation' the 'English' are fighting for.

Of course, as many scholars have noted, the play itself does well enough:

MACMORRIS   What ish my nation? Who talks of my nation? (3.3.62–3).[33]

Of course, too, the play contains the unsettling implications of such questions, not least through its deployment of music:

> The concluding scene of this history play provides a (temporary) harmonious solution to the war between England and France thanks to the marriage between Henry and the daughter of French King. In a play dominated by battles and military sound effects, the focus on music at this point is all the more appropriate.[34]

---

[30] N. McLaughlin and M. McLoone, 'Hybridity and national musics: The case of Irish rock music', *Popular Music*, 19:2 (2000), 181–200, 191.

[31] S. Campbell, *'Irish Blood, English Heart': Second Generation Irish Musicians in England* (Cork University Press, 2011), 63, 2, 46; citing Seamus Heaney, *Finders Keepers: Selected Prose, 1971–2001* (London: Faber and Faber, 2002), 368.

[32] Ibid. 147, 9.

[33] See, for example, J. Joughin, ed., *Shakespeare and National Culture* (Manchester University Press, 1997).

[34] C. R. Wilson and M. Calore, *Music in Shakespeare: A Dictionary* (London and New York: Continuum, 2005), 304.

And yet the play itself ends in the knowledge that harmony rings true only temporarily: 'they lost France' (Chorus, Epilogue, 12). Preluding this, though, we hear that even the union promised by marriage involves all kinds of breaks, sonic and social disconnections, as well as new bonds:

> KING HENRY V Come, your answer in broken music; for thy voice is music, and thy English broken. Therefore, queen of all, Katherine, break thy mind to me in broken English (5.2.220–3).

Hence this production's use of popular music brought into earshot the play's own ambiguous realisations of the power of music, and the nature of power. In other words, questions we might ask about this play we might also ask about this production, as reviewers like Paul Taylor did: 'Jingoistic jamboree or anti-war drama?' Such questions were all the more acute in 2011–12, a period including many events that were seen to celebrate or consolidate pride in national identity: the Royal Jubilee, the World Shakespeare Festival, the Olympics and the Cultural Olympiad, in which, as Morra notes, both Shakespeare and popular music figured prominently (and often together).[35] Propeller's production would therefore appear to speak directly about the ways in which popular music, not to mention Shakespeare, can be implicated in problematic constructions of national identity.

Macbeth: 'Confusion Now Hath Made His Masterpiece' (2.3.62)

But popular music exists beyond Britain, and beyond the 'British bubble' other political questions were more pressing at the same time. Deployment of popular music to convey crises in national identity is not evident solely in British productions, as we can see by considering *Macbeth: Leïla and Ben – A Bloody History* (directed by Lofti Achour for the Artistes Producteurs Associés at Northern Stage, Newcastle upon Tyne, 2012). *Macbeth* depicts a time and space of ambiguity, where there is much talk of confused and mixed atmospheres:

ALL   Fair is foul, and foul is fair,
       Hover through the fog and filthy air.   (1.1.12–13)

However, 'air' may imply 'a musical meaning' as well as atmosphere.[36] To put this differently, we might consider how *Macbeth* resounds to conflicting types of music some more atonal than others. The witches

---

[35] See Morra, *Britishness*, 17–30.   [36] Wilson and Calore, *Music in Shakespeare*, 29.

make *'Music and a song'* (3.5.33.SD), and follow Hecate's advice (voiced through Thomas Middleton's later contribution to the play) to 'now about the cauldron sing / Like elves and fairies in a ring' (4.1.41–2). And just as it is possible to argue they orchestrate Macbeth's actions, as he becomes their tool, so the dagger Macbeth imagines is 'an instrument' (2.1.43), both an implement and a device to create noise, however discordant. These arrangements mean Scotland is a country in despair, enduring terrors of 'Great tyranny' (4.3.33), registered aurally:

MACDUFF   Each new morn
               New widows howl, new orphans cry   (4.3.5–6)

Counterposed to these sounds of fury, however, another form of music offers resistance:

MALCOLM   This tune goes manly. . . .
                    our power is ready: . . .
                          Macbeth
               Is ripe for shaking, and the powers above
               Put on their instruments.   (4.3.238–42)

The military, personal, and political might figure in musical terms. These harmonising, resolute, and gendered motifs are so potent that by its end there is little else for the play to do but enact a *'Retreat and flourish'* as Macbeth's nemeses triumph *'with drums and colours'* (5.9.0.SD). Macbeth may despair that human life is 'full of sound and fury / Signifying nothing' (5.5.27–8), but sounds, when properly regimented under masculine authority, can also signify something.

These audible conflicts made *Macbeth* a suitable vehicle for Artistes Producteurs Associés' exploration of Tunisian history and socio-political struggle under the rule of Ben Ali (from 1987–2011) leading up to what has been called the 'Arab Spring'. *Leïla and Ben* juxtaposed registers, dialects, local and international languages, as it also combined theatrical modes of documentary drama, film and interview footage, puppetry, and live songs and music. Some of these songs were traditional, some were notorious for their implication in shoring up the old regime, and some were created specifically for this production: but all were, in consumption or idiom, 'popular'. According to one of the artistic directors, Jawhar Basti, these popular songs performed particular functions in this production:

> We wanted to work on rural popular music (but once again musically
> speaking our own personal reading of popular music), so we decided I'd

be writing songs inspired by popular and rural Tunisian music to be sung by singers from a more traditional background. The function of the songs would be then to convey the voice of the people, the "street mythologies", but also to talk about the function of the propaganda song and the role of the artist during Ben Ali's reign.[37]

In practice, this meant some songs were performed to underscore how Ben Ali's regime consolidated 'popular' support. Yet *Leïla and Ben* also contested alignments between tyranny and popular music: one song performed by Walid Soltan praised Ben Ali's predecessor (and patron) ex-President Bourguiba as 'handsome' and 'cute' (set against images of him on a hospital bed), but with Bourguiba's demise Soltan changed mid-flow to herald the succession of 'Maczine' (Ben Ali). While popular song was implicated in celebrating political power, the self-conscious shifts in such songs showed the mutability and transience of such power. Pieces created specifically for the production had a similarly disjunctive effect, as Basti affirms:

> [W]e decided to find a guitarist and I contacted Hamza Zeramdini (who has rather a Jazz background but who of course as a Tunisian musician knows something about our popular songs) who took up the material and interpreted it brilliantly and often quite personally. I just had to urge him at the beginning not to make it too beautiful, to leave things harsh and quite brute [sic], in short to play it rock in order to be nearer to the social and political realities we were living then.[38]

In these musical and *political* contexts, and since the production explicated the ways foreign interventions have shaped Tunisian politics, Artistes Producteurs Associés' choice of a non-Tunisian popular music idiom for part of the production's soundtrack was both ironic and appropriate:

> ['Rock' music in Tunisia is] marginal of course. But probably that was part of the aim. A marginal lonely and distorted voice as an instrumental background for our Tunisian Macbeth.[39]

Popular music was part of this production's polyphony, generating sympathy for murderous devils, while also evoking dissent, and thereby exposing historic (and all-too relevant) fractures. Basti notes that 'Tunisia saw the uprising of the Tunisian rap movement which grew during the revolution'; yet in 2013 a Tunisian rapper was sentenced to two years'

---

[37] J. Basti, Correspondence with the author (13–21 November 2012).   [38] Basti.   [39] Basti.

imprisonment for maligning the police.[40] In this regard, *Leïla and Ben*'s score enabled the 'promotion of the play' and helped it transplant specific aspects of Tunisia's musical cultures and material conditions into new contexts.[41] In a way different to Propeller's 'band' of collaborative 'brothers', for Artistes Producteurs Associés, popular music provided 'the mutual culture in the absence of other mutual cultures and links, social and political, under regimes which don't encourage social cohesion':

> Music in the Tunisian culture is very important of course. It is one of those things that subdue the many hurts that the people are living with everyday.[42]

Conclusions and Questions

This chapter has tried to address some questions regarding the interactions of Shakespeare and popular music in contemporary productions, but many remain. Describing Propeller's *Henry V*, Nick Asbury claimed 'We created contemporary soldiers' songs which allude to contemporary music'.[43] But 'London Calling' is over thirty years old, so while the production may be contemporary, is the music? Indeed, much of iconic popular music's power comes from how it now draws upon or represents older contexts and resonances. What are the costs or opportunities of this? Similarly, given Shakespeare's current global dimensions, and the development of forms and discourses of 'world music' (however problematic that term is), we might also speculate about what happens when productions employ music that is popular in one context, but esoteric or exotic in another.

Lindley suggests: 'If all performance history is a species of archaeology, then the traces of music in the record are particularly fragmentary.'[44] Thinking about this might lead us to consider the differences between a production's popular music that is diegetic (in the scene, done by the performers, whether original or a cover) or non/extra-diegetic (incidental, underscoring, pre-existing)? But, more fundamentally, how valid, feasible or *desirable* is the analysis of music, popular or otherwise, in productions of Shakespeare? Perhaps the internet age (and especially websites such as Reviewing Shakespeare) mean it is easier to gather and interpret fragments

---

[40] Basti; 'Rapper Weld EL 15 gets two years in jail for calling police dogs in song', *The Independent* (22 March 2013): www.independent.co.uk/arts-entertainment/music/news/rapper-weld-el-15-gets-two-years-in-jail-for-calling-police-dogs-in-song-8546156.html (accessed 23 April 2014).
[41] Basti.   [42] Basti.   [43] Asbury, 'The process of the Music'.
[44] Lindley, 'Sounds and Sweet Airs', 59–60.

now. However, what are the continuing challenges of retrieving past productions' soundscapes; and since those fragments are part of a more or less coherent whole can it make sense to isolate one aspect of a performance as we do?

When productions do use popular music this is now perhaps motivated less by a concern for what Shakespeare can do for or to it, and more by a need to impress upon audiences in a demanding marketplace that popular music can do engaging things to or for Shakespeare, including bringing him down from some lofty (and lonely) peak of high culture. Alternatively, we might argue that Shakespearean productions use popular music not to trivialise Shakespeare, or make him more accessible, or give gravitas to pop music, because those battles are over. As we identify significant uses of popular music preceding 'contemporary' productions as discussed here, recovering the histories of popular music in Shakespearean production, and as we recognise the prevalence of popular music in recent Shakespearean productions, we might find that distinctions between Him and It are now conclusively erased. Yet even with those histories might we still be asking: at what point and why did it become appropriate to appropriate popular music in appropriations of Shakespeare? Indeed, has it; and are we able to hear such appropriations when they occur? Maria Aberg's 2012 *King John* for the Royal Shakespeare Company was saturated with, and choreographed to, diverse forms of popular music, with diverse connotations ranging from the likes of Frankie Valli and P.J. Harvey to Bill Medley and Jennifer Warnes. This excited some audience members: 'the kind of dance of death to [Valli's] "Begging You" was ... surprisingly powerful'.[45] Yet others were appalled: 'The RSC is lost. They ... have little understandsing [sic] of the depths of Shakespeare's plays, which is why they think that stag and hen party pop entertainment ... is the way to interpret them.'[46] While many commentators noted what the staging had to say about the state of the nation, it was also described by one reviewer as 'radical, flashy and defiantly feminising'.[47] Was its use of popular music part of this, and if so, what does this say about the relations between Shakespeare, popular music and concerns only touched on briefly

---

[45] C. Morton, comment in response to W. Sharpe, 'Review: *King John*, Royal Shakespeare Company' (14 May 2012); available at bloggingshakespeare.com/year-of-shakespeare-king-john-at-the-rsc (accessed 24 August 2015).

[46] C. Smith, comment in response to Sharpe.

[47] D. Cavendish, 'King John', *The Telegraph* (23 April 2012): www.telegraph.co.uk/culture/theatre/theatre-reviews/9221716/King-John-RSC-Swan-Theatre-Stratford-upon-Avon-review.html (accessed 24 August 2015).

here: gender and sexuality? Popular music has the power to coalesce these matters. For example, dreamthinkspeaks' 2012 version of *Hamlet, The Rest is Silence*, featured Gertrude and Claudius smooching to Chris Montez's 1966 hit 'The More I See You', wherein the androgynous-voiced singer confesses to feeling daily 'more mad' about their beloved. As the Ghost knows too well, poison comes 'in the porches' of one's 'ears' (1.5.63): such cloying expressions of desire, couched in popular song, mortify Hamlet in his 'unmanly grief' (1.2.94), not least because they confound his already unsettled sense of gender distinctions, further motivating his misogyny.

This chapter has covered a history play and a tragedy, raising questions about the ways genre affects the sorts of popular music contained within or referenced by a production. The Royal Shakespeare Company's 2013 *As You Like It* (a comedy, albeit a rough one, and also directed by Aberg) featured neo-folk settings of songs from the play by Laura Marling. These songs soundtracked the apparently bucolic community the play conceives, and worked against the sombre electronica pervading the early court scenes, thereby juxtaposing what seemed like the wholesomely 'organic' with the troublingly 'synthesised'. More broadly, do particular plays, theatres, companies (like Propeller), directors (like Aberg) or indeed audiences, invite or problematise the use of popular music in productions? Such questions might offer prompts for further investigations, in scholarship and on stage.

CHAPTER 16

In Practice IV

'Sounds Like' – Making Music on Shakespeare's Stage Today

Jon Trenchard with Carol Chillington Rutter[1]

I

It was an insult, but when Robert Green accused William Shakespeare of early modern megalomania, aiming in 1592 to succeed as the 'absolute *Iohannes fac totum*' of the London stage, he wasn't far wrong.[2] From the beginning to the end of his career Shakespeare didn't write just for actors. He wrote for performance, jobs today's theatre assigns to 'creatives' in a dozen theatrical departments from wigs to wardrobe to props and stage management. Shakespeare was his plays' first designer. He thought about location ('Hail Rome!'; 'What country, friends, is this?'; 'In Troy there lies the scene'; 'This is the forest of Arden'; 'make him stand upon this molehill here'). Costume ('Petruccio is coming in a new hat and an old jerkin'; ''Tis not alone my inky cloak, good mother'; 'Pluck off, pluck off, / The seven-fold shield of Ajax'). And objects ('That handkerchief'; 'This same skull'; 'This shoe'; 'This ring'; 'what book is that?'; 'Are there balance here to weigh the flesh?'). He was his plays' first choreographer, arranging scenic effects big and small: 'Enter . . . the masquers'; 'Blow, wind, and crack your cheeks!; 'Enter . . . Cleopatra . . . with eunuchs fanning her'; 'Thunder and lightning. Ariel like a harpy'; ''Tis time. Descend. Be stone no more'; 'He holds her by the hand, silent'. Shakespeare was his plays' first lighting designer ('But soft, what light through yonder window breaks?'; 'Give me some light!'); first fight arranger ('To it, Hal!'; 'Once more, unto the breach'); first animal

---

[1] This article is edited from a conversation between Jon Trenchard and Carol Rutter before an audience at David Lindley's 'Shakespeare and Music' conference at the Globe in April 2013. Here, Part I is Rutter; Part II, Trenchard.

[2] *Greenes Groats-Worth of Witte, bought with a million of Repentance* (1592), G.B. Harrison, ed., Bodley Head Quartos VI (1923), 46–47.

handler ('When a man's servant shall play the cur with him'; 'Exit, pursued').

Withal, he was his plays' first musical director, cueing vocals and instrumentals; songs; sound effects; music to dance or attend to; music to stir memory and thought; sounds harsh or sweet or strange, to appal, terrify, madden or heal; noises 'off', and on. Like all his other 'original' writing for performance, Shakespeare's musical direction was permissive. It yields itself, latterly, to wide interpretation, reimagining and riffing. So how do subsequent performers make Shakespeare's music on today's stage?

Here, the actor-musician Jon Trenchard talks about the practical business of picking up Shakespeare's music cues and reperforming them.[3] He's worked as Musical Director (MD) on five Propeller theatre company productions, making music 'with' Shakespeare, 'after' Shakespeare but specifically 'for' Propeller, a company whose signature rules of engagement both constructively limit an MD and liberate him.[4] For starters, every Propeller production has a 'modern aesthetic': the design typically will bring together elements of periods and settings within the last hundred years or so, but is never Elizabethan. This eclecticism invites the music to be similarly eclectic: anything from plain-song to pop, folk ballad to rap can turn up in the mix. Next, Propeller is an all-male touring Shakespeare company, usually fourteen- or fifteen-strong. Vocal arrangements, then, are for all-male voices (some of which can, on demand, reach to falsetto). But since neither an ability to sing a note or play an instrument is tested in auditions, what turns up on the first day of rehearsal is what the MD has to work with. (Some Propeller actors are ex-choir boys; some come with tin ears; some, like Trenchard, play several instruments and can jam on any of them; some have never lifted a maraca.) That said, some part of every company will be a quantity known to the MD given Propeller's trademark 'first refusal' casting policy, which offers actors

---

[3] Trenchard was choral scholar at St Johns College, Oxford where he acted in OUDS productions and was president of Mummers. He joined Propeller in 2006 for *The Taming of the Shrew* tour. He has since written and arranged music for four further productions (*Twelfth Night*, 2006, *The Merchant of Venice*, 2008, *Richard III*, 2010, *The Comedy of Errors*, 2010). He played Puck in Propeller's revival of *A Midsummer Night's Dream* (2008).

[4] Launched in 1997 at the Watermill Theatre in Newbury, Berkshire, Propeller toured twenty-five productions of ten Shakespeare plays across the UK and around the world until 2016. Productions were directed by Edward Hall, designed by Michael Pavelka, and Lighting Designed by Ben Ormerod. Caro Mackay was Executive Producer; Nick Chesterfield, General Manager. Currently, the company is in suspension.

in the current production first option on the next. The MD, then, can count on skills taught in one season being developed and extended in the next.

He can count, too, on another signature feature of Propeller productions. Conceptually, every play is a story told by a 'chorus' who have an ensemble identity that's registered in the design and costuming:[5] members of a wedding metamorphosed Crazy Gang in *The Taming of the Shrew*; lager louts in football shirts and sombreros on holiday on the Costa-del-Grunge in *The Comedy of Errors*; prison inmates in prison blues in *The Merchant of Venice*; faceless 'lurkers' in half masks and formal evening wear hanging around Illyria, holding *Twelfth Night* in a kind of suspended animation and working as Feste's zanies, inhabiting a 'fool zone'; asylum, morgue (or abattoir?) assistants in *Richard III*, dressed in white meat packers' (or anatomists'?) coats over natty bow ties, their faces covered in stretch masks, their hands clutching instruments ancient and modern to cut, saw, drill, slice the human body on its way to being healed or turned into dead meat: so, physicians curing the nation, or butchers dismembering it?

This 'chorus' is always onstage. Individuals drop out of it to step into the action (with some addition of costume) as principals before stepping (with a return of anonymising coat, mask or sombrero) back into it. This means that in Propeller productions characters are always both a part of the ensemble and a product of the ensemble. It also means the whole company is constantly at work, making the play. Which further means for the MD that, when he's scoring diegetic or extra-diegetic arrangements, he always has a full orchestra and choir at his disposal. He can rely on company input from an ensemble that functions democratically. Every Propeller actor is called for every rehearsal. So, just as the permanent 'chorus' levels out differences in performance terms between 'main' and so-called 'bit' parts, the ensemble gives equal voice to every actor in the creative process. This makes for a rehearsal room where ideas for musical themes, motifs, instrumentation, period and style are pitched in to the devising process by everyone: a Schubert lullaby, a Pogues' classic; gospel, plainsong, madrigal; *a cappella* or accompanied by accordion, Spanish brass, harmonica, acoustic guitar, waterphone. The MD is never working solo; and never working without 'auditioning' ideas in rehearsal on a daily basis. In performance, all the music, all the sound effects Propeller produces

---

[5] For more on Pavelka's design work, see C. C. Rutter 'Michael Pavelka (in Conversation with Carol Chillington Rutter)', *Shakespeare Survey 66* (2013), 129–44.

are played live by actors onstage. In a real sense, then, in a Propeller production, when the ensemble is making the music, the music makes the ensemble.

But where does this musical process begin? Jon Trenchard picks up the narrative.

II

When we're rehearsing, we take the last hour of the day for musical rehearsal, to talk about musical ideas, bring in material from outside, jam together, try out arrangements, practise. But the whole process begins with deciding what kind of music to use, and here our inspiration comes from four major sources: the production design; the themes, language and music cues Shakespeare gives us; the actors' and director's interpretations of Shakespeare's writing; and the practical business of performance (for example, where the production needs music to cover a scene change or as a 'curtain-raiser' after the interval). I'm going to try to think about these separately, but of course, as what follows shows, they constantly overlap.

1   Design

We get a look at the model box on day 1 of rehearsals, which starts us thinking about the music. *The Comedy of Errors* was set on a hot, trashy, 1980s Ibiza-like holiday island catering to Brits, where constantly partying football louts in their team's away strips and sombreros 'Ruled, OK'. The place suggested Agadoo-style, cheesy 80s anthems and tasteless mariachi band covers of British pop, the acoustic accompaniment to heat, holidays, hilarity and hot tempers.

The Taming of the Shrew was loosely 1970s – 'loosely', because in design terms every Propeller show is a mash-up that resonates with different eras and ideas. We never work in 'period'. *Shrew*'s 1970s meringue wedding dresses and frilly shirts suggested disco and glam rock. But in the background, our designer had given this production another visual idea to work with. On the back wall was a massive blow-up of Titian's 'Venus and Adonis'. The original dates from 1553. It's erotic. And on our set it was hung crazily askew: from the off, things in Padua were visibly out of kilter. In a world where punk rockers could parade in front of Titians, we were free to recruit to performance *any* music, from Clash to standard wedding classics like Mendelssohn's 'Wedding March' and Pachelbel's 'Canon'.

Illustration 6 Tony Bell, Kelsey Brookfield, Chris Myles, Jon Trenchard, Dugald Bruce Lockhart, John Dougall and Tom Padden in Propeller *Comedy of Errors*. Photograph by Manuel Harlan

Twelfth Night's design was based on the French new-wave classic *Last Year at Marienbad*, a film whose characters are trapped in a monochrome world, in a hotel, repeating the same behavioural cycles day after day. I wanted to recapture this atmosphere for Illyria, of claustrophobia, of people stuck in behavioural patterns: Olivia in her grief, Orsino in his unrequited love, Sir Toby in his revelry, Malvolio in his puritanical pedantry. So I set all the music in the same minor key of C, with two main chord cycles that were repeated through most of the songs and the underscore. In the beginning, spectators saw a world covered in dustsheets, a massive chandelier crashed to the floor of a derelict ballroom left over from an age of elegance. A single figure – Feste – was alone on stage playing a simple tune on his little violin that would return at the end as 'When that I was a little tiny boy'. Underneath Feste's tune was heard a single note, a C, hummed by the full company of half-masked 'zanies'. This produced a drone effect that we sustained and developed across the opening (wordless) scenario as the dustsheets were whipped off and turned into sails torn by a storm that wrecked a ship and 'drowned' a pair of twins. And it carried on with Orsino's entrance, his call for music and his instruction to 'play on'. Later, we used echoes of that drone to enhance the atmosphere of entrapment and melancholy. 'O Mistress Mine' began with Feste accompanying himself on pizzicato violin, then another violin coming in, then Feste's 'zanies' imitating the sound in vocal harmony. Finally, Aguecheek joined the chorus and echoed Feste's lines – slightly off-key. When the outsiders, the twins Viola and Sebastian, arrived in Illyria and started interrupting the patterns, stirring the stagnation, their influence was *heard*. It began transforming the musical landscape. The C minor drone gradually edged towards A flat major, resolving the chord cycles, until finally Feste's song, sung when the twins have worked their magic on all the Illyrians, resolved the minor chord cycles to a calm A flat major chord. It was that note that was left resonating in the theatre.

2   *Textual Instruction*

We begin the rehearsal period with a full read-through of the script when we start getting to grips with the text, the language, the verse, the story. This can last a couple of days or even a week and a half of a four-to-five-week rehearsal period. As we go along, Ed Hall [Propeller's Artistic Director] reveals some of his ideas about where we might want music. Obviously, there is the music Shakespeare has scripted in the text. But there are also scene changes that will need music to cover them and places for occasional atmospheric sound or underscore (though the latter is rare in Propeller productions). Then too the director will suggest additions. There's normally a song at the start of the second half of a Propeller show to ease the audience back into the action. But Ed frequently wants music to point a textual moment, like King Edward's (doomed) attempt in 2.1 of *Richard III* to get his brawling family to make peace, which we introduced with the lyrics of a jolly eighteenth-century English folk tune, 'Here's a health to the King and a lasting peace, / To faction an end, to wealth increase.'

Working on the text we find linguistic themes to inspire our choice of music, or inspire lyrics if we need to write additional songs, as in *The Comedy of Errors* where we made the 'conjurer' Dr Pinch (who's supposed to be able to be perform exorcisms) a bible-bashing Evangelist backed by a doo-wop gospel choir. The lyrics I wrote for his big revival meeting-style 'number' in 4.4 were a mash-up of images, ideas, and lines heard in the play earlier ('mad', 'stranger', 'strange', 'slave'; loss, shipwreck, jealousy, deceit; 'I to the world am like a drop of water / That . . . in quest of them (unhappy) lose myself'; 'I greatly fear my money is not safe'). The song went like this, first Pinch solo, then the backing group kicking in:

> I was lost upon the ocean
> I was a stranger to myself
> I was jealous and deceitful
> I was mad for gold and wealth
> But I prayed to the Lord to save me
> To take me by the hand
> To lead me to my brothers
> Back to the promised land.
> I was mad (He was mad!)
> I was a sinner (He was bad!)
> I was a slave (He was a slave!)
> But I prayed (But he prayed!)
> And now I'm (Saved by the power of the Lord!).

To open the second half of *The Merchant of Venice* we found an American Negro spiritual, 'Didn't My Lord Deliver Daniel?' whose lyrics connected with themes in the play's trial scene: judgement, mercy, deliverance. The lion's den of the spiritual suggested the 'den' of our prison, built of cages to keep humans, like animals, in captivity. It seemed fit that our black Duke/Prison Governor, Babou Ceesay, in a white linen suit, would start singing this spiritual, praying for mercy, and that the rest of the prison would join in. At the end of *Richard III*, the lyrics we used for Richmond's hymn were set, appropriately, to the Welsh tune, 'Rhuddlan',

> Judge eternal throned in splendour
> Cleave our darkness with thy sword . . .
> Cleanse the body of this nation
> Through the glory of the Lord.

But here the words and harmonies in the vocals played off and against the last (unsettling) line in our production (which we put some twenty lines short of Shakespeare's more resolved ending), Richmond's ambiguous rhetorical question, 'What *traitor* hears me, and says not amen?' (5.5.22).

3   Interpretation

As actors we're constantly listening to each other: responding in rehearsal to actors' interpretations, coming up with ways to use music to enhance the mood created by actors for a scene. As Robert Hands played Adriana, the spurned wife in *The Comedy of Errors*, she was an outrageous diva in leopard skin leggings, stilettos, Dame Edna glasses, Margaret Thatcher handbag, and attitude to match. We marked her entrances with a brash Latin brass flourish accompanied by a *passionata* violin, which said everything you needed to know about her shrill jealousy (and which we set up to be hilariously wrong-footed by Shakespeare's next line, delivered by the man she thinks is her husband: 'But soft, who wafts us yonder?'). Chris Myles's Abbess was the kind of nun who'd wear a mini-length habit over fishnet stockings: so we gave her 'Heaven is a Place on Earth' for her first entrance. And we backed Antipholus of Ephesus's drunken encounters with the Courtesan with a brass quintet riffing in the style of Etta James's 'I just want to make love to you.'

In *The Taming of the Shrew* we opened with a wedding: the conceit was that it was Christopher Sly's wedding, but the drunkard hadn't turned up. We wanted to mark the human meltdown across this fifteen-minute sequence (which was all extra-textual) with music, so we used Giordani's 'Caro Mio Ben' for the 'Here Comes the Bride' moment. The first time the wedding guests heard it, everyone was on their feet, expectant. By the third repeat, the bride had stormed out, her father (frantically ordering the replays) was fuming, the guests were sagging, the soloist hoarse – and the groom still absent. To accompany the intrigue of the subplot of the second half of the play we reworked themes from Bach's double violin concerto into a jazz piccolo and electric double bass duet that sounded suspiciously like 'Inspector Gadget'. When we revived *Twelfth Night* with a new set of actors, their interpretation of the play put much more emphasis on the play's light humour than its melancholy, so we rescored the music to reflect this. We added a guitar underscore for the first half of 'Mistress Mine', leaving Feste to his own devices to be as humorous as he liked. But then in the second stanza, when our original choral parts kicked in, there was a sense of the whole mood plummeting: 'Youth's a stuff will not endure'.

4   Practicalities

Finally, then, when we're thinking about how music is going to serve a production, we have to think about practicalities. First, we need to take stock of our musical resources. Some Propeller companies are gifted, musically. Others are definitely musically challenged. In our *Comedy* company we had a fantastic Latin guitarist, a great violinist, a whole brass section, and an accordion, which gave us our mariachi band. We also had someone who'd never struck a note on any instrument – so we handed him the woodblock. By contrast, the original *Twelfth Night* company had hardly any musicians available for music cues. One good reason for starting that production on a single note – the C drone – was that we had only a few confident vocalists in the company. But as musical director I thought, '*Everyone* can sing *one* note, right?' It was a start. By contrast, the *Richard III* company was full of brilliant vocalists, so we could attempt dissonant harmonies.

Other practicalities we have to consider: we need music to cover scene changes – all of it played live onstage while actors also move scenery – and to respond to specific moments in the play. We also need to think about the music cues Shakespeare gives us, for songs (like the several in *Twelfth Night*), sounds (flourishes marking entrances), noises off (battles, clocks chiming, crowds shouting), musical business (the music lesson in *Shrew*). When we started rehearsing *Shrew*, the moment our director told us we needed music to introduce Padua, Jason Baughan picked up his guitar and played an exquisite Latin run, Dugald Bruce Lockhart added a tune, and the whole ensemble leaped into action with trombones, clarinet, trumpet, euphonium, tambourines, and woodblock to complete the impression of heat, sequins and bull-fighting. (Bull-fighting? Padua? Well, never mind.) This became Tranio's leitmotif, announcing his entrances – disguised as a toreador. Gremio's signature (he's *Shrew*'s geriatric suitor) was an *oom pah pah* on a euphonium; Bianca's, a sad flute tune.

In *Shrew*, Shakespeare scripts a scene where Hortensio (disguised as a music teacher) tries to teach Bianca the 'gamut', the basic scale, probably originally on a lute. But since we were in 70s territory, our Hortensio had a bass guitar, so when he started playing a funky bass line, I (as Bianca) started singing her lines in a soul-gospel falsetto. This sort of musical mayhem later punctuated the madness of the Lucentio-Bianca subplot, and contrasted starkly with Katherine's much darker story, which had far less musical accompaniment. One exception was the sun/moon scene (4.5), where country harmonica/guitar improvisations produced the acoustic atmosphere for Katherine's long, hot road-trip home. When the production was revived, we began the second half, after Petruccio has dragged Kate away from the wedding feast, with the accompaniment of an upbeat *a cappella* soul number that asked, 'Did he marry her for money / Or did he marry her for love?' We reprised this later, but in a gloomy minor key, to mark Kate's bewilderment: 'Did he marry me to famish me?'

Illustration 7 Tam Williams, Jon Trenchard and Jack Tarlton in *The Taming of the Shrew*. Photograph by Philip Tull ©Propeller Company

In *The Comedy of Errors* we used music to punctuate the action. We wanted sound to mark the play's textual rhythms and the way the plot accelerates so we introduced stings and stabs from what we called 'percussion corner'. In contrast to the awful violence of *Richard III*, which played opposite *Comedy* on tour, we wanted the violence in *Comedy* to be farcical. So we put together a full orchestra of cowbells, slapsticks, cymbals, and woodblocks to produce the kind of sound effects you get in kids' cartoons, and we had loads of fun in rehearsals deciding which sound (cowbell? woodblock?) would best accompany a bang on the head as against a smack on the jaw or punch to the stomach. We also introduced a running acoustic gag as the aural accompaniment to the tangled visual joke Shakespeare spins out in the play about the gold chain – the one that one Antipholus (of Ephesus) orders from the goldsmith who delivers it to the other, totally mystified Antipholus (of Syracuse). Every time the chain was mentioned, a glockenspiel 'dinged', first so you were hardly aware of it. But as the absurd mis-takings in the plot got more and more knotted and the arguments about the whereabouts of the chain got more and more furious, the 'dings' came faster and faster:

ADRIANA: Where is thy master, Dromio? . . . was he arrested on a band?
DROMIO: Not on a band but on a stronger thing: A chain [ding], a chain [DING]. Do you not hear it ring?
ADRIANA: What, the chain [dong]?
DROMIO: No, no, the bell . . . the clock strikes one. (4.2.49–53)

The 'dings' in 5.1 were the acoustic rendering of Antipholus/Ephesus's frustration when he was making long protestation to the Duke ('That goldsmith there'; 'parted with me to fetch a chain [ding]'; 'the chain [ding]'; 'I saw not'). Then, when the others piled in to dispute his account, the 'dings' were like maddening wasps in his brain:

DUKE: But had he such a chain [ding] of thee, or no?
GOLDSMITH: He had . . . / These people saw the chain [ding] about his neck.
MERCHANT: Besides, I . . . / Heard you confess you had the chain [ding] . . .
ANTIPHOLUS: . . . I NEVER SAW THE CHAIN [DING]! (5.1.257–268)

In *Richard III*, we spent a lot of time putting corpses into body bags and getting them off stage – which required musical cover. In *The Merchant of Venice*, when we shifted the mobile cages that made the prison in different configurations (the rec room, the lock-down corridor, Shylock's cell, the chapel) again we covered the scene changes with music, mostly scored as noise. Prisoners banged whatever they had to hand on their cell bars (bits of crockery, cutlery) which also suggested the enforced feminisation of male inmates and 'naturalised' Portia and Jessica to this setting.

Shakespeare himself scripts significant music in this play to cover the huge mood shift from the tragic end of the trial scene (for Shylock) to the gracious (and gritty) comic resolutions in Belmont. Earlier, we'd located the play's themes of religious difference, prejudice, and hatred in our music. We put the deeply plangent minor-key 'Kol Nidrei', sung on Yom Kippur, the Jewish Day of Atonement and the most solemn day in the Hebrew calendar, against a full-throated, triumphalist major-key 'Onward, Christian soldiers!', a kind of anthem for the Christians' revelry. 'Didn't My Lord Deliver Daniel?' brought in a different spiritual quality of voice and set of expectations. Its refrain, after all, repeatedly asks, if Daniel was delivered, then 'Why not every man?'. The spiritual's question poses a black challenge to white supremacism, and in our production, it was an oblique anticipation of Portia's universalism: 'We do pray for mercy / And that same prayer doth teach us all to render / The deeds of mercy'. (Doesn't it?) Coming home to Belmont, Portia hears music ('Music, hark!'), and the music we gave her was a Catholic plainsong chant that then overlapped with the Jewish atonement theme and the Spiritual's deliverance/forgiveness theme we'd heard earlier. The music didn't resolve the play's religious differences; but it combined them into some kind of sensible, that is, feel-able, continuum. It was as if the hope Lorenzo and Jessica saw in the stars and knew they couldn't sustain, and the music of the spheres they couldn't hear (being mortals 'close[d]' in a 'muddy vesture of decay' they were deaf to it) yet resonated in the earthly music.

5   *Making Music in* Richard III

It might be useful to think about the process of finding, arranging and performing music for Shakespeare by looking at a single Propeller production, *Richard III* (2010).

Cast as Lady Anne, I had to stifle a 'whoop' of excitement: it's a role I've always thought was difficult, and therefore a brilliant challenge. But I was also going to be musical director on the show, which focussed my attention on getting down to business. What musical ideas did Ed have for the play? He wanted an acoustic landscape similar to what they'd created in *Rose Rage*, Propeller's two-play adaption of Shakespeare's *Henry VI* trilogy, which tells the story of the original English civil war, the Wars of the Roses, and ends where *Richard III* begins. Ed's aspiration was eventually to stage a six-part history cycle, to include *Henry V* and *Edward III* (a play attributed to Shakespeare that tells the back story to the troubles in the houses of Lancaster and York). The music he had in mind would be one of the ways of achieving continuity across the planned cycle – and of course, *discontinuity*. So: choral music, especially madrigals and ecclesiastical music, and anything traditionally English.

I hadn't seen *Rose Rage* but managed to locate a recording of the music, and listening to those old Propeller boys singing 'Kyrie' and 'Sanctus', music originally written to be sung during the Catholic mass, I was struck by the idea that for *Richard III* we could compose a whole Requiem Mass to mourn Richard and everyone who'd died in the Wars of the Roses and to express through music the play's themes of conscience, repentance, vengeance, the Day of Judgement, and ultimately (ambiguously?) peace ('requiem'). I listened again to Benjamin Britten's '*War Requiem*', a piece I've always loved, and Britten got me excited about giving *Richard III* a more modern, discordant soundscape than anything Propeller had attempted to date.

I had to keep myself from getting carried away, imagining complex atonal harmonies and Britten-esque orchestrations because at this point I had no idea who else was cast, whether we'd have a musically accomplished set of musicians or a gang like some of the original *Twelfth*

Night company who clung to the C drone like the shipwrecked twins clung to the wreckage in the storm. But I made a start: converting five-part English madrigals to four parts, rearranging mixed choir carol harmonies for all-male voices, finding modern religious pieces that could be adapted and shortened for scene changes – all the while trying to make everything as simple as possible for my 'unknown quantity' of actors to learn and perform. As it turned out, I needn't have worried. The *Richard* company was probably the most accomplished, musically, that Propeller had ever cast, with experience ranging from West End and Broadway musicals to cathedral choirs, including a member of a classical boy band and a very fine Welsh tenor. This talent let me get on with composing and arranging numbers for a production the company would mock me by dubbing *Richard: The Musical!* They weren't far wrong. When it came to the first performance, we had forty sung musical cues involving eleven different tunes and multiple arrangements.

Much of it had been chosen because the lyrics seemed appropriate to the play, but with the songs I suggested and arranged, I tried to keep two musical themes running: descending scales and semitone intervals. These were prompted by something Ed Hall said to me before rehearsals began, that this production might track Richard's descent into hell.

When we got a look at the design, we could see just how violent that descent would be. Michael Pavelka had designed a set that suggested both a Victorian mental institution and an abattoir. Because Propeller is always on tour, sets are built out of component parts and mobile units that can be taken apart and rearranged by us actors in performance, which means that the traffic on our stage is non-stop and very busy and that when we're singing, we're likely to be shifting furniture. For *Richard*, the basic skeleton was a set of metal gantries lining three walls of the stage that we could climb on, with catwalks we could access from ladders that connected 'below' to 'above'. Centre stage, there was a double-decker cage-on-wheels, curtained on three sides with the kind of heavy plastic sheeting they use for doors in hospital corridors and in meat-packing units. This cage could be shoved downstage or upstage, and gave us a space 'within'. It also had a platform on top – a place for speech making, like Richmond's final 'hurrah' to England. Practically, the only other stuff onstage was an evil-looking piece of last-century furniture that could be opened flat (into a hospital gurney) or folded into a chair (think: executioner's chair; our 'throne') and a set of mobile hospital screens – the kind nurses wheel into place in NHS wards to give patients 'privacy', and you always wonder what awful procedure is happening behind them. In performance, these screens were scene-shifters. They literally uncovered scene changes, working like the slide mechanism on an old-fashioned manual projector, discovering new views behind them every time they were shifted. The effect was like camera cuts in a horror film. Indeed, the whole set had a horror film quality: grey, shadowed, gloomy.

These ideas were picked up in the costume designs. The principals wore Edwardian tailcoats on their torsos, which gave us all the same shape and silhouette above the waist; but below, where the men wore trousers, the women had skirts. As for the 'Chorus' who'd be telling *Richard*'s story, the design sketches showed a pair of lads in white gowns with masks over their faces covering not just their mouths but their whole faces: surgical balaclavas. One of them held a decapitated head; the other a hacksaw. So: a chorus of the 'faceless'. Armed and violent. Who, it emerged, would function as psychic extrapolations of Richard's bloody mind. Or, more prosaically, they were 'Orderlies' (their name in the programme) working in a Dickensian psychiatric unit, first performing Richard's insanity, then resisting it, then finally carrying him from the hell on earth he'd made of England to the eternal hell of the Last Judgement.

My notion, then, was to track the trajectory of Richard's fall by setting it to music that continuously repeated descending scales. I took from Bruckner's nineteenth-century motet '*Locus Iste*' the descending chromatic scale that forms the bass line of 'Irreprehensibilis est' ('It is beyond reproach') to underscore various deaths in the first half of the play. Our arrangement of 'Dies Irae' at Buckingham's death (the climax of Richard's killings) employed the same descending chromatic scale but in a higher vocal line. The spivs who murdered Clarence worked to 'Down Among the Dead Men', an eighteenth-century British folk tune whose refrain ('Down, down, down, down . . . ') is written to another descending scale.

I continued this theme of chromaticism in the modern close-harmony arrangements I wrote. Close harmony explores the relationship between two notes a semitone apart, notes very close in pitch. When I was growing up, my brother and I (both choir boys) used to play out our sibling rivalry by one of us singing a note, and the other singing the semitone next to it: the resultant discord forced one of us to change our note to achieve harmony. I thought that the juxtaposition of discordant semitones – a feature of modern harmony – could reflect the civil discord caused by Richard's and Richmond's rivalry for the crown. We gave Richmond-the-Welshman 'Rhuddlan' complete with nineteenth-century lyrics about 'cleansing the nation', words with disturbing resonances in the modern world, so I wanted to write a modern arrangement with lots of scrunchy harmonies based on semitones sung together or consecutively. Their clashing and resolving would be the acoustic complement to Richmond's ambiguous character – beautifully persuasive, yet deeply unsettling.

The older songs we sang – a sixteenth-century madrigal by Thomas Morley, 'Now is the Month of Maying' (which produced lots of 'fa-la-la-la-las' useful for scene changes), and the 'Coventry Carol' (traditionally sung in fifteenth-century Mystery plays) – both oscillate between major and minor keys, hinging on a semitone difference in harmony, which both surprises listeners and makes them ill-at-ease. The 'Coventry Carol' (with its beautiful melody and appalling lyrics telling of Herod's slaughter of the innocents) prophesied the murder of the boy-princes in the Tower, who in our production were puppets. Our assassin, a *Pillowman* figure with a tool belt hung with children's toys and a see-through plastic mask that turned him, bizarrely, into a kid's party entertainer, worked to a Schubert lullaby set against a sung 'tick tock, tick tock' that was both a nursery clock and the (mechanical) puppet-boys' time running out. Again, a mismatch between what spectators were seeing and what they were hearing ratcheted up the scene's intensity.

So, what about my initial idea for a Requiem Mass? When it came down to it, we used just the first three lines of the 'Dies irae', from the thirteenth-century Catholic liturgy, sung in Latin to the original plainsong tune: 'Dies irae, dies illa, solvet saeculum in favilla, teste David cum Sibylla / A day of wrath that day will be, when the age will dissolve into dust, as David and the Sibyl foretold.' But we kept reprising this text over the course of the play in arrangements that developed in complexity to underscore various curses and deaths. And I wrote a modern close-harmony arrangement of the final words of the 'Dies Irae' to bookend the production, 'O pie Jesu Domine, dona eis requiem aeternam': 'blessed Lord Jesus, grant them eternal rest'. Every performance of *Richard III* began with the 'Orderlies' coming silently onstage by ones and twos, almost in slow motion, like ghosts, to lurk or climb up the gantries or crouch; all staring out at the audience from behind their masks, cradling, clutching, swinging the killer weapons they carried. The threat they embodied was palpable, menace made flesh, strangely terrifying. Then in the wings I hit a tuning fork, the choir of Orderlies took the note, the gorgeous, heart-stopping melody of 'O Pie Jesu' swelled in the theatre. The horror film set the audience was looking at was suffused with sounds like the music of the spheres, the grace of God. That's when the audience knew what kind of production they were in for. Five acts later, after gallons of blood had washed across our stage and splattered every plastic surface, and victims had been garroted, drowned, smothered, decapitated (their heads preserved in specimen jars), eviscerated with chainsaw (to 'fa-la-la-la-la' accompaniment), it was 'O Pie Jesu', a sound like hope, that ended the slaughter: accompanying the death of Richard, leading to the 'nation-cleansing' Welsh hymn underscoring Richmond's final, uneasy 'amen'.

CHAPTER 17

Music in the 2012 Globe-to-Globe Festival

Bill Barclay

In the Olympic summer of London 2012, Shakespeare's Globe hosted thirty-seven theatre companies from around the world to perform a different play by Shakespeare in their own language, producing an unprecedented six-week complete works cycle beneath the halos of the Cultural Olympiad. The Globe-to-Globe Festival produced a magnetic parade of wonders, each humming with resonance along London's ethnic fault lines, leaving Bankside awash in linguistic rarities, cultural reunions, political lightning rods, and nationalistic celebrations. The festival was also a maelstrom of musical industry, featuring rarely heard ethnic genres, instruments, and songs that dynamically served Shakespeare's stories in fresh and integrative ways. In the deliberate absence of a common tongue, music's role as universal emotional storyteller smoothed and enabled international communication and understanding. But music was to play an even more intriguing role than narrator of the heart. The festival demonstrated that Shakespeare in translation meant Shakespeare in freer adaptation than is commonly seen in English speaking theatre. Adaptation was regularly the most common sponsor of musical ingenuity; in nearly every major detour from the original, music was employed as a chief binding agent in the forging of a new theatrical logic. Such free and powerful uses of music inspired us at the Globe; this essay aims to convey some of those lessons for future productions both faithful and freely divergent.

The strands of discourse that swirled about the festival were many and occasionally charged; the Cultural Olympiad's World Shakespeare Festival echoed the Olympics in further welcoming the plurality of the world to share a stage in all its harmonies and controversies, disappointing in neither.[1] The particular glory of London's hosting was the amplification

---

[1] Particular fault lines: hosting an Israeli and Palestinian company in the same festival (and hosting an Israeli company at all); the Belarus Free Theatre performing *King Lear* in exile and in Belarusian; Afghanis who couldn't rehearse in their country because of having women onstage, and many more such flashpoints.

of its own immense multiculturalism, and for one spotlit summer it held itself up to nature as the leading representative microcosm that it is. The structure of the festival was designed somewhat to enhance this effect; visiting companies were partly selected by what Festival Director Tom Bird called 'London languages': those that are widely spoken throughout the city. Each company varyingly brought out fellow speakers from the wood-work in a constant linguistic revolve ensuring that everyone played to crowds who both could and could not understand what was being spoken. A geographic balance was further sought to represent productions from six continents as equally as possible.

Various conventions affected everyone: surtitling (though only of short scene synopses) in two boxes far stage right and left; an allowance of recorded music if they wished – a rare embrace of amplified audio at that time in the Globe;[2] access to Globe Associates of Voice, Text, and Movement; and a mere three days to rehearse once and perform twice. They all performed rain or shine, saw as many other productions as they could, socialised at the bar, and fully soaked in their extraordinary moment. There is a densely littered trail of press and publications detailing each production and its unique context in the festival, but although the current state of international Shakespeare performance was (through the Globe darkly) on acrobatic display, few writers have surveyed the festival as a whole.

In freely comparing the various musical approaches at play, it feels barely possible to glimpse the state of music in Shakespeare internationally – from 1991, the birth of its oldest production, to those newly produced for the festival twenty years later.[3] My method was to review the entire archive (I had seen sixteen of the thirty-eight shows live), and catalogue each production by certain metrics of musical approach: number of musicians, recorded music or live, musical genre, musicians' positions onstage, and whether the production predated the festival or was created for it. I particularly noted scores comprised of traditional musical styles native to their respective countries, and examined productions that brought music into moments in the plays that typically go without.

---

[2] Each production was given printed guides to the space that detailed, among other wisdoms, the naturally responsive acoustic to the human voice, inspiring them to use live music but offering a sound system if they wanted one. This and the Globe's reputation surely encouraged more companies to incorporate live music than a random cross-section of international approaches otherwise would.

[3] Grupo Galpão's *Romeo & Juliet* began rehearsal in 1991. Their first performance was in 1993 and they have been travelling sporadically since.

Those curious to see or relive the immense cultural exchange that took part in the early summer of 2012 have several options that all contributed to this chapter. There are first and foremost the productions themselves available on the Globe's online GlobePlayer.[4] There is the informative collection of essays entitled *Shakespeare Beyond English; A Global Experiment* (Cambridge), edited by Susan Bennett and Christie Carson. Finally there is a host of online reviews, features, and interviews chronicling Globe-to-Globe's crowning of the World Shakespeare Festival and discussing the many ethnic pockets of London that resonated with it. As an introduction to the field, the thirty-eight productions[5] can be roughly grouped into five families of musical approach. First, there are the through-composed[6] productions that relied on music practically throughout, including Isango Ensemble's operatic *Venus and Adonis* from Cape Town, Deafinitely Theatre Company's *Love's Labours Lost* in British Sign Language, and Q Brothers' Hip-hop *Othello* from Chicago. Second are productions with an incidental musical score directly inspired by traditions native to their company's countries: the Māori *Troilus and Cressida*, South Korean *A Midsummer Night's Dream*, Gujarat *All's Well That Ends Well*, *Henry IV pt 1* from Mexico City, the Armenian *King John*, and the Globe's own *Henry V*. A third category comprises productions that used only recorded sound and were mostly built for indoor theatre runs at home: Vakhtangov Theatre's *Measure for Measure*, the Italian *Julius Caesar*, German *Timon of Athens*, Polish *Macbeth*, Palestinian *Richard II*, and director Eimuntas Nekrošius' iconic *Hamlet* from Lithuania (on tour since 1997). The fourth are productions that featured strikingly little sound and music at all including the Kenyan *Merry Wives of Windsor*, Argentine *Henry IV pt II*, and South Sudan's *Cymbeline*. A fifth category includes productions that for exciting reasons fail to sit naturally in any of the former groupings: the exiled Belarus Free Theatre's *King Lear* and Grupo Galpão's circus-inspired *Romeo & Juliet* from Brazil.

The festival began with a bang. Isango Ensemble's production of Shakespeare's poem, *Venus and Adonis*, performed in several languages including IsiZulu, IsiXhose, Afrikaans, and English, shook the Globe alive with

---

[4] www.GlobePlayer.tv

[5] The Globe's own *Henry V* was the thirty-eighth production. *Venus and Adonis* was added to the most commonly accepted canon of thirty-seven plays (without *Two Noble Kinsmen* or *Edward III*), owing to the pre-existing (and phenomenal) *U Venas No Adonisi* from Cape Town's Isango Ensemble.

[6] I use the term to indicate productions that used music almost from beginning to end. Each of these productions was also varyingly leitmotific using repeated material.

a through-sung adaptation of the poem, emphasising sexual duality and showcasing the theatrical power of multidisciplinary performers. Composer and Music Director Mandisi Dyantyis, in collaboration with Pauline Malefane and the company, created a soaring score that featured all twenty-three company members singing, dancing and playing in a kaleidoscope of musical styles, accompanied by a family of marimba/balafons, bass to soprano, along the music gallery. Astonishing leaps of genre from western operatic traditions to rhythm and blues, traditional African polyrhythms, South African *a cappella* styles, war chants and lullabies mingled and leapt from one to the next, representing the Rainbow Nation as an ecstatic swirl of coexisting identities. Isango had been in London before with their adaptive takes on *The Magic Flute* and *The Mysteries*. Here their eclectic musical style truly reflected the townships of Cape Town as a complex matrix of colliding influences. As a house style the ensemble makes memorable use of musically gifted actors – a common theme throughout the festival that perhaps had its apogee of virtuosity here. Like Globe naturals, these multi-talented performers demonstrated the 'wooden O's' affinity for big group storytelling in a full, direct embrace of the audience with all the comic and emotional spontaneity it engenders. In spite of never hearing one single English stanza, the musical prosody of this long-form narrative poem nonetheless felt authentically represented by the buoyancy of the score, using music as a proxy for poesy.

The Māori *Troilus and Cressida* followed in another display of the unique synergy that can be unearthed between an indigenous culture and a play's natural logic. Opening with a charged choreographed sequence of *kapa haka* (Māori performing arts), the company regularly returned to elements of the *haka*, the famous pre-war intimidation ritual of Aotearoa,[7] complete with stomping, grimacing, and thundering testosterone on overdrive (see Illustration 8). In the *haka*, the company found the perfect metaphor for the play's backdrop of aggression and its imbalance of male over female energies. It may have surprised some to see New Zealanders teaching the English how to realise war with thematic precision. As Rawiri Paratene (Pandarus and the show's producer) said in a post-show interview: 'It's very easy for New Zealanders to think that we are a peaceful nation but we're a nation that's founded on war.'[8] Culture and dramatic

---

[7] Aotearoa is today the commonly accepted indigenous name for New Zealand.
[8] From an interview with Catherine Silverstone, printed in *Shakespeare Beyond English*.

Illustration 8 The company Ngākau Toa performing the *Haka* in *Troilus and Cressida* in the Globe-to-Globe Festival, 2012. Photograph by Simon Annand
© Shakespeare's Globe

context became one, rendering the sacrifice of the eponymous characters' love all the more tragic.

The actors made iconic use of ceremonial objects in Māori culture, many of which have mixed aural and visual symbolism. The show began with a light drone of the didgeridoo and a knife-shaped green bell, made of the precious stone *kahurangi pounamu*, chimed like a knell to bring the aggravated players into the space. The many alarums in the script were played by a modified conch shell that Aeneas bears into the camp of the Greeks as a prop. This status object is doubly gendered – a long mouthpiece is affixed to the ear-like shell adorned with feathers. It is a symbol of war and of both sexes, as well as of the elemental air and group communication. Objects from the natural world provided musical punctuation throughout, mostly by a single musician placed upstage right between the centre and stage right doors of the Globe. Slumped over a table and partially under furs, this onstage band of one provided the tempi of several sequences with the simple clicks of small shells, framing the inherent theatricality of the tale with a measured degree of precise simplicity, giving the Globe a masterclass in tension.

Tension and simplicity also marked Cassandra's few but stirring moments; a simple shamanic bone flute accompanied her half-sung prophetic declamations. During the battle sequences she ritualistically whipped round her wrist a thick bunch of reeds making one rhythmic brush sound in her hand per second while observing the proceedings like a witch. This was the only music in the major battle sequence, and far from leaving a busy scene aurally exposed, the brushes focused the audience and allowed us to hear the actors' intense vocalisations. As the battle broke off, all four women entered to the unified pulse of their own reeds while a bullroarer spun and moaned upstage right. This eerie hum was enhanced by masks worn by the warriors to further theatricalise – and with explicit overtones of Greek tragedy (an appropriate overlay for a play about the Trojan war in a Renaissance theatre) – the blinding aggression resulting in Hector's climactic mutilation.

Another production that powerfully used native sounds to illuminate a challenging play from within was the National Academic Theatre's *King John* from Yerevan. Musicians strolled in with the actors at the top to establish the narrative device of a travelling company arriving with their suitcases, arguing and settling in until they suddenly began the play. Luggage would become the reconfigurable set, creating a casual space for the musicians and actors to live on the outskirts of the story. The band of three comprised two reed players, alternating between the *duduk* (Armenia's signature sound), clarinets and *zurnas*, with a drummer playing the *dhol* almost always from upstage right but away from the back wall to encourage inclusion in the story. The music was typically diegetic, announcing entrances of royalty and providing the wedding band for Blanche and Louis the Dauphin. The wailing of the *zurnas* proved wonderfully flexible for this story, able to conjure the ululations of a festival, the swirls of a mighty church organ, and the alarums of great armies with equally pungent dramatic power.

All of the most compelling musical moments in this production were in places at which no music is called for in the play. When King John asked Hubert to kill Arthur (the famous shared line: 'Death. / My Lord? / A grave. / He shall not live. / Enough.'), one of the most moving moments of the play took place: Albert Safaryan's Hubert suddenly registered the request and became emotionally petrified, wrenching his face and body in horror. The *duduk* began at precisely this moment, releasing the theatre into his deeply personal experience of grief: he was bound to kill or be killed. The *duduk* carries with it cultural meaning; it is synonymous with both individualistic spirituality and the collective mourning inherent in the story of modern Armenia. Hubert's drama was the inner grief of an assassin, externalised to include the whole Globe, and perhaps capturing the silhouette of Armenia itself in one utterly heartbreaking music cue.

Another mesmerising moment of the production, Blanche's seduction of Louis, was a radical departure from the original play. Here she straddles him downstage centre, sexually climaxing over him in a breathtaking act of manipulation to stop him from going to war against her uncle John. The drum was a genius touch of musical restraint, framing the moment as a spellbinding turn for Liana Arestakyan's Lady Blanche. When the drum (and Blanche) were finished, the whole cast suddenly applauded, out of character and in pure appreciation of this virtuosic cadenza. By the end of the play, when the combined *duduk, dhol*, and clarinet crescendo into the anarchic ending with Hubert, of all people, taking the crown, the band's aural chaos took us back to the chatty chaos of downtown Yerevan, and the cycle of political abuse poised to repeat itself again.

Constance's famous laments, underscored with solo and paired clarinets, felt similarly charged with cultural resonance. While it is common enough for these expansive arias of grief to receive support from something musically sustained, here the clarinets seemed to link the story of Constance to the story of Armenia itself, its proud history raked by genocidal loss.[9] It was a further gesture of cultural identification that validated the play's resonances in ways an English production could not. Armenians have an uncommonly profound relationship with Shakespeare dating back nearly a hundred years and owing to decades of Soviet censorship of Armenian writers. This multi-generational adoption (many Armenians alive today of all ages have middle names taken from Shakespearean characters) created a production rich with ownership of England's most exportable poet. Their nuanced account of the play mined its pitch-black comedic layers as perfectly as its themes of crude manipulation and authoritarian injustice. Much like *Troilus and Cressida*, such solutions to difficult material proved one of the most pleasurable victories of the festival.

Many other productions unfurled their traditional colours in Globe-to-Globe. The National Theatre of China's (NTC) *Richard III* was perhaps

---

[9] Interestingly, *Antony and Cleopatra* from neighbouring Turkey also used a live clarinet for moments of grief and inner anguish. Would that Turkey and Armenia agreed on more than how to express their grief.

most notable for being separated from their set and costumes at the airport. The nonetheless electrifying performance featured just one percussionist, Wang Jianan from the China Opera Company, who was also the composer. Director Wang Xiaoying's production, an effective mélange of Chinese cultural arts, styles, and symbols, drew heavily from Peking Opera (*jing ju*), showcasing the same percussion arsenal based around the onomatopoeic *gu* and *ban* – large skinned drums sitting beneath various cymbals and woodblocks.[10] The intricately choreographed interplay between movement and percussion was played from above and behind the action in the music gallery. When they returned to the Globe in 2014 with the same production – set and costumes this time in tow – they moved Wang to the down stage left corner, exciting the theatre with a more dynamic inclusion of the musician in the performance. The benefit of comparison was a lesson for us all, but it was notable for another reason: every Globe-to-Globe production that featured onstage musicians placed them stage centre or stage right with the exception of the radically reinterpreted Lithuanian *Hamlet*, which featured a lone pianist in the far stage left corner of the music gallery, nearly out of sight. Of twenty-three shows with a separate corps of live musicians, seven lived stage right, ten centre, and one stage left (the rest freely roamed throughout, though typically hovering stage right). The obvious penchant for a musical stage right as demonstrated by this international festival mystically appeared as somewhat of an unspoken universal constant.

The NTC effectively blended influences of Peking Opera with *xi qu* (Chinese Opera) and *hua ju* (spoken drama), often counterpoising them in the same scene for striking effect. Three *jing ju* actors joined the cast, including Queen Anne, whose intricately choreographed presentation of grief gave Zhang Dong-Yu's Duke of Gloucester (later Richard III) quite the formal challenge to overcome. In each instance, the inclusion of an older Chinese arts form required vividly attentive musical detail. Much was made of the two Clarence murderers, portrayed as *xi qu* acrobatic clowns, who returned again for the messier business of killing the princes instead of Tyrell in the original play. These intensely trained clowns served similar roles to the mischievous twinned spirit Duduri (Puck) in the South Korean *Dream* (see below). In a striking comparison, Zhang's Richard was without deformity, makeup, or gimmickry. A leading 'straight drama' *hua ju* actor, he remained psychologically modern, present and accountable to his

---

[10] If one is to choose just a single musician, in a Peking Opera orchestra the percussionist who plays the *gu* and *ban* drums is also the conductor of the ensemble.

audience, beautifully navigating the great swaths of history and styles so carefully mingled within this East-meets-West production.[11]

Several Asian companies arrived particularly attuned to exporting an impressive example of their cultural art forms as if it were the Shakespeare Olympics. Such a 'UN Pavilion' approach to representing their home countries abroad was a boon for music's role in the festival; it encouraged musical participation and gave close-up views of instruments rare even in London. Yohangza Theatre Company's *A Midsummer Night's Dream* could be described this way, although this production has been inspiring the international theatre festival circuit with its infectious energy and charms since 2002. This wildly playful, adventurously physical 'brand production' wooed the Globe with a heavily adapted, true-of-heart performance by an interdisciplinary group of actor/dancer/musicians. Freely drawing from a broad combination of Korean performing arts including the *Talchum* (mask dance), *Taekkyon* (Korean martial arts) and *Cocdoo Nolum* (puppet dance) not to mention Kabuki and Beijing Opera, the company unfurled an elaborately conceived series of dance, mime, song, acrobatics and clowning, impeccably supported by a combination of live and recorded music. Nearly every actor at some point sat on the upstage centre rug containing three places occupied by different actor-musicians in turn. Every minute of this pacey production could boast of several percussive (if not melodic) moments of punctuation, all without printed music. The performers from the fairy world (the Dokkaebi, borrowed from the mythical demons of Korean folklore) were elaborately costumed with Kabuki or clown-like presentationalism, consistent with an emphasis of visual storytelling over narrative in traditional Korean drama.[12] One observes again a distinctly featured role for music in visually oriented performance styles (often marked by elaborately choreographed movement or codified stylistic gesture), that de-emphasise language while elevating the role of sound and music. As if for proof, there is even a correlation between makeup and music throughout this festival – witness elaborate face painting from Brazil to China – in each case correlating with a very musical production.

Instrumentation in Yohangza's *Dream*, much like its melding of forms, included the *kayegum* (Korean zither), traditional Korean drums and

---

[11] The percussionist featured some western instruments in his mostly *jingju* arsenal, and the theatre's set design (once it arrived in 2014) drove home the East-meets-West theme. The Chinese artist Xu Bing designed calligraphic words on the backdrop of the set that appeared to be in Chinese but were in fact character-like renderings of English words.

[12] Adele Lee, *Shakespeare Beyond English*.

assorted cymbals, gongs, woodblocks, chimes, and some other funny noisemakers (the kazoo and swannee whistle both got their laughs). Highly attentive musical pivots allowed surprising avenues into comedy, further lofting the tale into a hyper-physicalised poetic space that supported both precise detail and a charismatically inclusive/responsive relationship to the audience. One moment featured a traditional Korean Pansori song, and then of a sudden a modern, cinematic recorded drumbeat would interrupt the formalised mood, raising the decibel level in the theatre while the whole company swirled in highly choreographed dance, thrilling the space. The mix of approaches worked in part because of the duality of mortals and Dokkaebi, of prosaic humanity and mystical magic. Their success integrating recorded and live music was proved by the jig. 'Jigs' are customary closing dances at the Globe; unlike the comedic postludes of Shakespeare's day that featured a few comedian/singers, bawdy jokes and rhymed folksong mash-ups, modern Globe jigs are full company dances (often outlining some of the play's themes and relationships), typically choreographed to up-tempo music and generously concluding a Globe show with gusto. This production's jig was an extended and ecstatic celebration of everything: the show, us, them, and their moment at the Globe all at once. They even had their recalls choreographed with more dancing and gifts liberally thrown at the audience. Both the slickness and heart on display emblematised a production that had been the exclamation point of many a theatre festival before Globe-to-Globe. It provided meaningful contrast to the NTC's *Richard III* – both conscious fusions of their country's traditions, both eager to connect and share their nation's treasures, but one utterly new and untried (not to mention naked without its trimmings), and the other radiantly self-assured.

To ensure that one doesn't equate Asian involvement in this festival with a broad presentation of nationalistic performing arts, the other two central Asian entries – Tang Shu Wing's *Titus Andronicus* from Hong Kong, and the minimalist Japanese *Coriolanus*, were both contractions of restraint. *Titus*, accompanied only by the occasional solo flute played by Canadian multi-instrumentalist Heidi Chan, presented the story with the raw cultural bareness we may associate with post-colonial Hong Kong's relationship to their history, while Kyoto's Chiten company presented *Coriolanus* in an aggressively stripped down and rebuilt adaptation, barely perceptible as Shakespeare's story even to Japanese speakers. Chiten's avant-garde condensation of Shakespeare's tale featured two musicians frequently busy with instruments and noisemakers of many kinds (an emphasis on the miniature and prosaic was clear in the selection of toy drums and pianos, a frying pan, shells and small bits of hand percussion), in service of achieving director Motoi Miura's impenetrably reconstructed essence of the drama via his own essentialist prism. Four actors (named Choros in the programme), alternatively blew or sang through natural trumpets slung about their shoulders (as trumpeting tribunes?), creating the shape-shifting world around Dai Ishida's baguette-wielding, basket-headed Coriolanus. The production had a vestigial flavour of presenta-tional Asian high art forms, but for audiences at the Globe, it carried little of their attendant logic, unity, or storytelling clarity.

Deeply contrasting in populism and accessibility from *Titus* and *Coriolanus* were three productions from south Asia that boasted full embraces of music as a joyful, ebullient extension of group storytelling, albeit abetted by the comedic aspects of the plays they performed. All featured a wedding, and in many ways, it was this special celebratory energy that pervaded their productions from start to finish. Mumbai's Company Theatre brought an explosively colourful *Twelfth Night* (see Illustration 9) richly alive with full-ensemble musical energy that pedalled the highly adapted story along with cheerful delight, mixing in music and

Illustration 9 Musicians Gagan Riar, Rahul Sharma and Saurabh Nayyar accompany *Twelfth Night*, performed by Mumbai's Company Theatre. Photograph by Simon Annand © Shakespeare's Globe

song at almost every articulated joint in the story. Loosely inspired by the traditional Indian theatre form of Kathakali, the show played alternatively like a Bollywood movie, a modern TV sitcom, and the most festive Hindi wedding one could imagine. Using the same upstage centre position for music as the Korean *Dream* (and Japanese *Coriolanus*), three musicians warmed up the space with drums, ankle bells (played with hands) and a harmonium. Act I, Scene II, where the Captain consoles a shipwrecked Viola ('What country, friends, is this?'), clearly demonstrated the ensemble's expanded involvement throughout: the whole ensemble played the captain, pulsing to an exciting and genial beat as if to say, 'You're going on a thrilling journey.' Viola, rather than mournful over her lost brother, was ecstatic – after all, it was exciting. Thenceforth, ensemble members could freely join for songs, dances, and commentary that were dramatically unexplained, but who could care? Joyful participation was the master of these revels. The company, when not directly involved in the action, lived in the musicians' area, singing, commenting, and cheering on the performance throughout. Songs formed so much a part of this world that when Toby, Andrew, and Feste carol late into the night, they were backed by a whole family of singers and players. Of course Malvolio can't sleep.

Also from Mumbai and equally euphoric was *All's Well That Ends Well* performed in Gujarati by the company Arpana, who incorporated song and dance in the style of Bhangwadi theatre from the nineteenth century. The similarly populist presentation of this story focused most of its musical might in a deeply delightful necklace of songs sung by Heli (Helena), played by the beguiling singer/actor Mansi Parekh. Her sung monologues, examining her plight and contrasting her truth of heart with Bharatram's (Bertram's) ambitious opportunism, powerfully served to connect her arc with the audience and congeal the rest of the play around her. Parekh's passionate performance was electrifying, and this 'problem' comedy leapt off the page, using music to smooth out the play's difficult bear traps, and engaging the Globe's audience like masters, showing their hosts how it can be done.

Dhaka Theatre's Bangla *Tempest* offered another ubiquitously musical treatment, building off Shakespeare's equation of music as magic and weaving sound into as many moments of the play as possible. There are seven songs called for in the play – the most among his complete works – and by adapting this musical romance to *panchali*, a traditional amalgamation combining many Bangladeshi art forms, Dhaka presented one of the most cohesive and memorably musical entries of the festival. The company trained for seven months in a difficult Manipuri dance style called *natapala*, often accompanied by two dancer/drummers in Bangladesh, who in this production provided a spectacular accompaniment to the play, leaping and twirling in unison while virtuosically playing a pair of *pungs*, double-sided drums strung around the neck that guided the choreography and punctuated the story. Any moment of magic seemed as good a reason for a full-blown song as any other, such as Prospero's putting Miranda to sleep in the second scene which stopped the action with a full company number. The Act IV masque/wedding sequence capped this musical momentum in a triumphant, full company explosion of song and dance, showing a clear cultural affinity with the Mumbai productions and reinforcing the magnetism of deeply integrated musical conception.

Though the entire festival spoke compellingly on behalf of the power of the multi-talented actor, Indian productions were particularly notable for a porousness between narrative acting and musical skill. While these productions did include some professional musicians, musical involvement was fundamentally decentralised and non-exclusive, reflecting priorities not only within their performing arts traditions but also in their culture. A value system of integration between music, dance, and story was one of the most compelling threads that connected a surprisingly large number of offerings from disparate parts of the world. Indeed, actor-musicianship may rarely have been on such radiant display as in this festival. When live music was integrated at its most compelling, it was actors who were often the reason. Entries from Brazil and Belarus both demonstrated this trend to powerful effect.

Grupo Galpão's stunning *Romeo & Juliet* is the oldest production of the festival's thirty-eight (see Illustration 10). Begun in 1991 and first arriving to the Globe in 2000, this freely adapted, heartrending and surprisingly joyful show featured ten musical quasi-circus clowns, all of whom could play something and sing. The group's aesthetic mixes street theatre, circus arts and acrobatics, forging a populist fusion of ideas that creates a completely unique chemistry with the classics. Romeo made his first entrance singing on stilts while playing the accordion, and – as if it weren't enough already – shading himself with an umbrella. Singing his heart out for Rosalind, his head was 'in the clouds' while effortlessly achieving something it would take anyone months if not years to attempt. In a production where Shakespeare himself was a (flute-playing) character, and in which simple grave crosses and chalk lines featured prominently downstage centre to highlight fate's unstoppable

Illustration 10 Grupo Galpão's production of *Romeo and Juliet* in which actors, singers, musical instruments and other disciplines freely intermixed. Photograph by Ellie Kurttz © Shakespeare's Globe

hand, music constantly framed the actors as sympathetic storytellers, weaving in and outside the tale, and provided emotion where naturalistic acting typically would. Counterpoising Romeo's stilts, Juliet spent most of the play on pointe, no doubt inspired by the Friar's line, 'Oh so light of foot will ne'er wear out the everlasting flint.' The fool-like Friar accompanied his solitude on the harmonica and three clowns played guitar (the Lark scene featured this trio singing a Brazilian serenade, an ode to a love that could never again experience itself). At the end, the band of ten resurrected a teary Globe with the inherently cyclical nature of song and story, endlessly repeating one of the leitmotific choruses in an evident celebration of life itself. This writer found himself laughing through tears at the play's end without really knowing why. A vivid palette of virtuosic skill was on display all evening long – utterly in service of the story – but it was composer Fernando Muzzi's music (none of which Shakespeare called for), that framed the performers' relationship with the audience, gluing the many pastiche-like elements together into a single, magical effect. At the end, the company processed out the same way they processed in, 'strumming, drumming, tooting, fluting and snaking through a packed yard of excited groundlings who clap them to the stage like a returning battalion of clown soldiers.'[13]

A final superlative example of actor-musicianship could be found in the dynamically deconstructed *King Lear* presented by The Belarus Free Theatre, performing in exile from their country and still on the road as of this writing. Performing not in Russian, but in Belarusian – an incendiary political affirmation in defiance to the Lukashenko regime (and the festival's original wishes), the company leveraged Lear's displacement as a theme of their own. This was not a weak, aging Lear but a virile, powerful, masculine leader in the person of leading company actor Aleh Sidorchyk – separated from his home in the prime of his life.

The Act I, Scene I entrance of the court began with characters singing warmups while a pianist and Kent on accordion (pushing himself around on a cart without use of his legs) got comfortable as the onstage band. We later discover this pianist to be the Fool, though here he is the court musician, a conflation completely in line with his role in the court, his musical persona, and his notable absence from this scene in the text. Lear makes a comedic entrance, first hunched in age beneath an old wizard's wig, then jocularly revealing his younger, completely healthy self to a round of applause from his family and a piano/accordion fanfare. Now the real entertainment begins; this production's 'love test' features rounds of X Factor-esque singing in garish presentation of show and spectacle. Goneril and Regan do their parts in the vein of tawdry music hall numbers and intriguingly appear to sing known folk tunes to new lyrics – a nod to Shakespeare's own practice of doing the same. All the actors clap along and Lear rewards the daughters – hysterically – by doling out actual handfuls of earth from his huge metal gauntlet into their outstretched skirts. It is Cordelia's turn next and she refuses. At Lear's provocation she performs a bit of adolescent air guitar and sits back down. Goaded further, she jaunts into a sardonic tune, dripping with sarcasm and ending with an anthemic battle cry of revolt that shatters any remaining illusion of compliance. The three songs create an architecture for the dynamics of the play as a whole, drawing attention to the performance (the daughters) of the performance (the production) of the performance (rebellion against Lukashenko as Lear, 'the last dictator of Europe').[14] The fact that music

---

[13] Jacquelyn Bessell, *Shakespeare Beyond English*.
[14] This particular condemnation of Lukashenko has been repeated often by western journalists since 1994.

could make such nesting of meaning clear is perhaps the most powerful example of its symbolic force in the festival.

The rest of the production continued to push the musical envelope. Lear's 'I will do such things' exit to the heath from Regan's court was frighteningly self-accompanied by a little menacing bird whistle he kept in his pocket, beckoning the storm to rage on as he left. The Fool, also a talented tenor saxophonist, passionately delivered the emotional weight of the fiercely violent and sexual killing of Cordelia – a searing moment that cannot possibly be described adequately here – by wailing an unhinged jazz solo before being stifled and killed in an act of artistic censorship. Perhaps most thrillingly, all three daughters at various moments led the company in visceral and stridently patriotic (and unsanctioned) Belarusian folk song, channelling the freest spirit of Belarus through censored tunes sung high in a keening, full-throated defiance against anything anywhere that sought to control them. The heterophonic anthem at the very end of the production was a true revolution in song, hollered with indestructible abandon.

The much-abused piano featured prominently throughout; the Fool's songs were manically pianistic; Lear, Oswald and others pounded on it as a noisemaker to command others to enter the stage; Goneril began her first domestic scene by slamming down the piano lid on the Fool in a gesture of domestic abuse, and everyone seemed to use the easy access of the instrument for their own devices. The piano is still at the Globe – its keyboard completely separated from its casing – as a testament to music so dynamically present in a story of dysfunction that after merely two performances it too would never be the same.

Two other productions merit musical discussion before all is said and done here, for in both cases music helped contextualise a bold decision on the part of the Globe to include them as languages: The Deafinitely Theatre's *Love's Labours Lost* in British Sign Language, and Q Brothers' *Othello* from Chicago performed 'in Hip Hop.'

Deafinitely Theatre is a deaf-led English theatre company that was deliberately tasked with performing one of the wordiest plays in the canon. *Love's Labours Lost* is a witty display of linguistic acrobatics, from endless rhyming couplets to the byzantine humour of its academically-minded clowns, Holofernes and Nathaniel. Watching this talented company navigate such a dexterous terrain through gesture was an Olympic sport all of its own. Deafinitely produces plays not just for deaf audiences, however; it celebrates deaf talent by producing works accessible to all. For the hearing crowd, the aural through-line was supplied by a quintet of musicians (guitar, accordion, violin, cello, and percussion) that never stopped playing and roved freely through the space with light-hearted repetitive folk patterns to accompany the athletic miming. In a fleeting and very funny two-hour performance, what was musically notable was the score's flexible structure – strophic loops that could expand and contract to give the actors freedom to do the same. The costumed and theatrically engaged band served as a vital conduit connecting hearing audience members with the story, joyfully framing the play as a gilded fable in which we saw dynamic performers achieving something so exquisitely rare, that those who had never seen nonverbal Shakespeare before were not likely to ever forget it.

Q Brothers' *Othello* was also through-composed, one might say, though here text and music became one as only hip-hop can make them. There is a deeply intriguing affinity between Shakespeare and hip-hop – both are known for linguistic pirouettes by various turns playful, onomatopoeic, anarchic, and spontaneously expressive. Actors of Shakespeare would be wise to take inspiration from the free-flowing spirit of invention in hip-hop that marries speeds of thought, wit, and discovery in performance. On the other hand, Shakespeare's influence on hip-hop seems inescapable (howsoever indirect), though this is a story for another time. Notably, hip-hop is a combined musico-linguistic form – vowels and consonants become tune and percussion – featuring a beat that entrains a crowd in all its diversity to the pulse of the performance, shifting our mode of spectatorship from a play to a gig.

The Globe proved the perfect space for these dynamics to play out, and the timing of the production could partly be a reason for its extraordinary reception. Having just navigated the controversy and gravitas of Ashtar Theatre's *Richard II* from Palestine, an afternoon of amplified beats, rhymes and jokes blew open a gasket of pent-up energy the Globe may not have recognised it was suppressing. Audiences came in droves and wildly celebrated this production that featured just four actors and DJ Clayton Stamper. The play wasn't really the thing; women were marginalised, the tragedy was trivialised, and the story's original relationships could hardly be recognised, and yet music's role in regaling the story with levity, flash, surprise, and the energy of a stadium show made it one of the exclamation points of the festival, and one of music's most transcendent moments.

The Shakespeare canon may only explicitly call for fifty-one songs and a dozen dances, but one would never know that at Globe-to-Globe. The freedom of translation, adaptation, then realisation in a populist open-air venue created new spaces of opportunity in which music was a chief beneficiary. In many cases this musicalised Shakespeare turned to plague the inventor, reminding English speakers just how predictable our productions often are by comparison. As such, there are far too many moments of musical success to represent everyone here, but it is worth mentioning that several festival entries used only recorded sound. These productions' geographic similarities – the avant-garde Italian *Julius Caesar*, the radically conceptualised German *Timon of Athens*, the epic and epically reconfigured Lithuanian *Hamlet*, the ghoulish Polish *Macbeth* and anguished Russian *Measure for Measure* featured the most prominent sound designs – tell a story of their own with repeated notes of psychological examination, cinematic influence, and quotational pop-culture references, revealing popular trends of continental indoor theatre that are common today nearly everywhere. As a sharp contrast, some productions used very little music at all, which rarely disappointed the Globe in spite of their context within a mostly musically vibrant festival. The table included at the end of this chapter is meant to help represent those sound and music designs that don't receive much prose here.

Two years later, the Globe went on to produce *Hamlet Globe-to-Globe*, a tour to every country in the world, which played to 197 countries. That effort was a direct encouragement of all the international relationships the Globe had cultivated through the Globe-to-Globe Festival. In a reflexive way, *Hamlet Globe-to-Globe* is its spiritual response: build the network, then hope the net will appear. The Globe-to-Globe brand – an incomparable achievement of outgoing Artistic Director Dominic Dromgoole and then-Festival Director (now Executive Producer) Tom Bird, continues to reincarnate in mini-festivals held by companies inspired by the Globe's pioneering example. It certainly lives on in the hearts and minds of tens of thousands of audience members at the Globe and around the world. Where connections of nationality or language do not define us, music and its transcendent terrains of emotion always can.

Table 2 *Globe-to-Globe Festival Productions*

PLAY	TOURING COMPANY	LANGUAGE	COMPOSER/ SOUND DESIGNER	NUMBER OF MUSICIANS	MUSICIAN PLACEMENT	RECORDED OR LIVE?	ELEMENTS OF STYLE/ INSTRUMENTATION
Antony & Cleopatra	Oyun Atölyesi	Turkish	Tolga Çebi	3 actor/musicians	Throughout the stage	Both	Prominent cinematic recorded sound of modern Turkish instruments w/ actors playing clarinet, violin & daff.
All's Well That Ends Well	Arpana (Mumbai)	Gujarati	Sada Mulik	3	Downstage right	Live	Bhangwadi 19th century theatre style; Helena sings all new heterophonic songs. Band: tablas, dholak, and harmonium
As You Like It	Marshanishvili Theatre	Georgian	Vakhtang Kakhidze	All single/play SFX & percussion	Throughout the stage	Both	Dynamic singing with percussive noisemakers and live sounds. Occasional leitmotific recorded cues for transitions
Comedy of Errors	Roy-e-Sabs (Kabul)	Dari Persian	The musicians	3	Downstage right	Live	Relaxed, responsive, frequent live playing. Band: *rabab, zerbaghali* (drum), flutes
Coriolanus	Chiten	Japanese	The musicians	3	Upstage centre	Live	Miniature/toy constant percussion score; chorus bore small trumpets throughout.
Cymbeline	South Sudan Theatre Company	Juba Arabic	none	1	Upstage right between doors	Live	Very little sound, simple percussion 3 drums, ankle bells & group singing
Hamlet	Meno Fortas	Lithuanian	Tadas Šumskas	1	Music gallery (far stage left)	Both	Highly conceptual production/ recorded score, with live eclectic piano constantly underscoring & commenting

Table 2 (cont.)

PLAY	TOURING COMPANY	LANGUAGE	COMPOSER/ SOUND DESIGNER	NUMBER OF MUSICIANS	MUSICIAN PLACEMENT	RECORDED OR LIVE?	ELEMENTS OF STYLE/ INSTRUMENTATION
Henry IV Part I	Compañía Nacional de Teatro, Mexico	Spanish (Mexican)	Juan Ernesto Díaz	4	Music gallery (entire)	Live	Big Latin percussion (timbales, cymbals) w/ bass clarinet, trombone, trumpet & tuba. Tuba for Falstaff, marimba *ostinati* for Henry. Mariachi colours.
Henry IV Part II	Elkafka Espacio Teatral	Spanish (Argentine)	Barbara Togander	All sing, play few instruments	Throughout the stage	Live	Very few music cues; some singing, live snare, crude offstage brass fanfares.
Henry V	Shakespeare's Globe	English	Claire van Kampen	5	All around the Globe, most often in music gallery	Live	An 'Original Practices' musical approach. Cornetts & sackbuts with cittern & lute; period selections (Agincourt Carol, etc.).
Henry VI Part 1	National Theatre in Belgrade	Serbian	Bora Dugic	3	Music gallery (centre)	Live	Folk/trad.: accordion, violin, and flutes. Actors thump on big set table, often sing, Greensleeves quoted for Mortimer's death.
Henry VI Part II	National Theatre of Albania	Albanian	Armand Broshka	1	Music gallery, Around the stage	Both	Synth-heavy recorded score punctuated by onstage clarinet/ recorder improvising Balkan motifs.
Henry VI Part III	National Theatre of Bitola	Macedonian	Miodrag Nećak	1 pianist, 2 actor/ drummers	Throughout the stage	Live	2 *govs* (national drum) played by actors. Pianist USR. Ample singing & musical numbers symbolically drive the narrative.
Henry VIII	Rakata	Castilian Spanish	Juan Manuel Artero	1	Music gallery (centre)	Both	Synth keyboard dressed as a pipe organ triggering period-inspired sounds/ styles, often playing to recorded tracks.

Play	Company	Language	Music director	No.	Location	Live/Recorded	Description
Julius Caesar	I Termini Co. Benvenuti/Lungta	Italian	Andrea Baracco & Vincenzo Manna	0	N/A	Recorded	Avant-garde dance theatre approach; orchestral, Italian cinema-inspired; culture quotational (Kraftwerk, etc.).
King John	Gabriel Sundukyan National Academic Theatre	Armenian	The musicians	3	Stage right	Live	Traditional: 2 reeds (*duduks*, clarinets, *zurnas*), 1 perc (*dhol*). Relaxed integration between actors and musicians.
King Lear	Belarus Free Theatre	Belarusian	The company	All sing, some play	Throughout the stage & gallery	Live	Onstage piano, Fool plays piano & sax, Belarusian folk songs & anthems. Extensive use of song & rudimentary SFX.
Love's Labours Lost	Deafinitely Theatre Co.	British Sign Language	Phillippa Herrick	5	Throughout the stage	Live	Through-composed strophic, diatonic folk music underscoring signing. Accordion, violin, percussion, guitar, etc.
Macbeth	Teat im. Kochanowskiego	Polish	Waldemar Wróblewski	0	N/A	Recorded	Pop/Quotational (Sinatra's 'Bang Bang'). Transvestite witches singing karaoke.
Merchant of Venice	Habima National Theatre (Tel Aviv)	Hebrew	Ori Vicislavski	4, w/ actor-musicians singing/playing	Music gallery (centre)	Both	Extensive use of band with company singing & colourful recorded music. Band: accordion, violin, piano, percussion.
Merry Wives Of Windsor	Bitter Pill & Theater Company Kenya	Swahili	N/A	0	N/A	Both	Four total music cues: National Anthem, Chariots of Fire, Falstaff *a cappella* song, Herne's Oak dance/song.
Measure for Measure	Vakhtangov Theatre	Russian	Faustas Latenas	0	N/A	Recorded	Cinematic, quotational playback with digital sampling.

Table 2 (*cont.*)

PLAY	TOURING COMPANY	LANGUAGE	COMPOSER/ SOUND DESIGNER	NUMBER OF MUSICIANS	MUSICIAN PLACEMENT	RECORDED OR LIVE?	ELEMENTS OF STYLE/ INSTRUMENTATION
A Midsummer Night's Dream	Yohangza Theatre Co.	Korean	Eun-Jung Kim	8 actor/musicians	Upstage centre (3 rotating places for musicians)	Both	Mix of Korean performing arts & instruments. Highly creative & whimsical accompaniment. Loud recorded drums for group dances.
Much Ado About Nothing	Hypermobile	French	Stéphanie Gilbert	0 (some actors sing, 1 plays guitar)	N/A	Both	Eclectic – modern synth design mixed w/ classical 19th century piano, some SFX, occasional songs to live guitar.
Othello	Q Brothers	American Hip Hop	The Company	4 rappers 1 DJ	Music gallery (centre)	Recorded	All actors on radio mic's, constant beat. Short show (75 min), music throughout.
Pericles	National of Theatre Greece	Greek	Melina Peonidou	All sing, some play	Throughout the stage	Live	Company like a big Greek chorus; actor-played instruments: *oud, doumbek*.
Richard II	Ashtar Theatre	Palestinian Arabic	Majaz Album, Trio Jubran	0	N/A	Recorded	Rich solo recorded *oud* (or two), for transitions, often with a *tompak* drum.
Richard III	National Theatre Of China	Mandarin	Wang Jianan	1	Music gallery (centre)	Both	Peking Opera-inspired percussion; highly choreographed/stylised movement; performed by composer.
Romeo & Juliet	Grupo Galpão	Portuguese	Fernando Muzzi	10 actor-musicians	Throughout the stage	Live	Ensemble of singing, playing clowns. Brazilian serenades. Flute, accordion, harmonica, *surdo*, three actor/guitarists.

Play	Company	Language	Musicians	Number	Stage position	Live/Recorded	Notes
Taming of the Shrew	Theatre Wallay (Lahore)	Urdu	6, the Mekaal Hasan Band		Downstage right	Live	Ample accompaniment, some dances Broad storytelling style. Band: sitar, sarod, guitars, flutes, dholak, harmonium
The Tempest	Dhaka Theatre	Bangla	The company	2 drummers, all sing	Throughout the stage	Live	Professional musicians play two *pungs*; all sing and play many other smaller drums, cymbals and noisemakers.
Timon of Athens	Bremer Shakespeare Company	German	N/A	0	N/A	Recorded	Modern/eclectic. All pulled, ironic music, from 19th century piano trios to German anthems, 'I Will Survive', etc.
Titus Andronicus	Tang Shu-Wing Theatre Studio	Cantonese (Hong Kong)	Heidi Chan	1	Music gallery (centre)	Live	Mostly solo flute: exposed, depersonalised and abstractly expressive.
Troilus and Cressida	Ngakau Toa, Auckland, New Zealand	Māori	James Webster	1 musician	Upstage right between doors	Live	Traditional Māori (*kapa haka*). Sacred objects and symbolic instruments. didjeridoo, rushes, shells.
Twelfth Night	Company Theatre (Mumbai)	Hindi	3 'Music Assistants'	3 musicians, all sing	Upstage centre	Live	Bollywood-inspired singalong. Dances, homophonic call & response; music at every possible juncture.
Two Gentlemen of Verona	Two Gents Productions (Zimbabwe)	Shona	N/A	0	N/A	Live	Two actors play all roles. Bits of campy/comedic song, Proteus plays *kalimba*.
Venus and Adonis	Isango Ensemble (Cape Town)	IsiZulu, IsiXhose, Afrikaans, English	Mandisi Dyantyis & Company	23 actor/singer/ Music gallery percussionists	Music gallery (entire)	Live	Opera theatre, multiple song styles; Family of marimba/balafons; through-composed original adaptation.

Table 2 (*cont.*)

PLAY	TOURING COMPANY	LANGUAGE	COMPOSER/ SOUND DESIGNER	NUMBER OF MUSICIANS	MUSICIAN PLACEMENT	RECORDED OR LIVE?	ELEMENTS OF STYLE/ INSTRUMENTATION
The Winter's Tale	Renegade Theatre (Lagos)	Yoruba	The company	1 musician, supplemented often by cast	Upstage right between doors	Live	Nigerian folk tale tradition w/ songs. Variety of West African drums/ percussion; much ensemble singing/ dancing/playing.

Index